# CURRENCIES, CRISES, FISCAL POLICY, AND COORDINATION

# CURRENCIES, CRISES, FISCAL POLICY, AND COORDINATION

*Editor*

## Paul R Masson
*University of Toronto, Canada*

World Scientific

NEW JERSEY • LONDON • SINGAPORE • BEIJING • SHANGHAI • HONG KONG • TAIPEI • CHENNAI

*Published by*

World Scientific Publishing Co. Pte. Ltd.

5 Toh Tuck Link, Singapore 596224

*USA office:* 27 Warren Street, Suite 401-402, Hackensack, NJ 07601

*UK office:* 57 Shelton Street, Covent Garden, London WC2H 9HE

**British Library Cataloguing-in-Publication Data**
A catalogue record for this book is available from the British Library.

ISBN-13 978-981-4350-15-0
ISBN-10 981-4350-15-X

Printed in Singapore.

# Introduction

This book assembles a selection of my papers in international money and finance, some published in journals or conference volumes that make them less accessible than they perhaps deserve to be. In particular, the IMF *Staff Papers* had the right of first refusal to publish papers written by staff of the International Monetary Fund during at least the first ten years of my employment, explaining why many of my papers are published there. Moreover, there are several threads to my work that I would like to describe in more detail, by grouping together papers written over a span of years. Though distant in time, they nevertheless are inspired by the same preoccupations and attempts to probe in ever greater depth the same issues. I also try to identify areas where I think further research would be fruitful. The introduction discusses the context in which each of the articles were written and sketches their context. A final chapter draws on my experience in policy institutions over three decades, discussing the role of research and models in policymaking and speculating on the evolution of the international monetary and financial system.

## Part I. Exchange Rate Dynamics and Currency Regime Choice

Part I is composed of papers that provide empirical models for explaining the determination of exchange rate levels and the choice of exchange rate regimes. For at least the decade after the breakdown of the Bretton-Woods system and the move to generalized floating of currencies in 1973, a key issue that economists grappled with was what drives exchange rates. The simple models that were available at that time, such as purchasing power parity or the monetary theory of the exchange rate, were quickly seen to be inadequate. The set of determinants included in these models was too limited, and they did not pay enough attention to dynamics. Exchange rates seemed at times not to reflect fundamentals at all; at others, they seemed to overshoot in response to fundamentals. Dornbusch's 1976 model of overshooting with respect to price shocks was influential, as were various portfolio balance models (e.g., Branson, Halttunen and Masson, 1977) that amplified the monetary model to include a richer set of assets.

Chapter 1 uses a portfolio balance model to consider whether a country's net foreign asset position matters qualitatively for dynamic adjustment to shocks. In particular, if a country is a net debtor, does it face a potentially explosive adjustment of debt deflation, as exchange rate depreciation makes foreign debts more onerous, lowering wealth and causing further depreciation? In other words, a net creditor country could be self-adjusting because a negative current account shock would lead to a depreciation that would re-establish equilibrium. In contrast, a depreciation in the case of a net debtor country would lead to lower wealth, reducing desired foreign borrowing, which itself would lead to further depreciation (until the explosive process was somehow brought to an end by factors not captured in the model). It should be emphasized that the model was very simple — the menu of assets included only domestic money and bonds, and foreign bonds (or borrowing, if negative) — and it was assumed that all foreign assets/liabilities were denominated in foreign currency.

The article gives a nuanced view as to whether net foreign liabilities could be the source of instability. While rational expectations would rule out such instability (as the exchange rate would jump to a saddle path leading directly to the new equilibrium), if expectations had an adaptive element to them, then instability could result. Learning behavior, for instance, could introduce adaptive expectations in some form. Interestingly enough, the instability highlighted in this paper was very much in evidence almost two decades later during the Asian crisis of 1997–98. Countries such as Thailand and Indonesia, which had borrowed in foreign currency in order to invest in domestic property markets, saw a downward spiral of their currencies that proceeded for many months until external assistance helped bring it to an end.

The second chapter also considers economic dynamics, but in a model in which the authorities intervene by selling foreign currency in order to stabilize the rate. What should be the form of their intervention rule? Is there evidence that countries were in fact stabilizing their exchange rates? It concludes that foreign exchange market intervention aimed to resist movements in the deutsche mark's real exchange rate, but that this intervention had very little effect on the path for exchange rates over the period from 1973 to 1983.

The third and fourth chapters address a more general issue, namely the choice of the exchange rate regime itself. By the end of the 1990s, more and more countries with implicit or explicit exchange rate pegs were forced to abandon them in the face of speculative attacks. This led some (e.g., Eichengreen, 1994; Obstfeld and Rogoff, 1995) to suggest that only the polar cases of a "hard" peg (like a currency board, or perhaps only a currency union) and a freely flexible exchange rate were viable alternatives. This was termed the "hollowing out hypothesis." However, their contention was never tested in a formal sense, other than by observing the exits from pegged rate regimes. My 2001 paper propounded an explicit test for hollowing out, namely that one or both of the poles should be absorbing states, or together they should form a closed set (in a Markov transition model with three exchange rate regime states — fixed, intermediate and floating), and that the intermediate exchange rate regime itself should *not* be an absorbing state. If the hypothesis were true, all intermediate regimes would disappear in the limit as time went to infinity.

It turned out that this hypothesis was not in fact supported by the data. The estimated transition matrix implied that neither of the two poles was an absorbing state. While it suggested that there might be some further decline in intermediate regimes in the future, they would not disappear entirely. There seemed to be a good intuitive explanation for why this might be so: even if not ultimately sustainable, adjustable pegs served a useful purpose, in particular, in facilitating what are called "exchange-rate-based stabilizations." When countries with weak central banks experience a wage-price spiral that risks getting out of hand, they benefit like Odysseus from "tying themselves to the mast" with an exchange rate peg, limiting the scope for monetary accommodation. Though not a permanent solution, it seems likely that some countries periodically need that sort of imported discipline for a period of time.

The final chapter in Part I attempted to confirm this story by explaining the transitions between exchange rate regimes using a set of common macroeconomic variables. The distinction was made between voluntary and involuntary transitions: the decision to undertake an exchange-rate-based stabilization described above would clearly be voluntary, while a speculative attack might provoke an involuntary transition. The empirical estimates uncovered an interesting regularity in transitions: unsatisfactory macroeconomic outcomes (low growth or high inflation) tended to increase the *transitions away from all regimes* — whatever they were. In other words, unsatisfactory macro performance leads to major policy changes. This helps us understand why intermediate regimes are likely to continue to exist in the future, as countries continue to face severe negative shocks.

## Part II. Currency Crises, Credibility, and Contagion

The decade of the 1990s brought a revival of interest in currency crisis models — that is, models that attempt to explain why speculative attacks occur and whether they will be successful or not. The first generation of such models (Krugman, 1979; Flood and Garber, 1984) made precise predictions about the moment a speculative attack would occur: arbitrage would ensure that it would occur no later than the date when super-normal profits would be eliminated. The timing would be dictated by the trend deterioration in economic fundamentals, in particular, the growth in domestic credit to finance government deficits that was in excess of growth in money demand.

Though first generation models shed some light on earlier balance of payments crises, the crisis in the European Monetary System was hard to explain using such models, since the economic fundamentals of countries like France were good — the fiscal position was in balance, the trade account was in surplus, and inflation was low. Instead, it seemed necessary to allow for self-fulfilling expectations by market participants — if they thought the peg was sustainable, then it was; while a crisis of confidence brought on a speculative attack that brought down the peg. Obstfeld (1994) was the first to formalize a model that made such a situation understandable in the European context. He showed under what conditions self-fulfilling expectations were possible: fundamentals should be neither very good nor very bad, but had to be in an intermediate range for multiple equilibria driven by shifts in expectations to be possible.

If expectations by market participants were key, then it was clearly in the interest of the authorities to attempt to influence those expectations by establishing their credibility and commitment to the exchange rate peg. If speculators were convinced that the central bank and government would do everything possible to defend the peg, then they would hesitate to speculate against the currency. Therefore, by acting "tough," such as through implementing fiscal austerity and imposing high interest rates, the authorities could convince speculators to back off.

To Allan Drazen and myself, this explanation seemed much too simplistic to be a useful guide for government policy. Our paper (Chapter 5), completed in August, 1992 — before the EMS crisis had really taken hold — developed a model in which acting tough might be precisely the wrong thing to do to establish credibility. As in Obstfeld's work, commitment to an exchange rate peg was viewed as only instrumental — wider objectives were satisfactory output growth and low inflation. So credibility of that commitment could be hurt, not helped, by fiscal austerity and high interest rates, since they had persistent negative effects on output. Hence, there was a trade-off here for governments; they needed to recognize that at some point, there was little they could do to make the exchange rate peg sustainable, since their actions would be seen as self-defeating. Our empirical work tended to confirm this broader framework for understanding policy credibility (one which could also be applied to a wider set of policy issues than just exchange rate pegs).

The next chapter, Chapter 6, applied this notion of policy credibility to the United Kingdom's abandonment of its peg in September 1992 by using a dynamic version of the above model. The unobserved variable, policy credibility, was allowed to change over time, and it was estimated using a Kalman filter. In this way, the mapping between economic fundamentals and financial variables could be made more complex, helping to explain a deterioration in the latter despite no change in the former. This technique allowed one to trace the market's increasing scepticism with respect to the UK authorities' commitment to the peg — ending in its ultimate abandonment. The same model was also applied to Mexico's move to a floating exchange rate in December 1994 (Agénor and Masson, 1999).

A different approach was taken in Chapter 7, written with Olivier Jeanne. We tested whether a model with multiple equilibria due to self-fulfilling expectations fit the data for France better than a single-equilibrium model based on economic fundamentals alone. The model here is a generalization of the Obstfeld model and of Jeanne's previous work; unlike those models, it is dynamic and implies that there are potentially an infinite number of equilibria, some of which may be associated with chaotic dynamics. The empirical testing rejects the hypothesis of a unique equilibrium and thus tends to confirm the existence of self-fulfilling expectations (also termed "sunspots," since they are driven by random variables that are extraneous but nevertheless influence outcomes by affecting expectations) in the determination of pressures on France's exchange rate parity within the EMS.

The currency crises in Asia in 1997–98 highlighted a feature evident in a number of earlier crises (including those in the EMS and Mexico): a crisis in one country often triggers crises in others. My paper aimed to do two things: 1) to distinguish contagion from interdependence, that is, the normal spillovers that occur through international trade or capital flows; and 2) to provide a simple model in which contagion that was completely unrelated to economic interdependence was possible. The key is to work with a model in which self-fulfilling expectations can occur, such as that of the previous chapter. I extended this model to a multi-country context in Chapter 8, allowing the sunspots to be correlated. The model has empirical predictions; contagion requires a country's fundamentals to be in the intermediate zone — neither too good nor too bad (otherwise the attack would already have occurred). Simple calculations showed that many of the Asian countries affected by contagion during 1997–98 were indeed in the intermediate zone in which — according to the model — self-fulfilling attacks were possible.

While models with self-fulfilling speculative attacks are clearly a useful generalization of the unique-equilibrium models, they have had some unsatisfactory features. The models discussed above all assume that there is a representative agent — that is, everyone is essentially the same. This precludes a consideration of how expectations can differ among investors who interact with one another and influence one another's behavior. Heterogeneity of expectations is essential to understand why trading occurs and how agents come to focus on one or another equilibrium.

The final chapter in Part II introduces heterogeneity and moves away from the assumption of rational expectations. Instead, agents are assumed to modify their expectations in the light of their investment success and by imitating the strategies of others (but only episodically). The resulting interaction of many agents is thus very complex and can produce complex dynamics in asset prices. The model requires simulation techniques to solve, but some features can be determined analytically. An earlier paper of mine with Jasmina Arifovic (Arifovic and Masson, 2004) demonstrated that the distribution of expectations could be important for understanding currency crises; when expectations were bunched together with a few outliers, the exchange rate peg was fragile. For some values of the parameters, boom and bust cycles — that is, self-reinforcing expansions followed by crises — were possible.

Chapter 9, written with Tim Gulden and Shubha Chakravarty, extended that model by adding another country and a market maker dealing in both countries' bonds, and it considered the possibility of contagion. For some parameterizations, the actions of the market maker could trigger coincident crises; moreover, the simulations uncovered the interesting feature that the interactions among agents could cause the distribution of interest rate changes to be fat-tailed. Fat tails, that is kurtosis in excess of that of the normal distribution, are a feature of many asset prices, but there are few models that are capable of explaining it. Models with interacting agents need to be explored further in the quest for a deeper understanding of financial markets.

## Part III. Fiscal Policy in Currency Unions

An important area of research over the last two decades — largely inspired by the European Union but with applications to other regions — focussed on the interaction between national fiscal policies and a supranational central bank in the context of a currency union. This is an area that has fascinated me by its subtle complexities, which are still being played out in the EU as policymakers have come to see the need for institutional reform in the light of failures of the Stability and Growth Pact and debt crises facing Greece, Ireland, and Portugal.

The papers in Part III explore two aspects of that interaction. Chapter 10 examines whether, in fact, Europe's national governments are able to carry out fiscal policy adequately — using as benchmarks, the states and provinces in the monetary unions constituted by the United States and Canada, respectively. Here it is necessary to try to distinguish empirically between two roles of fiscal policy: stabilization, that is, reducing the amplitude of the business cycle, and redistribution between regions, which involves transfers to those areas that are negatively affected by shocks from those better off.

It turns out that Canada and the United States differ importantly from Europe in one of those dimensions, namely redistribution. A fiscal federation does a fair amount of redistribution through collecting higher tax revenues from better-off regions, and it also spends more in the regions suffering from a negative shock (unemployment benefits, among others). Neither of these channels is important in Europe, however, suggesting to Tamim Bayoumi and myself that lack of redistribution might well generate strains within the euro zone. A decade and a half later, we are seeing exactly that, in response to severe downturns in Greece and other countries. This has led the euro zone to put in place an initial mechanism to assist countries in difficulty (the exact form this will take in the future is still being worked out as this introduction is being written in late 2010). As for stabilization, countries in Europe seem to do at least as much as states and provinces in the United States and Canada.

Chapter 11, also written with Tamim Bayoumi, goes further in its exploration of fiscal policy in currency unions by considering how Ricardian equivalence impacts the relative effectiveness of stabilization policy at the regional and sub-regional levels. The advocates of Ricardian equivalence argue that tax cuts (or financing spending by running deficits rather than raising taxes) have no effect because agents anticipate having to pay higher taxes later. But the key to understanding fiscal policy in a federation is that those paying the higher taxes later may not be those benefiting today, thus suggesting that to be most effective, stabilization policy should be operated at the highest level of government. Using data for Canada, we confirm this view as we find that stabilization at the local level is only one-third to half as effective as stabilization at the national level. Again, this suggests that Europe may need to adapt its fiscal institutions.

A second aspect discussed in Part III is whether a country would gain from entering into monetary union with others having different degrees of fiscal discipline. Fundamental to the analysis here is the notion that central banks are never completely independent of the financing needs of governments (this is most obviously true for Africa, which is the subject of Chapter 12, but recent events have also shown its relevance even for Europe). This chapter, which was written jointly with Xavier Debrun and Catherine Pattillo, develops a model in which fiscal asymmetries may interfere with the feasibility of monetary unions. A country's welfare is assumed to depend on keeping inflation low and increasing output, as well as achieving a target for government spending. There may, in addition, be an element of government spending that corresponds to non-productive expenditure, fueled, for instance, by corruption. The model expands the criteria that should be satisfied by a successful monetary union: not only should countries not face shocks that are very different (as in an optimum currency area à la Mundell), they should also not face very different financing needs (due to both productive and non-productive spending and tax inefficiency). When we applied these criteria to monetary union projects in Africa, we found that in many cases, the fiscal asymmetries, combined with a low level of regional trade, made creating a common currency welfare-deteriorating — calling into serious question the enthusiasm in Africa for emulating the euro zone. Even if a generous estimate is made of the trade creation induced by a common currency was taken into account, monetary unions are judged to be undesirable (Masson, 2008).

## Part IV. International Economic Policy Coordination and Uncertainty

In the 1970s and 1980s, policy coordination was an active area of economic research, consistent with the interest shown by policymakers, who recognized the deficiencies of the "non-system" created by the move to generalized floating of exchange rates. The empirical academic research generally concluded that policy coordination, defined as the joint maximization of welfare by two countries acting together, could be beneficial, but that the gains were likely to be small — typically less than one percent of GDP (McKibbin, 1997). Other work pointed to the obstacles to reaching agreement, including disagreement as to the correct model of the economy (Frankel and Rockett, 1988).

In a joint work with Atish Ghosh, we argued that it was essential to distinguish disagreement over the true model from uncertainty about the effects of policy — and that uncertainty itself could increase, not decrease, the gains from coordination. The seminal work of William Brainard for a closed economy provides the intuition (Brainard, 1967): while only one instrument is needed to target one variable in the case of certainty (or if uncertainty relates only to additive shocks), with uncertainty about the effects of policy, using several instruments is necessary to achieve the best outcomes. With such uncertainty, policymakers need to be concerned with both the mean error in hitting the target and its variance around the target. In a global context with more than one country, governments would also like to have more instruments, precisely in order to avoid the negative welfare effects of greater variance around targeted variables. Policy coordination with other countries gives them partial control over additional instruments that affect domestic variables — namely foreign governments' policies. Gains from coordination are particularly large when uncertainty attaches to the international *transmission effects* of policy, rather than just their domestic effects.

Chapter 13 quantifies the gains from policy coordination in the context of model uncertainty, using a small two-country model of the world economy. Confidence regions around the parameters quantify the degree of model uncertainty. Ghosh and I show that uncertainty can increase the discounted present value of welfare gains from policy coordination by as much as a factor of two, relative to the certainty case. So gains could in fact be considerably larger than earlier estimated.

While that chapter assumed that the expected value of the true model's parameters was given by the unique set of model estimates, in Chapter 14, we assume instead that the structure of the true model is unknown, but can take one of three alternative forms suggested by economic theory. Each model is a variant of the mainstream Oudiz-Sachs model, but differs in terms of the form of the Phillips curve and the money demand function. Not knowing the true model, policymakers are assumed to learn from the macroeconomic outcomes and update their priors concerning the probability of each model being the correct one. We confirm the results of Frankel and Rockett, that having a large prior on an incorrect model could lead policy coordination to reduce welfare. However, with the additional assumption (which seems plausible) that policymakers learn from experience, policy cooperation dominates non-cooperation or simple uncoordinated policy rules (like a Friedman rule for money growth).

Chapter 15 makes the idea of model uncertainty more concrete by focusing on uncertainty in financial markets. Not only is uncertainty a central feature of investment decisions, it also seems to rise dramatically in times of financial crisis. As discussed in the previous two chapters, greater uncertainty can give rise to increased gains from policy coordination, helping to explain why international economic policy coordination is episodic. In normal times, potential gains may not be worth the time and resources involved in reaching agreement, but that may change when uncertainty spikes up. This chapter analyses the 1987 stock market crash in this light, explaining with the aid of a micro-founded model why countries coordinated their interest rate declines. The recent global financial meltdown of 2008–09, which led to unprecedented coordination of monetary and fiscal policies, are a further confirmation of the posited effect of uncertainty on coordination. The G20 summits at the height of the crisis showed an unusual unity of purpose, which, as the crisis receded, also tended to dissipate.

## Conclusion

This last chapter attempts to pull together some lessons from the development of academic-style models and their application to real world policy issues, drawing on my experience from working in official institutions and at a university. Comparisons are drawn between policy research and academic research, concluding that they are not the same — nor should they be. In addition, the chapter includes some speculation on how the international monetary and financial system may evolve in coming decades and discusses research topics in that light.

# References

Agénor, Pierre-Richard, and Paul Masson, "Credibility, Reputation, and the Mexican Peso Crisis," *Journal of Money, Credit and Banking*, Vol. 31(1) (February 1999), pp. 70–84.

Arifovic, Jasmina, and Paul Masson, "Heterogeneity and Evolution of Expectations in a Model of Currency Crisis," *Nonlinear Dynamics, Psychology, and Life Sciences*, Vol. 8 (April 2004), pp. 231–258.

Brainard, William, "Uncertainty and the Effectiveness of Policy," *American Economic Review*, Vol. 57 (May 1967), pp. 411–425.

Branson, William H., Hannu Halttunen, and Paul Masson, "Exchange Rates in the Short Run: The Dollar-deutschemark Rate," *European Economic Review*, Vol. 10(3) (1977), pp. 303–324.

Dornbusch, Rudiger, "Expectations and Exchange Rate Dynamics," *Journal of Political Economy*, Vol. 84 (December 1976), pp. 1161–1176.

Eichengreen, Barry, *International Monetary Arrangements for the 21st Century*, Washington, DC: Brookings Institution, 1994.

Emerson, Michael, *et al.*, *One Market, One Money*, Brussels: European Commission, 1990.

Flood, Robert and Peter Garber, "Collapsing Exchange-rate Regimes: Some Linear Examples," *Journal of International Economics*, Vol. 16 (1984), pp. 1–13.

Frankel, Jeffrey, and Katharine Rockett, "International Macroeconomic Policy Coordination when Policymakers Do Not Agree on the True Model," *American Economic Review*, Vol. 78 (June 1988), pp. 318–340.

Krugman, Paul, "A Model of Balance of Payments Crises," *Journal of Money, Credit and Banking*, Vol. 11(3) (1979), pp. 311–325.

Masson, Paul R., "Currency Unions in Africa: Is the Trade Effect Substantial Enough to Justify their Formation?" *The World Economy*, Vol. 31(4) (2008), pp. 533–547.

Masson, Paul and Francisco J. Ruge-Murcia, "Explaining the Transition between Exchange Rate Regimes," *Scandinavian Journal of Economics*, Vol. 107(2) (2005), pp. 261–278.

McKibbin, Warwick, "Empirical Evidence on International Economic Policy Coordination," in *Handbook of Comparative Economic Policies*, M. Fratianni, S. Salvatore, and J. Von Hagen, eds., Vol. 5, Westwood, CT: Greenwood Press, 1997.

Obstfeld, Maurice, "The Logic of Currency Crises," *Cahiers Economiques et Montaires*, Vol. 43 (1994), pp. 189–213.

Obstfeld, Maurice and Kenneth Rogoff, "The Mirage of Fixed Exchange Rates," *Journal of Economic Perspectives*, Vol. 9(4) (1995), pp. 73–96.

# Contents

# Acknowledgments

## Chapter 1
### Dynamic Stability of Portfolio Balance Models of the Exchange Rate

## Chapter 2
### Exchange Rate Dynamics and Intervention Rules

## Chapter 3
### Exchange Rate Regime Transitions

## Chapter 4
### Explaining the Transition between Exchange Rate Regimes

## Chapter 5
### Credibility of Policies Versus Credibility of Policymakers

## Chapter 6
### Gaining and Losing ERM Credibility: The Case of the United Kingdom

## Chapter 7
**Contagion: Macroeconomic Models with Multiple Equilibria**
Copyright 1999 by Elsevier Limited. Reprinted with permission from the *Journal of International Money and Finance*, Vol. 18 (August 1999), pp. 587–602.

## Chapter 8
**Currency Crises, Sunspots and Markov-switching Regimes**
Copyright 2000 by Elsevier Limited. Reprinted with permission from the *Journal of International Economics*, Vol. 50, No. 2 (April 2000), pp. 327–350.

## Chapter 9
**The Normal, the Fat-Tailed, and the Contagious: Modeling Changes in Emerging-Market Bond Spreads with Endogenous Liquidity**
Copyright 2005 by Oxford University Press. Reprinted with permission from *Identifying International Financial Contagion*, edited by Mardi Dungey and Demosthenes Tambakis, pp. 188–215.

## Chapter 10
**Fiscal Flows in the United States and Canada: Lessons for Monetary Union in Europe**
Copyright 1995 by Elsevier Limited. Reprinted with permission from the *European Economic Review*, Vol. 39 (February 1995), pp. 253–274.

## Chapter 11
**Liability-creating versus Non-liability-creating Fiscal Stabilisation Policies: Ricardian Equivalence, Fiscal Stabilisation and EMU**
Copyright 1998 by John Wiley and Sons. Reprinted with permission from *The Economic Journal*, Vol. 108 (July 1998), pp. 1026–1045.

## Chapter 12
**Monetary Union in West Africa: Who Might Gain, Who Might Lose, and Why?**
Copyright 2005 by John Wiley and Sons. Reprinted with permission from *The Canadian Journal of Economics*, Vol. 38, No. 2 (May 2005), pp. 454–481.

**Chapter 13**
**International Policy Coordination in a World with Model Uncertainty**
Copyright 1988 by Palgrave Macmillan. Reprinted with permission from IMF *Staff Papers*, Vol. 35, No. 2 (June 1988), pp. 230–258.

**Chapter 14**
**Model Uncertainty, Learning, and the Gains from Coordination**
Copyright 1991 by the American Economic Association. Reprinted with permission from the *American Economic Review*, Vol. 81, No. 3 (June 1991), pp. 465–479.

**Chapter 15**
**Portfolio Preference Uncertainty and Gains from Policy Coordination**
Copyright 1992 by Palgrave Macmillan. Reprinted with permission from IMF *Staff Papers*, Vol. 39, No. 1 (March 1992), pp. 101–120.

# Part I

# Exchange Rate Dynamics and Currency Regime Choice

Journal of International Economics 11 (1981) 467–477. North-Holland Publishing Company

# DYNAMIC STABILITY OF PORTFOLIO BALANCE MODELS OF THE EXCHANGE RATE

## Paul R. MASSON

*Bank of Canada, Ottawa, Ontario K1A 0G9, Canada*

Received April 1980, revised version received March 1981

The conditions for stability of a portfolio balance model of exchange rate determination with an endogenous current account are examined for various expectational assumptions. It is shown that unless strongly stabilizing expectational assumptions are made, if the economy is a net debtor in foreign currency assets there is the possibility that its exchange rate will exhibit instability.

## 1. Introduction

An increasingly important strand of theoretical work on open economies views the exchange rate as being determined in asset markets, rather than in goods markets.[1] Portfolio balance models imply that exchange rates, jointly with interest rates, result from the equilibrium of supply and demand for domestic and foreign assets, where these assets are allowed to be imperfect substitutes for each other.[2] Dynamic adjustment of the exchange rate over time results from the fact that current account surpluses (deficits) correspond to accumulation (decumulation) of foreign assets, and that the current account itself depends on both the exchange rate and the stock of foreign assets. The purpose of the present paper is to elucidate the conditions for the stability of this dynamic process, under various assumptions about expectations formation. In particular, stability under several plausible expectations hypotheses is shown to depend in a crucial way on a country's initial position in foreign currency assets. Provided foreign holdings of domestic bonds are ruled out (they are assumed not to be internationally traded here), stability cannot be assumed if a country is a net debtor abroad in assets denominated in foreign currency. More generally, if a country is a large net debtor, so that its borrowings in foreign currency exceed foreign holdings of domestic bonds, a similar possibility of instability will exist. The latter case is not treated here, however.

[1] A representative sample of this literature can be found in *The Scandinavian Journal of Economics*, vol. 78, No. 2 (1976).
[2] See Dornbusch (1979, pp. 14–19), and references therein.

The question of stability of such a dynamic system is considered by Kouri (1976), but in his model the crucial effect of the sign of the net foreign asset stock is not brought out. Ethier (1979) considers stability in an asset market model with various expectations assumptions; however, wealth is exogenous and so current account dynamics are not included, nor is the possibility of a negative net foreign asset position.[3] Boyer (1976) stresses the importance of the currency composition of portfolios for stability in a full-employment model of a small country producing traded and non-traded goods: an economy which is a net debtor in foreign currency may be unstable. However, only static expectations are treated. Lapan and Enders (1978) derive stability results for a two-country model, but each country is assumed to hold non-negative amounts of the other country's assets, and expectations are static, so the system is always stable. Branson, Halttunen and Masson (1979) and Martin and Masson (1979) discuss the significance of the net debtor case for modelling of the exchange rate, but the analysis of stability is limited to the financial sector with the current account exogenous, and expectations are assumed static. Section 2 presents a model that is representative of portfolio balance models with dynamic current account adjustment; section 3 discusses local stability for rational and adaptive expectations, static expectations, regressive expectations and a hybrid model where foreign assets are valued at the 'long-run' exchange rate. Section 4 sketches some conclusions.

## 2. The model

The model presented here is taken from Branson, Halttunen and Masson (1977). It assumes that the economy in question is 'small' in both assets and goods markets. Its bonds are not internationally traded so that it borrows and lends in foreign currency at an exogenous interest rate; imports/exports face infinitely-elastic world supply/demand schedules. The small-country assumption is a convenient one because it simplifies the analysis considerably, and general conclusions on stability are not likely to be materially affected.[4]

The portfolio of domestic residents thus is composed of domestic money ($M$), one-period domestic bonds ($B$) and one-period bonds or liabilities

---

[3]Ethier claims to present a very general class of asset models, but his assumption that wealth is exogenous means that exchange rate changes do not in themselves (given expectations and the current account) unbalance portfolios, unlike the model in this paper. Also his equilibrium condition for the domestic bond market [Ethier (1979, p. 261, eq. (3))] implies that domestic holdings of foreign bonds equal foreign holdings of domestic bonds, hardly a general case.

[4]Enders (1977) claims that in this context a two-country model may give quite different answers, but Masson (1980) argues that empirical magnitudes are unlikely to make this so. Also, see Martin and Masson (1979) for a multi-country model with similar properties to the one presented here.

denominated in foreign currency $(F)$, where negative $F$ corresponds to a net liability position. The domestic price of foreign currency is $e$; expected holding period yields are zero for money, $r$ for domestic bonds, and $\bar{r} + x$, for foreign bonds, where $\bar{r}$ is the exogenous world interest rate and $x$ is the expected rate of change of $e$. It is assumed that each of the asset demands are functions of the two holding-period yields and wealth, and are homogeneous in the latter.[5] Asset demands can be considered the result of expected utility maximization, so that demand parameters will be functions of the covariances of returns. Demand for a particular asset may be negative, given a certain pattern of interest rates, and liabilities are viewed as negative assets, as in Parkin (1970). Wealth $(W)$ is the sum of the values in domestic currency of the three assets, foreign currency assets being valued at the rate $e$. Asset markets are assumed to clear continuously; the result is equations determining the domestic interest rate, the exchange rate, and wealth. The equation for the exchange rate, which is of interest to us, can be linearized about initial values to obtain a reduced form, with coefficients that are functions of the initial values of asset holdings and of the exchange rate (zero subscripts):

$$e = a_0 + a_1 M + a_2 B + a_3 F + a_4 (\bar{r} + x),\qquad(1)$$

where $a_0 = $ a constant depending on initial conditions

$$a_1 = \frac{e_0}{f_0 W_0} \alpha_1,$$

$$a_2 = \frac{e_0}{f_0 W_0} \alpha_2,$$

$$a_3 = \frac{-e_0^2}{f_0 W_0},$$

$$a_4 = \frac{e_0}{f_0} \alpha.$$

It is assumed that all assets are gross substitutes, implying that $\alpha > 0$. For all but extremely large net debtors, $\alpha_1 > 0$, while $\alpha_2$ is ambiguous as to sign.[6]

---

[5] A straightforward extension would allow for transactions demand, and thus make each of the asset demands depend on the level of the exchange rate, through an endogenous domestic price. Such an assumption complicates the model, but does not change the conclusions.

[6] It can be shown that $\alpha_2 < 0$ if $f_0 < 0$. See Martin and Masson (1979, p. 14).

However, none of the coefficients $a_1-a_4$ is signable *a priori*, as each depends on the sign of the initial net foreign asset position ($f_0 \equiv e_0 F_0/W_0$).

Since only the foreign currency bond is tradable, the change in $F$ is identical to the current account balance, which will be equal to domestic output minus absorption (the trade balance) plus the interest receipts/payments on foreign assets/liabilities. Domestic output is assumed exogenous, but not national income, since debt service is endogenous. This is the reason for writing the current account as the sum of trade and services, rather than directly as national income minus absorption. It is assumed that the domestic economy produces only one good, priced in world markets (the world price is normalized at unity), so domestic prices are determined by purchasing power parity; nominal costs are assumed to rise with domestic prices, so that there is no effect of the exchange rate on real output ($Y$). Absorption is assumed to be a positive function of real wealth. The model could be expanded to allow deviations from purchasing power parity to affect output and real absorption in the short run, but the stability analysis is not materially affected. The current account, expressed in units of foreign currency, can be written symbolically as follows (where D is the differential operator $d/dt$):

$$DF = Y - A(W/e) + \bar{r}F.$$

We linearize and substitute for $W$ to obtain

$$DF = Y - A_{\rho} + A' \frac{(1-f_0)W_0}{e_0^2} e - (A' - \bar{r})F, \tag{2}$$

where $A' = dA/dW > 0$. The analysis of local stability that follows is performed on eqs. (1) and (2), the linearized exchange rate and current account equations.

## 3. Local stability

What is meant by local stability is the property of the linearized system (1) and (2) to return to an equilibrium position when shocked, *assuming that the coefficients of the linearized equations do not change*. For the analysis to be relevant requires first that the shock not be too large, and second, that the coefficients not be very sensitive to changes in the state variables. The latter will not be true, in our model, if $f$ is close to zero. The discussion will focus on the values of initial conditions and behavioural parameters that are consistent with local stability, i.e. that imply that the system of differential equations (1) and (2), incorporating an assumption for expectational dynamics, has characteristic roots with negative real parts.

## 3.1. Adaptive and rational expectations

As in Scarth (1977) adaptive expectations on the rate of change of the exchange rate converge to perfect foresight in the limit.[7] Rational expectations in this non-stochastic model are equivalent to perfect foresight. Symbolically, if expectations are revised in the following way,

$$Dx = \mu(De - x),$$ (3)

where $0 < \mu < \infty$, and we substitute (1) into (2) to get an equation for $DF$, differentiate (1), substitute into it (2), and substitute the result into (3) to get an equation for $Dx$, we can express the dynamics of the system as

$$
\begin{bmatrix} Dx \\ DF \end{bmatrix} =
\begin{bmatrix} -\mu(A'(1-f)\alpha + f^2)/f(f - \mu\alpha) & \mu(A' - \bar{r}f)/fW(f - \mu\alpha) \\ A'(1-f)W\alpha/f & -(A' - \bar{r}f)/f \end{bmatrix}
$$
$$
\times \begin{bmatrix} x \\ F \end{bmatrix}
$$

or $Dy = Sy$. Zero subscripts have been omitted on variables in the $S$ matrix, and $e_0$ has been set to unity. The Routh–Hurwitz conditions for stability require both that the trace of $S$ be negative, and that the determinant of $S$ be positive. It can be shown that the following expressions hold:

$$\text{tr } S = ((\bar{r} - \mu)f - A'(1 - \mu\alpha) - \mu\alpha\bar{r})/(f - \mu\alpha),$$

$$\det S = \mu(A' - \bar{r}f)/(f - \mu\alpha).$$

It is assumed that $A' > \bar{r}$, i.e. that an accumulation of wealth in the form of a change in $F$ will increase absorption more than it increases interest receipts, so that the net effect on the current account is negative. Therefore, $\det S > 0$ if and only if $f > \mu\alpha$, so that if the initial values of $x$ and $F$ are given, only a net creditor can be consistent with stability. There may be no range of foreign asset positions satisfying this condition, however, as by assumption money and domestic bond stocks are non-negative, so that $f$ must be less than unity. Hence, stability is only possible if $\mu\alpha < 1$, and clearly as the speed of adjustment of expectations becomes large this no longer holds. In particular, under perfect foresight the model is unstable for arbitrary initial conditions.

Now if the determinant condition is satisfied (and therefore also $\mu\alpha < 1$), it can be shown that $\text{tr } S < 0$ so that the model is stable under adaptive

[7]It can be verified that the result for $\mu \to \infty$ is the same as that obtained by setting $x = De$. See Evans and Yarrow (1979).

expectations if and only if

$$\mu x < f < 1. \tag{4}$$

If this condition is satisfied, then there are two stable roots. However, there is no reason to take the initial values of $x$ or $e$ to be given by the past. Rather, they should be allowed to jump discretely in response to new information ($F$ is of course given by past current account flows). An analogous procedure for the price level in perfect foresight models is proposed by Sargent and Wallace (1973). Unlike the perfect foresight case, however, this does not allow us here to specify uniquely the initial value of $x$ consistent with stability, since any combination of the two roots in the general solution of the differential equation system will be stable. Therefore, the paths for $F$ and $x$ (and hence $e$) are indeterminate in this case.[8]

If condition (4) is not satisfied, namely when $\mu$ is too large or $f$ is negative under adaptive expectations and *a fortiori* when rational expectations prevail, then the determinant is negative, and the two characteristic roots have opposite signs. The equilibrium is a saddlepoint, a property common to a number of rational expectations models; see, for instance, S.W. Black (1973), Kouri (1976), and Scarth (1977). Here one can determine a unique solution, provided one imposes the further condition that only the stable root appears in the solution, which implies a unique initial value for $x$. This further condition involves the assumption that speculators act in such a way as to bring about the discontinuous jump in $x$ needed to remain on the stable path.

On the one hand the assumption of adaptive expectations, if stable, runs into the problem of indeterminacy, while on the other, saddlepoint stability, common to rational expectations and adaptive expectations under certain parameter values, in effect assumes away the stability problem by imposing further conditions necessary to eliminate the unstable root. For these reasons it is also of interest to consider alternative expectational schemes which have some plausibility but attribute less knowledge to participants in the market. At one extreme the hypothesis of static expectations assumes that investors think the current rate is likely to persist, so that the expected change is zero. At the other end of the spectrum, investors look ahead to the long-run effect of exogenous variables on the exchange rate, after the current account and exchange rate changes have settled down to zero, and assume that in the short run the exchange rate regresses towards this value. These two hypotheses, static and regressive expectations, are considered below.

### 3.2. Static expectations

If speculators take the current exchange rate as the best forecast of its

---

[8] I am indebted to an anonymous referee for this point. See also F. Black (1974).

future value, so that $x = 0$, the system reduces to a single differential equation in $F$, which results from substituting (1) into (2):

$$DF = k - A' \frac{(1 - f_0)}{f_0} F - (A' - \bar{r})F$$

$$= k - (A'/f_0 - \bar{r})F, \tag{5}$$

where $k$ depends on exogenous variables. For the single characteristic root to be negative it is necessary and sufficient for initial foreign asset holdings to be such that

$$0 < f < A'/\bar{r}. \tag{6}$$

Thus, a net debtor position is inconsistent with stability in this case.

### 3.3. Regressive expectations

It is clear that the behaviour of the exchange rate in a portfolio balance model is linked to the valuation of foreign assets, and that the perverse effects of a negative net foreign asset stock result from this. Therefore, it is of interest to consider a case where domestic residents value their foreign assets at some long-run exchange rate. If the exogenous variables are constant, the asset demand and current account equations can be solved, for $DF = 0$ and $x = 0$, to give equilibrium exchange rates and foreign asset stocks $\bar{e}$ and $\bar{F}$:

$$\bar{e} = \frac{(A' - \bar{r}f\,(L(\bar{r})B/M, \bar{r}))(M + B)}{(Y - A_0)(1 - f\,(L(\bar{r})B/M, \bar{r})}\,,$$

$$\bar{F} = \frac{(Y - A_0)f\,(L(\bar{r})B/M, \bar{r})}{A' - \bar{r}f\,(L(f)B/M, \bar{r})}\,,$$

where $L(\cdot)$ is a function such that $L' > 0$, and $f(\cdot)$ is the demand function for net foreign assets. It is assumed that absorption at zero wealth $(A_0)$ is less than income so that $\bar{e}$ is positive. These long-term levels are thus independent of current $e$ and $F$, and can be treated as constants provided expected $M$, $B$, $Y$ and $\bar{r}$ tend to constant values. If people form their expectations in such a way that they assume that the exchange rate will move to its long-run level, then we can write

$$x = \mu(\bar{e} - e), \qquad 0 \leqq \mu \leqq 1.$$

If foreign asset stocks are valued at the current exchange rate, as has been assumed thus far, then it can be shown that for stability, the proportion of wealth held in the form of foreign assets initially must fall in the interval

$$-\alpha\mu < f < A'/\bar{r} + \alpha\mu(A'/\bar{r} - 1). \tag{11}$$

Under the assumptions made before, any positive $f$ (less than 1) is admissible, as are some negative values of $f$.

An alternative is to assume that investors value their foreign assets not at this period's exchange rate but rather at some combination of this period's rate and the long-run exchange rate $\bar{e}$, the weight $\mu$ being consistent with the expected exchange rate change. So in this case one could write

$$\hat{e} = (1 - \mu)e + \mu\bar{e},$$

$$\hat{e}F = f(r, \bar{r} + x)W,$$

$$W = M + B + \hat{e}F.$$

If $\mu$ is close to one this 'strongly regressive valuation'[a] can be expected further to stabilize the model. The results confirm this; the stability region is given by

$$-\alpha\mu/(1 - \mu) < f < ((A' - \bar{r})\alpha\mu + A')/\{(A' - \bar{r})\mu + \bar{r}\}. \tag{12}$$

As people's estimate of the speed with which the exchange rate will return to equilibrium increases (i.e. as $\mu$ approaches unity), so the stability region becomes larger.

## 4. Concluding comments

It has been shown elsewhere [see Branson, Halttunen and Masson (1979)] that portfolio balance models with non-traded domestic bonds, exogenous current account balances and static expectations require a country to be a net creditor in foreign currency assets for its exchange rate to be stable. The analysis here has confirmed that when current account dynamics are included in the model with static expectations, a net debtor position is still inconsistent with stability, and that, furthermore, the same is true for adaptive expectations with arbitrary initial values. For negative net foreign assets to be consistent with stability requires either the belief that the exchange rate will return to an exogenous long-run level, the case of regressive expectations, or the assumption that speculators rule out the

---

[a] This idea and the term 'strongly regressive valuation' was suggested in private correspondence by Ron McKinnon in a comment on Martin and Masson (1979).

explosive paths under rational or adaptive expectations. Neither set of conditions is entirely satisfactory: the former, because the current exchange rate is likely to embody some information relevant to its long-run level; the latter, because the assumptions required to produce saddlepoint stability are extremely strong.

It is therefore the case that for certain reasonable expectations assumptions the model is locally unstable for negative $f$. However, there is still the possibility that the model has stabilizing forces, resulting from changes in the coefficients of the linearized exchange rate equation, due to the essential non-linearity of asset demand and current account equations. This turns out not in fact to be true; if initially the country is a net debtor, and the stabilizing expectational assumptions mentioned above do not hold, its net foreign position will move increasingly negative, producing coefficients which are further and further from the region consistent with stability. It is not the case, for instance, that a large debtor position will make wealth negative [which would therefore re-establish a negative coefficient $a_3$ in eq. (1)], because in the model the value of wealth will be determined jointly with the interest rate by the demand for money and bonds, given the expected rate of change of the exchange rate. A large negative $F$ will mean that foreign assets will be valued at a very small $e$, not that wealth will be negative.

There is, however, a more serious sense in which the model may be reasonable locally but not globally.[10] Static or adaptive expectations, or other non-rational ways of forming anticipations, may hold for moderate changes away from the prevailing exchange rate. However, when large deviations from the exchange rate that would balance the current account occur, it is reasonable to presume that investors will look ahead to their effect on future values of the current account, and hence on $F$, and that this will influence their expectations of future exchange rates. Hence, explosive movements in $e$ may tend to be self-reversing because they are expected to bring about future changes of asset holdings through current account flows. Even if investors are uncertain about the magnitude of the effect, they will (correctly) anticipate that large movements in $e$ will cause large movements in the same direction in D$F$. In particular, if a country is a net debtor, an upward shock to $e$ will increase the domestic-currency value of its debts and reduce wealth, and the wealth reduction will decrease the demand for liabilities to the rest of the world. The 'incipient capital outflow' will further increase $e$: this is the source of the instability. But a higher $e$ will eventually produce a current account surplus that will allow the desired reduction of liabilities. If this effect on future current account surpluses is anticipated, it will tend to put a bound on the unstable process.[11] Very large or very small values of $e$ will be expected to reverse themselves. The problem for the

[10]This paragraph has been added after discussion with John Helliwell.
[11]There is still the possibility of oscillatory movements, and these may be explosive.

model-builder is specifying a model that embodies correct qualitative anticipations without imposing full rationality. The author would argue that full rationality is too strong an assumption, so that the instability associated with the other expectational assumptions mentioned in section 3 above and with net debtor positions is relevant for observed exchange market fluctuations. However, the stabilizing effect of anticipated future current accounts and hence future asset holdings should take hold beyond a certain range of values for the exchange rate, helping to ensure global stability.

Another possible stabilizing force might be foreign exchange intervention by the authorities. This would modify eq. (2) by making the left-hand-side $DR + DF$ (where $R$ is reserves) instead of $DF$ alone. A proportion of $R$ should be added to the money stock and subtracted from the bond stock in the exchange rate equation (1); if sterilization is complete, only the bond stock is affected. Intervention may, for instance, be directed at smoothing rate fluctuations, at producing a target foreign asset stock or a target exchange rate. Although such interventions may change the range of values of $f$ consistent with stability, they do not change the result that the more negative are foreign assets, the more likely is instability

In summary, therefore, the possibility of instability of the portfolio balance model of exchange rates is not a property due to either: (a) exclusion of expectations, or (b) neglect of current account adjustment. Rather, it is an intrinsic property of the portfolio balance model that negative holdings of foreign currency assets may have a destabilizing effect, at last in the short run, unless offset by strong expectational assumptions. There is no reason to think that the net debtor case is empirically unimportant; on the contrary. casual observation indicates that this case may apply to a number of developing and industrialized countries since the increase in the price of oil. It is quite possible that the stabilizing expectational forces mentioned above would not prevail, so that as a consequence the exchange rates of net debtor countries would exhibit short-term instability.

## Acknowledgements

I am grateful to Paul Krugman, David Longworth, Kevin Lynch and John Martin for comments on earlier drafts.

## References

Black, Fischer, 1974, Uniqueness of the price level in monetary growth models with rational expectations, Journal of Economic Theory 7, 53–65.

Black, Stanley W., 1973, International monetary markets and floating exchange rates, Princeton Studies in International Finance, No. 52.

Boyer, Russell, 1976, Net foreign assets and the exchange rate regime, Paper prepared for the SSkC–Ford Foundation Conference on Macroeconomic Policy and Adjustment in Open Economies, Ware, England.

Branson, William H., Hannu Halttunen and Paul Masson, 1977, Exchange rates in the short run: The dollar–deutschemark rate, European Economic Review 10, 303–324.

Branson, William H., Hannu Halttunen and Paul Masson, 1979, Exchange rates in the short run: Some further results, European Economic Review 12, 395–402.

Dornbusch, Rudiger, 1979, Monetary policy under exchange rate flexibility, NBER Working Paper No. 311, Cambridge, Mass.

Enders, Walter, 1977, Portfolio balance and exchange rate stability, Journal of Money, Credit and Banking 9, 491–499.

Ethier, Wilfred, 1979, Expectations and the asset-market approach to the exchange rate, Journal of Monetary Economics 5, 259–282.

Evans, J.L. and G.K. Yarrow, 1979, Adaptive and rational expectations in macroeconomic models, The Manchester School 47, 24–32.

Kouri, Pentti, 1976, The exchange rate and the balance of payments in the short run and in the long run: A monetary approach, Scandinavian Journal of Economics 78, 280-304.

Lapan, Harvey and Walter Enders, 1978, Devaluation, wealth effects, and relative prices, American Economic Review 68, 601–613.

Martin, John P. and Paul R. Masson, 1979, Exchange rates and portfolio balance, NBER Working Paper No. 377, Cambridge, Mass.

Masson, Paul R., 1980, Portfolio balance and exchange rate stability: Comment, Journal of Money, Credit and Banking 12, 228–230.

Parkin, Michael, 1970, Discount house portfolio and debt selection, Review of Economic Studies 37, 469–497.

Sargent, Thomas J. and Neil Wallace, 1973, The stability of models of money and growth with perfect foresight, Econometrica 41, 1043–1048.

Scarth, William M., 1977, Expectations and the wage-price spiral in a simple monetary model, The Manchester School 45, 208–219.

BLUNDELL-WIGNALL, A., *Exchange Rate Dynamics and Intervention Rules*, International
Monetary Fund Staff Papers, 32:1 (1985:Mar.) p.132

# Exchange Rate Dynamics
# and Intervention Rules

A. BLUNDELL-WIGNALL and P.R. MASSON*

THE PERIOD of generalized floating of exchange rates, which
began in early 1973, has been associated with wider fluctuations of both nominal and, especially, real exchange rates than
early advocates of exchange rate flexibility had anticipated
(Shafer and Loopesko (1983)). There is considerable debate concerning the causes of these fluctuations, and the extent to which
they have exerted unfavorable effects. Erratic fluctuations in relative prices—including real exchange rates—may be undesirable
because they have unfavorable effects on economic activity.[1] A
different question that has arisen is whether exchange rate levels
are appropriate; that is, whether they are consistent with some
notion of underlying equilibrium.

Williamson (1983) has argued strongly that the real exchange
rates of the largest industrial countries have been significantly and
persistently out of line with what he calls "fundamental equilibrium," and he advocates that policies be directed at narrowing
these misalignments. Williamson defines the fundamental equilibrium exchange rate as "that which is expected to generate a
current account surplus or deficit equal to the underlying capital
flow over the cycle [in the absence of abnormal internal demand
conditions or trade restrictions]" (Williamson (1983, p. 14)).
There may of course be considerable uncertainty, both on the part

* Mr. Blundell-Wignall is employed at the Economic Planning Advisory Council in Canberra, Australia; he holds a Ph.D. from Cambridge University.
Mr. Masson, an economist in the Research Department, received his Ph.D.
from the London School of Economics and Political Science. This work was
begun when the authors were employed by the Organization for Economic
Cooperation and Development (OECD), Paris.
[1] However, a recent study by the International Monetary Fund (1984a) reviews
exchange rate variability and international trade and concludes that there is little
evidence of adverse effects.

BLUNDELL-WIGNALL, A., *Exchange Rate Dynamics and Intervention Rules*, International
Monetary Fund Staff Papers, 32:1 (1985:Mar.) p.132

EXCHANGE DYNAMICS AND INTERVENTION　　　133

of central banks and private investors, as to what is the appropriate value for the equilibrium exchange rate. For instance, during
the period of fixed rates for the currencies of major industrial
countries, it may well have been the case that incorrect assessments of underlying values led central banks to defend inappropriate exchange rates. This issue will not be discussed here,
however; it will be assumed that the fundamental equilibrium rate
is known by all, and hence that there is agreement about the
magnitude of misalignments.

One of the sources of misalignments may be government policies themselves: for instance, a policy of monetary restraint often
causes real exchange rate appreciation during the transition period while domestic prices adjust (Williamson (1983, p. 54)).
Though Williamson favors subordinating monetary policy, to a
greater or lesser extent, to exchange rate objectives, another instrument that has often been put forward as a possible means of
limiting misalignments is sterilized intervention. However, the
effectiveness of this policy is in general thought to be quite limited,
as Williamson himself notes. A recent study by a working group
set up at the Versailles summit also concludes that the effect of
sterilized intervention on the exchange rate is likely, at best, to be
very modest (Report (1983)). Nevertheless, if the authorities are
unwilling to adjust monetary policy in order to achieve their exchange rate objectives, those who wish to make a case for greater
exchange rate management must address the question of the effectiveness of the sterilized intervention and, more generally, of
the extent to which the behavior of the economy differs depending
on whether such intervention takes place.

The present paper considers the effect of sterilized intervention
in a model where it is assumed that changes in monetary policy
can produce misalignments. The model also assumes imperfect
substitutability between domestic and foreign bonds, which implies that the changes in stocks of assets brought about by sterilized intervention have some effect on the equilibrium value of
the exchange rate. In contrast to much of the theoretical work in
this area, sterilized intervention is viewed in this paper not as a
one-time exchange market operation, but rather as a rule that the
authorities consistently follow in attempting to limit departures of
the real exchange rate from its long-run equilibrium level, subject
to a "reserves constraint." This constraint requires that reserves
lost by the central bank through sales of foreign exchange must
eventually be replenished.

BLUNDELL-WIGNALL, A., *Exchange Rate Dynamics and Intervention Rules* , International
Monetary Fund Staff Papers, 32:1 (1985:Mar.) p.132

134          A. BLUNDELL-WIGNALL and P.R. MASSON

It should be made clear at the outset that several issues will not
be considered in this paper. There is another rationale for intervention: to stabilize "disorderly markets." This role is of a very
short-term nature and involves the central bank giving "tone" and
"breadth" to the market. On occasion there may be few active
traders, leading to erratic swings in the exchange rate as the
random arrival of new orders meets little demand on the other
side of the market. Intervention may dampen these swings and
decrease the magnitude of bid-ask spreads. We will not be concerned with this aspect of intervention; our focus will be longer
term. Furthermore, it is assumed here that both the monetary
authorities and private investors correctly assess the long-run
equilibrium value for the exchange rate.[2] In practice, of course,
the problem of determining the sustainable level of a country's
real exchange rate is a formidable one; for a detailed discussion of
this issue, see International Monetary Fund (1984b). Furthermore, the possible costs of either volatility or misalignment of
exchange rates are not discussed; an intervention policy directed
at limiting misalignments is assumed to be given, and its implications for the dynamic behavior of the economy are examined.

The now-familiar overshooting model (see Dornbusch (1976))
implies that financial shocks, such as a shift in asset preferences or
a change in monetary policy, will produce a larger initial change
in the exchange rate than is necessary for long-run equilibrium.
Overshooting occurs in his model because prices in goods and
labor markets are more sluggish than those in financial markets.
A money supply shock makes the nominal exchange rate initially
overshoot its long-run equilibrium level while the domestic price
level changes very little. As a result, the real exchange rate di-
verges from its long-run equilibrium level. If the speed of adjustment of prices is very slow, this misalignment in the real exchange
rate may persist for a considerable period.

The Dornbusch model cannot be applied in its original form to
the questions addressed in this paper since it only provides a role
for intervention if intervention changes the money supply;
sterilized intervention has no effect. To examine the effects of
sterilized intervention, Dornbusch's model needs to be extended
to include assets denominated in domestic and foreign currencies

---

[2] Quite a different approach is used in Boughton (1984), where it is assumed
that speculators do not have a firm notion of long-run equilibrium. Instead, they
are assumed to readjust their assessments of the equilibrium exchange rate
in line with observed exchange rate movements.

BLUNDELL-WIGNALL, A., *Exchange Rate Dynamics and Intervention Rules*, International
Monetary Fund Staff Papers, 32:1 (1985:Mar.) p.132

EXCHANGE DYNAMICS AND INTERVENTION          135

that are not perfect substitutes, so that their uncovered interest
parity relationship is modified by a risk premium that depends on
the relative supplies of the assets. Such a model is usually called
the portfolio-balance model, and it has been applied a number of
times to observed exchange rate movements.[3] In the portfolio-
balance model, sterilized intervention has a role because it alters
the mix of domestic and foreign currency assets held by private
investors. In effect, the central bank that carries out the sterilized
intervention swaps a bond in domestic currency for one in foreign
currency. As long as investors do not consider that the two bonds
are perfect substitutes, the change in the relative supply of the two
assets requires an exchange rate change for equilibrium to be
re-established.

It is important to note at the outset that the existing empirical
evidence is weak concerning the existence of significant effects of
sterilized intervention on the exchange rate (see Tryon (1983)). It
has not been conclusively proved that sterilized intervention is
useless as a policy instrument, however, and the model for the
Federal Republic of Germany reported below provides an element of support for the hypothesis that sterilized intervention can
influence the value of the exchange rate.

In the Dornbusch model, as has been mentioned, overshooting
occurs because goods prices adjust more slowly than asset prices.
The portfolio-balance model provides an additional reason for
overshooting, namely the slow accumulation of assets, in particular the claims on foreigners that are the counterpart of current
account surpluses. The dynamics of exchange rate adjustment
arising from this channel were developed by Kouri (1976) and
Branson (1976), and a synthesis of the two types of overshooting
models is attempted in Henderson (1981) and Frenkel and Rodriguez (1982). The Henderson article explicitly considers the
effect of intervention in a general overshooting model; however,
intervention is treated as a once-and-for-all asset swap—in particular, a purchase of foreign money with home money—rather than
the ongoing dynamic process, described here, aimed at limiting
departures of the real exchange rate away from its long-run equilibrium level.

We proceed by first attempting to analyze a theoretical model

---

[3] For an early survey, see Isard (1978). See also Branson and Halttunen (1979);
Branson, Halttunen, and Masson (1977); Frankel (1982); Hooper and Morton
(1982); Obstfeld (1983); and Blundell-Wignall (1984).

BLUNDELL-WIGNALL, A., *Exchange Rate Dynamics and Intervention Rules*, International
Monetary Fund Staff Papers, 32:1 (1985:Mar.) p.132

136        A. BLUNDELL-WIGNALL and P.R. MASSON

that is the simplest possible generalization of that in Dornbusch
(1976); a risk premium variable and an intervention rule of the
type discussed above are included. Subsequently, a more complicated version of that model (with an endogenous current account)
is estimated for Germany. The estimation results suggest that data
for the floating rate period are consistent with the hypothesis that
the Deutsche Bundesbank intervenes in such a way as to resist
movements of the real exchange rate away from some "normal"
level of international competitiveness; furthermore, sterilized intervention seems to have a small but statistically significant effect
on the value of the deutsche mark. We then proceed to simulate
the model's behavior in the face of a monetary shock in order to
gauge its economic significance, and to examine its effect on the
dynamic behavior of the economy.

## I. The Dynamics of Sterilized Intervention

The literature on foreign exchange market intervention is now
voluminous. A long series of articles has considered Friedman's
(1953) contention that intervention should also be profitable to
central banks (see Taylor (1982) for a recent contribution). On the
question of whether sterilized intervention has any effect at all, a
task force of representatives of the seven major industrial countries (Report (1983), cited above, and various background studies) has provided new empirical evidence, as well as a discussion
of the rationale for intervention. Two recent papers have also
surveyed the empirical literature on the effectiveness of sterilized
intervention (Genberg (1981) and Solomon (1983)); that is,
whether such intervention constitutes an additional instrument,
separate from overall monetary policy, that is capable of moving
the exchange rate in the direction desired by the authorities. All
of the studies found that existing empirical evidence indicates at
most a very limited degree of effectiveness for sterilized intervention. Genberg also raises the issue of a possibly destabilizing
role for sterilized intervention if it is combined with a target for
holdings of international reserves (see Genberg (1981, p. 458)).
This point is not amplified by Genberg, beyond a reference to
similarities between this case and the case of nonsterilized intervention with a preannounced path for a monetary target, treated
in an earlier paper (Genberg and Roth (1979)). The idea behind
each case is that if there are other targets that force intervention

BLUNDELL-WIGNALL, A., *Exchange Rate Dynamics and Intervention Rules* , International
Monetary Fund Staff Papers, 32:1 (1985:Mar.) p.132

EXCHANGE DYNAMICS AND INTERVENTION      137

to be reversed at some future date, then its effects on the exchange rate will also be reversed, at a possibly inconvenient time.

There is general agreement that nonsterilized intervention does have an effect on the exchange rate; the effect of sterilized intervention, however, is more controversial. (Henceforth in the paper, "intervention" is used as shorthand for "sterilized intervention.") The effect of intervention is illustrated in a model that is as close as possible to that of Dornbusch (1976), in particular his model with sticky prices and output that is driven by aggregate demand. Using his notation, the model in the appendix to his paper can be written:

$$-\lambda R + \phi y = m - p \tag{1}$$

$$R = R^* + x \tag{2}$$

$$y = u + \delta(e - p) + \gamma y - \sigma R \tag{3}$$

$$\dot{p} = \Pi(y - \bar{y}). \tag{4}$$

The variables $R$, $y$, $m$, $p$, and $e$ are the domestic short-term interest rate, real output, money supply, prices, and the nominal exchange rate (defined as the domestic currency price of foreign currency), respectively; starred variables are foreign; dots over variables indicate rates of change, bars long-run equilibrium levels. Greek letters refer to positive parameters, and lowercase letters refer to natural logarithms of variables. The model assumes a world without trend inflation and with constant potential real output and money supply; consequently, expected inflation does not appear in equations (3) and (4) as would otherwise be appropriate. The foreign price level is normalized at unity, so it does not appear explicitly in the model. Expectations of the change in the exchange rate, $x$, are formed rationally; they are given by:

$$x = \theta(\bar{e} - e). \tag{5}$$

Rational expectations make $\theta$ a known function of the other parameters in the model.

We proceed by first making minor extensions to this model to introduce expectations of domestic price inflation explicitly and to take into account official intervention in the foreign exchange market. Instead of equation (2), which states that uncovered interest parity holds, we introduce a risk premium, assumed to depend on the private stock of net claims on foreigners, $K - F$, where $K$ is total net foreign assets (assumed to be denominated in

BLUNDELL-WIGNALL, A., *Exchange Rate Dynamics and Intervention Rules* , International
Monetary Fund Staff Papers, 32:1 (1985:Mar.) p.132

138          A. BLUNDELL-WIGNALL and P.R. MASSON

foreign currency) and $F$ is the net foreign claims of the central
bank, or foreign exchange reserves:

$$R = R^* + x - \psi(K - F). \tag{2a}$$

Such a specification could result from a portfolio-balance relationship where domestic and foreign interest-bearing assets are not
perfect substitutes in the portfolios of the private sector. In order
to be induced to hold more of foreign assets, domestic residents
require a higher expected return on them; alternatively, the foreign portfolio preferences could be reflected in the risk premium
term. In either case, this term should be scaled by portfolio size,
but for simplicity it is specified here as being linear in $K$ and $F$.
The theory underlying such an equation is taken as given.[4] In
addition, an equation explaining the endogenous intervention behavior of the authorities is introduced, where $s$ is defined as the
real exchange rate ($s = e + p^* - p$):

$$\dot{F} = \beta(\bar{s} - s) + \mu(\bar{F} - F). \tag{6}$$

Central banks are assumed to resist movements away from the
long-run equilibrium *real* exchange rate, which we assume to be
a constant, $\bar{s}$; in addition, they try to prevent reserves from deviating too far above or below some target level, $\bar{F}$. For the time
being, the current account is exogenous, so net foreign assets are
too.

As for the formation of expectations, for the moment Dornbusch's specification for the expected exchange rate is retained in
terms of the expected *real* exchange rate:

$$\dot{s}^e = \theta(\bar{s} - s). \tag{5a}$$

Then, an equivalent specification written in terms of nominal
exchange rates is:

$$x = \dot{p}^e - (\dot{p}^*)^e + \theta(\bar{s} - e - p^* + p).$$

For the time being, we assume that expectations of inflation are
exogenous with respect to the endogenous variables of the model.
For instance, expectations of inflation could be based on the rate
of growth of the money supply, as in Buiter and Miller (1982).[5]

---

[4] A mean-variance model with a similar property is described in Dornbusch
(1983). The adjustments necessary to go from a model framed in terms of assets
denominated in different currencies to a model using balance of payments data
are discussed in the appendix to Hooper and others (1983).
[5] In the empirical work reported in Section II, we generalize the model in a
number of ways. In particular, it is assumed that both exchange rate and inflation
expectations are formed rationally, conditional on the same information set.

BLUNDELL-WIGNALL, A., *Exchange Rate Dynamics and Intervention Rules* , International
Monetary Fund Staff Papers, 32:1 (1985:Mar.) p.132

EXCHANGE DYNAMICS AND INTERVENTION      139

Expected inflation also appears in equations for both output and actual inflation:

$$y = u + \delta(e + p^* - p) + \gamma y - \sigma(R - \dot{p}^e) \tag{3a}$$

$$\dot{p} = \Pi(y - \bar{y}) + \dot{p}^e. \tag{4a}$$

The model of equations (1), (2a) through (5a), and (6) can be reduced to a pair of differential equations in $p$ and $F$. Equations (1), (2a), and (3a) express $R$, $y$, and the real exchange rate $s$ in terms of $p$, $F$, and exogenous variables. First note that equations (2a) and (5a) can be solved for $s$:

$$s = \bar{s} + [R^* - \dot{p}^{*e} - (R - \dot{p}^e)]/\theta - (\psi/\theta)(K - F). \tag{7}$$

The real exchange rate may differ from its equilibrium level either because real interest rates differ at home and abroad or because private net claims on foreigners are nonzero. The LM and IS curves, equations (1) and (3a) respectively, can be solved jointly to express $R$ and $y$ as functions of other endogenous variables and of $m$ and $\dot{p}^e$ (the demand shift variable $u$ is ignored from now on):

$$R = \frac{1}{\Delta}[(1 - \gamma)p - (1 - \gamma)m + \theta\delta s + \theta\sigma\dot{p}^e] \tag{8}$$

$$y = \frac{1}{\Delta}[-\sigma p + \sigma m + \lambda\delta s + \lambda\sigma\dot{p}^e], \tag{9}$$

where $\Delta = \phi\sigma + \lambda(1 - \gamma) > 0$.

Equations (7), (8), and (9) can be solved together to express $s$, $R$, and $y$ as quasi-reduced-form functions of $p$ and $F$ and exogenous variables. Substituting the results into equations (4a) and (6) (omitting exogenous variables) yields

$$\begin{bmatrix} \dot{p} \\ \dot{F} \end{bmatrix} = \begin{bmatrix} \overset{-}{-\Pi(\delta + \sigma\theta)/\Gamma} & \overset{+}{\Pi\psi\lambda\delta/\Gamma} \\ \overset{+}{\beta(1 - \gamma)/\Gamma} & \overset{-}{-\beta\psi\Delta/\Gamma - \mu} \end{bmatrix} \begin{bmatrix} p \\ F \end{bmatrix}, \tag{10}$$

where $\Gamma = \Delta\theta + \delta\phi > 0$, with the relevant signs above each element.

The trace is negative, and it can also be shown that the determinant is positive. Therefore the Routh-Hurwicz conditions for stability are satisfied, and the model is stable whatever the value of the intervention parameter $\beta$. Furthermore, it can be shown that the two roots must be real because the discriminant is always positive, whatever the parameter values.

Given its assumptions, this simple generalization of the Dorn-

BLUNDELL-WIGNALL, A., *Exchange Rate Dynamics and Intervention Rules* , International
Monetary Fund Staff Papers, 32:1 (1985:Mar.) p.132

140          A. BLUNDELL-WIGNALL and P.R. MASSON

busch model implies that the authorities can help to guide the
exchange rate toward its long-run equilibrium value without inducing short-run fluctuations in that rate. Although the model
makes the simplifying assumption that both the authorities and
the private sector have a correct assessment of the long-run equilibrium, it also assumes that private investors either do not anticipate the intervention behavior of the authorities or, if they do,
consider it has no effect. This unrealistic feature can be modified
by considering a model with intervention *and* fully rational expectations regarding the exchange rate.

If expectations correctly take account of intervention, the order
of the system increases from second to third order. Instead of
equation (5a) we would have $x = \dot{e}$, and equation (2a) would
constitute a differential equation describing the rate of change of
the exchange rate:

$$\dot{e} = R - R^* + \psi(K - F). \tag{11}$$

Using equations (8) and (9) to substitute out for $R$ and $y$, the
model becomes a system of three first-order differential equations
(ignoring the exogenous variables):

$$\begin{bmatrix} \dot{e} \\ \dot{p} \\ \dot{F} \end{bmatrix} = \begin{bmatrix} \phi\delta/\Delta & [(1-\gamma)-\phi\delta]/\Delta & -\psi \\ \Pi\lambda\delta/\Delta & -\Pi(\sigma+\lambda\delta)/\Delta & 0 \\ -\beta & \beta & -\mu \end{bmatrix} \begin{bmatrix} e \\ p \\ F \end{bmatrix}. \tag{12}$$

The characteristic equation can be written as follows:

$$D^3 + [\mu + B]D^2$$
$$+ [\mu B - C - \beta\psi]D - [\beta\psi\Pi\sigma/\Delta + \mu C] = 0, \tag{13}$$

or

$$D^3 + a_1 D^2 + a_2 D - a_3 = 0, \tag{13a}$$

where

$$B = [\Pi(\sigma + \lambda\delta) - \phi\delta]/\Delta$$
$$C = \Pi\delta/\Delta > 0.$$

The signs of the coefficients of the characteristic equation depend
on the sign of $B$, which in turn depends on a number of parameters in the IS, LM, and Phillips curves. Now, $a_3$ is the product of
the characteristic roots; since $\Delta > 0$, it is clear that $a_3$ is positive.
Hence there are either three roots with positive real parts or one

BLUNDELL-WIGNALL, A., *Exchange Rate Dynamics and Intervention Rules* , International
Monetary Fund Staff Papers, 32:1 (1985:Mar.) p.132

EXCHANGE DYNAMICS AND INTERVENTION          **141**

positive and two negative ones; in the latter case the model has the
saddle-point property. In any case, it is clear that one root must
be real. Coefficients $a_1$ and $a_2$ have ambiguous signs. If $B$ is positive, then $a_1 > 0$, but the sign of $a_2$ is ambiguous; if $B$ is negative,
$a_1$ is ambiguous, but $a_2$ is negative. In either case, however, there
is only one change of sign in the coefficients of the characteristic
equation, which implies, by Descartes's rule of signs, that there
must be only one positive real root. It can also be shown that the
other roots, if they are complex, must have negative real parts.
Hence the model has the saddle-point property: there is one unstable root, associated with the rationally expected exchange rate;
the other roots are stable.

We can isolate the effect of intervention—that is, nonzero values of $\beta$—using the root locus method (Krall (1970)). If we let

$$g(D) = D^3 + (\mu + B)D^2 + (\mu B - C)D - \mu C$$

$$h(D) = D + \Pi\sigma/\Delta$$

and $K = -\beta\psi$ (abandoning an earlier notation to be consistent
with Krall's), then equation (13) can be rewritten as:

$$F(D) = g(D) + Kh(D) = 0. \tag{14}$$

When there is no systematic intervention, $\beta = 0$, and the characteristic equation can be factored to give:

$$(D + \mu)(D^2 + BD - C) = 0. \tag{14a}$$

Since $C$ is positive, it is clear that the roots to the quadratic must
be real, since the discriminant $B^2 + 4C$ will be positive whatever
the sign of $B$, and that one of them will be positive and the other
negative, as was discussed above. The remaining root is equal
to $-\mu$.

We can differentiate equation (14) to evaluate the effect of a
nonzero value of $\beta$ on the characteristic roots. Evaluated at $\beta = 0$,
the effect of increasing $\beta$ on any one of the three roots $Z$ will be
given by:

$$\frac{dZ}{d\beta} = \psi(Z + \pi\sigma/\Delta)^2/[(Z^2 + BZ - C)(\pi\sigma/\Delta - \mu)$$
$$+ (Z + \pi\sigma/\Delta)(Z + \mu)(2Z + B)].$$

Consider first the pair of roots to the quadratic factor in equation
(14a); that is:

$$Z^2 + BZ - C = 0.$$

BLUNDELL-WIGNALL, A., *Exchange Rate Dynamics and Intervention Rules* , International
Monetary Fund Staff Papers, 32:1 (1985:Mar.) p.132

142          A. BLUNDELL-WIGNALL and P.R. MASSON

If $Z$ is positive, then clearly $dZ/d\beta > 0$, so increasing $\beta$ will tend
to increase the value of the positive (unstable) root. The root is in
some sense a discount factor applied to future information (Sargent (1979)); intervention can be interpreted as making the distant future less important when forming expectations. The other
root to the quadratic $Z$ is negative, and the effect of intervention
on it is ambiguous. On the one hand, if $|Z|$ is either greater or less
than both $\mu$ and $\Pi\sigma/\Delta$, so that $Z + \mu$ and $Z + \Pi\sigma/\Delta$ have the same
sign, then increasing $\beta$ will make $Z$ more negative—that is, will
tend to speed up the adjustment to past shocks. This is necessarily
the case when $\mu = \Pi\sigma/\Delta$. On the other hand, if $|Z|$ is included in
an interval bounded by $\mu$ and $\Pi\sigma/\Delta$, so that $Z + \mu$ and $Z + \Pi\sigma/\Delta$
have opposite signs, then increasing $\beta$ will have the opposite ef-
fect: it will tend to slow down adjustment speed. Turning to the
third root to equation (14a), $Z = -\mu$, the effect of making $\beta$
nonzero is also ambiguous because both numerator and denominator of $dZ/d\beta$ can have either sign. However, when $\mu$ is
either very large or close to zero, $dZ/d\beta < 0$.

Turning now to the other limiting case, we can use the negative
root locus to discover what happens when intervention resists
exchange rate movements very strongly (Krall (1970, p. 66)). As
$\beta\rightarrow\infty$, and hence $K\rightarrow-\infty$, arbitrarily good estimates of two of the
roots will be given by:

$$Z = -(\mu + B - \Pi\sigma/\Delta)/2 + (\beta\psi)^{1/2} \qquad (15)$$

$$Z = -(\mu + B - \Pi\sigma/\Delta)/2 - (\beta\psi)^{1/2}. \qquad (16)$$

The root described by equation (15) obviously becomes un-
bounded in a positive direction as $\beta\rightarrow\infty$, while the root given by
equation (16) is increasingly negative as $\beta\rightarrow\infty$. Thus, in the limit,
intervention does not lead to cyclical behavior in this model. The
possibility exists, however, of an intermediate range for $\beta$ where
cyclical behavior may obtain.

This analysis suggests that in a Dornbusch model modified to
include a risk premium, an intervention rule to stabilize the real
exchange rate is likely to help lessen overshooting, if the latter
occurs, and is unlikely to induce any subsequent cyclical patterns.
These results seem to favor intervention. However, it should be
borne in mind that the model is unrealistically simple, especially
in two respects: expectations of inflation are exogenous, and,
though intervention has been endogenized, the current balance
has not, despite the two variables appearing symmetrically in the

BLUNDELL-WIGNALL, A., *Exchange Rate Dynamics and Intervention Rules* , International
Monetary Fund Staff Papers, 32:1 (1985:Mar.) p.132

EXCHANGE DYNAMICS AND INTERVENTION     143

exchange rate equation. Now the dynamics of the current balance, and especially its perverse short-run response to exchange rate changes, are a key factor in the economy's dynamic behavior when subject to shocks (Levin (1983)). To account properly for the J-curve, as well as for dynamics resulting from sticky prices, a fifth- or higher-order system is called for, and this takes us beyond the bounds of analytical tractability. A more complex, empirical model is therefore used in what follows, and is analyzed numerically.

## II. Intervention in a Modified
## Dornbusch Model for Germany

Recent data suggest that, while the Deutsche Bundesbank may not have attempted to stabilize the real exchange rate of the deutsche mark explicitly, ex post intervention was consistent with the reaction function analyzed in the preceding section. For example, after substantial real appreciation of the deutsche mark in 1978, the Bundesbank began to purchase U.S. dollars on the foreign exchange markets more actively. Conversely, in late 1980 and early 1981, sharp nominal and real depreciation of the deutsche mark led to persistent official sales of dollars. The evidence presented below also suggests that the risk premium variable seems to be important in the case of Germany, so that intervention may have been effective in influencing the exchange rate. The intervention function and portfolio-balance equation for the exchange rate are estimated simultaneously with a small set of equations representing a macroeconomic model of the German economy. The model is estimated subject to rational expectations for the exchange rate and for the price level.

### The Estimated Model

For purposes of estimation, a discrete-time system analogous to the Dornbusch model was specified. As discussed in Wickens (1984), unless additional lags are arbitrarily introduced into the price equation, the model in this form may not produce overshooting, whereas the Dornbusch model, written in continuous time, would. The reason is that in discrete time the price level can in fact jump—for instance, at the point of a monetary shock—

BLUNDELL-WIGNALL, A., *Exchange Rate Dynamics and Intervention Rules* , International
Monetary Fund Staff Papers, 32:1 (1985:Mar.) p.132

144 A. BLUNDELL-WIGNALL and P.R. MASSON

Table 1.  *Modified Dornbusch Model:*
*Equations and Error Statistics, 1973–82*

| Equation | Root Mean-Square Error Statistic |
|---|---|
| (C1) $e = \hat{e}_{+1} + (R^* - R)/4 - \psi(a_0 k - b_0 f - c_0 t)/4$ | 0.0179 |
| (C2) $\Delta f = \beta_1(p - p^* - e) - \mu f_{-1}$ | 0.0475 |
| (C3) $\Delta p = \Pi\Delta p_{-1} + (1 - \Pi)[\eta\Delta\hat{p}_{+1} + (1 - \eta)(\Delta e + \Delta p^*)]$ $+ \xi(y_{-1} - c_1 t)$ | 0.0111 |
| (C4) $y = c_1 t + \sigma(R - 4\Delta\hat{p}_{+1}) + \delta(e + p^* - p)$ | 0.0092 |
| (C5) $\Delta m = \beta_3(\phi y + \lambda R - m_{-1} + p_{-1}) + \Delta p$ | 0.0197 |
| (C6) $\Delta R = \beta_4(R^* - R_{-1}) + \beta_5(m_{-1} - c_0 t)$ | 0.0050 |
| (C7) $\Delta k = -\beta_6 Q + \beta_7 y^* - \beta_8 y + \Delta p + c_1$ | 0.0243 |
| (C8) $Q = \beta_9 Q_{-1} - \beta_{10}Q_{-2} - \beta_{11}(p - e - p^*)$ $+ \beta_{12}(p - e - p^*)_{-1}$ | 0.1016 |
| (C9) $e_{+1} = fn$ (exogenous variables) | 0.0334 |
| (C10) $p_{+1} = fn$ (exogenous variables) | 0.0096 |
| Full model fit statistics | |
| Carter-Nagar $R^2$ | 0.9993 |
| Log-likelihood test of overidentifying restrictions[1] | 668.0 |

Note: Estimates are obtained by applying the full information maximum likelihood method to data for the Federal Republic of Germany from the third
quarter of 1973 through the second quarter of 1982.
[1] Critical value at the 1 percent level equals 164.7.

even if it does not immediately attain its equilibrium level.
Whether or not overshooting occurs in Wickens's model depends
on the amount the price level jumps: if it increases sufficiently to
cause real balances to *fall* in response to a positive monetary shock
(and, as a result, the interest rate *rises*), then the exchange rate
undershoots—admittedly not a very plausible case. In our model
the price equation, discussed below, allows for jumps because it
depends contemporaneously on the exchange rate as well as on
the expected value of the price level in the following period, and
these expectations are formed rationally. As we shall see below,
whether the exchange rate overshoots or not depends on more
than just the behavior of real balances in a model where output is
endogenous and where there is a J-curve phenomenon in the
determination of the current balance, as is the case in our model.
   Table 1 contains a list of the equations of our generalization of
the Dornbusch model, written in discrete time. This model has

BLUNDELL-WIGNALL, A., *Exchange Rate Dynamics and Intervention Rules* , International
Monetary Fund Staff Papers, 32:1 (1985:Mar.) p.132

EXCHANGE DYNAMICS AND INTERVENTION          145

been estimated using the full information maximum likelihood
method on a sample of data for Germany for the third quarter of
1973 through the second quarter of 1982, and parameter estimates
are reported in Table 2. In what follows, $\Delta$ is the first-difference
operator, with $\Delta x = x - x_{-1}$, and $\hat{x}_{+1}$ indicates the expectation
formed at $t$ for the value of $x$ in period $t + 1$. We use $\Delta \hat{x}_{+1}$ as a
shorthand for $\hat{x}_{+1} - x$.

Equation (C1) in Table 1 is the interest parity condition augmented by a risk premium; the expected (log) change in the
exchange rate was multiplied by 4 to convert to annual rates for
comparability with interest rates, and then both sides of the equation were divided by 4. The exchange rate is a trade-weighted
effective rate; the foreign interest rate is taken to be the Euro-
dollar rate. The risk premium on foreign currency assets,
$\psi(a_0 k - b_0 f - c_0 t)$, is assumed to be proportional to net foreign
assets (the current account, cumulated from a benchmark figure,
minus foreign exchange reserves) minus a time trend that proxies
the growth in wealth, where, as before, lowercase letters denote
variables in natural logarithms. This term is a log-linear approximation to $(K - F)/W$, where $K$, $F$, and $W$ are the *levels* of the
cumulated current account, foreign exchange reserves, and wealth,
respectively. The coefficients $a_0$ and $b_0$ are constants used in the
log-linearization of net foreign assets through a Taylor series expansion about sample means. Coefficient $c_0$ is also imposed; it was
estimated as the trend growth in money over the sample period,
roughly 8 percent at an annual rate. The constant term in the
equation captures the difference in scale of money and wealth.

Table 2.   *Modified Dornbusch Model:
Parameter Estimates, 1973–82*

| Parameter Estimates (ratio to standard error in parentheses)[1] | | | | | |
|---|---|---|---|---|---|
| $\psi$ | 0.0521 (2.40) | $\xi$ | 0.0631 (0.72) | $\phi$ | 1.6555 (32.04) |
| $\beta_1$ | 0.2512 (2.00) | $\sigma$ | −0.3554 (12.84) | $\lambda$ | −0.2045 (2.17) |
| $\mu$ | 0.2532 (3.87) | $\delta$ | 0.0462 (4.41) | $\beta_4$ | 0.1853 (4.29) |
| $\Pi$ | 0.8056 (16.93) | $\beta_3$ | 0.3582 (7.59) | $\beta_5$ | 0.0832 (1.01) |

| Imposed Coefficients | | | | | |
|---|---|---|---|---|---|
| $a_0$ | 1.23 | $c_1$ | 0.00604 | $\beta_9$ | 0.8660 |
| $b_0$ | 2.23 | $\beta_6$ | 0.1623 | $\beta_{10}$ | 0.1430 |
| $\eta$ | 0.30 | $\beta_7$ | 0.3071 | $\beta_{11}$ | 1.5960 |
| $c_0$ | 0.02052 | $\beta_8$ | 0.4316 | $\beta_{12}$ | 1.8780 |

[1] See Note to Table 1.

BLUNDELL-WIGNALL, A., *Exchange Rate Dynamics and Intervention Rules*, International
Monetary Fund Staff Papers, 32:1 (1985:Mar.) p.132

146          A. BLUNDELL-WIGNALL and P.R. MASSON

The intervention function (C2) is specified such that movements away from the equilibrium level of the real exchange rate
are resisted, but that intervention is constrained by the level of
foreign exchange reserves. Excessive declines or increases in reserves are symptomatic of exchange rate pressure and may lead to
destabilizing expectations. Moreover, when reserves are zero, intervention would cease to be possible while, from the point of
view of the economy as a whole, very high levels of reserves may
be associated with large forgone earnings on alternative investments. It is assumed that there is some target reserve level $\bar{f}$.
Since in the sample reserves exhibited little trend, $\bar{f}$ is taken to be
a constant that is subsumed in a composite constant term, whose
value is not reported.

The price equation (C3) combines elements of price stickiness
and forward-looking expectations. Variable $p$ is a value-added
deflator, the largest component of which is wages. Average wages
are assumed to contain an element of inertia because of emulation
and overlapping contracts, for instance; it is also assumed that
they anticipate future developments of consumer prices. The
value-added deflator is therefore modeled in the following way:

$$\Delta p = \Pi \Delta p_{-1} + (1 - \Pi)\Delta \hat{pc}_{+1} + \beta(y - \bar{y})_{-1}. \tag{17}$$

Since domestic residents consume both domestic and foreign
goods, the consumption deflator $pc$ can be written as follows:

$$pc = \eta p + (1 - \eta)(e + p^*)_{-1}, \tag{18}$$

on the assumption that there is a one-quarter lag between the
production of foreign goods and their consumption domestically,
and that the deflator is a fixed-weight geometric average of the
domestic and foreign components. It is further assumed that expectations of consumer prices are formed rationally; combining
equations (17) and (18) yields equation (C3). It is clear that the
price level in this formulation is not predetermined (unless $\Pi = 1$)
because it is affected by contemporaneous movements in the exchange rate as well as by anticipation of future movements in $p$
itself. There is an element of sluggishness to the response of price
movements that increases with increases in the value of $\Pi$.

The standard lagged adjustment formulation for the demand
for real money balances is given in equation (C5), while the domestic short-term interest rate is explained by a policy reaction
function in equation (C6). The latter assumes that interest rates
are adjusted both to resist movements in the differential with rates

BLUNDELL-WIGNALL, A., *Exchange Rate Dynamics and Intervention Rules*, International
Monetary Fund Staff Papers, 32:1 (1985:Mar.) p.132

prevailing abroad and to limit deviations from monetary targets, here proxied by a uniform trend over the sample period. Monetary settings may be adjusted to external factors so as to avoid potential pressures on the exchange rate brought on by large interest differentials vis-à-vis other countries; if so, monetary aggregate targets may not be hit exactly. It should be noted that in this form the model relaxes the assumption made by Dornbusch that interest rates move instantaneously to equate money demand with exogenous money supply. Here interest rates respond to other factors, including external ones, and some monetary accommodation on the part of the authorities will tend to limit the degree of overshooting, as has been discussed by Papell (1983). Such behavior seems to characterize the historical period more accurately than strict monetary targeting. The simulations performed below will, however, replace this reaction function by the Dornbusch assumption that interest rates are set solely to achieve monetary targets, based on the equilibrium demand for money function. This is discussed more fully below.

Equations (C7) and (C8) represent the determination of the cumulated current balance. The coefficients of these equations are imposed on the small macroeconomic model, being derived through partial simulations of a much larger model of the German economy.[6] The variable $Q$ is a synthetic competitiveness variable which is a function of current and lagged values of the real exchange rate; its second order lag structure incorporates the J-curve effect implicit in the larger model. The rest of the model is estimated subject to the prior restrictions imposed on the trade submodel. Given the highly aggregated nature of the cumulated current balance, the coefficients necessarily had to be derived (in the manner described) from the considerably more disaggregated model.

In treating next period's expected exchange rate $\hat{e}_{+1}$ and price level $\hat{p}_{+1}$, the assumption is made that expectations are unbiased so that next period's *realized* values can be taken as measures of the expectations, subject to white-noise errors. The model is esti-

---

[6] The current account equation is derived by simulation of the OECD INTER-LINK model. See OECD (1984). Variables for domestic income, foreign income, and the real exchange rate were successively shocked, holding other variables constant. The resulting values for the current account were compared with their baseline values, and the difference between them regressed on the shocks applied to the exogenous variables, with lags where appropriate; see Masson and Richardson (1985).

BLUNDELL-WIGNALL, A., *Exchange Rate Dynamics and Intervention Rules* , International
Monetary Fund Staff Papers, 32:1 (1985:Mar.) p.132

148          A. BLUNDELL-WIGNALL and P.R. MASSON

mated using what Wickens (1982) calls the "errors in variables
method." Two additional unrestricted reduced-form equations are
included in the model, where next period's exchange rate and
price level, respectively, are set equal to functions of the exogenous variables. These equations appear in Table 1 as equations
(C9) and (C10). Wickens shows that using a subset of the exogenous variables, rather than the full set, also gives consistent
estimates of the model's parameters. Because of collinearity problems, we restricted the subset of exogenous variables to lagged
values of domestic prices, current and lagged values of foreign
prices, a lagged value of the competitiveness index, the lagged
exchange rate, and a time trend.

As is evident from the above description, the model is quite
parsimonious. The aim was to keep it as small as possible, and to
keep it linear without sacrificing too much realism or explanatory
power. Some experimentation was necessary concerning the lag-
ging of variables—for instance, output is lagged in the price
equation—and the form of reaction functions. Rather than including unrestricted time trends, we fitted trends to the money supply
and to real output over the sample: the estimated slope coefficients, $c_0$ and $c_1$, respectively, were imposed in the estimation of
the full model. It proved impossible to estimate sensible parameters for the price equation when all were unrestricted. We therefore imposed a value for $\eta$, 0.3. This parameter measures the
purely domestic cost influences on consumer prices; while somewhat implausibly low, it gave a higher likelihood for the full model
than values of $\eta$ closer to unity.

Table 2 presents estimates of the model's parameters obtained
by the full information maximum likelihood method.[7] The estimates have the expected signs, and most are significantly different
from zero. The estimate of $\psi$ in equation (C1) tends to support the
hypothesis that there is a risk premium related to net foreign asset
stocks. The intervention equation, (C2), seems to correspond to
Bundesbank behavior over the sample period; a more general
equation (not reported) also included the change in the nominal
exchange rate as an explanatory variable, consistent with the hypothesis that the authorities attempt to smooth short-run fluctu-

---

[7] Using the RESIMUL program developed by C.R. Wymer (1977). Estimates
of the parameters for expectations of the exchange rate and of the price level are
not reported, nor are intercept coefficients, which are, however, included in all
equations. Ratios of the parameter estimates to their standard errors, reported
in Table 2, are asymptotically normally distributed.

BLUNDELL-WIGNALL, A., *Exchange Rate Dynamics and Intervention Rules* , International
Monetary Fund Staff Papers, 32:1 (1985:Mar.) p.132

ations. Such behavior does not show up in our sample of quarterly
data, however, because the parameter estimate was insignificantly
different from zero.[8] The estimated price equation, (C3), implies
considerable inertia, since II is closer to unity than to zero; it is,
however, significantly different from both polar cases and does
include a forward-looking element. The effect of excess demand
is positive, as expected, but not statistically significant; such was
also the case when current, rather than lagged, excess demand was
included. The output equation, (C4), was originally estimated to
allow lagged adjustment. However, the speed of adjustment parameter was insignificantly different from unity, and the equation
was simplified to its current form. It implies a strong negative
effect of the real interest rate on economic activity and a significant positive effect of the real exchange rate, both operating
within the current quarter. Such a strong contemporaneous effect
seems somewhat implausible. The money demand estimates are
conventional, and resemble those reported for Germany in
Atkinson and others (1984). Finally, the interest rate reaction
function embodies the effects of foreign rates and of domestic
money targets, but the parameter capturing the latter is not well
determined.

Clearly, of primary interest here is the possible effect of intervention on the exchange rate. The risk premium parameter, $\psi$, is
of the correct sign and is significantly different from zero at the
1 percent level. It suggests that a 1 percent change in the cumulated current account will lead to a 0.05 percent change in the spot
exchange rate, other factors given. Evaluated at the mean level of
reserves for 1983, this would imply that a once-and-for-all
DM 1 billion purchase of foreign currency assets by the Bundesbank would lead to an immediate depreciation of roughly 0.08
percent in the deutsche mark's effective exchange rate. As a standard of comparison, two previous studies imply that (sterilized)
intervention of a similar size would cause a depreciation of 0.07
percent (Branson, Halttunen, and Masson (1977)) and 0.003 percent (Obstfeld (1983)).[9] The small size of this coefficient seems,

[8] Artus (1976) reports estimates of a similar equation over a shorter sample
period of monthly data (April 1973–July 1975) in which both the deviation of the
deutsche mark from its purchasing power parity level *and* the rate of change of
the nominal exchange rate have significant coefficients.
[9] These two studies model the bilateral dollar–deutsche-mark rate, and not the
effective rate as is the case here. The effect quoted above for Obstfeld was
obtained by scaling the number quoted in Tryon (1983) by the reserve money
stock for 1983; it includes other model feedbacks and is not directly comparable,
however, to our parameter $\psi$.

BLUNDELL-WIGNALL, A., *Exchange Rate Dynamics and Intervention Rules*, International Monetary Fund Staff Papers, 32:1 (1985:Mar.) p.132

on the face of it, to be consistent with the negligible effect found by many previous studies (see also Tryon (1983)). That the risk premium parameter is very small does not necessarily imply that the impact of intervention will be small when the model is solved under rational expectations. It should be stressed that, in principle, agents solve for the entire future path of the economy under rational expectations, so knowledge that the authorities will intervene to limit real exchange rate movements in the future may bring about substantial changes in current variables relative to a situation where the authorities do not resort to such intervention. It is hard to judge on the basis of this one parameter estimate what will be the influence of an intervention rule, as opposed to the effect of a one-time intervention.

In order to examine its effect, the model was simulated with and without official intervention in the foreign exchange market on the assumption that market participants know the structure of the model and the future values of the exogenous variables. In the absence of uncertainty about parameters and about exogenous variables, our simulations therefore involve calculating perfect-foresight solutions to the model. We do so using the algorithm of Blanchard and Kahn (1980).[10]

In Dornbusch's overshooting model the monetary authorities are assumed to target the money supply strictly, and interest rates adjust to equate money demand with the exogenous supply. The historical data imply that interest rates have not been determined in this way; in practice the authorities also attempt to achieve other objectives, and the money supply is to some extent endogenous, with interest rate fluctuations limited by central bank accommodation. It is for this reason that it proved necessary to estimate the interest rate as a policy reaction function with the money supply adjusting partially to demand.

For the purposes of subsequent policy analysis, however, the interest rate reaction function is suppressed, and the estimated money demand equation, in its equilibrium form, is inverted to determine the interest rate. In other words, lags are eliminated

---

[10] The exchange rate and the price level are the only truly "forward-looking" variables; however, the other state variables $X$ are not predetermined in the sense that Buiter (1982) uses the concept, because they can jump in response to news available at $t$. We avoided this problem by creating a vector of new state variables $X1$ composed of the lagged values of the variables $X$. The elements of $X1$ are predetermined, and the model can then be written in the Blanchard-Kahn notation, with initial conditions imposed on $X1$ at time 0 and transversality conditions imposed on $e$ and $p$ such that they do not exhibit explosive behavior.

BLUNDELL-WIGNALL, A., *Exchange Rate Dynamics and Intervention Rules* , International
Monetary Fund Staff Papers, 32:1 (1985:Mar.) p.132

EXCHANGE DYNAMICS AND INTERVENTION        151

from the demand for money equation, and the long-run demand
for money function is used. While this may seem to be an arbitrary
procedure, the justification for it is that if money were strictly
controlled, it is doubtful that interest rates would exhibit the
dynamic behavior implied by the inverted money demand function. Laidler (1982) has argued that estimated lags in short-run
"money demand equations" do not reflect lags in adjustment of
demand so much as the stickiness of prices, captured elsewhere in
our model; they may also result from the money supply process
(Gordon (1984)).

The dynamic properties of the model can conveniently be examined by calculating its characteristic roots, since the model is
linear. A conventional model in difference-equation form will be
stable provided all roots have modulus less than unity; a perfect-
foresight model will be stable provided there are only as many
characteristic roots with modulus greater than unity as there are
nonpredetermined variables—in this case two (the exchange rate
and the price level), since transversality conditions are imposed on
these variables to prevent them from exhibiting explosive behavior. Complex roots are evidence that some variables will respond in cyclical fashion when the model is subjected to shocks.
The characteristic roots of the model with the modifications described above, both with and without the estimated reaction function for intervention, are presented in Table 3. As expected, there
are two unstable roots corresponding to the rationally expected
exchange rate and domestic price level. Intervention increases the
size of one of these roots, as was the case for the theoretical model
developed in the first section. The other roots have modulus less

Table 3.   *Characteristic Roots of the Estimated Model*
*with the Long-Run Money Demand Function Renormalized*
*on the Interest Rate*

| Without Intervention | | With Intervention | |
|---|---|---|---|
| Root | Modulus | Root | Modulus |
| 14.018 | 14.018 | 14.018 | 14.018 |
| 1.194 | 1.194 | 1.211 | 1.211 |
| $0.984 \pm 0.056i$ | 0.986 | $0.963 \pm 0.059i$ | 0.965 |
| 0.838 | 0.838 | 0.910 | 0.910 |
| 0.747 | 0.747 | $0.689 \pm 0.013i$ | 0.689 |
| 0.670 | 0.670 | 0.221 | 0.221 |
| 0.221 | 0.221 | | |

BLUNDELL-WIGNALL, A., *Exchange Rate Dynamics and Intervention Rules* , International
Monetary Fund Staff Papers, 32:1 (1985:Mar.) p.132

Table 4.  *Simulated Effects of a Sustained 10 Percent Increase in the German Money Supply*

(Percentage deviations from baseline)

| Variable | Time Period (quarter) | | | | | | | | | |
|---|---|---|---|---|---|---|---|---|---|---|
| | 0 | 1 | 2 | 3 | 4 | 7 | 11 | 15 | 19 | ∞ |
| | Without Intervention | | | | | | | | | |
| $e$ | 9.87 | 8.27 | 6.87 | 5.68 | 4.68 | 2.69 | 1.81 | 2.22 | 3.39 | 10.00 |
| $f$ | 0.00 | 0.00 | 0.00 | 0.00 | 0.00 | 0.00 | 0.00 | 0.00 | 0.00 | 0.00 |
| $p$ | 1.42 | 2.69 | 3.81 | 4.81 | 5.69 | 7.76 | 9.56 | 10.71 | 11.45 | 10.00 |
| $e + p^* - p$ | 8.45 | 5.58 | 3.06 | 0.87 | −1.01 | −5.07 | −7.75 | −8.49 | −8.06 | 0.00 |
| $y$ | 4.41 | 3.76 | 3.18 | 2.66 | 2.21 | 1.14 | 0.23 | −0.34 | −0.70 | 0.00 |
| $R$ | −6.25 | −5.34 | −4.55 | −3.85 | −3.23 | −1.73 | −0.30 | 0.72 | 1.46 | 0.00 |
| $k$ | −2.68 | −3.80 | −3.48 | −2.33 | −0.83 | 3.27 | 5.15 | 3.52 | 0.06 | 0.00 |
| | With Intervention | | | | | | | | | |
| $e$ | 9.82 | 8.28 | 6.99 | 5.92 | 5.05 | 3.46 | 3.05 | 3.84 | 5.25 | 10.00 |
| $f$ | −2.11 | −2.98 | −3.02 | −2.52 | −1.70 | 1.44 | 4.92 | 6.68 | 6.99 | 0.00 |
| $p$ | 1.41 | 2.68 | 3.83 | 4.86 | 5.79 | 8.07 | 10.14 | 11.41 | 12.09 | 10.00 |
| $e + p^* - p$ | 8.41 | 5.60 | 3.16 | 1.06 | −0.74 | −4.61 | −7.09 | −7.57 | −6.84 | 0.00 |
| $y$ | 4.42 | 3.77 | 3.18 | 2.66 | 2.18 | 1.04 | 0.00 | −0.01 | −0.01 | 0.00 |
| $R$ | −6.24 | −5.28 | −4.41 | −3.61 | −2.89 | −1.08 | 0.63 | 1.69 | 2.26 | 0.00 |
| $k$ | −2.67 | −3.80 | −3.50 | −2.35 | −0.83 | 3.49 | 6.02 | 5.20 | 2.51 | 0.00 |

BLUNDELL-WIGNALL, A., *Exchange Rate Dynamics and Intervention Rules* , International
Monetary Fund Staff Papers, 32:1 (1985:Mar.) p.132

EXCHANGE DYNAMICS AND INTERVENTION          153

than unity, but there are complex roots, indicating cyclical behavior. We will see below that a monetary shock does in fact induce quite long and pronounced cycles. Interestingly enough, intervention adds a pair of complex roots, suggesting that it may itself be the source of cyclical fluctuations in response to shocks.

The results of simulating the model when it is subjected to a domestic money supply shock are presented in Table 4.[11] The nominal exchange rate does not overshoot its equilibrium value, either with or without intervention. In contrast to Wickens (1984), this is not the result of real balances falling in response to a positive shock to nominal balances but is due to some rise in the domestic price level and a substantial rise in output, combined with a large income elasticity of money demand (see Table 2). As noted above, the size of the contemporaneous output effect is somewhat implausible; however, estimation results rejected the hypothesis of lagged adjustment of output to the real interest rate and real exchange rate. The subsequent behavior of output and prices is not that of monotonic adjustment toward their equilibrium levels: there are strong cycles, and the exchange rate appreciates for a time before depreciating once again. The price level moves fairly steadily upward, but it exceeds its equilibrium level after three years; in consequence, the real exchange rate, which had depreciated by over 8 percent initially, has appreciated relative to baseline by almost that amount after five years. The cumulated current account balance is strongly cyclical, as expected given the J-curve.

The effect of intervention is small, especially over the initial few periods. Even though the Bundesbank intervenes by an amount exceeding 2 percent of its reserves in the initial quarter (over $1 billion), the effect on the exchange rate is only 0.05 percent. Differences widen as the simulation progresses, and after 20 quarters the exchange rate in both nominal and real terms is almost 2 percent higher (and hence closer to its equilibrium) than in the absence of intervention. Note that at this point reserves are some 7 percent *higher* than in the baseline, and that other variables—the price level, the nominal interest rate, and the cumulated cur-

[11] The effect of a foreign monetary shock is perhaps more interesting, because in this case the open market operation and the intervention operation are performed by different monetary authorities. Since our model does not contain equations for foreign income and money demand, this experiment could not be made, but its results should be qualitatively similar to the one performed but reversed in sign.

BLUNDELL-WIGNALL, A., *Exchange Rate Dynamics and Intervention Rules* , International
Monetary Fund Staff Papers, 32:1 (1985:Mar.) p.132

154          A. BLUNDELL-WIGNALL and P.R. MASSON

rent account—are *farther* from their equilibrium values than in the absence of intervention. It is also the case that the amplitude of the cyclical swings in the cumulated current account is larger for the simulation where the central bank intervenes.

The qualitative response of the model to the monetary shock will in fact depend on the values taken on by the parameters. Overshooting is more likely the less output and prices respond in the first instance, and the less sensitive is money demand to their movements. Conversely, the more interest elastic is money demand, the less interest rates must move to equate money demand and money supply, and hence the less period-to-period movement in the exchange rate there will be. The presence or absence of cycles will also depend on the configuration of parameter values.

Though our results are specific to a particular set of parameter values—in most cases estimated on the basis of historical data—they are suggestive of the following broader conclusions. First, the possibility of significantly limiting deviations of real exchange rates from their equilibrium levels—even assuming that these are known—seems extremely limited. Though our estimation results show a statistically significant effect for intervention on the exchange rate, the economic significance of the result seems small. Evidence presented in other papers cited also gives very little support for the effectiveness of intervention. Second, to the extent that intervention does have an effect, resisting movements in the real exchange rate may have perverse effects on other variables, slowing down their adjustment toward equilibrium (see also Frenkel (1983)). The simulation results of a positive monetary shock imply that the authorities, by intervening to resist real exchange rate misalignments, would have caused interest rates to be higher after 20 quarters than rates would otherwise have been, and the level of net foreign claims to be higher than its equilibrium value, implying subsequent current account deficits.

More generally, whatever the reason for the less than instantaneous adjustment in the economy—price stickiness, slow adjustment of trade volumes, gestation lags for investment—the dynamic effects of an intervention rule will be very complex, and may have unintended consequences for other variables. An evaluation of the consequences for economic welfare must go beyond just considering the costs of a misaligned real exchange rate. Even if (sterilized) intervention is an effective policy instrument independent of monetary policy itself, using it still incurs costs as well as benefits. Inhibiting movements in one variable has repercus-

BLUNDELL-WIGNALL, A., *Exchange Rate Dynamics and Intervention Rules*, International
Monetary Fund Staff Papers, 32:1 (1985:Mar.) p.132

EXCHANGE DYNAMICS AND INTERVENTION          155

sions for the rest of the economy that must be evaluated from a
general welfare perspective. Furthermore, the simulation results
suggest that an intervention rule such as the one specified may be
the source of cyclical fluctuations, since the characteristic roots in
this case include an extra complex pair. If there are costs to such
fluctuations, then they must be set against the costs of the misalignments that are being reduced by the intervention.

## III. Conclusions

In this paper, the Dornbusch model (1976) was extended to
include a role for asset supplies through a risk premium variable,
and the dynamics of an intervention rule whereby the authorities
attempt to resist movements in the real exchange rate were analyzed under assumptions of both regressive and rational exchange
rate expectations. It was shown that the generalized model was
stable under regressive expectations, whether or not the authorities intervened, and that the intervention rule did not itself generate cycles. Similarly, the model was shown to have the saddle-
point property under rational expectations and, provided that
intervention was sufficiently strong, intervention would not lead
to cyclical fluctuations. These results tended to provide analytical
support for the view that attempts to limit overshooting—through
intervention rules to stabilize the real exchange rate—may be
helpful.

To examine these results empirically, a more complete macroeconomic model was estimated for Germany under the assumption of rational expectations for both the exchange rate and for the
gross domestic product (GDP) deflator. The risk premium parameter, through which intervention may have an impact on the exchange rate, was shown to be small but statistically significant by
the usual criteria. The estimation results also suggest that, during
the first decade of generalized floating, the intervention behavior
of the Bundesbank, while possibly motivated by other concerns,
has been consistent with resistance to real exchange rate movements. This model was then solved under the perfect-foresight
assumption for a 10 percent permanent increase in the domestic
money supply.

Instead of overshooting of the nominal exchange rate in response to a domestic monetary shock, the model produced a
smaller nominal depreciation in the short run than in the long run,

BLUNDELL-WIGNALL, A., *Exchange Rate Dynamics and Intervention Rules*, International Monetary Fund Staff Papers, 32:1 (1985:Mar.) p.132

156     A. BLUNDELL-WIGNALL and P.R. MASSON

but the real exchange rate did depreciate substantially as prices took time to adjust. The intervention rule did tend to limit the deviation of the real exchange rate from its equilibrium level—which was unaffected by the monetary shock. However, the effects were small and were initially negligible. If the purpose of intervention is to limit nominal exchange rate overshooting, the model simulations provide little justification for its use. Furthermore, in the medium term the intervention rule produced adverse side effects, in particular slower adjustment of the current account balance and an increased tendency for cyclical fluctuations. The greater complexity of the empirical model, including a J-curve phenomenon on current balances, would seem to explain why there was a tendency toward cyclical behavior even though it did not exist in the simplest analytical examination of intervention.

It is important to underline the limitations of the analysis. A particularly simple strategy for intervention was examined—though one that has been advocated. If intervention does indeed have some identifiable effect, however small, other more complicated feedback rules—perhaps involving much larger intervention operations—might have clearly beneficial effects. Put somewhat differently, in a deterministic context, if there is an additional independent instrument, then its use will in general help to attain a higher value for the objective function that policymakers maximize. Optimal feedback rules were not derived, however, because such a deterministic setting is clearly not appropriate for that purpose. In particular, there was no attempt to model how behavior of individuals might change in response to changing uncertainty. In this paper the intervention rule is only allowed to affect the expectations of agents because the private sector is assumed to anticipate correctly the authorities' actions. However, it may be a deliberate part of an intervention strategy to change the degree of uncertainty concerning exchange rate fluctuations: either by limiting transitory fluctuations and hence providing a more stable planning environment, or by adding an erratic element to exchange rate movements, to discourage speculation.

## APPENDIX

### Data Definitions and Sources

All data, unless otherwise stated, are for the Federal Republic of Germany and are taken directly from the magnetic tape corresponding to the series shown in the *Monthly Report* of the Deutsche Bundesbank.

BLUNDELL-WIGNALL, A., *Exchange Rate Dynamics and Intervention Rules*, International
Monetary Fund Staff Papers, 32:1 (1985:Mar.) p.132

EXCHANGE DYNAMICS AND INTERVENTION     157

Endogenous Variables

| | |
|---|---|
| E | Effective exchange rate against 23 trading partners |
| F | Net external assets of the Deutsche Bundesbank, in billions of deutsche mark |
| P | GDP deflator |
| Y | Real GDP |
| M | M3 |
| R | Three-month interbank interest rate |
| K | Cumulated current account, in deutsche mark, calculated by summing current account flows from a benchmark figure |
| Q | Synthetic competitiveness variable, calculated from data for the real exchange rate and parameters derived from the INTERLINK model of the Organization for Economic Cooperation and Development (OECD). |

Exogenous Variables

| | |
|---|---|
| $R^*$ | Three-month Eurodollar deposit rate |
| $P^*$ | Import price index in foreign currency terms |
| $Y^*$ | Real GDP of the seven major OECD economies excluding Germany (source: OECD, *Main Economic Indicators*) |
| $t$ | Time trend (equals 0 in third quarter of 1973, 1 in fourth quarter of 1973, and so on). |

## REFERENCES

Artus, Jacques R., "Exchange Rate Stability and Managed Floating: The Experience of the Federal Republic of Germany," *Staff Papers*, International Monetary Fund (Washington), Vol. 23 (July 1976), pp. 312–33.

Atkinson, P.E., A. Blundell-Wignall, M. Rondoni, and H. Ziegelschmidt, "The Efficacy of Monetary Targetting: The Stability of Demand for Money in Major OECD Countries," *OECD Economic Studies* (Paris), No. 3 (1984), pp. 145–76.

Blanchard, Olivier Jean, and Charles M. Kahn, "The Solution of Linear Difference Models Under Rational Expectations," *Econometrica* (Evanston, Illinois), Vol. 48 (July 1980), pp. 1305–11.

Boughton, James M., "Exchange Rate Movements and Adjustment in Financial Markets: Quarterly Estimates for Major Currencies," *Staff Papers*, International Monetary Fund (Washington), Vol. 31 (September 1984), pp. 445–68.

Branson, William H., "Asset Markets and Relative Prices in Exchange Rate Determination," Seminar Paper No. 66 (Stockholm: Institute for International Economic Studies, 1976).

———, and Hannu Halttunen, "Asset Market Determination of Exchange Rates: Initial Empirical and Policy Results," in *Trade and Payments Adjustment Under Flexible Exchange Rates*, ed. by J.P. Martin and A.D. Smith (London: Macmillan, 1979).

———, and Paul R. Masson, "Exchange Rates in the Short-Run: The Dollar Deutschemark Rate," *European Economic Review* (Amsterdam), Vol. 10 (December 1977), pp. 303–24.

BLUNDELL-WIGNALL, A., *Exchange Rate Dynamics and Intervention Rules* , International Monetary Fund Staff Papers, 32:1 (1985:Mar.) p.132

158       A. BLUNDELL-WIGNALL and P.R. MASSON

Buiter, Willem H., "Predetermined and Non-Predetermined Variables in Rational Expectations Models," *Economics Letters* (Amsterdam), Vol. 10 (Nos. 1–2, 1982), pp. 49–54.

———, and Marcus Miller, "Real Exchange Rate Overshooting and the Output Cost of Bringing Down Inflation," *European Economic Review* (Amsterdam), Vol. 18 (May-June 1982), pp. 85–123.

Dornbusch, Rudiger, "Expectations and Exchange Rate Dynamics," *Journal of Political Economy* (Chicago), Vol. 84 (December 1976), pp. 1161–76.

———, "Exchange Risk and the Macroeconomics of Exchange Rate Determination," in *The Internationalization of Financial Markets and National Economic Policy*, ed. by R. Hawkins, R. Levich, and C. Wihlborg (Greenwich, Connecticut: JAI Press, 1983).

Frankel, Jeffrey A., "In Search of the Exchange Risk Premium: A Six Currency Test Assuming Mean-Variance Optimization," *Journal of International Money and Finance* (Guildford, England), Vol. 1 (December 1982), pp. 255–74.

Frenkel, Jacob A., "Flexible Exchange Rates: The State of Research and Implications for Macroeconomic Policy," in *Floating Exchange Rates in an Interdependent World*, a symposium sponsored by the General Accounting Office (Washington, D.C., February 18, 1983).

———, and Carlos A. Rodriguez, "Exchange Rate Dynamics and the Overshooting Hypothesis," *Staff Papers*, International Monetary Fund (Washington), Vol. 29 (March 1982), pp. 1–30.

Friedman, Milton, "The Case for Flexible Exchange Rates," in *Essays in Positive Economics* (Chicago: University of Chicago Press, 1953).

Genberg, Hans, "Effects of Central Bank Intervention in the Foreign Exchange Market," *Staff Papers*, International Monetary Fund (Washington), Vol. 28 (September 1981), pp. 451–76.

———, and Jean-Pierre Roth, "Exchange Rate Stabilization Policy and Monetary Target with Endogenous Expectations," *Schweizerische Zeitschrift für Volkswirtschaft und Statistik* (Basle), Vol. 115 (September 1979), pp. 527–45.

Gordon, Robert J., "The Short-Run Demand for Money: A Reconsideration," *Journal of Money, Credit and Banking* (Columbus, Ohio), Vol. 16 (November 1984), pp. 403–34.

Henderson, Dale W., "The Dynamic Effects of Exchange Market Intervention Policy: Two Extreme Views and a Synthesis," *Kredit und Kapital* (Berlin), Heft 6 (1981), pp. 156–209.

Hooper, Peter, Richard D. Haas, S.A. Symansky, and L. Stekler, "Alternative Approaches to General Equilibrium Modeling of Rates and Capital Flows: The MCM Experience," *Zeitschrift für Nationalökonomie* (Vienna), Suppl. 3 (1983), pp. 29–60.

Hooper, Peter, and John Morton, "Fluctuations in the Dollar: A Model of Nominal and Real Exchange Rate Determination," *Journal of International Money and Finance* (Guildford, England), Vol. 1 (April 1982), pp. 39–56.

International Monetary Fund (1984a), *Exchange Rate Volatility and World Trade*, Occasional Paper No. 28 (Washington, 1984).

——— (1984b), "Issues in the Assessment of the Exchange Rates of Industrial Countries," Occasional Paper No. 29 (Washington, 1984).

Isard, Peter, *The Process of Exchange-Rate Determination: A Survey of Popular Views and Important Models*, Princeton Studies in International Finance No. 42 (Princeton, New Jersey: Princeton University, 1978).

BLUNDELL-WIGNALL, A., *Exchange Rate Dynamics and Intervention Rules* , International
Monetary Fund Staff Papers, 32:1 (1985:Mar.) p.132

EXCHANGE DYNAMICS AND INTERVENTION          159

Kouri, Pentti J.K., "The Exchange Rate and the Balance of Payments in the
     Short Run and in the Long Run: A Monetary Approach," *Scandinavian
     Journal of Economics* (Stockholm), Vol. 78 (No. 2, 1976), pp. 280–304.
Krall, A., "The Root Locus Method: A Survey," *SIAM Review* (Philadelphia),
     Vol. 12 (January 1970), pp. 64–72.
Laidler, David E.W., *Monetarist Perspectives* (Deddington, England: P. Allan,
     1982).
Levin, Jay H., "The J-Curve, Rational Expectations and the Stability of the
     Flexible Exchange Rate System," *Journal of International Economics* (Am-
     sterdam), Vol. 15 (November 1983), pp. 239–51.
Masson, Paul R., and Peter Richardson, "Exchange Rate Expectations and
     Current Balances in the OECD INTERLINK System," in *International
     Macroeconomic Modelling for Policy Decisions*, ed. by P. Artus (The
     Hague: Nijhoff, 1985).
Obstfeld, Maurice, "Exchange Rates, Inflation and the Sterilization Problem:
     Germany 1975–1981," *European Economic Review* (Amsterdam), Vol. 21
     (March 1983), pp. 161–89.
Organization for Economic Cooperation and Development, *OECD INTER-
     LINK System: Structure and Operation* (Paris, 1984).
Papell, David H., "Activist Monetary Policy, Imperfect Capital Mobility and the
     Overshooting Hypothesis," NBER Working Paper No. 1244 (Cambridge,
     Massachusetts: National Bureau of Economic Research, December 1983).
"Report of the Working Group on Exchange Market Intervention" (Washing-
     ton: Board of Governors of the Federal Reserve System, 1983).
Sargent, Thomas J., *Macroeconomic Theory* (New York: Academic, 1979).
Shafer, Jeffrey R., and Bonnie E. Loopesko, "Floating Exchange Rates After
     Ten Years," *Brookings Papers on Economic Activity: 1* (1983), The Brook-
     ings Institution (Washington), pp. 1–86.
Solomon, Robert, "Official Intervention in Foreign Exchange Markets: A Sur-
     vey," Brookings Discussion Papers in International Economics No. 1
     (Washington: The Brookings Institution, 1983).
Tryon, R.W., "Small Empirical Models of Exchange Market Intervention: A
     Review of the Literature," Staff Studies No. 134 (Washington: Board of
     Governors of the Federal Reserve System, 1983).
Wickens, M.R., "The Efficient Estimation of Econometric Models with
     Rational Expectations," *Review of Economic Studies* (Edinburgh), Vol. 49
     (January 1982), pp. 55–67.
———, *Rational Expectations and Exchange Rate Dynamics*, Discussion Paper
     No. 20 (London: Centre for Economic Policy Research, 1984).
Williamson, John, *The Exchange Rate System*, Study No. 5 (Washington: Insti-
     tute for International Economics, 1983).
Wymer, Clifford R., "Full Information Maximum Likelihood Estimation with
     Nonlinear Restrictions and Computer Programs: Resimul Manual" (un-
     published; Washington: International Monetary Fund, 1977).

Journal of Development Economics
Vol. 64 (2001) 571–586

JOURNAL OF
Development
ECONOMICS

www.elsevier.com/locate/econbase

# Exchange rate regime transitions

## Paul R. Masson [*]

*Research Department, International Monetary Fund, Washington, DC 20431, USA*

Received 1 April 2000; accepted 1 August 2000

### Abstract

The "hollowing-out", or "two poles" hypothesis is tested in the context of a Markov chain model of exchange rate transitions. In particular, two versions of the hypothesis—that hard pegs are an absorbing state, or that fixes and floats form a closed set, with no transitions to intermediate regimes—are tested using two alternative classifications of regimes. While there is some support for the lack of exits from hard pegs (i.e. that they are an absorbing state), the data generally indicate that the intermediate cases will continue to constitute a sizable fraction of actual exchange rate regimes. © 2001 Elsevier Science B.V. All rights reserved.

*JEL classification:* F33
*Keywords:* Exchange rates; Regimes; Pegs; Floating

## 1. Introduction

Some have argued that the only sustainable regimes are free floating and hard exchange rate commitments—essentially currency boards or monetary unions (Eichengreen, 1994, 1998; Obstfeld and Rogoff, 1995). For instance, Eichengreen (1994, pp. 4–5) says that " ... contingent policy rules to hit explicit exchange rate targets will no longer be viable in the twenty-first century ... [C]ountries ... will be forced to choose between floating exchange rates on the one hand and monetary unification on the other." Similarly, Obstfeld and Rogoff (1995, p. 74)

---

[*] Tel.: +1-202-623-7483; fax: +1-202-623-7271.
*E-mail address:* pmasson@imf.org (P.R. Masson).

state " ... there is little, if any, comfortable middle ground between floating rates and the adoption of a common currency." Hence, in the view of these authors, in the future we will see a disappearance of the middle ground that corresponds to soft commitments to some sort of intermediate exchange rate regime-adjustable pegs, crawling pegs, or bands, and perhaps also managed floating. This view is sometimes called the "two poles" or "hollowing out" (e.g. Eichengreen, 1994, p. 6) theory of exchange rate regimes, and is based on the observation that higher capital mobility makes exchange rate commitments increasingly fragile. However, like the optimal currency area literature, which is essentially static, an explicit or implicit assumption is made that regimes are chosen to last forever, and from this perspective, one would only choose a regime that could be sustained once and for all. Only the hardest peg and the absence of any exchange rate commitment whatsoever are likely to qualify on that basis. Thus, Eichengreen (1994, p. 5), states "This will rule out the maintenance *for extended periods* of pegged but adjustable exchange rates, crawling pegs, and other regimes in which governments pre-announce limits on exchange rate fluctuations... " (italics added).

However, exchange rate regimes, like other aspects of economic policy, are not chosen once and for all. In fact, history shows us that countries change their regimes frequently, either voluntarily or involuntarily.[1] A particular exchange rate regime may suit the country's needs at the time—for instance, a peg may be the only way to halt a hyperinflation—but eventually be abandoned even though inflation has been brought down, because there has been a substantial loss of competitiveness.[2] This is the typical sequence with exchange rate based stabilizations—only rarely do they lead to "permanent" pegs. For instance, Poland in 1990 introduced a fixed peg to the dollar to provide an anchor for the price level, which was followed a year later by a crawling band introduced to limit appreciation of the real exchange rate, and, more recently, has moved to flexibility of the zloty exchange rate. Similarly, Brazil succeeded in eradicating hyperinflation in the mid-1990s through the "real plan", which involved a dollar peg with a very slow rate of crawl. Since 1999, this regime has been replaced by a flexible rate accompanied by inflation targeting. Only if we believed that countries will never be in the situation of using an exchange peg to disinflate (or never again suffer strong inflationary shocks) would it make sense to argue that countries will never use adjustable pegs as a temporary strategy, but instead will always be at one of the two poles.[3]

---

[1] For instance, Klein and Marion (1997) look at the duration of *pegs* (not *regimes*, as is done here), and find that the Latin American pegs in their sample last on average 10 months.

[2] Their have been few formal attempts to model transitions between regimes. A notable exception is Bhandari et al. (1989).

[3] Of course, using a peg in this way requires an exit strategy, something considered in Eichengreen et al. (1999).

P.R. Masson / Journal of Development Economics 64 (2001) 571–586

573

Regimes intermediate between a hard fix and a clean float may also be chosen as part of a regional integration strategy. The Exchange Rate Mechanism (ERM) of the European Monetary System, and its predecessor, the Snake, are examples of this. While the ERM has led to membership in a currency union (one of the poles) for 11 of the countries concerned, it lives on in the form of the ERM2 for countries that may subsequently want to join EMU. And it remains an open question whether for other regions integration may stop short of monetary union, and only involve limiting fluctuations among members' currencies.

Transitions between regimes may also reflect the shifting preferences of policymakers (and the public): a populist government may attempt to stimulate output at the expense of exchange rate stability, only to be followed by a more conservative and stability-oriented administration. The exchange rate regime chosen in each case need not be at one or another of the poles. Indeed, for many developing countries, free floating is not a viable option because of a lack of well-developed financial markets and institutions, including a deep foreign exchange market, while the hard constraints of currency boards are not politically acceptable. As a result, the exchange rate regime is not necessarily stable, but fluctuates among various alternative intermediate regimes, depending on the relative weight given to sustaining activity or limiting inflation, and on the shocks hitting the economy.

It is therefore useful to think of exchange rate regime choice not as a once-and-for-all decision but rather in terms of the likelihood of moving from one regime to another. In what follows, it is assumed that the probability of being in one or another regime next period depends only on the current regime. While somewhat restrictive, it supposes that the typical country will face the same likelihood that some shock will push it from its current regime to one of the others —independent of past history. As a first approximation, this would seem an adequate framework for testing hollowing out, which is a hypothesis concerning the direction of transitions, not their cause. Here, the historical data gives us some evidence on the transition between regimes. If we divide the regimes into three categories: hard pegs, floating, and a middle category that includes adjustable or crawling pegs and bands, and managed floats, we can see what the likelihood was in the past of remaining in each of the regimes, or of moving to the two others.

At any point in time, the distribution of regimes reflects these probabilities. However, if the probabilities have changed over time (for instance, as a result of increased capital mobility), the current distribution may not be the same as the *steady-state distribution* of regimes.[4] The latter is of interest also, because it tells us what the long-run equilibrium should look like, if the current transition

---

[4] In addition to the fact that our sample of countries is finite, so that the observed frequency distribution of regimes may not correspond to the theoretical population density.

probabilities remain unchanged. This steady-state distribution is the natural way to test the hollowing-out hypothesis, since the latter implies that the proportion of countries in the middle should be zero in the long run.

We can begin by asking whether there are any cases of exits from hard pegs or pure floats to intermediate regimes. As a notable dissenter to the hollowing-out hypothesis, Frankel (1999) notes that there have been exits from monetary unions (when Czechoslovakia broke up, and when the ruble area became limited to Russia after the CIS states left it). If one goes back further, Canada, which had a free float in 1951–1962, had an (adjustable) peg from 1962 until 1970, when it went back to a float. Also, a number of colonies which had currency boards abandoned them upon independence in favor of intermediate regimes, but this was arguably a specific historical episode.

A more systematic test of the hypothesis would involve looking at the probabilities of regime transitions, and projecting them into the future. The two poles view would be strictly correct (if the past is a guide to the future), if there were no exits from either hard pegs or floats (or if so, only to each other). We can test these restrictions on the transition matrix formally, and also calculate the long-run probabilities of the regimes; if the hypothesis is correct, the long-run probability of the middle regime would be zero.

In what follows, data on exchange rate regimes over the past two-and-a-half decades are used for constructing transition matrices, whose properties are then examined, to see whether they support the hypothesis of the disappearance of intermediate regimes. Because classification of regimes is difficult and contentious, we use two different sources. In neither case do the data support a substantial or continuing move away from intermediate regimes.

## 2. Properties of Markov chains and transition matrices

### 2.1. Definition and basic results

It is useful to start with some definitions and basic results (see Feller, 1957, Chap. 15). We assume that the stochastic process for the choice of exchange rate regimes can be described by a Markov chain, such that the probability of a given country being in each of the $n$ regimes depends only on its regime in the most recent previous period.[5] It is convenient to write the probability of regime $s_t = j$ given $s_{t-1} = i$ as $p_{ij}$, and to collect the transition probabilities in a matrix

---

[5] However, by augmenting the state space, dependence of probabilities on the regime in earlier periods can be nested in a first-order Markov chain.

*P.R. Masson / Journal of Development Economics 64 (2001) 571–586* 575

$P = \{p_{ij}\}$, with the sum across each row equal to unity. In our case, we can represent the transition matrix as follows:

General case

| Regime in period $t-1$ | Probability of regime in period $t$ | | |
| --- | --- | --- | --- |
| | Fix | Intermediate | Float |
| Fix | $p_{11}$ | $p_{12}$ | $p_{13}$ |
| Intermediate | $p_{21}$ | $p_{22}$ | $p_{23}$ |
| Float | $p_{31}$ | $p_{32}$ | $p_{33}$ |

A transition matrix (and associated Markov chain) has an *absorbing state i* if there is no way to reach other states from that state. This would be evidenced by a row with $p_{ii} = 1$ and all other elements 0. For instance, it could be that currency boards are permanent, so that once one was adopted there would be no transitions to other states. If there was a positive probability of going from other regimes to a currency board, therefore, the world might end up being dominated by that regime (if there were no other absorbing states). This could be depicted as follows:

Fix as an absorbing state

| Regime in period $t-1$ | Probability of regime in period $t$ | | |
| --- | --- | --- | --- |
| | Fix | Intermediate | Float |
| Fix | 1 | 0 | 0 |
| Intermediate | $p_{21}$ | $p_{22}$ | $p_{23}$ |
| Float | $p_{31}$ | $p_{32}$ | $p_{33}$ |

More generally, there could be a *closed set* of states C such that no state outside of C can be reached from any state in C. The hypothesis of the hollowing out of intermediate regimes would be consistent with fixing and floating together constituting a closed set, from which there were no exits to intermediate regimes:

Closed set of fix and float

| Regime in period $t-1$ | Probability of regime in period $t$ | | |
| --- | --- | --- | --- |
| | Fix | Intermediate | Float |
| Fix | $p_{11}$ | 0 | $1 - p_{11}$ |
| Intermediate | $p_{21}$ | $p_{22}$ | $p_{23}$ |
| Float | $1 - p_{33}$ | 0 | $p_{33}$ |

Thus, transitions between hard fixes and floats could occur, but none back to the intermediate soft pegs, dirty floats, or bands. The hollowing-out hypothesis is satisfied if either fixes of floats are absorbing states, or if together they constitute a closed set. A transition matrix without closed sets (including absorbing states) is termed *irreducible*, that is, every state can be reached from every other state.

Finally, for a given Markov chain we can calculate the *long-run distribution* of regimes by repeatedly applying the transition matrix. If we start with some initial distribution of exchange rate regimes (in the three categories, fix, intermediate, and float)—call this the row vector $\pi_0$—then the distribution of regimes in period

1 will be $\pi_1 = \pi_0 \mathbf{P}$ and in period 2, $\pi_2 = \pi_1 \mathbf{P}$, etc. So the limiting (long-run) distribution will be $\pi = \lim_{n \to \infty} \pi_0 \mathbf{P}^n$. The long-run distribution for an important subset of Markov chains,[6] is independent of the initial distribution, and is also called the _invariant distribution_ (it is equal to any row of the matrix lim $\mathbf{P}^n$, as $n$ goes to infinity). For all of the subcases consistent with the hollowing-out hypothesis, the long-run distribution is invariant, and implies no regimes in the intermediate category.

It is relevant in any case to compare the current distribution to the long-run distribution. An interesting possibility, for instance, would be that the invariant distribution implied much greater regime polarization than what prevails now (even if the hollowing out hypothesis is not strictly true). As is well known from the persistence in the use of reserve currencies, exchange rate regimes are slow to change, so that the effects of a new economic environment (involving for instance capital account liberalization) might take a long time to be visible in the number of countries in each regime category. Thus, a trend toward polarization might not yet be evident in the actual regime distribution though it would show up in the invariant distribution (and in the transition matrix). Thus, testing of the hollowing-out hypothesis is best done using the latter.

## 2.2. Testing the hollowing out hypothesis

The hypothesis that eventually all regimes do converge to fixed or floating means that the intermediate regime gets a zero weight in the invariant distribution, and this is equivalent to the zero restrictions on the transition matrix described above. Strictly speaking, the existence of transitions toward the intermediate regime from fixes and floats (i.e. non-zero transition probabilities) would be incontrovertible evidence that the hypothesis is false. However, the approach to hypothesis testing taken in Bhat (1972) is to ignore those transition probabilities which are zero under the null, and instead test whether the remaining probabilities are consistent with the hypothesis. The relevant test of the hollowing-out hypothesis is that either fixes or floats are absorbing states or that fixing and floating together form a closed set. An absorbing state for one of the two regimes and a closed set constituted by the two of them together each involves two zero restrictions on the transition matrix. For an absorbing state, there are no transitions away from the regime in question, while for a closed set, there can be transitions from intermediate regimes to fix or float and the latter between themselves, but not from the latter to the intermediate regimes.

Ordering the three states as above into fix, intermediate, and float, respectively, we estimate two transition matrices, the first one unrestricted, $\mathbf{P} = \{p_{ij}\}$, and the second one $\mathbf{P}^0$ with two restrictions. In the case that fixed rates are an absorbing state, the restrictions are $p_{12} = 0$ and $p_{13} = 0$ (so $p_{11} = 1$). Only this case is

---

[6] Those for which the **P** matrix has a single unit eigenvalue.

P.R. Masson / Journal of Development Economics 64 (2001) 571–586          577

relevant, since (as we will see below) the data firmly reject the hypothesis of floating as absorbing state. For the hypothesis of fixes and floats jointly constituting a closed set, the restrictions are $p_{12} = 0$ and $p_{32} = 0$.

The log likelihood function for each of the estimates can be written as:

$$L(\mathbf{P}_{ij}) = \ln B(n_{ij}) + \Sigma_i \Sigma_j \, n_{ij} \ln \mathbf{P}_{ij}$$

Maximum likelihood estimates of the two matrices correspond to the sample frequencies of transitions between the regimes, with only the non-zero transitions being included in the restricted case (Bhat 1972, p. 99). A likelihood ratio statistic equal to twice the difference in the maximized values of log likelihood functions in the two cases is distributed as a chi-square with degrees of freedom equal to two, the number of restrictions. Since the first term (in $B$ above) is common to both, the likelihood ratio can be written

$$2 \, \Sigma_i \Sigma_j \, n_{ij} \ln \mathbf{P}_{ij}^0 / \mathbf{P}_{ij}$$

where the summation is taken only over the non-zero cells.[7] If this statistic is significant, we reject the hypothesis of hollowing out.

## 3. Classification of regimes

The problems with the official classification (tabulated in the IMF's International Financial Statistics and in more detail in the Annual Report on Exchange Arrangements and Exchange Restrictions) are well known. The official classification often does not correspond to the reality of exchange rate fluctuations. For instance, a number of Asian countries were classified as floaters before the 1997–1998 crisis, even though de facto they were pegging to the U.S. dollar. The fact that they were then forced to float does not therefore appear as a transition in the official data. A proposal to make the official classification more relevant is contained in IMF (1999), and the new classification has now been adopted. However, it mainly concerns the classification of the intermediate exchange rate regimes, bringing them more in line with actual practice and providing information on monetary policy strategies. Moreover, data only exist for 1997 and subsequent years.

We estimate transition matrices using two data sources that modify the official classification, due to Ghosh et al. (1997) and Levy Yeyati and Sturzenegger (1999). Their methodologies are very different, which should provide some sense

---

[7] The likelihood ratio has to be greater than zero, since the constrained estimates of the probabilities of transitions between fixes and floats will necessarily be greater than the unconstrained ones (and only those cells of rows 1 and 3 are included in the summation), while the estimates for the intermediate regime (the second row) are identical in the two cases.

of whether the results are robust. The former relies to some extent on the official classification, while the latter classifies regimes solely on the basis of the behavior of exchange rates and foreign exchange market intervention.

## 3.1. Ghosh et al. data

The Ghosh et al. (1997) study looks at actual exchange rate behavior as well as the official classification, and is available from 1960 to 1997 for a broad range of countries. Pegs are distinguished between single currency, SDR pegs, other official basket pegs, and secret basket pegs, and differentiated by the extent that parity adjustments are absent, infrequent or frequent (using as input an analysis of historical data). There is a separate category of cooperative arrangements (the EMS and its predecessor the Snake), while more flexible arrangements are divided into crawling pegs, target zones, managed floating (with or without heavy intervention), and independent floats.

Since we are interested in the three-way classification of hard pegs, floats, and intermediate regimes, we need to compress their classification. As in all work in this area, there can be serious debate about whether a particular country's regime should fall in one or another of the categories. We include among the hard peggers only those countries with a currency board, and announced pegs with virtually no changes in parities.[8] Those with some parity adjustments (frequent or infrequent) and secret basket pegs are included with the intermediate arrangements. We include in the other polar case only the "independent floats", and all other types of managed or dirty floats are included among the intermediate regimes. This latter group also includes the EMS, which historically has included parity changes and occasional wide fluctuations (in particular after the widening of the bands of fluctuation in July 1993).

In defining fixes and floats relatively narrowly, we are guarding against biasing the test of hollowing out towards rejection. A somewhat wider definition would tend to produce more transitions *away from* the poles, leading to a greater probability of rejection (as we will see below, there have been no exits from currency boards or monetary unions during the 1990s, which is consistent with fixes being an absorbing state). Of course, if the two poles were defined very widely, so that intermediate regimes did not exist in our sample, then hollowing out would follow automatically. But we are far from that extreme.

The transition matrix is first estimated using the whole of the post-Bretton–Woods sample, that is, using data from 1974 through 1997. The matrix is

---

[8] The CFA franc zone countries are classified in the Ghosh et al. data as hard peggers. Despite some changes in the composition of the zone, there have been no changes in parity among the African CFA franc countries (except for Comoros) since 1948, and only one adjustment of the peg to the French franc, in 1994.

*P.R. Masson / Journal of Development Economics 64 (2001) 571–586* 579

Table 1
Estimated transition matrix, 1974–1997

| | | |
|---|---|---|
| 0.9430 | 0.0544 | 0.0027 |
| 0.0114 | 0.9601 | 0.0285 |
| 0.0072 | 0.0885 | 0.9043 |

Table 2
Estimated transition matrix, 1980–1997

| | | |
|---|---|---|
| 0.9490 | 0.0474 | 0.0036 |
| 0.0097 | 0.9549 | 0.0354 |
| 0.0078 | 0.0940 | 0.8982 |

Test of fixes and floats being a closed set: $2*\log$ likelihood $= 119.3$ ($p$-value $< 0.0001$).
Test of fixing as absorbing state: $2*\log$ likelihood $= 54.5$ ($p$-value $< 0.0001$).

constructed on the basis of 3453 observations: 24 years and 167 countries (not all countries' regimes are available for all dates). Of these 3453 observations, 754 correspond to initial fixes, 418 floats, and 2281 intermediate regimes. The matrix in Table 1 is clearly irreducible: all regimes can be reached from each state. However, each of the three regimes is highly persistent, with at least a 90% chance of remaining in that regime in the following year. Interestingly, the float regime is the least persistent, however, and the intermediate one the most (based on the relative sizes of the diagonal elements).

A criticism of using such a long run of data may be that the early years of generalized floating involved some experimentation with regimes, as well as being affected by the turbulence following the oil price shocks. Starting in 1980 at least partially avoids this problem. It can be seen from Table 2 that the transition matrix is little changed, though fixes are somewhat more persistent, while intermediate regimes and floats are somewhat less.

Interestingly enough, the long-run (invariant) distribution of regimes looks much like the distribution that prevailed at the end of 1997 (Table 3). In fact, the former implies a somewhat higher frequency of intermediate regimes, and fewer fixes and floats, than prevailed in 1997, suggesting that we will see a move toward, not away from, intermediate regimes.

Table 3
Invariant distribution and current state

| | Fix | Intermediate | Float |
|---|---|---|---|
| Regimes in 1997 | 0.1677 | 0.5749 | 0.2575 |
| Invariant distribution, 1980–1997 | 0.1529 | 0.6246 | 0.2224 |

Table 4
Estimated transition matrix, 1990–1997

| 0.9909 | 0.0000 | 0.0091 |
|--------|--------|--------|
| 0.0055 | 0.9234 | 0.0711 |
| 0.0066 | 0.1093 | 0.8841 |

Test of fixes and floats being a closed set: $2*\log$ likelihood $= 62.3$ ($p$-value $< 0.0001$).
Test of fixing as absorbing state: $2*\log$ likelihood $= 3.98$ ($p$-value $= 0.137$).

Table 5
Invariant distribution and current state

|                                      | Fix    | Intermediate | Float  |
|--------------------------------------|--------|--------------|--------|
| Regimes in 1997                      | 0.1677 | 0.5749       | 0.2575 |
| Invariant distribution, 1990–1997    | 0.3954 | 0.3554       | 0.2492 |

We now turn to what is arguably the most relevant time period for considering the hollowing-out hypothesis, the 1990s, since it comprises a period during which many developing countries increased their integration with international capital markets, exposing their intermediate exchange rate regimes to greater risk of speculative attack. Using 1990–1997 data provides somewhat greater support for the two poles, or hollowing-out, hypothesis (Tables 4 and 5). Over this period, according to the Ghosh et al. data, there were no exits from fixed rates to intermediate regimes, so one of the constraints needed for hollowing out is satisfied in the sample. Nevertheless, the matrix is irreducible, since there are transitions from fixes to floats and from floats to intermediate regimes, and a formal test of the two constraints of the closed set overwhelming rejects it (though with a somewhat lower chi-square statistic). Turning to the hypothesis that fixed rates are an absorbing state, we can only reject this hypothesis at the 13.7% significance level given the few transitions away from fixes.[9] There are only two in the data: Trinidad and Tobago in 1992 (from a single currency peg to a float) and Sao Tomé and Principe in 1994 (from an official basket peg to a float). Despite this, the invariant distribution, while it gives greater weight to the two poles than one calculated over 1980–1997, still gives considerable weight to the middle—indeed, more than to floating rate regimes. Thus, though this data set does provide some support for the hypothesis that the past decade's experience foreshadows a reduction in the future of the proportion of intermediate exchange rate regimes (and also floats), it is not overwhelming.

---

[9] John Williamson has pointed out to me a problem with a classification that includes among the hard fixes only those with no changes in parity: this guarantees no transitions away from such regimes! However, the Ghosh et al. data also includes more objective criteria, such as the establishment of monetary unions or currency boards, and their data do not show any transitions away from these.

P.R. Masson / Journal of Development Economics 64 (2001) 571–586          581

Given that the trend is to a somewhat greater support for the hypothesis, it is also of interest to test the stability of the transition matrix when the 1990s are compared to the 1980s. Accordingly, we calculate a likelihood ratio test for the null hypothesis that the two subperiods have the same parameters.[10] The value of the test statistic, 86.6, is significant with a $p$-value $< 0.0001$, so that there is evidence of structural instability. Thus, there is some question whether a stable Markov process describes the data, and whether the lack of support for hollowing out even using the most recent data will persist into the future.

## 3.2. Levy Yeyati and Sturzenegger data

These authors completely ignore the official classification and use three variables: monthly percentage changes in the nominal exchange rate, the standard deviation of monthly percentage changes in the exchange rate, and the volatility of reserves—to classify countries into four exchange rate regimes (flexible, dirty float, crawling peg, and fixed) plus an "inconclusive" group in which the variability of reserves seemed to be irrelevant for exchange rate fluctuations. Exchange rate changes are calculated with respect to the US dollar, the French franc, the deutsche mark, the pound sterling, and Japanese yen, as well as, where relevant, some "local" anchor currencies (such as the Indian rupee for Nepal and the South African rand for Namibia). Cluster analysis is used to identify the groups; flexible rate regimes are assumed to be associated with large average percentage changes in the exchange rate, high exchange rate volatility, and low reserves volatility, and fixed rates the opposite constellation. The time period is 1990–1998; the list of countries (110 of them) includes all countries for which the relevant data were available in the IMF's International Financial Statistics. Since not all observations were available for all years, there is a total sample of 955 observations.

For our purposes, we need a three-way classification. We drop the inconclusive observations, and group the dirty float and crawling pegs in the intermediate regime. We lose one observation per country for the initial state, and calculate the transition matrix over 1991–1998. This gives 590 observations, of which 208 initially involve fixes, 227 floats, and the rest (155) in the intermediate regime category. The results for the transition matrix and the invariant distribution are given in Tables 6 and 7.

There is a notable difference with the Ghosh et al. data: regimes are much less persistent than in the latter study, as captured by smaller diagonal elements in the

---

[10] The test statistic is given in Bhat (1972), Eq. (5.3.23). As discussed in Section 5.3 of that book, observations of the transition matrix which are zero are ignored in the calculation, and the number of degrees of freedom is reduced accordingly (by two in this case, since for the first subperiod, $P(1,3) = 0$, while $P(1,2) = 0$ in the second subperiod). This yields a chi-square with 4, rather than $(T-1) * n * (n-1) = 6$ degrees of freedom.

Table 6
Estimated transition matrix, 1991–1998

| 0.8413 | 0.0913 | 0.0673 |
|--------|--------|--------|
| 0.1935 | 0.5290 | 0.2774 |
| 0.0440 | 0.1894 | 0.7665 |

Test of fixes and floats being a closed set: $2 * \log$ likelihood $= 113.5$ ($p$-value $< 0.0001$).
Test of fixing as absorbing state: $2 * \log$ likelihood $= 60.5$ ($p$-value $< 0.0001$).

transition matrix. This may well reflect the reality that actual regimes changed even though official pronouncements did not, perhaps because the official regime did not initially reflect reality. However, an example of this that was cited above, Thailand, is classified as an intermediate regime in 1997 and 1998, while in 1996 and before it was in the inconclusive range, and hence was dropped from our sample. Another reason for the apparent lower persistence in regimes is due to a difference in methodology, since fluctuations in exchange rates and reserves reflect external forces as well as the intentions of the authorities. So when exchange market pressures occur, the authorities' commitment is put to the test and the actual regime may diverge from the official one.

It is also notable that the intermediate regime has a lower probability of continuing next period than either fix or flex. However, there is no evidence that fixes or flexes are absorbing states, or together form a closed set; the data strongly reject these hypotheses (only the absorbing state hypothesis applied to fixed rates is reported). On the contrary, the probability of moving to the middle regime in any given year is about 10% when starting from a fix and 20% from a float, and as a result the invariant distribution attributes a weight of about a quarter to the intermediate regime, and three-eighths to each of the poles, very similar to the actual distribution, suggesting that no major changes are in the pipeline. Thus, there is no support here for the hollowing-out hypothesis, as Levy Yeyati and Sturzenegger themselves note.

### 3.3. Emerging market countries

An objection that can be made to the above empirical exercise is that it concerns a large and heterogeneous set of countries, while the hollowing out hypothesis may be intended specifically for the more advanced countries that are

Table 7
Invariant distribution and current state

|                                       | Fix    | Intermediate | Float  |
|---------------------------------------|--------|--------------|--------|
| Regimes in 1998                       | 0.3614 | 0.2289       | 0.4096 |
| Invariant distribution, 1991–1998     | 0.3865 | 0.2294       | 0.3840 |

*P.R. Masson / Journal of Development Economics 64 (2001) 571–586*          583

most open to international capital flows. In addition, it could be hypothesized that with the passage of time, more and more countries would be included in the category of advanced countries, so that hollowing out would extend eventually to the whole world. In this view, looking at the historical data on all regime transitions would not give a good indication of future trends, since it reflects the shifting composition of the set of countries. The rejection of structural stability between the 1980s and 1990s for the Ghosh et al. data might reflect this.

A useful way of examining this issue is to restrict the set of countries to the "emerging market countries," which are integrated with world capital markets. Therefore, the same transition matrix approach was applied to the 27 countries making up the JP Morgan Emerging Markets Bond Index Global.[11] These countries include the larger and most active developing country issuers of international bonds.[12] Of course, one might also include the industrial countries in this group, but interpreting the results would depend very much on whether the creation of EMU was viewed as a unique event or an example for other regions. The creation of the euro on January 1, 1999, is not in fact reflected in the data, which extend only to 1997 or 1998, and which therefore do not include a transition away from the intermediate regime constituted by the EMS towards monetary union. Hence, we focus on the emerging market countries.

Results for the 1990s are presented in Table 8 for both the Ghosh et al. and Levy Yeyati–Sturzenegger data. The table contains also a stability test for the former classification, when the 1980s are compared to the 1990s (this could not be done for the latter classification, given the shorter sample period). Interestingly enough, a stability test does not reject the hypothesis that the two decades' data in the Ghosh et al. classification are drawn from the same sample.

The test of the hollowing out hypothesis gives markedly different results in the two classifications. It is soundly rejected by the Levy Yeyati–Sturznegger data, but a variant of hollowing out—namely that fixed rates are an absorbing state—is satisfied by the Ghosh et al. data. This results from the fact that there are no transitions away from hard fixes in the Ghosh et al. classification, even though there are transitions to the intermediate regimes from floats. As a result, the Markov chain predicts that after a very long transition, all countries would have pegged rates, and there would be no floats or intermediate regimes. The short sample period and the restricted set of countries suggest caution in accepting this result; its relevance to the entire population of countries relies on the subsidiary hypothesis that all will eventually resemble this set of emerging market countries. Moreover, it should be noted that since intermediate regimes are very persistent, as

---

[11] The more widely quoted EMBI+ index only includes a representative handful of countries, for ease in updating the yield spread.

[12] The countries are Algeria, Argentina, Brazil, Bulgaria, Chile, China, Colombia, Cote d'Ivoire, Croatia, Ecuador, Greece, Hungary, Lebanon, Malaysia, Mexico, Morocco, Nigeria, Panama, Peru, the Philippines, Poland, Russia, South Africa, South Korea, Thailand, Turkey, and Venezuela.

Table 8
Emerging market countries in the 1990s: transition matrices and tests of hollowing out

| Ghosh et al. data | | |
|---|---|---|
| 1.0000 | 0.0000 | 0.0000 |
| 0.0097 | 0.9578 | 0.0325 |
| 0.0143 | 0.0857 | 0.9000 |

Test of structural stability, 1980s vs. 1990s: $2 * \log$ likelihood $= 2.14$ ( $p$-value $= 0.55$);
Test of fixes and floats being a closed set: $2 * \log$ likelihood $= 11.5$ ( $p$-value $= 0.003$);
Test of fixing as absorbing state: $2 * \log$ likelihood $= 0$ ( $p$-value $= 1.000$).

Long run distribution (distribution in 1997):

| | | |
|---|---|---|
| 1.0000 (0.1538) | 0.0000 (0.6154) | 0.0000 (0.2308) |

| Levy Yeyati and Sturzenegger data | | |
|---|---|---|
| 0.6667 | 0.1905 | 0.1429 |
| 0.1569 | 0.5490 | 0.2941 |
| 0.0192 | 0.3269 | 0.6538 |

Test of fixes and floats being a closed set: $2 * \log$ likelihood $= 34.9$ ( $p$-value $< 0.0001$);
Test of fixing as absorbing state: $2 * \log$ likelihood $= 11.4$ ( $p$-value $= 0.003$).

Invariant distribution (distribution in 1998):

| | | |
|---|---|---|
| 0.2046 (0.1875) | 0.3844 (0.3125) | 0.4110 (0.5000) |

evidenced by a value of 0.9578 on the diagonal of the transition matrix, it takes 83 years before the proportion of intermediate regimes, which is 62% initially, is reduced to 25% (and 166 years to 10%).

The Levy Yeyati–Sturzenegger classification, based on actual exchange rate and reserves behavior, has starkly contrasting implications. There are frequent transitions away from fixed rates, to both the intermediate regime and to floats, and the transitions from floats are mainly to the intermediate regimes. As a result, the hollowing out hypothesis in either form is soundly rejected, and the invariant distribution implies proportions of roughly 0.2, 0.4, and 0.4, for the three regimes, implying some future increase in the proportion of fixes and intermediate regimes, at the expense of floats.

## 4. Conclusion

Historical evidence of regime transitions gives an indication of whether the trend towards the poles of exchange rate regimes, which some commentators have divined in the 1990s, will eventually lead to the disappearance of intermediate regimes. Projecting transitions into the future does not produce such a hollowing out. The hypothesis that there are only transitions toward the two poles, and not toward the middle, can generally be overwhelmingly rejected by data samples

*P.R. Masson / Journal of Development Economics 64 (2001) 571–586* 585

based on the widest possible set of countries. We have guarded against the danger of arbitrary classification of regimes by using two different data sets that depart from the official classification. Both data sets suggest that a range of exchange rate regimes will be present for the foreseeable future, and will constitute roughly a quarter to a third of all regimes, though the Ghosh et al. data for the 1990s cannot reject the hypothesis of fixed rates as absorbing state. The Levy Yeyati–Sturznegger data set, which is based on what governments do, not what they say, overwhelmingly rejects all variants of hollowing out.

Of course, using historical data for transitions raises the danger that we are using data which are no longer relevant, or that the trends in capital mobility, which have affected some countries (emerging markets) will spread to others in the future, producing an irreversible movement toward the poles. We therefore also look at a restricted set of countries, those classified as emerging markets, in the 1990s. Results for the Ghosh et al. data set suggest that eventually fixed rates will prevail as the single exchange rate regime for these countries. This result emerges because of the small number of hard pegs and the short time period, leading to the absence of any exits from this regime. As mentioned in the Introduction, there are earlier examples of breakdowns of both monetary unions and currency boards, and this experience is still relevant to an environment with higher capital mobility (capital mobility can be expected to make all exchange rate commitments, including fixes, more fragile). The starkly different implications of the Levy Yeyati–Sturzenegger data set, which strongly rejects the two forms of hollowing-out hypothesis for even this restricted set of countries, also throw doubt on hard pegs as the solution for all countries. The evidence of transitions thus suggests that intermediate regimes will continue to constitute an important fraction of actual exchange rate regimes.

## Acknowledgements

The paper was written while I was Visiting Fellow at the Brookings Institution. I am grateful to Brookings for their hospitality, to Rex Ghosh and Eduardo Levy Yeyati for providing me with spreadsheets containing their data, and to Ralph Bryant, Susan Collins, Martin Evans, William Gale, Carol Graham, Olivier Jeanne, Eduardo Levy Yeyati, Paolo Mauro, John Williamson, and an anonymous referee for helpful discussions and comments. The views expressed are my own and do not commit any official institution.

## References

Bhandari, J., Flood, R., Horne, J., 1989. Evolution of exchange rate regimes. International Monetary Fund Staff Papers 36 (4), 810–835.

Bhat, U.N., 1972. Elements of Applied Stochastic Processes. Wiley, New York.

Eichengreen, B., 1994. International Monetary Arrangements for the 21st Century. Brookings, Washington, DC.

Eichengreen, B., 1998. The only game in town. The World Today (December).

Eichengreen, B., Masson, P., Savastano, M., Sharma, S., 1999. Transition strategies and nominal anchors on the road to greater exchange-rate flexibility, Essays in International Finance, No. 213. Princeton University, Princeton, NJ.

Feller, W., 1957. An Introduction to Probability Theory and Its Applications. 3rd edn. Wiley, New York.

Frankel, J.A., 1999. No single currency regime is right for all countries or at all times, Essays in International Finance, No. 215. Princeton University, Princeton, NJ.

Ghosh, A.R., Gulde, A-M., Ostry, J., Wolf, H., 1997. Does the nominal exchange rate matter? NBER Working Paper No. 5874. National Bureau of Economic Research, Cambridge, MA.

IMF, 1999. Exchange rate arrangements and currency convertibility: developments and issues, World Economic and Financial Surveys. International Monetary Fund, Washington, DC.

Klein, M., Marion, N., 1997. Explaining the duration of exchange rate pegs. Journal of Development Economics 54, 387–404 (December).

Levy Yeyati, E., Sturzenegger, F., 1999. Classifying exchange rate regimes: deeds vs. words, mimeo, available at http://www.utdt.edu/ ~ ely.

Obstfeld, M., Rogoff, K., 1995. The mirage of fixed exchange rates. Journal of Economic Perspectives 9 (4), 73–96.

Scand. J. of Economics 107(2), 261–278, 2005
DOI: 10.1111/j.1467-9442.2005.00407.x

# Explaining the Transition between Exchange Rate Regimes*

*Paul Masson*

University of Toronto, Toronto, ONT M5S 3E6, Canada
paul.masson@rotman.utoronto.ca

*Francisco J. Ruge-Murcia*

University of Montréal, Montréal, Québec H3C 3J7, Canada
francisco.ruge-murcia@umontreal.ca

## Abstract

This paper studies the transition between exchange rate regimes using a Markov chain model with time-varying transition probabilities. The probabilities are parameterized as nonlinear functions of variables suggested by the currency crisis and optimal currency area literature. Results using annual data indicate that inflation and, to a lesser extent, output growth and trade openness help explain the exchange rate regime transition dynamics.

*Keywords*: Hollowing out hypothesis; regime change; Markov chains; floating; pegs

*JEL classification*: F33

## I. Introduction

Advocates of the "hollowing out" hypothesis argue that an increase in capital mobility would tend to make intermediate exchange rate regimes (for example, adjustable pegs, bands, or dirty floating) disappear, in favor of the extremes of currency boards or monetary union on the one hand, and freely flexible exchange rates on the other; see Eichengreen (1994), Obstfeld and Rogoff (1995) and Fischer (2001). Underlying this view is the presumption that the abandonment of intermediate exchange rate regimes would not be the result of a voluntary choice. Instead, if countries attempted to maintain an intermediate regime until forced to exit, the exit would be the result of a speculative attack; see Eichengreen, Masson, Savastano, and Sharma (1999). The adoption of a regime would be less the result of official policy than of speculators' actions. An exchange rate peg would give way to a

* We are grateful to Susan Collins, Paolo Mauro, and an anonymous referee for comments, and to Grace Juhn, Haiyan Shi, and Saji Thomas for research assistance. Ruge-Murcia gratefully acknowledges financial support from the Social Sciences and Humanities Research Council and the Fonds pour la Formation de Chercheurs et l'Aide à la Recherche.

262    *P. Masson and F. J. Ruge-Murcia*

floating currency if the former became unsustainable as a result of over-expansionary domestic credit (as in first generation models), or low growth and high unemployment (as in second generation models). In principle, the abandonment of an intermediate exchange rate regime in a crisis could also involve a move to a currency board or monetary union, though in practice this is less frequent.

A parallel and equally influential literature on exchange rate regime choice is derived from Mundell's seminal paper on optimum currency areas (OCA). The structural characteristics of an economy should influence whether a country would choose to share a common currency with another. These characteristics include, for example, the correlation (symmetry) and effect of shocks and the mobility of labor; see Mundell (1961). Other factors have also been suggested as important for the choice of exchange rate regime, such as the existence of fiscal transfers, the degree of openness, and the extent of diversification of production; for a survey, see Masson and Taylor (1993). Although there have been numerous attempts to explain regime choice using OCA models, the variables implied by the theory have not been very successful in accounting for the observed exchange rate regimes; see, for example, Frankel and Rose (1998), Mussa, Masson, Swoboda, Jadresic, Mauro, and Berg (2000) and Juhn and Mauro (2001). Poirson (2001) reports some success of traditional OCA variables and political factors in explaining regime choice.

Masson (2001) argues that a strategy to test the hollowing out hypothesis is to look at the matrix of transition probabilities between different exchange rate regimes.[1] Specifically, it can be tested whether there are transitions away from intermediate regimes, but not towards them. This condition is both necessary and sufficient for hollowing out. Using two different exchange rate regime classifications, the data generally reject the hollowing out hypothesis for all time periods when all countries are included. When the sample is restricted to the decade of the 1990s for the emerging market countries only, and for only one of the two regime classifications, the data cannot reject the hypothesis that there are no exits from currency boards, implying that this regime would eventually dominate. Such a conclusion contrasts with the predictions of OCA models, which imply that a degree of exchange rate flexibility would be desirable, hence that countries would prefer an intermediate regime.

In this paper we estimate a Markov chain model of exchange rate regime transitions with time-varying probabilities. In particular, the transition probabilities between exchange rate regimes are specified to be nonlinear functions of the explanatory variables. The explanatory variables are those

---

[1] Markov chains have been used in other contexts to study the properties of long-run distributions, for instance by Quah (1993) and Kremer, Onatski, and Stock (2001).

implied by both OCA and currency crisis models. Results indicate that, in many cases, it is possible to reject the null hypothesis of constant transition probabilities, in favor of an alternative where inflation, trade openness, output growth, and/or reserves help determine exchange rate regime transitions. We also study whether, conditioning on unchanged explanatory variables, transitions have changed over time. For instance, if capital mobility has increased, then the currency crisis literature predicts that transitions away from intermediate regimes should increase. Finally, we test whether industrial and developing countries can be considered to be part of the same sample, or whether they form distinct groups. The latter point has been argued by, for example, Hausmann, Panizza, and Stein (2001) and Calvo and Reinhart (2002), who suggest reasons why developing countries do not benefit from exchange rate flexibility.

Markov chains are also a natural framework to test the predictive power of models that seek to explain the observed distribution of exchange rate regimes. According to currency crisis models, abandonment of pegs should be more frequent when countries with pegs experienced excessive domestic credit growth, overvalued exchange rates, or weak economic activity. According to OCA models, exchange rate regime transitions should result from changes in structural characteristics. These two models are not mutually exclusive. For example, if forced to exit from an adjustable peg, a country's authorities may then have the choice between a hard peg and a free float, so both currency crisis and optimum currency area criteria could be relevant. Second generation currency crisis models acknowledge that exit could be a deliberate choice of the authorities, even if provoked by speculation. Thus, a model explaining transitions between exchange rate regimes may include variables implied by both OCA (or other structural) models and currency crisis models.

The rest of the paper is structured as follows. Section II describes models of exchange rate regime choice that motivate our empirical analysis. Section III explains the use of Markov chains to model exchange rate regime transitions. Section IV reports empirical results and examines the ability of the estimated Markov chain model to forecast exchange rate regime transitions. Section V concludes and suggests avenues for future research.

## II. Models of Voluntary and Involuntary Exchange Rate Regime Choice

The main difference between OCA (and other structural) and currency crisis models is that in the former, the exchange rate regime choice is assumed to be the outcome of a voluntary decision by the monetary authorities. The latter explain the involuntary exit from an exchange rate peg as triggered by

264   *P. Masson and F. J. Ruge-Murcia*

the actions of speculators. If a forced exit involves a choice between the alternative regimes, then voluntary and involuntary elements would both be present.

Among the models of voluntary choice of regime, those broadly characterized as optimum currency area models have attracted the most attention. In principle, these models should use exogenous structural features of the economy to explain the voluntary choices of the policy authorities. Frankel and Rose (1998) question the exogeneity of some of these variables. Subject to this caveat, several OCA variables have unambiguous implications for the choice of exchange rate regime. Poirson (2001, Table A4) identifies trade openness, the existence of a dominant trading partner, labor mobility, and nominal flexibility as variables associated with a fixed exchange rate regime, while economic development, diversification of production and exports, and (large) size of the economy are variables associated with a floating exchange rate regime. Poirson identifies two other sets of models, namely those inspired by political economy, especially as in Collins (1996) and Edwards (1996), and by "fear of floating", as in Calvo and Reinhart (2002). Political economy or "fear of floating" variables that have been suggested to influence regime choice include the extent of foreign currency debt and dollarization, the degree of central bank credibility, and the size of reserves. However, some of these variables are very hard to measure, while others are clearly endogenous.

First generation currency crisis models describe the process by which foreign exchange reserves are depleted by speculators; see, for example, Krugman (1979). Speculators correctly anticipate that the authorities will not be able to maintain the peg. In the simplest monetary model, the peg is unsustainable because domestic credit expansion is too rapid. In more elaborate models, the peg is unsustainable because the real exchange rate is overvalued or the fiscal deficit is too large.

In second generation models, the authorities are assumed to decide whether to maintain a peg in the light of variables that enter their objective function. Assuming that they care about both the real economy (e.g. the rate of unemployment) and price (or exchange rate) stability, shocks to the real economy may affect the trade-off between objectives and lead to a greater willingness to sacrifice price (or exchange rate) stability and hence abandon an exchange rate peg.

Currency crisis models suggest a set of largely endogenous variables as determinants of the exchange rate regime. These variables include the rate of domestic credit expansion, the fiscal deficit, the level of reserves, the real exchange rate, the rate of unemployment, the growth rate of GDP, and the inflation rate. In addition, these models suggest that the degree of capital account openness should matter for the vulnerability to speculative attack. Most models assume perfect capital mobility, but if the economy is cut off

## Explaining the transition between exchange rate regimes 265

from world capital markets, it may not be forced to abandon a peg even in the face of a fundamental disequilibrium.

## III. Markov Chains

A Markov chain is a simple stochastic structure that can summarize the transition between exchange rate regimes. Define by $s_t$ the exchange rate regime in period $t$. In the subsequent analysis, $s_t$ is assumed to take either of three possible values: $s_t = 1$ denotes a fixed exchange rate regime, $s_t = 3$ denotes a floating exchange rate, and $s_t = 2$ denotes an intermediate exchange rate regime. The Markov chain is defined by three objects: first, the state-space set, $S_t$ that contains the possible values the state variable can take (in this case, 1, 2, or 3); second, the $3 \times 3$ matrix of transition probabilities, $\mathbf{P}$, with elements $p_{ij}$ for $i, j = 1, 2, 3$:

$$\mathbf{P} = \begin{bmatrix} p_{11} & p_{12} & p_{13} \\ p_{21} & p_{22} & p_{23} \\ p_{31} & p_{32} & p_{33} \end{bmatrix}. \tag{1}$$

The typical element $p_{ij} = \Pr(s_t = j | s_{t-1} = i)$ is the probability that the current regime is $j$ given that the regime in the previous period was $i$; third, the $1 \times 3$ vector $\boldsymbol{\pi}_t$ that records the proportion of countries in each of the three regimes at time $t$. The matrix $\mathbf{P}$ satisfies $\Sigma_j p_{ij} = 1$ for $j = 1, 2, 3$. That is, the elements of $\mathbf{P}$ add up to one across rows. The vector $\boldsymbol{\pi}_t$ satisfies $\Sigma_i \pi_{t,i} = 1$, where $\pi_{t,i}$ is the typical element of $\boldsymbol{\pi}_t$. The distribution of exchange rate regimes evolves over time following the law:

$$\boldsymbol{\pi}_t = \boldsymbol{\pi}_{t-1} \mathbf{P}. \tag{2}$$

Iterating forward on (2) delivers the distribution at some point in the indefinite future:

$$\boldsymbol{\pi} = \lim_{t \to \infty} \boldsymbol{\pi}_0 \mathbf{P}^t, \tag{3}$$

where $\boldsymbol{\pi}_0$ denotes the initial distribution at time $t = 0$. Provided that the Markov chain is ergodic, i.e., the matrix $\mathbf{P}$ has a single unit eigenvalue, the long-run distribution $\boldsymbol{\pi}$ is independent of the initial distribution and can be termed the *invariant distribution*.

The hypothesis of hollowing out of intermediate regimes implies that the second element of $\boldsymbol{\pi}$ is 0. That is, the long-run distribution of exchange rate regimes is concentrated in either one or both of the tails. This is possible, if (1) either the fixed, floating, or both regimes are *absorbing states* (i.e., $p_{11} = 1$ and/or $p_{33} = 1$) so that other states cannot be reached from them, or (2) fixed and floating exchange rate regimes together constitute a *closed*

266  *P. Masson and F. J. Ruge-Murcia*

*set*, i.e., transitions between them can take place but not towards the intermediate regime (i.e., both $p_{12} = 0$ and $p_{32} = 0$ with $p_{22} < 1$); see Masson (2001) for further details.

In the above discussion, the transition probabilities in **P** are assumed to be constant. However, it seems likely that economic variables could affect the probability of a country's transition from one exchange rate regime to another. A simple way to allow time-varying transition probabilities in Markov chains involves the nonlinear parameterization of the probabilities in terms of a set of predetermined explanatory variables. Pesaran and Ruge-Murcia (1999) follow this approach to model the realignment probability in exchange rate target zones. Variables suggested by the currency crisis and OCA literatures are natural variables to explain exchange rate regime transitions. This extension is important for examining the hollowing out hypothesis because transitions away or into intermediate exchange rate regimes might be less or more frequent depending on economic conditions.

In order to economize on notation, the function that links transition probabilities and explanatory variables is defined as $p_{ij}(\mathbf{X}_{t-1})$, where $\mathbf{X}_{t-1}$ is an $m \times 1$ vector of predetermined variables (including a constant) and $p_{ij}(\mathbf{X}_{t-1}) : R^m \rightarrow [0, 1]$. We adopt a functional form that imposes the constraints that the transition probability is bounded between zero and one, and that each row of the matrix **P** sums to one. For example, for row 3:

$$p_{31}(\mathbf{X}_{t-1}) = \exp(\boldsymbol{\beta}'_{31}\mathbf{X}_{t-1})/[1 + \exp(\boldsymbol{\beta}'_{31}\mathbf{X}_{t-1}) + \exp(\boldsymbol{\beta}'_{32}\mathbf{X}_{t-1})],$$
$$p_{32}(\mathbf{X}_{t-1}) = \exp(\boldsymbol{\beta}'_{32}\mathbf{X}_{t-1})/[1 + \exp(\boldsymbol{\beta}'_{31}\mathbf{X}_{t-1}) + \exp(\boldsymbol{\beta}'_{32}\mathbf{X}_{t-1})],$$
$$p_{33}(\mathbf{X}_{t-1}) = 1/[1 + \exp(\boldsymbol{\beta}'_{31}\mathbf{X}_{t-1}) + \exp(\boldsymbol{\beta}'_{32}\mathbf{X}_{t-1})],$$

where $\boldsymbol{\beta}_{ij}$ is an $m \times 1$ vector of coefficients. The case studied by Masson (2001) corresponds to the special case where the only element in $\mathbf{X}_{t-1}$ is a constant term.

Note that even if a given transition is infrequent (but nonzero) in the data, the nonlinearity of the model helps identify the coefficients of variables that determine this transition. To see this, suppose that the transition from floating to fixed exchange rates is infrequent, i.e., the econometrician does not have very many observations of this transition in the data set. In terms of the above equations, the coefficients in $\boldsymbol{\beta}_{31}$ might seem to be poorly (perhaps, not) identified. However, due to the restrictions that probabilities are bounded between zero and one, and that each row of the matrix **P** sums to one, $\boldsymbol{\beta}_{31}$ also appears in the equations that describe the transition probabilities $p_{32}$ and $p_{33}$. If these transitions are more frequent in the data, the coefficients in $\boldsymbol{\beta}_{31}$ can be identified.

The Markov property of the model implies that the probability of observing a given sequence of exchange rate regimes in country $k$ is given by:

$$L(k) = \pi_{0,i,k} \prod_i \prod_j (p_{ij,k}(\mathbf{X}_{t-1}))^{n_{ijk}}, \tag{4}$$

where $n_{ijk}$ is the number of times that there occurs a one-period transition from state $i$ to state $j$ in country $k$. For the complete sample of $K$ countries, the log-likelihood function is constructed by taking logs on both sides of (4) for each country and summing up over $k = 1, 2, \ldots, K$ to obtain:

$$\log L = \sum_k \log L(k) = A + \sum_k \sum_i \sum_j n_{ijk} \ln p_{ij,k}(\mathbf{X}_{t-1}),$$

where $A = \Sigma_k \log(\pi_{0,i,k})$ is a constant term. This log-likelihood function can be maximized numerically using standard procedures to obtain efficient and consistent estimates of the model parameters.

Note that when the relation between $p_{ij}$ and $\mathbf{X}_{t-1}$ is given by the logit function, this log-likelihood function corresponds exactly to that of a multinomial logit model. The parallel between discrete choice models and the Markov chain with time-varying probabilities means that a structural interpretation could be given to the model. Specifically, conditional on the current exchange rate regime and a set of observable variables, $\mathbf{X}_{t-1}$, each country chooses whether to remain in the current regime or to switch to either of the alternative regimes.[2]

## IV. Empirical Results

### The Data

For the estimation of the Markov chain models, we used data on exchange rate regime classification and four explanatory variables, namely, inflation, trade openness, growth, and reserves between 1975 and 1997 (inclusive). Excluding missing observations, the data set contains 2,430 exchange rate transitions for 168 countries. The classification of regimes was obtained from Ghosh, Gulde, Ostry, and Wolf (1997). The data for the explanatory variables were obtained from the *IMF International Financial Statistics*. Inflation was measured by the annual percentage change in the price level. Trade openness was measured by the ratio of imports plus exports to gross domestic product (GDP). Growth was measured by the annual real growth rate of GDP. Reserves were measured by international reserves minus gold

---

[2] Note, however, that we do not model the (potential) choice of $\mathbf{X}_t$, even though some of the variables in this vector could be endogenous. A formal treatment of this problem would require the complete specification of the government's optimization problem, for example, as in Burnside, Eichenbaum, and Rebelo (2001). At the econometric level, the possible endogeneity of $\mathbf{X}_t$ is addressed by including only lagged values of the variables among the regressors.

over GDP. In order to limit the effect of outliers on the results, the variables were reparameterized as $x/(1 + x)$ where $x$ is either inflation, trade openness, GDP growth, or reserves/GDP.[3]

The Ghosh *et al.* classification exhibits more stability in regimes than that of Levy Yeyati and Sturzenegger (1999), because the latter is based solely on the behavior of two indicator variables, the exchange rate itself and foreign exchange reserves. While *de facto* fixity or flexibility is of interest in itself, it ignores the stated commitment of the authorities. Arguably, it is this commitment that is central to the distinction between regimes. In addition, a feature of the Ghosh *et al.* classification identified in Masson (2001) was the possibility that there might be transitions toward currency boards (hard pegs) but not away from them, a feature that eventually would produce hollowing out. This highlights the interest in analyzing the determinants of these transitions.

### Preliminary Analysis of the Data

Panel A in Figure 1 plots the proportion of all countries in each exchange rate regime in each year of the sample.[4] In terms of the notation introduced in Section III, these figures correspond to the unconditional distribution of regimes $\pi_t$ in each year of the sample. Two observations are apparent from this panel. First, there has been a persistent decline in the proportion of countries under fixed exchange rate regimes, even after the breakdown of the Bretton Woods system. Second, there was a sharp increase in the number of transitions from intermediate to floating exchange regimes in the early 1990s. The proportion of countries under floating rose from 10.3 percent in 1990 to 33.9 percent in 1994. These numbers reflect both transitions in existing countries (like Finland's in 1992) and the addition to the sample of new countries that adopted floating exchange rate regimes (like Latvia and Lithuania). However, this trend has been partly reversed since 1994. This panel is not entirely supportive of the hollowing out hypothesis whereby intermediate exchange rate regimes would disappear in favor of either fixed or freely flexible exchange rates, and suggests a richer transition dynamics than this hypothesis would imply.

---

[3] We used annual data because, in contrast to quarterly or monthly data, they are readily available for almost all countries for a reasonably long sample period. However, it seems likely that higher-frequency data might provide a sharper picture of exchange rate regime transitions for the small number of countries for which these data are available. We intend to take up this issue in future work.

[4] Note that since there are missing observations for some countries, and some countries (e.g. Estonia) did not exist for the whole sample period, the total number of countries is not the same in all years, varying from 127 in 1975 to 168 in 1997.

Explaining the transition between exchange rate regimes　269

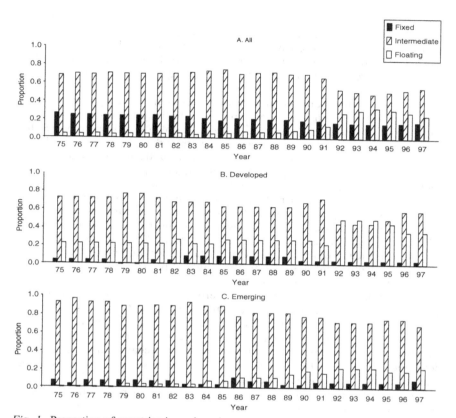

*Fig. 1.* Proportion of countries in each regime

Most of the evidence for hollowing out has been based on data from emerging and developed economies; see, for example, Fischer (2001). Panels B and C in Figure 1 plot the unconditional distribution of exchange rate regimes for developed and emerging countries in each year of the sample, respectively. The countries classified as "developed" are Austria, Australia, Belgium, Canada, Finland, Denmark, France, Hong Kong, Germany, Japan, Ireland, New Zealand, Italy, Norway, the Netherlands, Singapore, Portugal, Sweden, Spain, Switzerland, the United Kingdom, and the United States. This list was taken from Fischer (2001, p. 7), and is originally based on the list of developed market economies produced by Morgan Stanley Capital International (MSCI). The countries classified as "emerging" are Argentina, Bulgaria, Panama, China, Egypt, Jordan, Malaysia, Morocco, Pakistan, Qatar,

270  *P. Masson and F. J. Ruge-Murcia*

Greece, Turkey, Hungary, Israel, Poland, Sri Lanka, Venezuela, the Czech Republic, Nigeria, Brazil, Chile, Colombia, Ecuador, India, Indonesia, Korea, Mexico, Peru, Philippines, Russia, South Africa, and Thailand. This list was also taken from Fischer (2001, p. 8).[5] These are the economies included in the MSCI emerging market index and/or the emerging index plus (EMBI+) of J. P. Morgan.

Three observations are apparent from panels B and C. First, for both sets of countries there is no discernible time trend in the proportion of countries under fixed exchange rate regimes.[6] Hence the downward trend reported for the complete sample above is caused by countries that are neither developed nor emerging economies. Second, until the early 1990s, there was no trend in the proportion of developed economies under intermediate or floating exchange rate regimes. After the early 1990s, there is a strong downward (upward) trend in the number of developed economies under an intermediate (a floating) exchange rate regime, but these trends are partly reversed after 1994. Third, there is a persistent downward (upward) trend in the number of emerging economies under an intermediate (a floating) exchange rate regime. It is clear from this figure that further understanding of the determinants of exchange rate regime transitions would be desirable.

Table 1 also reports ML estimates of the Markov chain for all countries and the subsamples of developed and emerging market economies, under the assumption that the transition probabilities are constant. In most cases, the null hypothesis that the fixed and floating exchange rate regimes are absorbing states (that is, $p_{11} = 1$ or $p_{33} = 1$) is rejected by the data at standard significance levels. The exception is the fixed exchange rate regime for developed countries, for which the null hypothesis $p_{11} = 1$ cannot be rejected at the 5 percent significance level.[7] This means that after adopting a fixed or a floating exchange rate regime, there is a nonnegligible probability that the country will exit from that regime in finite time. Since $p_{12}$ and $p_{32}$ are statistically different from zero, but $p_{13}$ and $p_{31}$ are not, a country that exits one of the polar regimes is most likely to adopt an intermediate exchange rate regime. Since the fixed and floating exchange rate regimes are neither absorbing states nor form a closed set, the invariant distribution of regimes contains nonzero mass at the intermediate regime. In this sense, the hypothesis of hollowing out would be rejected.

---

[5] Our list of emerging countries differs from Fischer's, who also includes Taiwan.

[6] For example, if one runs an ordinary least squares (OLS) regression of these proportions on a constant and a time trend, the coefficient on the time trend is not significantly different from zero.

[7] As pointed out by the editor, the empirical observation that countries do exit fixed/floating exchange regimes (for example, Argentina in 2001) constitutes a direct rejection of this null hypothesis.

Explaining the transition between exchange rate regimes 271

Table 1. *Estimated transition matrix and invariant distribution, constant transition probabilities*

| All $N = 2,430$ | | | Developed $N = 478$ | | | Emerging $N = 604$ | | |
|---|---|---|---|---|---|---|---|---|
| | | | *A. Transition matrix* | | | | | |
| 0.934* | 0.064* | 0.002 | 0.857* | 0.143 | 0 | 0.857* | 0.143* | 0 |
| (0.011) | (0.011) | (0.002) | (0.093) | (0.093) | | (0.054) | (0.054) | |
| 0.010* | 0.960* | 0.030* | 0.003 | 0.972* | 0.025* | 0.008* | 0.966* | 0.025* |
| (0.002) | (0.005) | (0.004) | (0.003) | (0.008) | (0.009) | (0.004) | (0.008) | (0.007) |
| 0.006 | 0.076* | 0.918* | 0 | 0.029* | 0.971* | 0.016 | 0.078* | 0.906* |
| (0.004) | (0.015) | (0.015) | | (0.014) | (0.014) | (0.015) | (0.034) | (0.036) |
| | | | *B. Invariant distribution* | | | | | |
| 0.120 | 0.641 | 0.240 | 0.011 | 0.532 | 0.455 | 0.065 | 0.736 | 0.198 |

*Notes*: $N$ is the number of observations. The superscripts * and † denote statistical significance at the 5 and 10 percent levels, respectively. The figures in parentheses are standard errors.

## Endogenous Transitions, All Countries

We now endogenize the exchange rate regime transitions using explanatory variables suggested by the optimum currency area literature and currency crisis models. Since $p_{13}$ and $p_{31}$ are not statistically different from zero in Table 1, we now concentrate on the transitions from fixed and floating to intermediate exchange rate regimes, and on transitions away from intermediate exchange rate regimes.[8] The explanatory variables included are lagged annual inflation, lagged openness to trade, lagged GDP growth, and lagged foreign exchange reserves over GDP. Panel A in Table 2 reports the estimates of the coefficients on the explanatory variables for the complete sample.

Each of the variables has at least one significant coefficient, but the coefficient on inflation is statistically significant in all transitions. Estimates imply that *inflation* increases the probability of leaving a fixed exchange rate regime for an intermediate regime, and of leaving an intermediate regime for a freely floating exchange rate regime. This result reflects the fact that fixed and managed floating regimes might not be sustainable when the inflation rate is high. Interestingly, inflation also increases the probability of leaving an intermediate regime for a fixed exchange rate. An explanation of this result is that the fixed and managed

---

[8] Results obtained when the restriction $p_{13} = p_{31} = 0$ is not imposed are basically the same as those reported below. In preliminary work we also considered adding one explanatory variable at a time with similar results to those reported. All these results are available on request.

regimes might serve as commitment mechanisms to reduce inflation (for example, as in Israel in 1986 and Argentina in 1991).

*Trade openness* decreases and *low growth* increases the probability of going from a fixed to an intermediate regime, and from an intermediate to a floating exchange rate regime. It seems that, as with high inflation, the unpleasant consequences of low growth lead to a change in regime, whether initiated by the authorities or by private investors. Moreover, a low level of international *reserves/GDP* increases the probability of going from an intermediate to a floating exchange rate regime.

The null hypothesis of constant transition probabilities can be tested against the alternative of time-varying transition probabilities by means of a likelihood ratio (LR) test. This is basically a joint test of the restriction that the coefficients on inflation, trade openness, growth, and reserves are all zero. The test statistic is 72.08. Under the null hypothesis of constant transition probabilities, this statistic is distributed chi-square with 16 degrees of freedom. Since the statistic is well above the 5 percent critical value, the hypothesis can be rejected. Hence, variables implied by the OCA and currency crisis literature are helpful in explaining exchange rate regime transitions.

Results for the subsamples 1975–1989 and 1990–1997 are reported, respectively, in panels B and C in Table 2. The sample is split in 1990 for two reasons. First, many developing countries increased their integration with world markets during the 1990s. Second, this allows us to compare our results with those reported in previous literature, for example, Masson (2001). Note that results for both subsamples are qualitatively similar to those for the full sample. For a more stringent comparison of subsample results, we use the stability test proposed by Andrews and Fair (1988). Define by $\hat{\theta}_1$ and $\hat{\theta}_2$ the column vector of ML estimates of the transition probabilities obtained using data for the periods 1975–1989 and 1990–1997, respectively. Similarly, define by $\hat{\mathbf{V}}_1$ and $\hat{\mathbf{V}}_2$ the variance–covariance matrix of these estimates. Andrews and Fair show that under the null hypothesis $\theta_1 = \theta_2$, the Wald statistic

$$W = (\hat{\theta}_1 - \hat{\theta}_2)'(\hat{\mathbf{V}}_1 + \hat{\mathbf{V}}_2)^{-1}(\hat{\theta}_1 - \hat{\theta}_2)$$

is distributed chi-square with as many degrees of freedom as the number of elements in $\hat{\theta}$. The application of this stability test for our model yields a statistic $W = 51.047$, that is well above the 5 percent critical value of a chi-square variable with 20 degrees of freedom. Hence, the quantitative role of the variables that explain exchange rate regime transition appears to have changed after 1990 as capital mobility increased. In particular, the inflation coefficients in the second subsample are numerically smaller than in the first subsample for transitions into intermediate regimes but larger for transitions

*Explaining the transition between exchange rate regimes*     273

Table 2. *Coefficients of explanatory variables, time-varying transition probabilities*

| Coefficients | Inflation | Openness | Growth | Reserves |
|---|---|---|---|---|
| | | A. All countries (1975–1997) | | |
| $\beta_{12}$ | 6.47* | −2.37[†] | −5.28* | 2.17 |
| $\beta_{21}$ | 2.79* | −0.09 | −2.09 | −0.58 |
| $\beta_{23}$ | 1.49* | −2.11* | −3.75[†] | −2.84* |
| $\beta_{32}$ | 2.54* | 0.86 | −0.95 | 0.93 |
| | | B. All countries (1975–1989) | | |
| $\beta_{12}$ | 10.25* | −2.03 | −5.39[†] | 3.11* |
| $\beta_{21}$ | 2.21[†] | 0.86 | −4.74 | −0.42 |
| $\beta_{23}$ | −1.16 | −4.91* | 2.42 | −4.57 |
| $\beta_{32}$ | 15.22* | −3.25 | 0.90 | 4.18 |
| | | C. All countries (1990–1997) | | |
| $\beta_{12}$ | 1.14 | −3.49 | 9.41 | −6.05 |
| $\beta_{21}$ | 5.71* | −5.01 | 8.31 | −1.22 |
| $\beta_{23}$ | 2.02* | −2.19[†] | −2.74 | −3.84* |
| $\beta_{32}$ | 1.77[†] | 0.98 | 0.66 | 0.39 |
| | | D. Developed economies (1975–1997) | | |
| $\beta_{12}$ | 333.91 | 2,036.77 | 297.88 | −1,480.68 |
| $\beta_{21}$ | −6.48 | 2.04 | −9.23 | −3.84 |
| $\beta_{23}$ | −17.54 | −6.17[†] | −48.23* | 3.73 |
| $\beta_{32}$ | 0.53 | 5.43 | 25.37 | 2.05 |
| | | E. Emerging economies (1975–1997) | | |
| $\beta_{12}$ | 7.11[†] | 4.21 | 2.53 | 7.38[†] |
| $\beta_{21}$ | 8.89* | 10.65* | 3.96 | 10.44* |
| $\beta_{23}$ | 0.52 | −3.21 | −5.84 | −4.71 |
| $\beta_{32}$ | 3.52[†] | −2.24 | 4.88 | −2.45 |

*Notes*: See notes to Table 1. The fixed, intermediate, and floating exchange rate regimes are denoted by 1, 2, and 3, respectively. The 5 × 1 vector $\beta_{ij}$ contains the coefficients of the variables that might help explain the transition probability $p_{ij} = \Pr(s_t = j | s_{t-1} = i)$, namely lagged annual inflation, lagged openness to trade, lagged GDP growth, lagged foreign exchange reserves over GDP, and a constant term. The sample sizes for panels A, B, C, D, and E, are 2,430, 1,471, 959, 478, and 604, respectively.

out of intermediate regimes. These results are consistent with the finding by Masson (2001) that a fixed matrix of transition probabilities is unstable across the pre-1990 and post-1990 subsamples.

## Developed vs. Emerging Market Economies

Next we compare the exchange rate regime transitions for developed and emerging market economies. Since both sets of countries face a high degree of capital mobility, it is interesting to examine whether their transition dynamics are driven by the same factors.

Estimates for developed countries are reported in panel D in Table 2. Empirical results indicate that *low growth* increases the probability of going from an intermediate to a floating exchange rate regime in developed market

274   *P. Masson and F. J. Ruge-Murcia*

economies. No other variable explains transitions for this subsample. The large numerical values of the coefficients that explain the transition from a fixed to a managed floating regime reflect the small number of observations of this transition in the data set. Estimates for emerging countries are reported in panel E in Table 2. *Inflation, reserves/GDP*, and (in one case) *trade openness* are important in explaining the exchange rate regime transitions in emerging markets. Higher inflation not only makes the transition from a fixed to an intermediate regime more likely, but also makes the transition from intermediate to fixed, and from floating to intermediate regimes more likely. This would seem to reflect both the use by emerging market countries of exchange-rate-based stabilizations to disinflate after periods of high inflation, and the inability of many countries to maintain adjustable pegs in the face of high inflation.

*Reserves/GDP* appear to explain the transition between fixed and intermediate regimes for emerging markets but not for developed economies. This result suggests that freer access to international capital markets on the part of developed economies makes the level of reserves less of a constraint. On the basis of these point estimates, the exchange rate regime transition dynamics appear quite different in emerging markets as compared to those of developed economies.[9] In particular, these results provide some support for the views of Hausmann *et al.* (2001) and Calvo and Reinhart (2002) that developing countries may not benefit from exchange rate flexibility in the same way as developed economies.

## Forecasting

We now evaluate the ability of the time-varying Markov chain model to forecast exchange rate regime transitions. Since the Markov chain was estimated using variables lagged one year, the focus here is on the one-year-ahead forecast.[10] The strategy to evaluate the model is the following. First, *ex-ante* transition probabilities were computed using the parameter estimates reported in Table 2 and the realized (lagged) annual inflation, openness to trade, GDP growth, and foreign exchange reserves over GDP for each country and year. Then, these probabilities were converted into a discrete indicator using a probability threshold. As an example, if the

---

[9] Note, however, that the Wald statistic of the null hypothesis that the coefficients in both subsamples are the same is only $W = 17.25$. Since this statistic is below the 5 percent critical value of a chi-square variable with 20 degrees of freedom, the hypothesis cannot be rejected. Given the small number of countries in each sample and the imprecision with which some of the coefficients are estimated, it is possible that this result reflects low test power. We considered splitting these samples into pre-1990 and post-1990 subsamples, but the number of transitions in each subsample is too small to allow reliable results.

[10] Results for longer horizons are available on request.

*Explaining the transition between exchange rate regimes* 275

threshold is 0.5, the indicator takes a value of 1 when the *ex-ante* transition probability takes a value larger than or equal to 0.50 and 0 otherwise. Next, we computed the proportion of times that (1) the indicator predicts an exchange rate regime transition when one takes place the following year, and (2) the indicator predicts a transition when none takes place the following year. These statistics are, respectively, the "signal" and "noise" of the indicator. A perfect indicator has signal equal to 1 and noise equal to 0.

Table 3 reports results for all countries and the subsamples of developed and emerging economies for all transitions and for each transition separately. We consider two probability thresholds: (1) the natural, but arbitrary, value of 0.5, and (2) the optimal value that minimizes the noise-to-signal ratio. The optimal threshold was found using grid search between 0 and 1, with 0.01 increments. Note that the indicator is informative in the sense that the signal is larger than the noise in all cases. However, the proportion of true positives is relatively small for the complete sample (panel A). The indicator based on the Markov chain and a threshold of 0.5 predicts correctly only 2.5 percent of the time. The indicator constructed using the optimal threshold predicts correctly 5 percent of the time. Transitions from fixed to intermediate

Table 3. *Forecasting Exchange Rate Regime Transitions*

| | All | Fixed to interm. | Interm. to fixed | Interm. to float | Float to interm. |
|---|---|---|---|---|---|
| | | *A. All countries* | | | |
| Optimal threshold | 0.360 | 0.360 | 0.070 | 0.190 | 0.370 |
| Noise | 0.016 | 0.058 | 0.007 | 0.002 | 0.002 |
| Signal | 0.050 | 0.161 | 0.063 | 0.020 | 0.040 |
| Fixed threshold | 0.500 | 0.500 | 0.500 | 0.500 | 0.500 |
| Noise | 0.011 | 0.043 | 0.000 | 0.001 | 0.000 |
| Signal | 0.025 | 0.096 | 0.000 | 0.000 | 0.000 |
| | | *B. Developed economies* | | | |
| Optimal threshold | 0.090 | 0.720 | 0.010 | 0.340 | 0.250 |
| Noise | 0.111 | 0.244 | 0.004 | 0.006 | 0.055 |
| Signal | 0.467 | 1.000 | 0.000 | 0.125 | 0.250 |
| Fixed threshold | 0.500 | 0.500 | 0.500 | 0.500 | 0.500 |
| Noise | 0.074 | 0.247 | 0.000 | 0.002 | 0.044 |
| Signal | 0.133 | 1.000 | 0.000 | 0.000 | 0.000 |
| | | *C. Emerging economies* | | | |
| Optimal threshold | 0.440 | 0.440 | 0.270 | 0.120 | 0.450 |
| Noise | 0.042 | 0.146 | 0.013 | 0.003 | 0.013 |
| Signal | 0.185 | 0.666 | 0.500 | 0.083 | 0.200 |
| Fixed threshold | 0.500 | 0.500 | 0.500 | 0.500 | 0.500 |
| Noise | 0.034 | 0.126 | 0.003 | 0.000 | 0.008 |
| Signal | 0.037 | 0.167 | 0.000 | 0.000 | 0.000 |

*Notes*: Noise is the proportion of false negatives. Signal is the proportion of true positives. The optimal threshold is the one that minimizes the noise-to-signal ratio. All forecasts are in-sample and based on parameter estimates for the full sample.

exchange rate regime are forecasted more accurately, but the proportion of correct predictions is still below 20 percent. Regarding the subsamples of developed and emerging economies (panels B and C), the Markov chain is more successful in forecasting their exchange rate regime transitions, especially when the threshold is the optimal one. In some cases the signal is larger than 50 percent, but there is considerable variance across transitions. However, since the number of transitions in the subsamples is smaller than in the full sample, but the number of estimated parameters is the same, a high signal might to some extent reflect the overfitting of the model.

In summary, the indicator based on the Markov model with time-varying transition probabilities appears to be informative regarding exchange rate regime transitions one-year ahead, but, as in the case of indicators proposed in previous literature by, for example, Kaminsky and Reinhart (1999) and Berg and Pattillo (1999), it has modest predictive power.

## V. Conclusions

Our results suggest that a promising way of gaining some understanding of the distribution of exchange rate regimes is to try to explain transitions between regimes. Currency crisis models and the optimum currency area literature both imply that particular variables should help explain transitions. Estimates confirm that these variables have significant explanatory power, but our results nevertheless indicate that they do not have good forecasting power. When the sample includes all countries, high inflation and, to a lesser extent, low growth and low trade openness all tend to increase exits from the prevailing regime. This is consistent with currency crisis models (when considering the exits from intermediate or fixed regimes), but also with the voluntary use of fixed or quasi-fixed rates in exchange-rate-based stabilizations. In contrast, the level of reserves seems to have a less systematic impact. Reserves are significant in explaining transitions only for emerging market countries. This suggests that capital mobility may be lower for these economies than for the developed countries (which may have access to international capital markets even in a crisis).

What do these results have to say about hollowing out? Estimates suggest that low inflation and sustained growth may be the key to making intermediate (and other) regimes sustainable. To the extent that inflation decreases in emerging market economies (as it has done in many of them), and growth can be maintained, such regimes as soft pegs may be able to resist speculative attacks. It is in bad times, measured by both variables, that regimes are especially vulnerable.

We were unable to obtain a proxy for capital mobility for a sufficient number of countries to include it as an explanatory variable. However, to the extent that increasing capital mobility makes emerging market economies resemble the advanced countries in our sample, the level of reserves should become less important as a determinant for exchange rate regime transitions.

## References

Andrews, D. W. K. and Fair, R. C. (1988), Inference in Nonlinear Econometric Models with Structural Change, *Review of Economic Studies 55*, 615–640.

Berg, A. and Pattillo, C. (1999), Predicting Currency Crises: The Indicators Approach and an Alternative, *Journal of International Money and Finance 18*, 561–586.

Burnside, C., Eichenbaum, M. and Rebelo, S. (2001), Prospective Deficits and the Asian Currency Crisis, *Journal of Political Economy 109*, 1155–1197.

Calvo, G. and Reinhart, C. (2002), Fear of Floating, *Quarterly Journal of Economics 117*, 379–408.

Collins, S. (1996), On Becoming More Flexible, Exchange Rate Regimes in Latin America and the Caribbean, *Journal of Development Economics 51*, 117–138.

Edwards, S. (1996), The Determinants of the Choice between Fixed and Flexible Exchange Rate Regimes, NBER Working Paper no. 5756.

Eichengreen, B. (1994), *International Monetary Arrangements for the 21st Century*, Brookings Institution, Washington, DC.

Eichengreen, B., Masson, P., Savastano, M. and Sharma, S. (1999), Transition Strategies and Nominal Anchors on the Road to Greater Exchange-rate Flexibility, in *Essays in International Finance, no. 213*, Princeton University, Princeton, NJ.

Fischer, S. (2001), Exchange Rate Regimes: Is the Bipolar View Correct?, *Journal of Economic Perspectives 15*, 3–24.

Frankel, J. A. and Rose, A. (1998), The Endogeneity of the Optimum Currency Area Criteria, NBER Working Paper no. 5700.

Ghosh, A. R., Gulde, A.-M., Ostry, J. and Wolf, H. (1997), Does the Nominal Exchange Rate Matter? NBER Working Paper no. 5874.

Hausmann, R., Panizza, U. and Stein, E. (2001), Why Do Countries Float the Way They Float?, *Journal of Development Economics 66*, 387–414.

Juhn, G. and Mauro P. (2001), Determinants of Exchange Rate Regimes: A Simple Sensitivity Analysis, mimeo, International Monetary Fund, Washington, DC.

Kaminisky, G. and Reinhart, C. M. (1999), The Twin Crises: The Causes of Banking and Balance-of-payments Problems, *American Economic Review 89*, 473–500.

Kremer, M., Onatski, A. and Stock, J. (2001), Searching for Prosperity, NBER Working Paper no. 8250.

Krugman, P. (1979), A Model of Self-fulfilling Balance of Payments Crises, *Journal of Money, Credit, and Banking 11*, 311–325.

Levy Yeyati, E. and Sturzenegger, F. (1999), Classifying Exchange Rate Regimes: Deeds vs. Words, mimeo, Universidad Torcuato Di Tella, Buenos Aires.

Masson, P. (2001), Exchange Rate Regime Transitions, *Journal of Development Economics 64*, 571–586.

Masson, P. and Taylor, M. (1993), Currency Unions: A Survey of the Issues, in P. Masson and M. Taylor (eds.), *Policy Issues in the Operation of Currency Unions*, Cambridge University Press, Cambridge.

Mundell, R. (1961), A Theory of Optimum Currency Areas, *American Economic Review 51*, 657–665.

278   *P. Masson and F. J. Ruge-Murcia*

Mussa, M., Masson, P., Swoboda, A., Jadresic, E., Mauro, P. and Berg, A. (2000), Exchange
    Rate Regimes in an Increasingly Integrated World Economy, Occasional Paper no. 193,
    International Monetary Fund, Washington, DC.
Obstfeld, M. and Rogoff, K. (1995), The Mirage of Fixed Exchange Rates, *Journal of
    Economic Perspectives 9*, 73–96.
Pesaran, M. H. and Ruge-Murcia, F. J. (1999), Analysis of Exchange Rate Target Zones Using
    a Limited-dependent Rational-expectations Model with Jumps, *Journal of Business and
    Economics Statistics 17*, 50–66.
Poirson, H. (2001), How Do Countries Choose Their Exchange Rate Regime?, Working Paper
    no. WP/01/46, International Monetary Fund, Washington, DC.
Quah, D. (1993), Empirical Cross-section Dynamics in Economic Growth, *European
    Economic Review 37*, 426–434.

First version submitted June 2003;
final version received July 2004.

# Part II

# Currency Crises, Credibility and Contagion

# CREDIBILITY OF POLICIES VERSUS CREDIBILITY OF POLICYMAKERS*

## ALLAN DRAZEN AND PAUL R. MASSON

Standard models of policy credibility, defined as the expectation that an announced policy will be carried out, emphasize the preferences of the policymaker and the role of tough policies in signaling toughness and raising credibility. Whether a policy is carried out, however, will also reflect the state of the economy. We present a model in which a policymaker maintains a fixed parity in good times, but devalues if the unemployment rate gets too high. Our main conclusion is that if there is persistence in unemployment, observing a tough policy in a given period may *lower* rather than raise the credibility of a no-devaluation pledge in subsequent periods. We test this implication on EMS interest rates and find support for our hypothesis.

## I. INTRODUCTION

There is now an extensive literature on policy credibility, credibility being defined as the expectation that an announced policy will be carried out. Much of this literature has emphasized the role of a government's "type" (for example, the relative weights it puts on the losses from inflation versus unemployment) in determining the credibility of a policy. In this approach, introduced into the macroeconomics literature by Backus and Driffill [1985a, 1985b], a policymaker who assigns a relatively low cost to inflation may find it optimal to mimic the actions of a more inflation-averse policymaker to build "reputation." Observed monetary policy choices are thus taken to provide information about the government's (unobserved) inflation preferences, and they can therefore affect expectations about future policy. More specifically, when a policymaker delivers on an announced commitment to low inflation, this strengthens the belief that he really is inflation averse. Hence, a government that follows tough policies will see its reputation and the credibility of its commitment to anti-inflationary policies increase over time.[1]

---

*The authors would like to thank Robert Flood, Peter Isard, Peter Kenen, Donald Mathieson, and Bennett McCallum for helpful comments, as well as seminar participants at Boston University; the Hebrew University of Jerusalem; the International Monetary Fund; the University of Maryland; the University of California, Los Angeles; and the NBER Seminar on Monetary Economics. The views expressed are those of the authors and do not necessarily represent those of the International Monetary Fund.
1. The basic approach of Backus and Driffill has been extended in several directions. Whereas they considered the case where the "tough" policymaker cares only about inflation, Vickers [1986] showed that if both tough and "weak" types care about unemployment, tough governments tend to be even more restrictive.

736        *QUARTERLY JOURNAL OF ECONOMICS*

Whether or not an announced policy is carried out, however, reflects more than the policymaker's intentions. The situation in which he finds himself can be as important. Since even a "tough" policymaker cannot ignore the cost of very high unemployment, he may renege on an anti-inflation commitment in sufficiently adverse circumstances, that is, in times of weak activity, when pressures to restore high employment are strong.[2] In short, the credibility the public assigns to an announced policy should therefore reflect external circumstances as well.

In assessing the effect of observed policy choices on credibility, the role of external circumstances may be especially important when policies have persistent effects on the economic environment. The purpose of this paper is to investigate the effect of such *persistence* and to demonstrate that if tough policies constrain the room to maneuver in the future, then following a tough policy may actually harm rather than enhance credibility. For example, a tough anti-inflation policy today may raise unemployment well into the future, making the commitment to future anti-inflation policy less credible. Similarly, monetary tightening may increase government debt accumulation, making it more likely that an adverse shock will lead to a monetary easing in the future.

Our result may be illustrated by a simple story. One afternoon, a colleague announces to you that he is serious about losing weight and plans to skip dinner. He adds that he has not eaten for two days. Does this information make it more or less credible that he really will skip dinner? The model of types outlined in the first paragraph would imply that with each meal he skips, the "tough policy" of skipping the next meal becomes *more* credible, as each observation of playing tough raises the probability we assign to his being a fanatical dieter. Once we realize that his skipping one meal makes him hungrier at the next mealtime (i.e., that policy has persistent effects), we are led to the opposite conclusion, namely, that it becomes less likely he will stick to his diet the more meals he has skipped. We apply this point to the credibility of fixed parities in the European Monetary System. In the early years of the EMS, the willingness to accept the costs of unemployment in order to avoid realignments gave the system credibility by signaling the

---

Persson [1988] and Rogoff [1987, 1989] provide excellent surveys of models of credibility and reputation. An alternative approach is to define strength in terms of ability to precommit to a particular policy, as in Cukierman and Liviatan [1991].

2. A related point, made by Flood [1983] and Blanchard [1985], among others, is that if policies are too tough then current policymakers may be removed from power, leading to an easing of policies.

toughness of governments. More recently, however, mounting unemployment made it more likely that a further unfavorable shock would lead to a devaluation. Under these circumstances, the absence of a realignment, and the resultant further upward pressures on unemployment, were seen as lowering the credibility of fixed parities.[3] This reasoning suggests that credibility need not monotonically increase with the length of time there has been no devaluation, as it would if uncertainty about the "type" of government were the only factor affecting credibility.[4] Furthermore, interest differentials (taken as a measure of the credibility of the policy of fixed parities) should be interpreted as reflecting not only signaling, but also the perception that in certain circumstances, devaluation will be viewed as being desirable, even by a tough government.

In the next sections we consider the issue of signaling when effects of policy on employment are persistent. We show formally how persistent unemployment effects of a tough policy (maintaining a fixed parity), may lower rather than raise the credibility of a pledge of no devaluations in subsequent periods. In the final section we apply the theory to France. Regression results suggest that while the signaling model may apply in a period in the mid-1980s in which the stated priorities of the authorities changed, the alternative notion of credibility set out in the paper may help explain devaluation expectations and interest differentials in the late 1980s and early 1990s.

## II. A BASIC MODEL

To illustrate our points, we use a two-period open-economy version of the simple Barro-Gordon [1983a, 1983b] model, in which surprise devaluations decrease unemployment, but expected devaluations have no effect. (Modeling persistence requires a multiperiod model; a two-period version is sufficient.) We use the Barro-

---

3. The paper was initially drafted in mid-1992. Events of September 1992 provide strong support for our contention that credibility is never definitively established because in some circumstances governments will choose to devalue.
4. Froot and Rogoff [1991] suggest a number of reasons why the credibility of the EMS may not be increasing monotonically over time. A recent paper by Chen and Giovannini [1992] presents empirical evidence which suggests that tough policy and lack of realignments have not enhanced the credibility of fixed exchange rates in the EMS. Klein and Marion [1992] use duration analysis to study the credibility of a fixed exchange rate as a function of the length of time since the last devaluation. They do not consider a persistence effect, however, and their model has the credibility of the no-devaluation policy rising over time the longer there has been no devaluation.

Gordon model to facilitate comparison of our results with the existing macroeconomic literature on credibility, in which this model has been used extensively. To model the importance of external circumstances, we add a stochastic unemployment shock to the Barro-Gordon model, so that the government's choice of policy will depend on the realization of the shock, as well as the cost it assigns to inflation relative to unemployment. Our modeling of policy conditioned on the realization of shocks is based on Obstfeld's [1991] model of escape clauses, a model also used by Flood and Isard [1989] and Lohmann [1990].[5] In these models the government chooses between following a no-devaluation rule and following a discretionary policy: in the latter case it optimally chooses the magnitude of devaluation as a function of the realized state of the world.[6]

We depart from the basic escape-clause model by assuming that the choice is between the rule of a fixed parity, and the alternative of a devaluation of a fixed size. Formally, this is a state-contingent, two-part rule, so that devaluation at the preannounced trigger could be characterized as carrying out the "announced," or at least implicit, policy. In our opinion, this view, though semantically correct, misses the point—that even a tough policymaker who plans ex ante to keep the fixed parity (and makes public statements to that effect) will devalue in adverse circumstances. We therefore take devaluation to represent departing from the announced (no-devaluation) policy.

For EMS countries it is probably reasonable to consider a devaluation of an exogenously fixed size as representing the alternative to no realignment, since the EMS puts constraints on the realignments that are possible.[7] The problem of discretion always dominating does not arise here, since for small enough shocks, maintaining the existing parity will be preferred to a discrete devaluation. Moreover, limiting ourselves to two options does not change the qualitative nature of the results, and allowing other size realignments will leave our basic point intact.

5. For a general discussion of this type of model, one may refer to Persson and Tabellini [1989].
6. The policymaker is modeled as choosing between a rule and discretion on the basis of the realized state of the world, rather than as using a two-part rule, in order to capture the notion that all states of the world cannot be foreseen ex ante. Hence, a fully state-contingent rule cannot be specified. To avoid problems of time-consistency, it is assumed that the policymaker must pay a private fixed cost when choosing discretion. Otherwise a benevolent policymaker would always choose discretion ex post.
7. Throughout, references to the EMS should be taken to refer to the countries participating in the exchange rate mechanism of the EMS.

## POLICIES VERSUS POLICYMAKERS 739

We begin by supposing that unanticipated inflation reduces unemployment $u_t$ relative to the natural rate $u_N$, where $u_t$ is also subject to a stochastic shock $\eta_t$ and is affected by its lagged value:

$$(1) \qquad u_t = u_N + \eta_t - \sqrt{a}\,[(\pi_t - \pi_t^E) - \delta(u_{t-1} - u_N)],$$

where $\delta \geq 0$ is a measure of persistence in unemployment fluctuations ($\Delta = \delta\sqrt{a}$ is the autoregressive coefficient). (In the initial period $t = 1$ of the two-period model, the inherited unemployment gap $u_o - u_N$ is assumed to be zero, so that persistence only affects unemployment in the second period.)[8]

The government's objective is to minimize an expected discounted loss function, where each period's loss is quadratic in the deviation of unemployment from a target level below the natural rate, $u_N - K$ (where $K$ captures distortions leading to too high a natural rate), as well as in actual inflation. We assume that there can be different types of governments, implying possible uncertainty about the government's objective function.[9]

The tough government (with superscript $T$) cares about inflation with a weight $\theta^T$, while the weak government (superscript $W$) gives a lower weight $\theta^w$ to inflation in its objective function. The $i$-type government's objective function conditioned on information available at $t = 1$ is

$$(2) \quad \Lambda^i = L_1^i + \beta E L_2^i = (u_1 - u_N + K)^2 + \theta^i(\pi_1)^2$$
$$+ \beta E_1[(u_2 - u_N + K)^2 + \theta^i(\pi_2)^2].$$

Assume that the exchange rate is the policy instrument to influence the price level. For simplicity of exposition we suppose that the price level equals the exchange rate, so that if $e_t$ is the *log* of the

---

8. We model persistent effects of policy in the equation summarizing the *structure* of the economy. Alternatively, one could model the effects of persistence in the *preference* equation, by putting lagged unemployment in the loss function (2). Much of the policy discussion in Europe which takes past policy choices as constraining current choices implicitly takes this second route. Our results would be the same under this alternative specification, the key point being that the probability of a devaluation in the second period may depend positively on first-period unemployment.

9. An alternative approach is to use a trigger-strategy model of expectations with uncertainty, along the lines of Canzoneri [1985]. Though this allows the government to depart from tough monetary policy in response to observable adverse shocks without losing credibility and may be simpler than the Kreps-Wilson [1982] framework for some purposes, it does not allow a simple comparison with the signaling-of-type motive for tough policy, which we feel is important in understanding devaluation expectations.

exchange rate at $t$, the inflation terms in (1) and (2) can be written as

$$\pi_t = e_t - e_{t-1}$$

$$\pi_t - \pi_t^E = (e_t - e_{t-1}) - (E_{t-1}e_t - e_{t-1})$$

$$= e_t - E_{t-1}e_t.$$

We also define the transformed variables $\kappa = K/\sqrt{a}$ and $\epsilon_t = \eta_t/\sqrt{a}$. It is assumed that wages are set before the shock $\epsilon_t$ is realized; $E_{t-1}e_t$ is conditioned on information available at the end of the previous period.

### III. WILL A HISTORY OF TOUGH POLICY NECESSARILY RAISE CREDIBILITY?

The basic question is how the probability of a devaluation in the second period, denoted $\mu_2$, depends on the action of the government in the first period, once we consider not only the standard signaling of unknown government type, but also the effect of persistence. With uncertainty about types, we may write $\mu_2$ as

(3) $$\mu_2(j) = p_2(j)\, \rho_2^w(j) + (1 - p_2(j))\rho_2^T(j);$$

where

$p_2 \equiv$ probability the government is of type $w$,
$\rho_2^w \equiv$ probability a government of type $w$ will devalue (given the distribution of $\epsilon_2$),
$\rho_2^I \equiv$ probability a government of type $T$ will devalue.

The argument $j$ $(= D$ or $F)$ indicates whether the government devalued $(D)$ or kept the exchange rate fixed $(F)$ in period 1. To calculate $\rho_2^i$, we start by solving the government's second-period problem for given expectations of a devaluation $\mu_2(j)$. By substituting $\rho_2^i$ into (3), we can then solve for $\mu_2(j)$. The functional relation between policy choice and the realization of $\epsilon_t$ will become clear from this calculation. The public is assumed to know the values $\theta^T$ and $\theta^W$. We shall consider the case where the public does not observe the shock $\epsilon_1$. Let us denote the single-period loss function of a type $i$ government if it (for example) devalues in the second period by $L_2^{i,D}(j)$ (where $j$ was the first period action). Then the government will devalue in period 2 if $L_2^{i,D}(j) - L_2^{i,F}(j) < 0$. This defines a critical value of the shock $\hat{\epsilon}_2^i(j)$:

(4) $\qquad \hat{\epsilon}_2^i(j) = \dfrac{(a + \theta^i)s}{2a} - \kappa - \mu_2(j)s - \delta(u_1 - u_N),$

where $s$ is the fixed devaluation size and where the critical value is dependent both on the type of government (via $\theta^i$) and on previously observed policy. If the realization of $\epsilon_2$ is below this critical value $\hat{\epsilon}_2^i(j)$, a policy of maintaining the fixed parity is optimal; if it is above, a devaluation is optimal. If the distribution of $\epsilon$ is uniform between $-v$ and $+v$, we have (for an interior solution)

(5) $\qquad \rho_2^i(j) = \text{prob}(\epsilon_2 > \hat{\epsilon}_2^i(j)) = (v - \hat{\epsilon}_2^i(j))/2v.$

To calculate the probability of government type, we assume that the public uses a Bayesian approach, starting from uniform priors over the two types of governments. Expectations are conditioned on whether the government devalued or not in period 1, but not on the shock $\epsilon_1$, which we assume that the public does not observe.[10] The probability that the government is weak conditional on its first-period action may then be written as

(6) $\qquad p_2(D) = \dfrac{\rho_1^w}{\rho_1^w + \rho_1^T}, \qquad p_2(F) = \dfrac{1 - \rho_1^w}{2 - \rho_1^w - \rho_1^T},$

when we start with uniform priors. Note that $p_2(D) > p_2(F)$ as long as $\rho_1^w > \rho_1^T$, that is, as long as the probability that a weak government will devalue in the first period is greater than the probability that a tough government will devalue.

The probability that a given type would devalue in the first period is derived in an analogous way to the above calculation for $\rho_2^i$. We calculate a critical value of the shock in the first period, namely $\hat{\epsilon}_1^i$, such that $\Lambda^i(D) = \Lambda^i(F)$. In the Appendix details of this calculation are shown. $\rho_1^i$, the probability that $\epsilon_1 > \hat{\epsilon}_1^i$, can then be calculated, assuming the same uniform distribution as above.

To calculate $\mu_2(D) - \mu_2(F)$, we combine equations (3), (5), and

---

10. One can do an analogous calculation in the case where the shock $\epsilon_1$ is observed (or can be inferred). For $\theta^W$ not close to $\theta^T$, there will be a separating equilibrium for some realizations of $\epsilon_1$: action would be fully revealing, with a weak government finding it optimal to devalue and a strong government not to devalue at those realizations. For other realizations of $\epsilon_1$, there would be pooling, with both types choosing the same policy, as would also be the case for all realizations of $\epsilon_1$ for $\theta^W$ close to $\theta^T$. $p_2(j)$ would equal zero or one in the relevant regions of separation and would equal the prior in the region of pooling.

(6) to obtain, after some manipulation,

$$(7) \quad \mu_2(D) - \mu_2(F) = \frac{1}{1 - s/2v}$$

$$\times \left[ -\frac{\sqrt{a}\delta s}{2v} + \frac{(\rho_1^w - \rho_1^T)(\theta^T - \theta^w)(s/4av)}{(\rho_1^w + \rho_1^T)(2 - \rho_1^w - \rho_1^T)} \right],$$

where we have used $u_1(D) - u_1(F) = -\sqrt{a}s$. (Note that $1 - s/2v > 0$, for otherwise, the devaluation size would exceed twice the maximum size of the shock it was aimed to offset.)

The persistence parameter $\delta$ will affect both terms inside the brackets. The effect on $\rho_1^i$ ($i = T,W$) arises because the critical level $\hat{\epsilon}_1^i$ of the first-period shock depends on welfare in both periods and hence on $\delta$. In the case of *no persistence* of unemployment effects across periods ($\delta = 0$), so that there is only a signaling effect, the first term in brackets disappears, and the expression in (7) is unambiguously positive. The standard result on signaling of types will then hold: observing a tough policy (no devaluation) in the first period will raise the probability of no devaluation in the second. That is, in this case we see from (7) that $\mu_2(D)$ is greater than $\mu_2(F)$ as long as $\rho_1^w > \rho_1^T$; that is, as long as a weak government is more likely to devalue in the first period. This will be true since $\theta^T > \theta^w$. Hence absence of persistence and different preferences over inflation imply that the signaling motive alone contributes to the credibility of the fixed exchange rate, which is therefore enhanced in the second period if no devaluation was observed in the first.

To add persistence back in, set $\delta > 0$. The dependence of $\mu_2(D) - \mu_2(F)$ on $\delta$ is complicated, reflecting the contribution of both terms. Solving (7) with MATHEMATICA, one can show that for $\delta$ sufficiently large, the persistence effect will tend to dominate the signaling effect, and (7) will become negative. This result is illustrated in Figure I for two sets of parameter values. In the two cases, the following values were imposed: $\kappa = 0.02$, $s = 0.1$, $a = 0.25$, $v = 0.15$, $\beta = 0.95$, $\theta^T = 1$, and either $\theta^w = 0$ or $\theta^w = 0.5$. Figure I then plots $\mu_2(D) - \mu_2(F)$ as a function of $\Delta = \delta \sqrt{a}$ in the interval $[0, 1]$. It can be seen that at about $\Delta = 0.8$ (when $\theta^w = 0$) or $\Delta = 0.45$ (when $\theta^w = 0.5$), $\mu_2(D) = \mu_2(F)$, and for higher values of $\Delta$, not devaluing in the first period *lowers* credibility in the second.

To summarize, positive persistence of unemployment implies that no devaluation in the first period may raise rather than lower the public's expectation of a devaluation in the second period. Shocks that are not offset through a devaluation in period 1 have

$\mu_2(D) - \mu_2(F)$

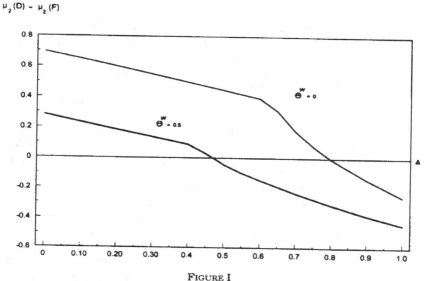

FIGURE I
Effect of Persistence on the Likelihood of Devaluation

further unfavorable effects in period 2, increasing the probability that a government of either type will devalue. If these persistence effects are sufficiently strong ($\delta$ large), not devaluing in the first period will raise the probability of a devaluation in the second. Thus, credibility will not necessarily be enhanced by "playing tough" in period 1.[11]

## V. EMPIRICAL EVIDENCE

We now turn to how one can empirically distinguish the two influences of tough policy on credibility—its role in signaling type versus its effect in constraining future room to maneuver due to persistence. The model we have developed above implies that the correlation between changes in unemployment rates and the expectation of a devaluation will be quite different depending on whether the signaling factor or the "external circumstances" factor in policymaking dominates. If there is great uncertainty

11. In the case where the shock is observed (see footnote 10), we shall see the same effect: if persistence effects are strong enough, playing tough in the first period will lower the credibility of the no-devaluation policy in the second.

about the government's type, then high unemployment may convincingly signal that the government is tough and determined to carry through on its policy commitment; therefore, policy credibility should improve. However, if the government's type is known (or if the difference in types is small), then increased unemployment reduces credibility, since it makes it less likely that either type of government will deliver on its policy commitments in the future.

The EMS provides a good application of the model, and interest rate differentials relative to Germany, the anchor for EMS monetary policy, provide a good proxy for expected devaluation, and hence for the lack of credibility of fixed parities.[12] Received wisdom suggests that the EMS went from an initial stage of low credibility, lack of policy convergence, and relatively frequent realignments, to a later stage in which there was considerable policy convergence and realignments were infrequent or did not occur at all. Giavazzi and Spaventa [1990], for instance, refer to the latter period as the "New EMS." If there is a change in behavior along those lines, our model suggests that the partial effect of unemployment on the interest rate differential should be quite different in the different periods.

France may be an especially good case for examining alternative models of credibility. Between the formation of the EMS in March 1979 and the present, France has had six realignments relative to the deutsche mark (September 24, 1979; October 5, 1981; June 14, 1982; March 21, 1983; April 7, 1986; and January 12, 1987). While in the early part of the period the long-term interest differential between the franc and the DM rose, since the end of 1982, the interest differential has been falling steadily and, at the end of 1991, stood at less than half of a percentage point (Figure II).[13]

In the early part of the EMS period, the socialist government which came to power in May 1981 followed strongly expansionary policies, making it clear that it had little commitment to fixed parities. Higher unemployment would signal the need to stimulate aggregate demand, and hence make a realignment more likely. It

---

12. Recent empirical analyses of EMS credibility include Bartolini and Bodnar [1992], Koen [1991], and Weber [1991, 1992]. Koen calculates credibility bands around interest differentials which take into account the freedom for exchange rates to change without realignments being necessary. For long-term interest rates, which we use in our empirical work, the bands are quite narrow, however.

13. It subsequently widened, in large part because of the considerations discussed in this paper.

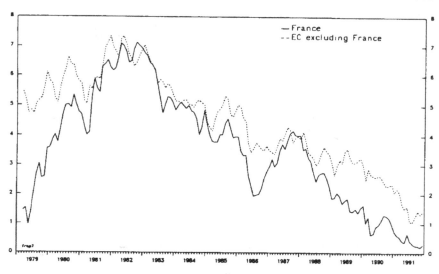

FIGURE II
Long-Term Interest Differentials Against Germany

should therefore have been associated with higher long-term interest rate differentials vis-à-vis Germany. However, there was an important change in behavior in June 1982, reinforced in March 1983, when France shifted to far tighter fiscal and monetary policies, the *politique de rigueur*. We would argue that this shift in policy was not immediately perceived as a long-term shift; that is, that it took time for policymakers to convince investors. They did so by showing that they accepted the unemployment costs without devaluing, and there were in fact no realignments for a three-year period, despite high unemployment, which rose above 10 percent (Figure III). The commitment to a strong franc made by the socialist government was reaffirmed by the conservatives, who were in power between 1986 and 1988.[14] After returning to power in May 1988, socialist finance minister Bérégovoy further asserted that the franc would not be realigned against the deutsche mark in the future. The consistency in French policy no doubt helped to establish a reputation for toughness. However, unemployment remained a problem; after declining to about 9 percent, it rose once

14. The fact that Mitterand was still President guaranteed some continuity in exchange rate policy. Besides, the conservatives already had a reputation of support for a strong currency.

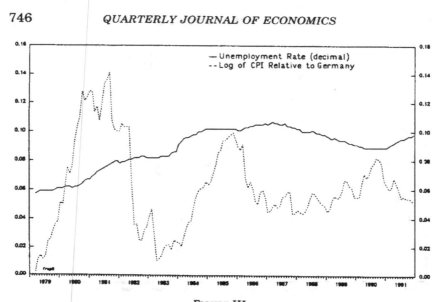

FIGURE III
France: Unemployment and Relative Prices

again to 10 percent as the economy slowed in 1990–1991. Though the reputation for toughness was established (so that $p$ was close to zero), there may have been legitimate concerns that restrictive policies could not be maintained. In these circumstances, higher unemployment should once again tend to raise interest differentials, since even a tough government might devalue if the unemployment costs became too high.

Our theory therefore implies that the relationship between unemployment and long-term interest differentials should change over time, perhaps going through three phases. In the initial period following the election of François Mitterand as President and the formation of a socialist government, the authorities were perceived as being neither tough with respect to inflation nor committed to resisting realignments. They were willing to devalue, and the higher was the unemployment rate, the more likely was a realignment. After the 1982–1983 switch to a *politique de rigueur,* however, the absence of devaluations in spite of high unemployment helped signal to the public the change in the type of government, so that higher unemployment should have raised credibility (by lowering $p$) and hence led to declining interest differentials relative to Germany. Once a reputation for toughness was established, devaluation in the face of an adverse shock or accumulated loss of competitiveness (as occurred in January 1987) should not have significantly damaged the credibility of the strong franc policy. However, despite this favorable effect on credibility, increases in unemployment would be associated with fears of an eventual devaluation (raising both $\rho^T$ and $\rho^w$) and hence would lead to higher interest differentials than would otherwise have prevailed.

This characterization of the difference in the relation between unemployment and interest differentials depending on which factor influencing credibility dominates suggests the following sort of empirical investigation: one can regress the long-term interest differential with Germany on variables which measure the policy stance to see how the relation changed over time. One can then ask whether such changes reflect political changes taking place in France which would operate in the direction predicted above.

Long-term interest differentials between France and Germany were regressed (using ordinary least squares in the first instance) on the unemployment rate and some other plausible measures of expected devaluation (see Panel A of Table I). These other indicators are a measure of competitiveness (the ratio of the CPI in France relative to that in Germany); the EC-wide interest differential (excluding France) with respect to Germany, which is intended to capture the overall credibility of the EMS commitment to fixed parities; and the lagged dependent variable, which can be expected to enter because the accumulation (or loss) of credibility can be expected to occur gradually.[15] (More general lag structures were tried, but in general other lagged dependent or independent variables were not significant.)

Changes in the relationship between the unemployment rate and interest differentials were examined in two ways. First, natural breaks in the series that correspond to the dating discussed above were imposed in estimation, using appropriately specified dummy variables. The discussion suggests an initial period ending in late 1982 or early 1983, a middle period extending to the most recent devaluation, in January 1987, and a final period since then. Second, tests of structural stability were performed, splitting the whole

---

15. The variables included, in particular the interest differentials, competitiveness, and unemployment, are nonstationary, I(1), variables in our sample, but they are cointegrated. Our dynamic equation can thus be interpreted as an error-correction model.

TABLE I

REGRESSIONS FOR THE FRENCH LONG-TERM INTEREST DIFFERENTIAL AGAINST GERMANY (ID), MAY 1979–DECEMBER 1991

(STANDARD ERRORS IN PARENTHESES)

$$ID = a_1 LRP + a_2 IDEC + a_3 ID_{-1} + DUM1(a_4 UR + a_5) + DUM2(a_6 UR + a_7) + DUM3(a_8 UR + a_9)$$

A. Ordinary least squares

| Independent variables[a] | | | | | | | | | Statistics[b] | | | | | |
|---|---|---|---|---|---|---|---|---|---|---|---|---|---|---|
| LRP | IDEC | $ID_{-1}$ | DUM1 | DUM1.UR | DUM2 | DUM2.UR | DUM3 | DUM3.UR | $R^2$ | SER | ARCH | LM(1,8) | Q(1,20) | LR(4) |
| **Whole sample** | | | | | | | | | | | | | | |
| 0.492 | 0.265* | 0.801* | −0.892* | 0.043 | — | — | — | — | 0.979 | 0.279 | 0.83 | 12.20 | 26.3 | — |
| (0.789) | (0.050) | (0.037) | (0.311) | (0.024) | | | | | | | | | | |
| **Subperiods: May 1979–Dec. 1982, Jan. 1983–Dec. 1986, Jan 1987–Dec. 1991** | | | | | | | | | | | | | | |
| 0.985 | 0.316* | 0.703* | −2.125* | 0.242* | 0.309 | −0.074 | −3.269* | 0.294* | 0.981 | 0.267 | 1.18 | 8.21 | 25.7 | 17.9* |
| (0.956) | (0.059) | (0.047) | (0.522) | (0.072) | (0.778) | (0.070) | (0.804) | (0.084) | | | | | | |
| **Subperiods: May 1979–Sept. 1981, Oct. 1981–Oct. 1986, Nov. 1986–Dec. 1991** | | | | | | | | | | | | | | |
| −0.670 | 0.359* | 0.717* | −3.449* | 0.425* | −0.333 | −0.026 | −2.486* | 0.207* | 0.982 | 0.262 | 0.96 | 9.40 | 29.3 | 23.5* |
| (1.044) | (0.060) | (0.043) | (0.828) | (0.120) | (0.694) | (0.057) | (0.707) | (0.075) | | | | | | |

B. Instrumental variables

| | Independent variables[a] | | | | | | | | | Statistics[b] | |
|---|---|---|---|---|---|---|---|---|---|---|---|
| LRP | IDEC | $ID_{-1}$ | DUM1 | DUM1.UR | DUM2 | DUM2.UR | DUM3 | DUM3.UR | | $R^2$ | SER |
| **Whole sample** | | | | | | | | | | | |
| 0.491 | 0.264* | 0.802* | -0.883* | 0.042 | — | — | — | — | | 0.979 | 0.279 |
| (0.789) | (0.050) | (0.037) | (0.312) | (0.024) | | | | | | | |
| **Subperiods: May 1979–Dec. 1982, Jan. 1983–Dec. 1986, Jan. 1987–Dec. 1991** | | | | | | | | | | | |
| 1.138 | 0.319* | 0.691* | -2.248* | 0.263* | 0.568 | -0.097 | -3.482* | 0.317* | | 0.980 | 0.267 |
| (0.962) | (0.059) | (0.048) | (0.526) | (0.073) | (0.793) | (0.072) | (0.821) | (0.085) | | | |
| **Subperiods: May 1979–Sept. 1981, Oct. 1981–Oct. 1986, Nov. 1986–Dec. 1991** | | | | | | | | | | | |
| -0.832 | 0.365* | 0.707* | -3.756* | 0.476* | -0.221 | -0.035 | -2.549* | 0.215* | | 0.982 | 0.261 |
| (1.052) | (0.060) | (0.043) | (0.838) | (0.122) | (0.705) | (0.058) | (0.719) | (0.076) | | | |

a. Variables names: $LRP$ = log of French CPI relative to Germany's; $IDEC$ = EC interest differential with Germany (excluding France); $ID_{-1}$ = lagged dependent variable; $DUM1$, $DUM2$, $DUM3$ = dummy variables, equal to unity within the relevant subperiods, zero otherwise; $UR$ = French unemployment rate.

b. Statistics: $R^2$ = explained sum of squares as a ratio to total sum of squares; $SER$ = standard error of regression; $ARCH$ = autoregressive conditional heteroskedasticity test, distributed as $F(1,150)$; $LM(1,8)$ = Lagrange multiplier test for serial correlation, lags 1 to 8, distributed as $\chi^2(8)$; $Q(1,20)$ = Ljung-Box test for serial correlation, lags 1 to 20, distributed $\chi^2(20)$; $LR(4)$ = likelihood ratio test of structural break, distributed $\chi^2(4)$, *assuming that break points are known.*

*Significant at 5 percent level.

sample into two subperiods by successively trying different break points. If breaks are significant at several dates, the one that gives the maximum value of the likelihood ratio is chosen. Then, each of the two subsamples is further tested for break points in the same fashion. In doing these tests, the coefficients of both the unemployment rate and the constant term were allowed to vary, but the remaining coefficients were assumed constant over the whole sample.[16]

Using the first approach, the unemployment rate and the constant are entered with separate coefficients for the three subperiods discussed above (1979:05–1982:12, 1983:01–1986:12, and 1987:01–1991:12). The likelihood ratio test indicates that there is a significant difference in the regression coefficients on the unemployment rate and the constant across the three subperiods.[17] In the first and third subperiods, higher unemployment is associated with _higher_ interest differentials, reflecting increasing concern with the possibility of realignment. In the second subperiod, when the authorities were attempting to signal a change in the priorities of the government and gaining credibility for a "hard currency" policy, a higher unemployment rate is associated with lower interest differentials, as the discussion above suggested that it should. However, the coefficient is not strongly significant.

The size of the coefficients in the first and third subperiods is also of interest. If a government is considered to be less concerned about the exchange rate and inflation (i.e., weak), then it is expected to resist movements away from a lower target for the unemployment rate. In the model the target unemployment rate is given by the ratio of the coefficients on the dummy variable and the product of the latter with the unemployment rate. That is, grouping the terms multiplied by each of the dummy variables as $a_4DUM1$ $(UR + a_5/a_4)$, etc., then $-a_5/a_4$ is the level of unemployment rate in the first subperiod above which there is a positive effect on the interest differential, and similarly for the other subperiods. The values for the transformed constant term are, respectively, 8.78 and 11.2 for the first and third subperiods.

Thus, the target rate of unemployment is higher in the third subperiod, confirming the reasoning described above. As for the

16. Tests that allowed _all_ of the coefficients to vary gave similar break points and test statistics.
17. On the assumption that the break points are known—see discussion below, however.

POLICIES VERSUS POLICYMAKERS          751

relative *size* of the unemployment rate effects (i.e., $a_8$ versus $a_4$), there is no unambiguous prediction: a tough government could conceivably be just as concerned about deviations of unemployment from its (much higher) target, and in fact, the estimates give a somewhat higher value for the third subperiod than the first.

The second approach identified the break points on the basis of the values of the likelihood ratio at the different dates (allowing for different coefficients on the unemployment rate and the constant before and after that date). The critical values of the likelihood ratio when the break point is not known have recently been tabulated by Andrews [1990]. For two degrees of freedom, they are 11.7 at the 5 percent level and 10.1 at the 10 percent level. Starting with the whole sample, the maximum likelihood ratio statistic (a value of 11.0) occurred when the sample was broken at 1986:9, and this is significant at the 10 percent level. If we then treat the first subperiod as a separate sample, the maximum likelihood ratio statistic (a value of 13.5) occurs when a further break is made at 1981:9. Using the second subperiod as a separate sample, the likelihood ratio has a maximum value of 8.1, well below the 10 percent critical value, suggesting no break point in this period. Therefore, the coefficients on unemployment and the constant were estimated over three subperiods: 1979:5–1981:9, 1981:10–1986:10, and 1986:11–1991:12. Interestingly, the second break point is very close to that suggested by our historical discussion.

Again the unemployment coefficients evolve over time as our model would suggest. Unemployment has a strongly significant, positive coefficient in the early and late periods. In contrast, in the middle period, when unemployment was rising strongly and the government was trying to establish credibility for greater exchange-rate stability and for limiting inflation, the coefficient is negative, though insignificant. Again, the target unemployment rate is higher in the third subperiod than in the first (12.0 percent versus 8.1 percent), though now the coefficient on unemployment is in fact lower in the later period than in the earlier one.

In order to correct for the possibility that the unemployment rate and the interest differential were jointly endogenous, instrumental variables estimation was also performed (see Panel B of Table I). Instruments used were the other regressors, plus time and the lagged unemployment rate. The results are very similar to the OLS results, and confirm the qualitative conclusions discussed above.

## VI. Conclusions

The initial work on modeling credibility stressed a policymaker's intentions as summarized by his "type." It enabled macroeconomists to understand better how a "tough" policy could yield benefits well into the future via enhanced reputation. We were always uneasy, as were others, with the picture of a tough policymaker who would adhere to his anti-inflation policy no matter what was happening to the economy.

A more realistic picture is that of a policymaker who will renege on his commitment if circumstances are bad enough. Credibility, namely the expectation that an announced policy will be carried out, then reflects not only the policymaker's intentions, but also the state of the economy, where stochastic shocks will be important. The purpose of this paper was to show that this view of policymaking and credibility implies that tough policies may have adverse effects on credibility in the future if they severely constrain the choices of future policymakers. Policies that raise unemployment into the future, for example, will lower the "threshold" level of the random shock at which a future policymaker will find it optimal to devalue.

Using interest differentials relative to Germany as a measure of the perceived credibility of a country's pledge to maintain a fixed parity in the EMS, we found support for this alternative view in the effect of unemployment on credibility in France. In fact, though there was some weak evidence of the signaling role of unemployment in a period in the mid-1980s in which the priorities of the authorities had changed, in the earlier and later subperiods there seems to be clear evidence of a negative association between credibility and the unemployment rate. This suggests that *both* a policymaker's reputation for pursuing a hard-currency peg *and* durably lower unemployment are necessary to convince investors of the credibility of policy. The results are far from conclusive. But they indicate that modeling credibility solely in terms of a policymaker's preferences or intentions is seriously incomplete.

## Appendix: The First-Period Decision Problem

The first-period decision for a government of type $i$ is to choose a critical value $\hat{\epsilon}_1^i$ such that $\Lambda^i(D) = \Lambda^i(F)$, where $\Lambda^i(\ )$ is defined by

(2) in the text. Using (2), one finds that

(A1)   $\hat{\epsilon}_1^i = -\kappa - \mu_1 s + \dfrac{a + \theta^i}{2a} s + \dfrac{\beta}{2as} [EL_2^i(D) - EL_2^i(F)],$

where $\mu_1$ is the probability of a devaluation in the first period, which depends on $\rho_1^w$, $\rho_1^T$, and the uniform priors. To evaluate the terms in brackets, we use

(A2)   $EL_2^i(j)$

$$= \frac{1}{2v} \int_{\epsilon_2=-v}^{\epsilon_2=\hat{\epsilon}_2^i(j)} a[-\mu_2(j)s - \epsilon_2 - \kappa - \delta(u_1(j) - u_N)]^2 \, d\epsilon_2$$

$$+ \frac{1}{2v} \int_{\epsilon_2=\hat{\epsilon}_2^i(j)}^{\epsilon_2=v} (a[s - \mu_2(j)s - \epsilon_2 - \kappa - \delta(u_1(j) - u_n)]^2 + \theta^i s^2) \, d\epsilon_2.$$

For ease of notation, define $m(j) = \mu_2(j)s + \kappa + \delta(u_1(j) - u_N)$. Using the fact that $\hat{\epsilon}_2^i(j) = -m(j) + (a + \theta^i)s/2a$, the integral (A2) may, after some manipulation, be evaluated as

(A3)      $EL_2^i(j) = a(m(j) + \kappa)^2 + \dfrac{av^2}{3} - \dfrac{as}{2v}(v - \hat{\epsilon}_2^i(j))^2.$

The term in brackets in (A1), $EL_2^i(D) - EL_2^i(F)$ then becomes

(A4)   $\dfrac{a(2v - s)}{2v} [(m(D))^2 - (m(F))^2] + \left( \dfrac{(a + \theta^i)s^2}{2} v - as + 2a\kappa \right)$

$$\times (m(D) - m(F)) = ((\mu_2(D) - \mu_2(F))s + \delta(u_1(D) - u_1(F)))$$

$$\times \left( \left( 1 - \frac{s}{2v} \right) [(\mu_2(D) + \mu_2(F))s + 2(\kappa - \delta u_N) \right.$$

$$\left. + \delta(u_1(D) + u_1(F)) - s] + \frac{\theta^i s^2}{2av} \right).$$

$\rho_1^w$ and $\rho_1^T$ may then be calculated from (A1), using (A4) and the uniform distribution.

UNIVERSITY OF MARYLAND AND NBER
INTERNATIONAL MONETARY FUND

## REFERENCES

Andrews, Donald W. K., "Tests for Parameter Instability and Structural Change with Unknown Change Point," Cowles Foundation Discussion Paper No. 943: Yale University, 1990.

Backus, David, and E. John Driffill, "Inflation and Reputation," *American Economic Review*, LXXV (1985a), 530–38.

Backus, David, and E. John Driffill, "Rational Expectations and Policy Credibility Following a Change in Regime," *Review of Economic Studies,* LII (1985b), 211–21.

Barro, Robert J., and David B. Gordon, "Rules, Discretion, and Reputation in a Model of Monetary Policy," *Journal of Monetary Economics,* XII (1983a), 101–21.

Barro, Robert J., and David B. Gordon, "A Positive Theory of Monetary Policy in a Natural Rate Model," *Journal of Political Economy,* XCI (1983b), 589–610.

Bartolini, Leonardo, and Gordon Bodnar, "Target Zones and Forward Rates in a Model with Repeated Realignments," *Journal of Monetary Economics,* XXX (1992), 373–408.

Blanchard, Olivier J., "Credibility, Disinflation, and Gradualism," *Economics Letters,* XVII (1985), 211–17.

Canzoneri, Matthew, "Monetary Policy Games and the Role of Private Information," *American Economic Review,* LXXV (1985), 1056–70.

Chen, Zhaohui, and Alberto Giovannini, "The Credibility of Adjustable Parities: The Experience of the European Monetary System," mimeo, Columbia University, 1992.

Cukierman, Alex, and Nissan Liviatan, "Optimal Accommodation by Strong Policymakers Under Incomplete Information," *Journal of Monetary Economics,* XXVII (1991), 99–127.

Flood, Robert P., "Comment on Buiter and Miller," in Jacob A. Frenkel, ed., *Exchange Rates and International Macroeconomics* (Chicago: University of Chicago Press, 1983), pp. 359–65.

Flood, Robert P., and Peter Isard, "Monetary Policy Strategies," *IMF Staff Papers,* XXXVI (1989), 612–32.

Froot, Kenneth A., and Kenneth Rogoff, "The EMS, the EMU, and the Transition to a Common Currency," in Olivier J. Blanchard and Stanley Fischer, eds., *NBER Macroeconomics Annual 1991* (Cambridge MA: MIT Press, 1991). pp. 269–317.

Giavazzi, Francesco, and Luigi Spaventa, "The New EMS," CEPR Discussion Paper No. 369, 1990.

Klein, Michael, and Nancy Marion, "The Duration of Fixed Exchange Rate Regimes," mimeo, Dartmouth College, 1992.

Koen, Vincent R., "Testing the Credibility of the Belgian Hard Currency Policy," IMF Working Paper WP/91/79, 1991.

Kreps, David, and Robert Wilson, "Reputation and Imperfect Information," *Journal of Economic Theory,* XXVII (1982), 253–79.

Lohmann, Susanne, "Monetary Policy Strategies–A Correction," *IMF Staff Papers,* XXXVII (1990), 440–45.

Obstfeld, Maurice, "Destabilizing Effects of Exchange Rate Escape Clauses," NBER Working Paper No. 3603, 1991.

Persson, Torsten, "Credibility of Macroeconomic Policy: An Introduction and Broad Survey," *European Economic Review,* XXXII (1988), 519–32.

Persson, Torsten, and Guido Tabellini, *Macroeconomic Policy, Credibility and Politics* (London: Harwood, 1989).

Rogoff, Kenneth, "Reputational Constraints on Monetary Policy," in K. Brunner and A. Meltzer, eds. *Carnegie-Rochester Series on Public Policy* 26 (Amsterdam: North-Holland, 1987), pp. 141–82.

——, "Reputation, Coordination, and Monetary Policy," in R. Barro, ed., *Modern Business Cycle Theory* (Cambridge, MA: Harvard University Press, 1989), pp. 236–64.

van Wijnbergen, Sweder, "Intertemporal Speculation, Shortages and the Political Economy of Price Reform: A Case Against Gradualism," mimeo, World Bank, 1990.

Vickers, John, "Signalling in a Model of Monetary Policy with Incomplete Information," *Oxford Economic Papers,* XXXVIII (1986), 443–55.

Weber, Axel, "Reputation and Credibility in the European Monetary System," *European Policy,* XII (1991), 57–102.

——, "The Role of Policymakers' Reputation in the EMS Disinflations: An Empirical Evaluation," *European Economic Review,* XXXVI (1992), 1473–92.

### Corrigendum to "Credibility of Policies versus Credibility of Policymakers" Quarterly Journal of Economics, August 1994

- On page 84 (740), the third identity under equation (3) should read

$\rho_2^T \equiv$ probability a government of type $T$ will devalue.

- On page 85 (741), equation (4) should read

$$\hat{\varepsilon}_2^i(j) = \frac{(a + \theta^i)s}{2a} - \kappa - \mu_2(j)s - \delta(u_1(j) - u_n)$$

- On page 97 (753), equation (A3) should read

$$EL_2^i(j) = a(m(j))^2 + \frac{av^2}{3} - \frac{as}{2v}(v - \hat{\varepsilon}_2^i(j))^2$$

and equation (A4) should read

$$\frac{a(2v - s)}{2v}[(m(D))^2 - (m(F))^2] + \left[\frac{(a + \theta^i)s^2}{2v} - as\right][m(D) - m(F)]$$

$$= a\{[\mu_2(D) - \mu_2(F)]s + \delta[u_1(D) - u_1(F)]\}\left\{\frac{2v - s}{2v}[(\mu_2(D) - \mu_2(F))s\right.$$

$$\left. +[2(\kappa - \delta u_N) + \delta(u_1(D) + u_1(F)) - s] + \frac{\theta^i s^2}{2av}\right\}$$

*The Economic Journal*, **105** (*May*), 571–582. © Royal Economic Society 1995. Published by Blackwell Publishers, 108 Cowley Road, Oxford OX4 1JF, UK and 238 Main Street, Cambridge, MA 02142, USA.

# GAINING AND LOSING ERM CREDIBILITY: THE CASE OF THE UNITED KINGDOM*

*Paul R. Masson*

The model of this paper highlights two aspects of credibility: signalling the type of government, which is assumed not to be known; and, for any type, the likelihood that if circumstances are sufficiently unfavourable a devaluation will be impossible to avoid, since not to do so would go against the government's interests. These two factors have opposite implications for the link between unemployment and interest differentials: high unemployment signals a tough government, but also makes it less likely that even a tough government will maintain an existing parity.

The United Kingdom is an interesting case for assessing the factors that affect credibility. Because the purpose of joining the European Monetary System's exchange rate mechanism, or ERM, in October 1990 was clearly to enhance the credibility of monetary policy so as to achieve a reduction of the high rate of inflation with minimum effects on unemployment, yet the speculative attacks leading to the withdrawal of the pound from the ERM two years later are clear evidence that credibility was not achieved, despite a substantial reduction in inflation. It has been argued that a peg to the deutsche mark should allow the monetary authorities to borrow the Bundesbank's credibility by tying their hands; (see, notably, Andersen and Risager (1988) and Horn and Persson (1988)). Moreover, Winckler (1991) has suggested that the entry of the pound into the ERM at an appreciated rate (2·95 DM) signalled the firm anti-inflationary intentions of the authorities. In the context of signalling models, the more the government shows a willingness to pay the costs of fighting inflation, the more effectively it signals its 'type', that is whether it is tough or weak.[1] A more appreciated rate would also produce more slack in output and labour markets, and this slack would tend to put downward pressure on inflation (over and above any favourable signalling effects).

Such an analysis would suggest that the U.K. government, by signalling its toughness initially and persisting with the ERM peg, should have established a measure of credibility initially for its policies, and continued to gain credibility as inflation declined. The annual inflation rate[2] fell from 9·5% in October 1990 to 3·6% in October 1992; moreover, the Chancellor of the Exchequer and the Prime Minister reinforced their commitment to maintaining the value of sterling against the deutsche mark by declaring that the

---

* The author is grateful to Marcel Cassard, Robert Corker, Stephen Hall, Brian Henry, Peter Isard, Svante Öberg, Ceyla Pazarbasioglu, Demosthenes Tambakis, Mark Taylor, Axel Weber, a referee of this JOURNAL, and seminar participants at the IMF, Federal Reserve Board, and Bordeaux, Tilburg and Warwick Universities for useful discussions and comments. The views expressed here are personal to the author and do not represent those of the International Monetary Fund.

[1] See Vickers (1985) and Backus and Driffill (1985a, b). In the United Kingdom context, a more usual terminology for the types of government would be 'dry' and 'wet'.

[2] Retail prices excluding mortgage interest payments.

pound would enter the narrow ERM band at that parity.[3] A measure of credibility of the exchange rate commitment is the interest rate differential relative to Germany, and there was indeed a fall in both the short-term and long-term differentials shortly after ERM entry. However, that fall came to an end in the summer of 1992, at which time the differential was between 0·5 and 1·0 percentage point; and speculative pressures in September forced the U.K. authorities to abandon their peg and to float the currency.[4]

The present paper considers a broader concept of credibility that includes not just signalling of its type by the government, but also the costs of sticking to its policies that any government – whether wet or dry – must take into account. In particular, though the U.K. authorities may have deliberately created slack in output and labour markets in order to achieve disinflation, the severity of the recession was greater than anticipated, and this unfavourable shock made the exchange rate peg costlier in terms of employment. Investors anticipated that employment considerations would eventually lead to an abandonment of the peg to the deutsche mark, despite the government's statements to the contrary, and this led to a rise in interest rate differentials and to capital outflows that were ultimately so large that they could not be offset by official intervention.

The paper thus integrates two aspects of credibility, whose relative importance can vary over time. The paper assumes that, in general, no government can put sole weight on the objective of controlling inflation, and completely ignore growth and employment objectives. Therefore, in adverse circumstances a government may be led to ease monetary policy, and an aspect of credibility that became increasingly important in 1991–2 was the realisation that economic activity and employment were severely depressed in the United Kingdom.[5] The paper thus follows in the lines of Drazen and Masson (1994), but in a multi-period context in which credibility evolves over time, and in which the updating is explicitly modelled. Maintaining the parity exchange rate in the face of inflation that is higher than in the anchor country affects credibility in two opposite ways: it signals the preferences of the authorities, but also makes the economy more vulnerable to future adverse shocks because losses of competitiveness have persistent effects on activity.

Other papers have also considered the tradeoff between 'big bang' and gradual policies from the point of view of credibility. Flood (1983) for example points out that too rapid a contraction in monetary policies (for instance, the Thatcher experiment of the early 1980s) could raise, not lower, inflation expectations because it might cause expectations of a change in government.

[3] The pound sterling entered the ERM with the wide fluctuation bands, plus or minus 6% of the central parity; these bands also applied until recently to the Portuguese escudo and Spanish peseta. The narrow band, which applied to the other ERM currencies, was plus or minus 2·25%. On 2 August 1993, bands of fluctuation around all bilateral central parities except the deutsche mark/Dutch guilder rate were widened to 15%.

[4] See Barrell et al. (1993) for a discussion of this period.

[5] This assumes that monetary policy has some effect on economic activity, at least in the short run, which is a feature even of natural rate models of the Barro–Gordon type.

Similarly, Blanchard (1985) considers the alternation of governments and its effect on inflation expectations, where each government is solely concerned with one objective, either inflation or employment. In the present paper, electoral considerations are ignored; it is assumed that there is a social consensus at least on the belief that both objectives are important – so that no government can ignore unemployment costs – even if relative weights are subject to disagreement. This seems realistic in the context of the early 1990s in Britain, since both major parties supported ERM membership, and the parity of the pound was not a major issue in the April 1992 general election.

The model is tested using Kalman filter estimation to account for the variation of credibility over time. Time-varying parameter models have been used before to model exchange rates and interest rates, for instance by Hamilton (1988), Lewis (1989), Engel and Hamilton (1990), Kaminsky and Peruga (1990), Haldane and Hall (1991), and Weber (1991, 1992). However, those papers have either not attempted to relate changes in parameters to optimising behaviour, or have been applied to floating exchange rates rather than to ERM parities.

The plan of the paper is as follows. Section I develops the theoretical model, which is estimated in Section II. Finally, brief conclusions are given in Section III.

## I. A MODEL OF CREDIBILITY

The model that follows is a simple setup that combines the two elements that are important in explaining the evolving credibility of the commitment of the U.K. monetary authorities to the ERM. In particular, the model incorporates the favourable effect on credibility of maintaining the parity and, initially, of accepting the resulting unemployment costs, but also the opposite effect that continuing unemployment has in making the commitment to a fixed parity more difficult to maintain, and hence less credible. As in Drazen and Masson (1994), the model is an elaboration of that in Obstfeld (1991), and is related to the 'escape clause' model of Flood and Isard (1989), but here assessments of the type of government are updated period by period; the model thus explains the evolution of credibility in a multi-period context.

The model is based on a simple relationship between devaluations and employment. Expected devaluations do not have a stimulative effect, but surprise devaluations do; such a relationship would prevail for given domestic (wage) inflation, in a model where only surprise inflation matters for output. A government therefore has the incentive to increase employment by devaluing; in the ERM context, the choice is assumed to involve maintaining the current parity or devaluing by a fixed amount $d$, which is exogenous to the government and a feature of the exchange rate system. Thus, the government has two discrete alternatives for the exchange rate in period $t$: $e_t = e_{t-1}$ or $e_t = e_{t-1} + d$. There may be a devaluation bias because, as in Barro and Gordon (1983), the central bank attempts to offset distortions that produce a higher-than-optimal unemployment rate; however, this feature is not critical to the model of this paper and is ignored.[6] There is also a stochastic shock $u$ to unemployment; the private sector is assumed not to observe this shock when forming its expectations, while the government (or central bank) knows the value of the shock when deciding whether or not to devalue in the current period. Crucial to our purposes, shocks and government policies have persistent effects on unemployment that extend beyond the current period; this assumption explains why policy choices constrain the room for manoeuvre in subsequent periods.

For simplicity, the model is written in terms of $ur_t$, the deviation of unemployment from the natural rate,[7]

$$ur_t = \sqrt{a}[-(e_t - E_{t-1} e_t) + u_t + \delta ur_{t-1}], \tag{1}$$

where $e$ is the log of the exchange rate ($\pounds/\mathrm{DM}$) and $u$ is an unemployment shock which is assumed to be uniformly distributed in the interval $[-v, v]$. Private sector expectations $E_{t-1} e_t$ are conditional on information available prior to $t$, which excludes current and past shocks. The private sector knows that the government is one of two 'types' (whose objective functions are known), but it does not know which, so it forms probability assessments of the government's type (described below).

The government is assumed for simplicity to minimise a one-period loss function[8] which depends on the squared deviations of unemployment from the natural rate and on the (squared) change in the exchange rate:

$$L_t = (ur_t)^2 + \theta(\Delta e_t)^2. \tag{2}$$

The second term reflects both the cost of inflation[9] and the policy-maker's concern for exchange rate stability. A tough government has a larger value for $\theta$ than does a weak government: $\theta^T > \theta^W$. These values are known by the private sector, which updates its assessment $\pi_t$ of the probability that a government is weak on the basis of observed behaviour.

Given the above assumptions, the government's optimal behaviour can easily be characterised. It devalues when a shock $u_t$ is large enough that the costs of maintaining the parity exceed those of incurring higher inflation. Let $L^F$ be the loss function value when the exchange rate is kept fixed, $L^D$ when the exchange rate is devalued by amount $d$: the government devalues when $L^D < L^F$. This implies that it will devalue if and only if

$$u_t > \frac{(a+\theta)\,d}{2a} - E_{t-1} e_t + e_{t-1} - \delta ur_{t-1}. \tag{3}$$

Let $\rho_t^w$ be the probability that a weak government will devalue in period $t$ and

---

[6] Its inclusion merely affects a constant term which is not restricted in estimation.

[7] Unlike the model of Obstfeld (1991), which is written in terms of employment.

[8] Allowing for a multi-period objective function, as in Drazen and Masson (1994), makes the problem considerably more complex, and precludes a closed-form solution to be used in estimation. It has the advantage, however, of allowing the government to choose policy with an eye to its future reputation.

[9] Exchange rate depreciation leads to higher import prices (as well as lower unemployment, if the depreciation was not fully expected).

$\rho_t^T$ the probability that a strong government will devalue; since $\pi_t$ is the private sector's assessment of the probability that a government is weak,

and

$$E_{t-1} e_t - e_{t-1} = [\pi_t \rho_t^W + (1 - \pi_t) \rho_t^T] d$$

$$\rho_t^i = \text{prob} \left[ u_t > y_t - \pi_t \rho_t^W d - (1 - \pi_t) \rho_t^T d + \frac{\theta^i d}{2a} \middle| \text{government is of type } i \right] \quad (4)$$

where

$$y_t \equiv \frac{d}{2} - \delta u r_{t-1}.$$

Recall that $u_t$ is distributed uniformly in the interval $[-v, v]$. Assuming an interior solution,

$$\text{prob}(u_t > u_t^*) = \frac{v - u_t^*}{2v}. \quad (5)$$

We can then solve equations (4) above for $\rho_t^W$ and $\rho_t^T$:

$$\rho_t^W = \frac{(v - y_t)}{2v - d} - \frac{\theta^W d/2a}{2v - d} + \frac{(1 - \pi_t)(\theta^W - \theta^T) d^2/2a}{2v(2v - d)}, \quad (6a)$$

$$\rho_t^T = \frac{(v - y_t)}{2v - d} - \frac{\theta^T d/2a}{2v - d} - \frac{\pi_t(\theta^W - \theta^T) d^2/2a}{2v(2v - d)}. \quad (6b)$$

Furthermore,

$$\rho_t \equiv \pi_t \rho_t^W + (1 - \pi_t) \rho_t^T = \frac{v - y_t}{2v - d} - \frac{\theta^T d/2a}{2v - d} + \frac{\pi_t(\theta^T - \theta^W) d/2a}{2v - d}. \quad (7)$$

It is useful to separate the time-varying part of (7) from the part that is independent of time, and moreover to decompose the latter into 'steady-state' probabilities of devaluation, $\bar{\rho}^W$ and $\bar{\rho}^T$, *assuming that the private sector knows the type of government* (i.e. $\pi = 1$ in $(6a)$ and $\pi = 0$ in $(6b)$) *and* $ur_{t-1} = 0$:

$$\bar{\rho}^W \equiv 1/2 - \frac{\theta^W d/2a}{2v - d}, \quad (8a)$$

$$\bar{\rho}^T \equiv 1/2 - \frac{\theta^T d/2a}{2v - d}. \quad (8b)$$

Then, the probability of a realignment in period $t$ can be written simply as

$$\rho_t = \bar{\rho}^T + \pi_t(\bar{\rho}^W - \bar{\rho}^T) + \frac{\delta u r_{t-1}}{2v - d}. \quad (9)$$

A variant of this equation is used below in estimation. Note that for a given assessment of type, higher unemployment raises expected devaluation next period, because it makes it more likely that a positive unemployment shock will push it into a region where devaluation will be more attractive than maintaining the parity.

576                    THE ECONOMIC JOURNAL                    [MAY

Next we consider how to formulate estimates of the probability that the government is of type $W$ or $T$. Starting from a prior estimate $\pi_{t-1}$, suppose that the government does not devalue in period $t-1$. Then Bayesian updating would imply that

$$\pi_t = \frac{1 - \rho_{t-1}^W}{(1 - \rho_{t-1}^W)\,\pi_{t-1} + (1 - \rho_{t-1}^T)\,(1 - \pi_{t-1})}\,\pi_{t-1}. \tag{10}$$

If we substitute equations (6) and (8), linearise (see Appendix), and add an error term $\eta_t$ we obtain

$$\pi_t = \alpha\pi_{t-1} + \beta ur_{t-2} + \eta_t, \tag{11}$$

where $\alpha$ and $\beta \leqslant 0$ are parameters to be estimated. Higher unemployment lowers the probability assessment that the government is weak: the willingness to accept unemployment without devaluing reinforces the government's reputation for toughness.

The analysis thus far has considered a single-period horizon; empirically the model is applied to long-term bonds, since the longer the term to maturity, the smaller is the impact of expected movements within the band on the yield to maturity, so yield differentials can be identified with expected devaluation.[10] What is the expected rate of depreciation over the maturity of a bond, given the assessment of the type of government made at time $t$? It will be approximately true in the absence of risk premia[11] that the annual yield differential on an $N$-month bond, $R_t^{(N)}$, will equal the average of the expected rate of depreciation in each of the next $N$ months, at an annual rate. Using (9) and the autoregressive process for $ur_t$, this allows us to express the yield differential on an $N$-period bond as follows, with the addition of an error term $\epsilon_t$:

$$R_t^{(N)} = \tilde{\rho}^T d + \pi_t(\tilde{\rho}^W - \tilde{\rho}^T)\,d + \gamma ur_{t-1} + \epsilon_t, \tag{12}$$

where

$$\tilde{\rho}^T = 12\bar{\rho}^T, \quad \tilde{\rho}^W = 12\bar{\rho}^W, \quad \text{and} \quad \gamma = \delta(1 - \delta^N)\,12d/[N(1-\delta)\,(2v-d)] > 0.$$

Note that, in this formulation, $\tilde{\rho}^T$ and $\tilde{\rho}^W$ are probabilities of devaluation over the course of the next year (not the maturity of the bond), since $R_t^{(N)}$ is calculated as an annual rate.

### II. ESTIMATION

Equation (12) constitutes the model to be estimated, where $\pi_t$ is an unobservable state whose transition is described by equation (11), and which can be estimated using a Kalman filter.[12] The variable $ur_t$ was measured as the deviation of unemployment from an estimate of the natural rate of 8%. It was verified that this was a stationary series for the United Kingdom. In estimation, it was further assumed that $\epsilon_t$ and $\eta_t$ were i.i.d. with $\epsilon_t \sim N(0, R)$, $\eta_t \sim N(0, Q)$.

The model is estimated by choosing a value for $d$ and estimating the other

---

[10] See, for instance, Koen (1991).

[11] Given the low U.K. public debt to GDP ratio over this period, credit risk is unlikely to have been a factor.

[12] For other applications of Kalman filtering to EMS credibility, see Weber (1991, 1992).

Table 1

*Parameter Estimates (October 1990–August 1992)*

| Coefficients | | Standard errors | Coefficient/ standard errors |
|---|---|---|---|
| $a_0$ | 1·1963 | 0·2319 | 5·159 |
| $a_1$ | 3·4065 | 2·2374 | 1·523 |
| $\gamma$ | 0·2627 | 0·4704 | 0·558 |
| $\alpha$ | 0·5092 | 0·1678 | 3·036 |
| $\beta$ | −0·0640 | 0·0397 | −1·612 |
| Adjusted parameter values | | | |
| $\tilde{\rho}^T$ | 0 | | |
| $\tilde{\rho}^W$ | 0·1703 | | |
| $\pi_0$ | 0·6826 | | |
| Q | 0·0035 | | |
| R | — | | |
| Test statistics | | | |
| Box–Pierce (lags 1 to 5) | 3·246 (0·66)* | | |
| Bera–Jarque normality | 0·259 (0·88)* | | |

\* p − values.

parameters, including the state variable, using the Kalman filter. The value of $d$ was imposed because the model needs additional identification restrictions. A higher value for $d$, and proportionately lower values for $\tilde{\rho}^T$ and $\tilde{\rho}^W$, give identical predictions for $R_t^{(N)}$. The value for the devaluation size $d$ was chosen to be 20 % against the deutsche mark, roughly the amount of the depreciation of sterling by early February 1993 relative to its ERM parity. As is discussed below, the level of $\pi_t$ is also not identified, and a further normalisation is needed.

It is necessary at the outset to note two limitations of the estimation procedure for the state variable $\pi_t$. First, only an approximation to the updating equation (10) is used (with the addition of an error term). This is justified by the extremely non-linear form of the equation, making it difficult to find maximum likelihood estimates of the parameters. Second, equation (11) can produce values of $\pi_t$ in estimation which are not bounded [0, 1], either because $ur_{t-1}$ takes on extreme values, or because the drawings of $\eta_t$, which are assumed to be Gaussian, are too large (note that this problem would also apply if a generalised Kalman filter were used to estimate the non-linear expression for $\pi_t$). The filter described by Hamilton (1990) and applied in Hamilton (1988, 1989) and Engel and Hamilton (1990) does produce a probability in the interval [0, 1]. However, it does not allow endogenous probabilities as modelled here.

Equations (11) and (12) were estimated in the following form:[13]

$$R_t^{(N)} = a_0 + a_1 \pi_t + \gamma ur_{t-1} + \epsilon_t, \tag{13}$$

$$\pi_t = \alpha \pi_{t-1} + \beta ur_{t-2} + \eta_t. \tag{14}$$

The coefficients and their standard errors are given in Table 1. Though $\alpha$ and

[13] Using the MAXLIK procedure in GAUSS 3.1, written by Aptech Systems.

$a_0$ are statistically significant, the coefficients on unemployment are not well determined. In deriving parameter values, it should be noted from equation (13) that increasing $\pi_t$ by $k$ and reducing $a_0$ by $a_1 k$ will not affect the fit of the equation; thus, additional assumptions are needed to pin down the level of $\pi_t$. The further assumption is made that $\tilde{\rho}^T = 0$, which implies $a_0 = 0$: in steady state, starting from a zero unemployment gap, no shock is large enough to cause a government which is known to be tough to devalue.[14] This allows the scaling of $\pi_t$ to be uniquely determined, and implies that in October 1990, i.e. at the time Britain entered the ERM, the private sector assessed a 68% probability that the government was weak (and would devalue with probability $\rho^W$). The estimate of the steady-state probability of devaluation for a weak government in any given year, $\tilde{\rho}^W = 0.17$, seems plausible.

Despite the relative insignificance of the unemployment variables, the model explains movements in the interest differential with Germany well (Fig. 1); all

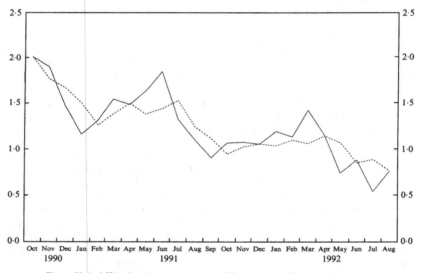

Fig. 1. United Kingdom long-term interest differential with Germany (% points), October 1990–August 1992. ——, Actual; – – – –, fitted.

of the residual variance is attributed to $\eta_t$, whose standard error is only 0.06. There is a downward trend in $\pi_t$ over the period; this variable (on the basis of the estimates in Table 1) is plotted in Fig. 2, with bands around the one-step-ahead estimates that correspond to plus or minus the state variable's standard error, when both filtering uncertainty and parameter uncertainty are taken

[14] Of course, this does not preclude that shocks outside of steady state would cause it to devalue, i.e. a succession of unfavourable shocks leading to high unemployment, or a 'credibility crisis' such that $\pi_t > 0$.

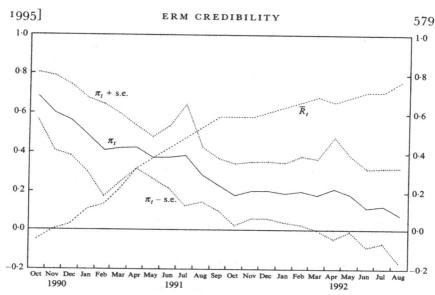

Fig. 2. United Kingdom measures of credibility, October 1990–August 1992. ——, Probability of a weak government $(\pi_t)$; ----, predicted interest differential if government is known to be tough $(\bar{R}_t)$.

into account.[15] By end-1991, $\pi_t$ is down to 20%, suggesting that the intentions of the authorities to stick with the parity had been fairly convincingly established by this time.

Though there is a slight increase in $\pi_t$ in April 1992, which may be associated with the general election (though neither the Conservatives nor Labour advocated devaluation), the probability of a weak government continues to decline in 1992. Despite this, the long-term interest differential remains high. The model explains this by the significant *positive* effect of lagged unemployment on the probabilities $\rho^W$ and $\rho^T$ that either a weak or a tough government will devalue, if further shocks to unemployment are sufficiently unfavourable – as captured by the positive coefficient $(\gamma)$ on $ur_{t-1}$. Suppose that the government's reputation for toughness had been established from the start of ERM membership, that is the value of $\pi_t$ estimated for 1992:08, namely $\bar{\pi} = 0.08$, had prevailed throughout the period. Then the model would have predicted an interest differential $\bar{R}_t$ equal to:

$$\bar{R}_t = a_1\bar{\pi} + \gamma ur_{t-1}. \tag{15}$$

This variable is plotted in Fig. 2, along with $\pi_t$. The chart supports the view that the relative stability of the interest differential resulted from two opposing influences: an enhanced reputation for toughness, but increasing concerns that

[15] Calculated from Monte Carlo simulations using 2,000 draws of the parameters. See Hamilton (1994, pp. 397–9), for a description of the method.

© Royal Economic Society 1995

rising unemployment was inconsistent with maintaining the parity. Though $\tilde{\rho}^T$ is assumed to be zero, according to the model the market attributed an increasing likelihood that a tough government would devalue because of the magnitude of unemployment, which rose steadily throughout the period. In the event this assessment turned out to be correct, and sterling left the ERM in September 1992.

### III. CONCLUDING REMARKS

The model highlights two aspects of credibility: signalling the type of government, which is assumed not to be known; and, for any type, the likelihood that if circumstances are sufficiently unfavourable a devaluation will occur, since not to devalue would be inconsistent with the government's objectives. These two factors have opposite implications for the link between unemployment and interest differentials: high unemployment signals a tough government, but also makes it less likely that even a tough government will maintain an existing parity.

This model is applied to long-term interest differentials relative to Germany for the two years of U.K. membership in the ERM. The model suggests that by the autumn of 1991, the commitment of the government to the existing parity was widely believed. However, in the summer of 1992 unemployment was increasingly seen as tying the hands of the authorities in defending the parity, and this helped to keep interest differentials high. Market expectations correctly reflected the belief that even a government committed to the ERM would decide to abandon its commitment to an exchange rate parity in sufficiently adverse circumstances.

It could be objected that the model predicts that the authorities would voluntarily devalue, while the events of September 1992 suggest that they tried to defend the pound, at least for a time, but faced speculative flows that were too large to be resisted. Thus, some would argue that the choice to leave the ERM was not voluntary but rather was forced on the authorities.

These two views are not in fact incompatible. To quote the Governor of the Bank of England:

> ...raising U.K. interest rates, when the economy was so weak and inflationary pressure so subdued...would have been regarded...as transparently perverse...[F]ar from adding to credibility, it was always likely to bring – indeed in the event it did bring – the latent pressure to a dramatic climax. (Leigh-Pemberton, 1992, p. 7).

There was surely a price at which sterling could have been defended – for instance, through much higher interest rates – but the authorities were unwilling to pay it given the weakness of economic activity, high private-sector indebtedness, and the fact that in the United Kingdom increases in official rates are quickly reflected in loan rates. Rational speculators knew this, so that they were induced to test the pound when other factors – the forthcoming French referendum, the devaluations of the Finnish markka and the Italian lira, and doubts about Bundesbank support – put the pound at risk. The model also contains a linkage which allows speculators to force the hand of the authorities, by making its policy dilemma worse: in the model, the larger the expected devaluation (for instance, because the government is thought to be weak) the higher is the unemployment cost of maintaining the parity, thus making a devaluation more likely.

The timing of speculative crises is not modelled in the paper, and it is clear that some fortuitous events combined to make September 1992 happen. An interesting extension of the model might involve two phases of speculative pressure: first, when the market tests the 'type' of the government, and, second, when the market thinks that the government's objective function does not allow it to raise interest rates sufficiently to counteract speculation because shocks to activity and employment have been adverse. The model could also include shocks to other variables and not just to unemployment: for instance, if shocks to interest rates indirectly affect activity, and hence unemployment, they also affect the credibility of the peg.

A further question, not considered here, is how the credibility of government policies was affected by the withdrawal of the pound from the ERM. A more general model with a multi-period objective function could also make the government's decision to defend the peg depend on the expected future loss (or gain) of credibility. In the context of the present model, there are, as before, two separate considerations: views about the 'toughness' of the government, which are influenced by the fact that it succumbed to exchange market pressures; and the increased room for manoeuvre that a depreciated exchange rate permits. However, analysis of the experience since 16 September 1992 goes beyond the scope of this paper, which is focused on expected parity changes in a pegged exchange rate system.

*International Monetary Fund*

*Date of receipt of final typescript: September 1994*

### REFERENCES

Andersen, Torben and Risager, Ole (1988). 'Stabilization policies, credibility, and interest rate determination in a small open economy.' *European Economic Review*, vol. 32 (March), pp. 669–79.
Backus, David and Driffill, E. John (1985a). 'Inflation and reputation.' *American Economic Reivew*, vol. 75 (June), pp. 530–8.
Backus, David and Driffill, E. John (1985b). 'Rational expectations and policy credibility following a change in regime.' *Review of Economic Studies*, vol. 52 (April), pp. 211–21.
Barrell, Ray, Britton, Andrew and Pain, Nigel (1993). 'When the time was right? The UK experience of the ERM.' National Institute of Economic and Social Research, Discussion Paper No. 58.
Barro, Robert J. and Gordon, David B. (1983). 'A positive theory of monetary policy in a natural rate model.' *Journal of Political Economy*, vol. 91 (August), pp. 589–610.
Blanchard, Olivier, J. (1985). 'Credibility, disinflation, and gradualism.' *Economics Letters*, vol. 17, pp. 211–7.
Cukierman, Alex and Liviatan, Nissan (1991). 'Optimal accommodation by strong policymakers under incomplete information.' *Journal of Monetary Economics*, vol. 27 (February), pp. 99–127.
Drazen, Allan and Masson, Paul R. (1994). 'Credibility of policies versus credibility of policymakers.' *Quarterly Journal of Economics*, vol. 109 (August) pp. 735–54.
Engel, Charles and Hamilton, James D. (1990). 'Long swings in the dollar: are they in the data and do markets know it?' *American Economic Review*, vol. 80 (September), pp. 689–713.
Flood, Robert P. (1983). 'Comment on Buiter and Miller,' in *Exchange Rates and International Macroeconomics* (ed. Jacob A. Frenkel), pp. 359–65. Chicago: University of Chicago Press.

Flood, Robert P. and Isard, Peter (1989). 'Monetary policy strategies.' IMF *Staff Papers*, vol. 36 (September), pp. 612–32.

Haldane, A. G. and Hall, S. G. (1991). 'Sterling's relationship with the dollar and the deutsche mark: 1976–89.' ECONOMIC JOURNAL, vol. 101 (May), pp. 436–43.

Hamilton, James D. (1988). 'Rational-expectations econometric analysis of changes in regime: an investigation of the term structure of interest rates.' *Journal of Economic Dynamics and Control*, vol. 12, pp. 385–423.

Hamilton, James D. (1989). 'A new approach to the economic analysis of nonstationary time series and the business cycle.' *Econometrica*, vol. 57 (March), pp. 357–84.

Hamilton, James D. (1990). 'Analysis of time series subject to changes in regime.' *Journal of Econometrics*, vol. 45 (July/August), pp. 39–70.

Hamilton, James D. (1994). *Time Series Analysis*, Princeton, N.J.: Princeton University Press.

Harvey, Andrew C. (1989). *Forecasting, Structural Time Series Models and the Kalman Filter*. Cambridge: Cambridge University Press.

Horn, Henrik and Persson, Torsten (1988). 'Exchange rate policy, wage formation and credibility.' *European Economic Review*, vol. 32 (October), pp. 1621–36.

Kaminsky, Graciela and Peruga, Rodrigo (1990). 'Can a time-varying risk premium explain excess returns in the forward market for foreign exchange?' *Journal of International Economics*, vol. 28 (February), pp. 47–70.

Koen, Vincent R. (1991). 'Testing the credibility of the Belgian hard currency policy.' IMF Working Paper WP/91/79 (August).

Leigh-Pemberton, Robin (1992). 'Speech given by the Governor of the Bank of England at the CBI Eastern Region annual dinner in Cambridge on 8/10/92.' *BIS Review*, No. 197 (15 October).

Lewis, Karen K. (1989). 'Can learning affect exchange rate behavior? The case of the dollar in the early 1980s.' *Journal of Monetary Economics*, vol. 23 (January), pp. 79–100.

Obstfeld, Maurice (1991). 'Destabilizing effects of exchange rate escape clauses.' NBER Working Paper No. 3603 (January).

Vickers, John (1986). 'Signalling in a model of monetary policy with incomplete information.' *Oxford Economic Papers*, vol. 38 (November), pp. 443–55.

Weber, Axel (1991). 'Reputation and credibility in the European Monetary System.' *Economic Policy*, no. 12 (April), pp. 57–102.

Weber, Axel (1992). 'The role of policymakers' reputation in the EMS disinflations: an empirical evaluation.' *European Economic Review*, vol. 36, pp. 1473–92.

Winckler, Georg (1991). 'Exchange rate appreciation as a signal of a new policy stance.' IMF Working Paper WP/91/32 (March).

## APPENDIX

### Linearising the Transition Equation

Starting from equation (10) in the text, we substitute for $\rho^T$ and $\rho^W$ using equations (6) and (8):

$$\pi_t = \frac{1 - \bar{\rho}^W - \dfrac{\delta u r_{t-2}}{2v-d} - (1-\pi_{t-1})(\bar{\rho}^T - \bar{\rho}^W)\dfrac{d}{2v}}{1 - \bar{\rho}^T - \delta\dfrac{u r_{t-2}}{2v-d} + \pi_{t-1}(\bar{\rho}^T - \bar{\rho}^W)}\pi_{t-1}.$$

Linearising this expression around $u r_{t-2} = 0$ and $\pi_{t-1} = \pi_0$, we obtain

$$\pi_t = \frac{\pi_0(1-\pi_0)(\bar{\rho}^T - \bar{\rho}^W)\,\delta/2v}{A^2}u r_{t-2}$$

$$+ \frac{(1-\bar{\rho}^T)[1-\bar{\rho}^W - (1-2\pi_0)(\bar{\rho}^T - \bar{\rho}^W)\,d/2v] + \pi_0^2(\bar{\rho}^T - \bar{\rho}^W)^2\,d/2v}{A^2}\pi_{t-1}$$

where $A = 1 - \bar{\rho}^T + \pi_0(\bar{\rho}^T - \bar{\rho}^W)$.

It can be verified that the coefficient of $u r_{t-2}$ is negative.

ELSEVIER

Journal of International Money and Finance
18 (1999) 587–602

Journal of
International
Money
and Finance

www.elsevier.com/locate/jimonfin

# Contagion:
# macroeconomic models with multiple equilibria

## Paul Masson[*]

*Research Department, International Monetary Fund, Washington, DC, 20431, USA*

**Abstract**

Several concepts of contagion are distinguished. It is argued that models that allow only a single equilibrium conditional on the macroeconomic fundamentals are not adequate to capture all forms of contagion, hence it is useful to formulate macro models that admit multiple equilibria and self-fulfilling expectations. A simple balance of payments model is presented to illustrate that phenomenon, and some back-of-the-envelope calculations assess its relevance to the coincidence of emerging market crises in 1994–95 and in 1997. © 1999 Elsevier Science Ltd. All rights reserved.

*JEL classification*: F3; F4

*Keywords:* Contagion; Spillovers; Multiple equilibria

## 1. Introduction

The balance of payments crises in Asia, beginning with pressures on the Thai baht and spreading to other countries in the region, have intensified the interest in models of contagion that began with Mexico's Tequila crisis in 1994–95. As Eichengreen et al. (1996) and others have pointed out, there are many reasons for crises to be contemporaneous in time. Using a terminology proposed in a companion paper, the macroeconomic linkages behind contagion can be divided into monsoonal effects,

---

[*] Tel.: + 1-202-623-7483; fax: + 1-202-623-7271; e-mail: pmasson@imf.org

0261-5606/99/$ - see front matter © 1999 Elsevier Science Ltd. All rights reserved.
PII: S 0 2 6 1 - 5 6 0 6 ( 9 9 )0 0 0 1 6 - 9

588            *P. Masson/Journal of International Money and Finance 18 (1999) 587–602*

spillovers, and jumps between multiple equilibria (Masson, 1999). The former effects emanate from the global environment (in particular, from policies in industrial countries), and sweep over all developing countries to a greater or lesser extent. Spillover effects explain why a crisis in one country may affect other emerging markets through linkages operating through trade, economic activity, or competitiveness. The third category is a residual: if the first two do not explain the coincidence of crises, it is argued that there is a role for self-fulfilling expectations in which sentiment with respect to a given country changes purely as a result of a crisis in another country. In Masson (1999), it is argued that macroeconomic fundamentals alone do not seem to have justified speculative attacks on other Latin American countries at the time of the Tequila crisis, nor the spread of crisis from Thailand to other East Asian countries in 1997. The magnitude and timing of developments in industrial countries (such as the tightening of US monetary policy in 1994 and the appreciation of the dollar in 1995–96) cannot plausibly explain these developments. Trade and competitiveness linkages within Latin America and East Asia are not strong enough for a crisis in one country to have worsened the fundamentals significantly in others in the region. Monsoonal and spillover effects therefore do not seem sufficient to understand the spread of contagion, suggesting the need to formulate models with multiple equilibria.

It is, of course, crucial to try to understand and model how shifts in sentiment occur, and the reasons why investors may exhibit herd behavior and be subject to contagion. However, theories of fads and herd behavior tend to be very microeconomic in their focus, and sensitive to assumptions concerning informational asymmetries and the order in which agents act (Banerjee, 1992; Bikchandani et al., 1992; Lee, 1997; Morris and Shin, 1998; Chari and Kehoe, 1998). They are therefore difficult to embed into macroeconomic models that are rich enough to include the spillover and monsoonal effects. In any case, it is important to understand how differences in the processing of information and the formation of expectations can influence macroeconomic outcomes. In macroeconomic models with a single equilibrium, it seems reasonable to suppose that rational learning behavior would lead expectations to converge to that equilibrium. Unless one accepts that expectations may differ systematically from macroeconomic outcomes, then macroeconomic models need to embody the possibility of multiple equilibria, so that shifts in expectations can be self-fulfilling.

In this paper, a simple balance of payments model is presented in which multiple equilibria are made possible through the plausible channel that expectations influence interest rates on external borrowing, and hence also the likelihood that reserves will decline below a threshold level, provoking a crisis. Because of its simplicity, the model can be solved analytically to yield clear implications concerning the factors that should influence the possibility of self-fulfilling expectations. Multiple equilibria can occur only in certain ranges for macroeconomic fundamentals, implying, in particular, conditions on reserves and the level of external debt. In the relevant ranges for the fundamentals, jumps between multiple equilibria, and hence contagion triggered by a crisis elsewhere, are possible—though the actual triggering of such jumps is assumed to be stochastic.

*P. Masson / Journal of International Money and Finance 18 (1999) 587–602* 589

Back-of-the envelope calculations for the fundamentals at the time of the Mexico and Asian crises are presented for emerging market countries to see if having fundamentals in the multiple equilibria region made a country more likely to suffer from contagion. While some of the results are suggestive, this criterion is not very good at discriminating between countries subject to the Asian crisis, especially since the crisis has now spread to most emerging markets.

A final section discusses possible extensions and conclusions.

## 2. A simple balance of payments model

In what follows, a simple two-country model is developed to illustrate the role of multiple equilibria and contagion, as well as monsoonal and spillover effects. In this model, a devaluation occurs when foreign exchange reserves approach a certain critical level (as in Krugman, 1979, or Flood and Garber, 1984). In this very simple model, there may be no trend for the fundamentals, but if the foreign debt that needs to be serviced exceeds a certain level, then shocks to the current account can be large enough to provoke a crisis. Expectations of a crisis show up in the borrowing cost paid to foreigners. Thus, the size of the stock of external debt (assumed, for simplicity, to be predetermined) is a crucial variable for the possibility of multiple equilibria, since higher interest rates by increasing debt service costs can push reserves below the level that triggers a devaluation.

### 2.1. The home country

The model includes two emerging market countries; the external environment (in particular, interest rates in industrial countries, $r^*$) are given to them. Consider first the home country (later on we will use superscript $a$ to distinguish it from the other emerging market country, $b$). It has accumulated external indebtedness $D$, paying a floating interest rate, but for simplicity there are assumed to be no new net capital flows. Up to a point that triggers a crisis, the authorities finance any current account deficit (or surplus) through changes in reserves. The source of uncertainty is shocks to the trade balance, $T$.[1] If they are large enough to cause reserves $R_t$ to fall below a critical level $R$ then a devaluation (by $\delta$ percent) occurs.[2] Algebraically, for liabilities in local currency, where $S_t$ is today's spot exchange rate (price of foreign exchange), and $S_{t+1}^d$ is its value next period in the event of a devaluation (otherwise $S_{t+1} = S_t$), the ex ante (ln) return on the asset is

---

[1] However, an easy extension is to make $r^*$ stochastic, so that the risk of a rise in world interest rates raises the probability of a crisis.

[2] An interesting possibility would be to endogenize $\delta$, by making it depend on the size of the current account imbalance. However, as will be seen below, the size of that imbalance is uncertain, since it depends on the possibility of contagion: the more crises occur elsewhere, the larger the loss of competitiveness at home, and hence also the size of the needed exchange rate change.

$$E_t\ln[(1 + r_t)/(S_{t+1}/S_t)] \simeq r_t - \pi_t\ln(S_{t+1}/S_t) - (1 - \pi_t)\ln 1. = r_t \quad (1)$$
$$- \pi_t\ln(1 + \delta) \simeq r_t - \pi_t\delta$$

Thus, risk-neutral investors demand to be compensated by an amount equal to the risk-free (foreign) rate, $r^*$, which we will assume is constant, plus the probability of a devaluation occurring, $\pi_t$, times the extent of the expected devaluation, $\delta$ (in percent).[3] As we will see below the probability of a crisis will also be influenced by those very same expectations, with the circularity leading to the possibility of multiple equilibria.

The change in reserves is therefore given by the following equation:

$$R_{t+1} - R_t = T_{t+1} - (r^* + \pi_t\delta)D. \quad (2)$$

A crisis occurs at $t + 1$ if:

$$R_{t+1} - R < 0. \quad (3)$$

Therefore, the probability, formed at $t$, of a crisis in period $t + 1$ is

$$\pi_t = Pr_t[T_{t+1} - (r^* + \pi_t\delta)D + R_t - R < 0]. \quad (4)$$

In considering both the Mexican and Asian crises, however, it needs to be recognized that *domestic currency* external debt was quantitatively not as significant as *foreign currency* debt. The latter is not subject to devaluation risk; interest rates on those countries' dollar debts nevertheless rose sharply, presumably reflecting fears of default. In practice, risks of devaluation and default are linked. Devaluation increases the domestic value of foreign currency debts and makes them more difficult to repay, provoking defaults. Conversely, a default on foreign debt (as in the debt crisis of the 1980s) leads to devaluation, as the country needs to adjust to a sharp fall in capital inflows by increasing net exports.

Default on private bank or corporate debt will occur if the value of indebtedness exceeds the value of assets, which for many of the relevant institutions were heavily concentrated in domestic currency assets, while their liabilities were in foreign currency. So increased risk of devaluation leads to increased risk of domestic insolvency and default on foreign currency obligations. At the same time, any risk that domestic assets are impaired (as occurred because of excessive lending for property speculation) would affect devaluation risk because it would raise the external borrowing costs of domestic banks and corporates on their foreign currency debt via the default risk premium. Higher borrowing costs on the latter would raise balance of payments outflows and lower reserves, making a devaluation more likely, through the same circularity as embodied in Eq. (2). So default and devaluation risk are linked, and we assume in what follows that expected devaluation size and the extent

---

[3] Implicitly, there is a market among nonresidents for these bonds that equalizes their expected return with the foreign interest rate.

P. Masson/Journal of International Money and Finance 18 (1999) 587-602          591

of partial default are the same, a percentage $\delta$, so that the borrowing rates on domestic and foreign currency debt move together. For liabilities in foreign currency, where $V_{t+1}^d$ is the value in the event of a partial default (of amount $\delta$) next period of an asset whose current value is $V_t$, then the ex ante (ln) return is

$$E_t\ln[(1 + r_t)/(V_{t+1}/V_t)] \simeq r_t + \pi_t\ln(V_{t+1}^d/V_t) - (1 - \pi_t)\ln 1.$$

$$= r_t + \pi_t\ln(1 + \delta) \tag{5}$$

$$\simeq r_t - \pi_t\delta$$

Thus, the default model is formally the same as the devaluation model.

The above model, though simple, has interesting implications concerning the relationship between the possibility of multiple equilibria and the values of key variables, in particular external debt $D$ (taken to include both domestic- and foreign-currency-denominated debt) and foreign exchange reserves $R$. The conditions for multiple equilibria in a model isomorphic to this one have been derived by Jeanne (1997), who tested whether the French franc/deutsche mark interest differential seemed to be subject to jumps between multiple equilibria in 1987–93. Letting

$$b_t \equiv T_t - r^*D + R_{t-1} - R, \ \alpha \equiv \delta D, \text{ and } \phi_t \equiv E_t b_{t+1},$$

then the model is formally identical to the one in Jeanne (1997), with

$$\pi_t = Pr_t[T_{t+1} - r^*D + R_t - R < \pi_t\delta D] = Pr_t[b_{t+1} < \alpha\pi_t]. \tag{6}$$

The possibility for multiple equilibria, as in that paper, depends on the values for $\alpha$ and $\phi_t$. If one assumes that the innovation in variable $b_t$, $\epsilon_t \equiv b_t - \phi_{t-1}$ has a cumulative distribution function $F$, we can write $\pi_t$ as:

$$\pi_t = F[\alpha\pi_t - \phi_t]. \tag{7}$$

In what follows, it will be assumed that $\epsilon_t$ is normally distributed with mean zero and variance $\sigma^2$, and $F_\sigma$ (.) will stand for its c.d.f.

Eq. (7) defines the formation of rational expectations by investors. Since both right and left sides of Eq. (7) depend positively on $\pi_t$, there may be multiple solutions.[4] A necessary condition for the latter (Jeanne, 1997) is that

$$z \equiv \frac{\alpha}{\sqrt{2\Pi}\sigma} > 1, \tag{8}$$

which requires that the slope of the cumulative distribution function [the right hand side of Eq. (7)] be steeper at some point than the left hand side, a 45° line from the origin. This condition can be interpreted as a condition on the size of foreign debt

---

[4] The normal distribution is convenient because its c.d.f. can exhibit enough curvature such that there are multiple solutions, depending on the variance $\sigma^2$. However, other distributions also allow multiple equilibria.

592            P. Masson/Journal of International Money and Finance 18 (1999) 587–602

and on the extent of default or devaluation in case of a crisis, since $\alpha \equiv \delta D$, relative to the standard deviation of shocks to the trade balance, $\sigma$. To give a numerical illustration, suppose that the time period is one year, so that $\pi_t$ refers to the probability of devaluation or default in the coming year. If the standard deviation of trade balance shocks is 2% of GDP, and the expected devaluation size is 25%, then multiple equilibria are possible if the stock of external debt exceeds about 20% of GDP. In contrast, if the stock of debt is too small or the variance of shocks to the trade balance is too large, the c.d.f. has an elongated shape with a slope that never exceeds 1, and hence only a single equilibrium exists.

Having a slope greater than unity is not sufficient for multiple equilibria, however. There is also a condition on $\phi_t$, which requires it to be within a certain range so that the c.d.f. on the RHS of Eq. (7) has a slope greater than unity in the region where it intersects the 45° line from the origin. This is illustrated in Fig. 1. If the fundamentals are very good ($\phi_t$ large), then the c.d.f. is shifted to the right and there is only one intersection, giving a low value for $\pi_t$. Alternatively, poor fundamentals shift the c.d.f. to the left, giving one (high $\pi_t$) intersection. The range of multiple equilibria is defined by two tangency conditions of the c.d.f. and the 45° line (the corresponding values for $\phi_t$ are labeled phimin and phimax in Fig. 1). In particular, if we let $w \equiv \sqrt{2 \log z}$, then the tangency conditions can be written as defining the following range for $\phi_t$ where multiple equilibria are possible:

$$\alpha F_1( - w) + \sigma w < \phi_t < \alpha F_1(w) - \sigma w. \tag{9}$$

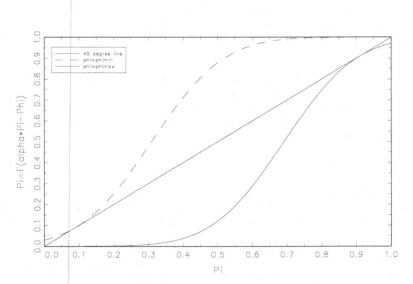

Fig. 1.   Solutions for $\pi$.

*P. Masson/Journal of International Money and Finance 18 (1999) 587–602* 593

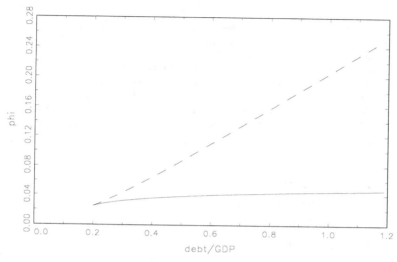

Fig. 2. Multiple equilibria region for $\pi$ ($\sigma = 0.02$).

Figs. 2 and 3 plot the dependence of this multiple equilibria region on $D$ and $\sigma$ respectively (the area between the two curves is the region where multiple equilibria are possible). Inequality (9) in essence defines a range for reserves. If they are higher than a certain value, then there is very little possibility of crisis, while if they are

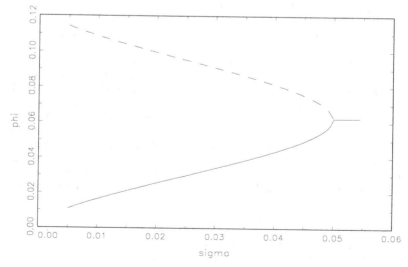

Fig. 3. Multiple equilibria region for $\pi$ ($D = 0.5$).

below a minimum, a crisis is virtually certain. In between, multiple equilibria can occur. To continue the numerical example cited above, the following table gives the values for the right and left hand sides of the inequality (9), labeled $\phi^{min}$ and $\phi^{max}$, respectively, for various values of $D$ which exceed the level of 20% of GDP, necessary for multiple equilibria. It is further assumed that the threshold level of reserves is zero, and that the expected value of the trade balance is equal to 1.25% of GDP (chosen so that it equals the product of the foreign interest rate, assumed to be 5%, and a debt level of 25% of GDP). The values $\phi^{min}$ and $\phi^{max}$ are translated into corresponding values for initial reserves, labeled $R^{min}$ and $R^{max}$, calculated as:

$$R^{min,max} \equiv \phi^{min,max} - E_t(T_{t+1}) + r^*D + R: \qquad (10)$$

| $D$ | $\phi^{min}$ | $\phi^{max}$ | $R^{min}$ | $R^{max}$ |
|-----|------|-------|------|-------|
| 25  | 2.91 | 3.34  | 2.91 | 3.34  |
| 50  | 3.81 | 8.69  | 5.06 | 9.94  |
| 75  | 4.23 | 14.52 | 6.73 | 17.02 |
| 100 | 4.50 | 20.50 | 8.25 | 24.25. |

Thus (assuming as before that $\sigma = 2\%$), for $D = 25\%$ of GDP, values for the initial level of reserves between 2.91 and 3.34% of GDP permit multiple equilibria to occur. Below 2.91, only a single (high) value of $\pi_t$ would prevail, while above 3.34, a devaluation would be viewed as unlikely and self-fulfilling crises could not occur. The range of values widens considerably as $D$ rises, as indicated in the table (though an increase in $D$ also increases the lower bound below which a single high probability equilibrium would prevail). For $D = 100\%$ of GDP a range of reserves between 8.25 and 24.25% of GDP would permit multiple equilibria.

## 2.2. Contagion: a jump between equilibria triggered by a crisis elsewhere

So far the model has not explained which equilibrium is chosen. One approach that is convenient for estimation is to treat jumps between equilibria as being stochastic, and having a simple Markov probability structure describing the likelihood of staying in a particular equilibrium or moving to another one (as in Jeanne and Masson, 1998). For instance, once a 'bad' equilibrium occurs (i.e. devaluation or default), it may be reasonable to suppose that a jump back to the 'good' equilibrium is not straightforward—the bad equilibrium could be an absorbing state. The experience of Mexico and Thailand suggests that an attack followed by a substantial depreciation seems to have enduring effects on confidence and also on the health of financial and nonfinancial corporations that have substantial foreign currency debt. Contagion would occur when the home country jumps to a 'bad' equilibrium as a result of a crisis in another emerging market country.

Such a way of modeling contagion for estimation purposes, and the balance of payments model given above, are not inconsistent with various micro theories that involve the revision of expectations or detailed models of the portfolio behavior of financial institutions. For instance, jumps between equilibria could occur because of

*P. Masson/Journal of International Money and Finance 18 (1999) 587–602*          595

small triggers which lead to herding behavior (Banerjee, 1992) or 'informational cascades' (Bikchandani et al., 1992) or 'avalanches' (Lee, 1997). Or, as discussed above, a crisis in one country might lead to a reassessment of the fundamentals in others (a 'wake up call' as in Goldstein, 1998). However, the micro theories need to be placed in a macroeconomic context, otherwise it is difficult to understand the severity of crises affecting the real economies of Latin America and East Asia in recent years, and why euphoria and pessimism in financial markets seem to be self-sustaining for extended periods. Rational learning of a single equilibrium would suggest in contrast that market sentiment should converge to the 'correct' view, and that the problems of Mexico and the subsequent Tequila crisis in 1994–95 would have made investors permanently wary of countries with large short-term external exposure. While Mexico's growth of GDP recovered quickly, serious banking sector problems have persisted, highlighting the deficiencies of supervision and regulation in many developing countries. Instead of learning these lessons, foreign investors in 1996 sent a record volume of capital flows to developing countries, and this continued into 1997, only to be abruptly reversed when the Thai baht depreciated early in July.

The model presented above, though not providing a theory of jumps between equilibria, has something to say about vulnerability to contagion. Multiple equilibria, and hence attacks triggered by crises elsewhere that go beyond the macroeconomic fundamentals (which themselves are influenced by monsoonal effects and spillovers) can occur only in certain ranges of the fundamentals. Vulnerability is greater when there is a large (floating rate) debt, when reserves are low, and when the trade balance is in deficit.

## 2.3. Links with other emerging markets

We now make more explicit monsoonal and spillover effects, and in particular introduce interactions between the home country ($a$) and emerging market economy $b$, through competitiveness effects on trade. For simplicity we will assume that all structural parameters are the same in the two countries, and omit superscripts for those parameters.

The home country trade balance is assumed to depend on the logarithm of the real exchange rate (RER), which gives a weight $w$ on country $b$, $x$ on the United States, and $u \equiv (1 - w - x)$ on the rest of the world. Nominal exchange rates $S_t^a$, $S_t^b$, $S_t$ (the rest of the world's exchange rate, assumed fixed) are expressed as the dollar price of local currency, so that an increase in $S$ (and in RER) is an appreciation. It is assumed that the currencies of $a$ and $b$ are, at least initially, pegged to the dollar. Prices are assumed fixed so that nominal devaluation produces an improvement in competitiveness. The equations for the trade balance and the real exchange rate are as follows:

$$T_t^a = T - \beta RER_t^a + \epsilon_t^a; \tag{11}$$

$$RER_t^a = S_t^a - wS_t^b - uS_t. \tag{12}$$

Similar equations exist for country $b$.

Now the assessment of the probability of devaluation is more complicated, since it depends on the possibility of devaluation for country $b$, captured through $\pi_t^b$. In particular, in place of Eq. (6), the probability of $R_{t+1}^a < R$ will be different depending on whether or not $b$ is expected to devalue (by $\delta$) next period:

$$\pi_t^a = (1 - \pi_t^b)Pr_t[T - \beta(S_t^a - wS_t^b - uS_t) + \epsilon_t^a - (r_* + \pi_t^a\delta)D^a$$
$$+ R_t^a - R < 0] + \pi_t^b Pr_t[T - \beta(S_t^a - wS_t^b + w\delta - uS_t) + \epsilon_t^a - (r* \quad (13)$$
$$+ \pi_t^a\delta)D^a + R_t^a - R < 0].$$

The model illustrates the three channels by which crises can coincide in time. Monsoonal effects can take the form of a change in $r*$ (e.g. US interest rates), or $S_t$ (e.g. the dollar–yen rate). Spillovers can take the form of changes in the initial level of the exchange rate of country $b$. The third channel works through the possibility of self-fulfilling expectations for $\pi_t^a$, since the latter variable also appears on the RHS of (13). The potential for contagion will also be affected by the expectation of devaluation in $b$ ($\pi_t^b$), which will have a direct effect on $\pi_t^a$; it can feed back onto itself through an equation analogous to (13) for country $b$.

As discussed above, the range ($\phi^{min}$, $\phi^{max}$) within which multiple equilibria are possible is determined by points of tangency with the 45° line from the origin. However, instead of Eq. (7) above, we now have a linear combination of it and a curve that is shifted to the right, by the amount of potential loss in competitiveness due to the possible devaluation of the currency of country $b$, $\beta w\delta$:

$$\pi_t^a = (1 - \pi_t^b)F_\sigma[\alpha^a\pi_t^a - \phi_t^a] + \pi_t^b F_\sigma[\alpha^a\pi_t^a - \phi_t^a + \beta w\delta], \quad (14)$$

where now $\phi_t^a = T - \beta(S_t^a - wS_t^b - uS_t) - r*D^a + R_t^a - R$ and $\alpha^a = \delta D^a$.

Fig. 4 plots solutions to Eq. (14), for $D = 25\%$ of GDP, $\beta w = 0.1$, $\delta = 25\%$, and either $\pi_t^b = 0.2$ or $0.5$. Relative to the original curve (labeled 'without contagion' in Fig. 4), Eq. (14) is shifted up further on the left side of the figure than on the right. As a result, both the lower and upper equilibria will involve a higher value for $\pi^a$ than when $\pi^b = 0$, but the lower equilibrium (if there are multiple equilibria) will be more affected.[5] Though points of tangency (determining $\phi^{min}$ and $\phi^{max}$) are not shown, this suggests that the value of $\phi^{min}$ (this is the lower tangency point) will be more affected than $\phi^{max}$ (corresponding to the upper tangency point), because the curve needs to be shifted more in the horizontal direction to compensate for contagion from country $b$. Numerical solutions confirm this intuition.

However, there is another possibility, shown for $\pi_t^b = 0.5$, namely that the fear of a devaluation in $b$ will eliminate the multiple equilibria region entirely in $a$, and produce a single, high value of $\pi_t^a$ indicating that a devaluation is very likely. We

---

[5] It is also possible that $\pi^b > 0$ would give two points of inflection to the RHS of Eq. (14), increasing the number of equilibria for $\pi^a$. This possibility was not relevant here, given the range of numerical values assumed.

*P. Masson/Journal of International Money and Finance 18 (1999) 587–602* 597

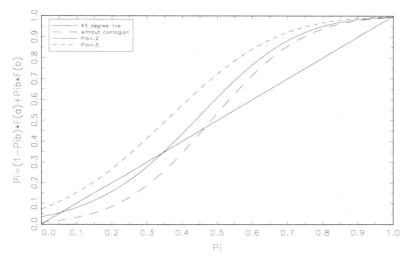

Fig. 4. Solutions for $\pi$, with and without contagion.

would still characterize this as contagion, since it is the fear of a crisis in $b$ that triggers a crisis in $a$, not spillover effects per se.

Fig. 5 pursues the relationship between devaluation expectations in $a$ and $b$, by calculating $\pi_t^a$ as a function of $\pi_t^b$ and vice-versa. If there is only a single equilibrium,

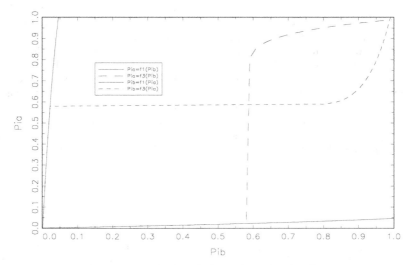

Fig. 5. $\pi^a$ as a function of $\pi^b$ and $\pi^b$ as a function of $\pi^a$.

then that is plotted, but for values where multiple equilibria exist, both the upper and lower intersections (as in Fig. 4) are plotted (the middle equilibrium, which is unstable, is ignored). In this example (unlike in Fig. 4), the fundamentals $\phi_t^a$ are good enough in the absence of contagion effects that there is only a single equilibrium (as long as $\pi_t^b < 0.58$). It can be seen that in this case, in which the countries are assumed identical, an equilibrium where the probability of devaluation in both $a$ and $b$ is roughly zero is possible: in the absence of fears of devaluation in the other country, each would not be vulnerable to self-fulfilling attacks. However, above $\pi_t = 0.58$ for the other, each country is in the range of multiple equilibria. Therefore, attacking *both* countries' currencies would also be rational, and two other equilibria are possible: one with $\pi_t^a = \pi_t^b = 0.58$, and a second where $\pi_t^a = \pi_t^b = 0.99$ (see Fig. 5). Thus, contagion effects amplify the possibility of self-fulfilling attacks in this model. Even if each country separately is not subject to multiple equilibria, together they may be, since the fear of crisis in one will increase the devaluation probability in the other, making a crisis more likely in both.

## 3. Applicability to the Tequila and Asian crises

We now turn to some simple calculations to see whether the fundamentals of emerging market countries at the end of 1994 and 1996 were such that the balance of payments model implies that multiple equilibria were possible. In assessing the possible relevance of the model we need to face whether the debt stock should be limited to domestic currency debt held by foreigners, all external debt, or all debt held by domestic and foreign residents. We choose the intermediate measure, since the model focuses on the overall balance of payments and the link between devaluation and default discussed above suggests that the broader measure of external indebtedness, in all currencies, would be the appropriate one.[6] Another important question is whether to distinguish between short-term and long-term debt. Presumably, the measure should include that debt which comes to maturity within the horizon over which $\pi_t$ is calculated, but should also include the *interest service* on longer term debt. In addition, any debt which is callable by the creditor should also be included in $D$. In practice, available classifications refer to original term to maturity and do not take account of call features. We therefore include both short- and long-term debt. Limiting $D$ to short-term debt would narrow the implied region for multiple equilibria, so that the calculations that follow may, if anything, overstate the scope for such contagion.

---

[6] Another approach, adopted in their theoretical modeling by Sachs et al. (1996), is to consider domestic currency debt, regardless of whether it is held domestically or abroad. However, it seems clear that the Asian crisis, at least, had an important external dimension, and most external debt was in foreign currency.

P. Masson/Journal of International Money and Finance 18 (1999) 587–602          599

Table 1 summarizes some of the relevant data for the end of 1994 and the end of 1996, the latest full years preceding the crises in Mexico and East Asia. We use the simplest version of the model to see whether it implies that multiple equilibria were possible [using Eq. (4) above]. The model suggests that a composite fundamental, called $\phi_t$, needs to be in a certain range for multiple equilibria to occur. The fundamental depends positively on the level of reserves and the expected trade balance, and negatively on the stock of debt and the foreign interest rate. The calculation assumes that the threshold level of reserves, $R$, is zero; that is, a devaluation does not occur until reserves are completely exhausted. This is unrealistic, and a positive value for this threshold level would tend to reduce the values of $\phi_t$ calculated below. The possibility for multiple equilibria also depends on the value for $z_t$, which in turn depends on the debt, the size of a potential devaluation $\delta$, and the variance $\sigma^2$ of innovations to the trade balance—as does the range for $\phi_t$ within which multiple equilibria are possible. In implementing these calculations, for each country a first-

Table 1
External debt, reserves, trade balance, and criteria for multiple equilibria, 1994 and 1996 (in % GDP)

| Country ($\sigma$) | Date | $D_t$ | $R_t$ | $T_t$ | $z_t$ | $\Phi_t^{\min}$ | $\Phi_t^{\max}$ | $\Phi_t$ |
|---|---|---|---|---|---|---|---|---|
| Argentina (2.12) | 1994 | 31.9 | 5.1 | −2.5 | 1.51 | 3.38 | 4.62 | 1.93[a] |
| | 1996 | 34.4 | 6.1 | −0.3 | 1.60 | 3.47 | 5.03 | 4.71[b] |
| Brazil (1.69) | 1994 | 28.0 | 6.6 | 1.1 | 1.65 | 2.80 | 4.20 | 6.04 |
| | 1996 | 28.0 | 7.8 | −1.8 | 1.65 | 2.80 | 4.20 | 5.83 |
| Chile (3.05) | 1994 | 46.2 | 25.1 | 1.4 | 1.51 | 4.87 | 6.67 | 23.10 |
| | 1996 | 37.1 | 20.6 | −2.2 | 1.21 | 4.37 | 4.90 | 18.03 |
| Colombia (2.68) | 1994 | 30.3 | 11.0 | −3.1 | 1.13 | 3.68 | 3.90 | 6.40 |
| | 1996 | 32.6 | 11.0 | −2.1 | 1.21 | 3.84 | 4.31 | 7.44 |
| India (0.46) | 1994 | 33.3 | 6.7 | −0.7 | 7.22 | 1.11 | 7.22 | 3.50[b] |
| | 1996 | 27.2 | 5.8 | −1.6 | 5.90 | 1.07 | 5.73 | 2.80[b] |
| Indonesia (1.23) | 1994 | 55.5 | 6.9 | 2.3 | 4.54 | 2.71 | 11.29 | 4.72[b] |
| | 1996 | 46.9 | 8.1 | 1.3 | 3.81 | 2.61 | 9.14 | 7.46[b] |
| Korea (2.38) | 1994 | 14.9 | 6.7 | −0.7 | 0.62 | – | – | 5.43 |
| | 1996 | 21.2 | 7.0 | −4.0 | 0.88 | – | – | 3.20 |
| Malaysia (3.53) | 1994 | 39.5 | 35.1 | −1.6 | 1.12 | 4.85 | 5.15 | 31.97 |
| | 1996 | 38.6 | 27.0 | 0.7 | 1.46 | 4.77 | 4.98 | 26.30 |
| Mexico (3.29) | 1994 | 37.3 | 1.5 | −4.9 | 1.13 | 4.50 | 4.75 | −3.86[a] |
| | 1996 | 48.0 | 5.8 | 2.5 | 1.10 | 5.17 | 6.83 | 5.54[b] |
| Philippines (2.76) | 1994 | 57.9 | 9.4 | −6.3 | 2.10 | 4.98 | 9.52 | −0.72[a] |
| | 1996 | 51.1 | 12.0 | −9.8 | 1.84 | 4.77 | 7.98 | 0.44[a] |
| South Africa (3.05) | 1994 | 15.3 | 1.4 | 1.8 | 0.50 | – | – | 3.08 |
| | 1996 | 18.0 | 0.7 | 0.7 | 0.59 | – | – | 2.08 |
| Thailand (2.47) | 1994 | 46.2 | 20.9 | −4.3 | 1.86 | 4.28 | 7.22 | 13.57 |
| | 1996 | 50.1 | 20.9 | −5.7 | 2.02 | 4.40 | 8.10 | 13.47 |
| Turkey (1.91) | 1994 | 50.1 | 5.5 | −6.3 | 2.61 | 3.68 | 8.82 | −5.15[a] |
| | 1996 | 44.3 | 9.1 | −10.0 | 2.30 | 3.55 | 7.45 | −1.73[a] |

Source: WEO and IFS databases, and author's calculations.
[a] Fundamental is below multiple equilibria region, i.e. in crisis region.
[b] Inside region of multiple equilibria.

order autoregressive process was estimated for the trade balance as a percent of GDP, with innovations assumed to be normally distributed, and the standard error of estimate of this regression (over 1980–96) was the estimate of $\sigma$. The US one-year rate on Treasury securities was used as the foreign interest rate, $r^*$. Data for reserves, debt, and the trade balance, all as ratios to GDP, are given in Table 1. It is hard to gauge ex ante devaluation expectations, but it was assumed that the expected devaluation size $\delta$ was 25%. This is much smaller than ultimately occurred in Mexico and several Asian countries, but roughly the extent of initial currency adjustments. A larger value for $\delta$ would increase the value of $z$ and the range ($\phi^{min}$, $\phi^{max}$).

It is interesting that in most, but not all, cases, there is a range of values for $\phi_t$ for which multiple equilibria can occur: that is, $z_t$ is generally greater than unity as a result of substantial foreign debt. The exceptions are Korea and South Africa, which have relatively low external indebtedness, giving values for $z_t$ that do not allow multiple equilibria. Neither of them was significantly affected by the Mexican crisis. Korea was strongly affected by the Asian crisis, though relatively late, while South Africa was not.

Nevertheless, the value of the fundamental $\phi_t$, which reflects among other things the level of reserves, was not in all cases in the multiple equilibria region. Brazil, Chile, Colombia, and Malaysia, though admitting of multiple equilibria, had fundamentals above the admissible range in which they are predicted to occur, mainly because their reserve levels were high. Of these latter countries, only Malaysia was significantly affected by the 1997 crisis, while though Brazil was subjected to the 1994–95 'Tequila effect,' it did not suffer the loss of confidence experienced by Mexico.[7] Thailand also belongs in this latter group on the basis of the end of 1996 data, but subsequent intervention changed the picture markedly, especially when forward commitments are taken into account, with net reserves falling close to zero in June 1997. Mexico, interestingly enough, has a value at the end of 1994 for $\phi_t$ that is so low that it implies a very high probability of a crisis (essentially because reserves were so low and the trade deficit large), but by 1996 its fundamentals had put it in a much more favorable position (though still in the multiple equilibria region). The Philippines and Turkey are estimated to have fundamentals that imply in both years a high probability of crisis, which would be consistent with high interest rates on their borrowing.

The results are suggestive that contagion effects were possible at the time of the 1994–95 and 1997 crises, though it does not in any way test for contagion. The model has implications for the vulnerability to jumps between equilibria, but does not explain how or why they occur. The pervasiveness of contagion, however, makes it plausible that vulnerable countries would be attacked. In partial confirmation of the model, the countries spared the worst effects of crisis generally come out well in terms of the fundamentals identified by the balance of payments model as being important. This is true of such countries as Brazil, Chile, and Colombia. Korea and

---

[7] Brazil, like a number of other countries, was also subjected to speculative pressures following Russia's failure to service its debts in August 1998.

*P. Masson/Journal of International Money and Finance 18 (1999) 587–602* 601

Malaysia, in contrast, should have been immune to multiple equilibria when considered in isolation, suggesting that other factors came into play. In particular, Korea's crisis may be better modeled as a Diamond and Dybvig (1983) bank run, where concerns about liquidity and access to foreign exchange, in the presence of government guarantees which were not viewed as credible, led to a loss of confidence of foreign investors.

## 4. Conclusions

In considering the phenomenon of contagion and what to do to limit it, it is important to understand its causes and the linkages through which it operates. There are some aspects of contagion that seem hard to explain on the basis of macroeconomic fundamentals. This suggests that it may be useful to formulate models that do not imply a unique equilibrium mapping between those fundamentals and crisis expectations. In this paper, a simple balance of payments model allowing for self-fulfilling devaluation or default expectations is presented. The model has clear implications for the range of fundamentals (principally reserves and external indebtedness) where changes in such self-fulfilling expectations—perhaps triggered by a crisis elsewhere—are possible.

In several respects the model deserves elaboration, and more complicated models would no doubt not have such stark implications for the ranges of the fundamentals where countries are vulnerable to contagion. Greater attention should be paid to financial intermediation (Agenor and Aizenman, 1997; Kaminsky and Reinhart, 1996), bank runs (Diamond and Dybvig, 1983), the maturity of government debt (Cole and Kehoe, 1996), rollover risk (Calvo and Mendoza, 1996), the role of government guarantees on deposits and private foreign borrowing (Dooley, 1997), self-fulfilling expectations of volatility (Flood and Marion, 1996), and moral hazard issues. The absence of consideration of these linkages may help to explain why the range of fundamentals implied by the model is not completely successful in discriminating between countries strongly affected by recent crises and those (mainly) spared.

## Acknowledgements

I am grateful for comments, especially to Mike Dooley, Olivier Jeanne, Rick Mishkin, and Deepak Mishra. The views expressed here are my own and should not be attributed to the International Monetary Fund or other official institutions.

## References

Agenor, P.-R., Aizenman, J., 1997. Contagion and volatility with imperfect credit markets. NBER Working Paper No. 6080.

Banerjee, A., 1992. A simple model of herd behavior. Quarterly Journal of Economics 107 (August), 797–817.

Bikchandani, S., Hirshleifer, D., Welch, I., 1992. A theory of fads, fashion, custom, and cultural change as informational cascades. Journal of Political Economy 100 (5), 992–1026.

Calvo, G., Mendoza, E., 1996. Mexico's balance-of-payments crisis: a chronicle of a death foretold. Journal of International Economics 41, 235–264.

Chari, V.V., Kehoe, P., 1998. Hot money. Mimeo. Research Department, Federal Reserve Bank of Minneapolis.

Cole, H., Kehoe, T.J., 1996. A self-fulfilling model of Mexico's 1994–95 debt crisis. Journal of International Economics 41, 309–330.

Diamond, D., Dybvig, P., 1983. Bank runs, deposit insurance, and liquidity. Journal of Political Economy 91, 401–419.

Dooley, M., 1997. A model of crises in emerging markets. NBER Working Paper No. 6300.

Eichengreen, B., Rose, A., Wyplosz, C., 1996. Contagious currency crises. NBER Working Paper No. 5681.

Flood, R., Garber, P., 1984. Collapsing exchange rate regimes: some linear examples. Journal of International Economics 17, 1–13.

Flood, R., Marion, N., 1996. Speculative attacks: fundamentals and self-fulfilling prophecies. NBER Working Paper No. 5789.

Goldstein, M., 1998. The Asian financial crises: causes, cures, and systemic implications. Institute for International Economics, Policy Analyses in International Economics 55, Washington, D.C.

Jeanne, O., 1997. Are currency crises self-fulfilling? A test. Journal of International Economics 43, 263–286.

Jeanne, O., Masson, P., 1998. Currency crises, sunspots and markov-switching regimes. CEPR Discussion Paper No. 1990.

Kaminsky, G., Reinhart, C., 1996. The twin crises: the causes of banking and balance-of-payments problems. Mimeo, Board of Governors of the Federal Reserve System.

Krugman, P., 1979. A model of balance of payments crises. Journal of Money, Credit, and Banking 11, 311–325.

Lee, I.H., 1997. Market crashes and informational avalanches. Paper presented at a CEPR/ESRC/GEI Conference on The Origins and Management of Financial Crises, Cambridge, UK, July 11–12.

Masson, P., 1999. Contagion: monsoonal effects, spillovers, and jumps between multiple equilibria. In: Agenor, P.R., Miller, M., Vines, D., Weber, A. (Eds), The Asian Financial Crisis: Causes, Contagion and Consequences. Cambridge University Press, Cambridge, UK.

Morris, S., Shin, H.S., 1998. Unique equilibrium in a model of self-fulfilling attacks. American Economic Review 88 (June), 587–597.

Sachs, J., Tornell, A., Velasco, A., 1996. Financial crises in emerging markets: the lessons from 1995. NBER Discussion Paper No. 5576.

ELSEVIER    Journal of International Economics 50 (2000) 327–350

Journal of
**INTERNATIONAL
ECONOMICS**

www.elsevier.nl/locate/econbase

# Currency crises, sunspots and Markov-switching regimes

Olivier Jeanne*, Paul Masson

*Research Department, International Monetary Fund, Washington, DC 20431, USA*

Received 20 February 1997; received in revised form 19 August 1998; accepted 28 January 1999

**Abstract**

This paper investigates the theoretical properties of a class of escape clause models of currency crises as well as their applicability to empirical work. We show that under some conditions these models give rise to an arbitrarily large number of equilibria, as well as cyclic or chaotic dynamics for the devaluation expectations. We then propose an econometric technique, based on the Markov-switching regimes framework, by which these models can be brought to the data. We illustrate this empirical approach by studying the experience of the French franc between 1987 and 1993, and find that the model performs significantly better when it allows the devaluation expectations to be influenced by sunspots. © 2000 Elsevier Science B.V. All rights reserved.

*Keywords:* Currency crises; Self-fulfilling speculation; Sunspots; Markov-switching regimes; European Monetary System; French franc

*JEL classification:* F3; F4

## 1. Introduction

The crisis of the European Monetary System in 1992–1993, the collapse of the Mexican peso in 1994 and the Asian crises have heightened academic interest in the determinants of currency crises. Much debate has focused on whether the speculation was essentially determined by the fundamentals or whether it was, at

*Corresponding author. Tel.: +1-202-623-4272; fax: +1-202-623-6334.
*E-mail address:* ojeanne@imf.org (O. Jeanne)

least to some extent, self-fulfilling.[1] Some analytical support for the self-fulfilling view was provided by the development of new models of currency crisis that generically give rise to multiple equilibria. These models, regrouped under the name of 'escape clause' or 'second generation' approaches to currency crises, have been used extensively in recent discussions of self-fulfilling speculation (Obstfeld, 1994; Velasco, 1996; Jeanne, 1997).[2] One reason for the success of these models is their simplicity. But they have also been criticized for their lack of realism and robustness; Krugman (1996), in particular, presents an escape clause model that does not give rise to multiple equilibria and questions the theoretical robustness of the self-fulfilling view. Attempts at estimating escape clause models, furthermore, have been few,[3] which is due in no small part to the difficulty of estimating non-linear models with multiple equilibria.

The contribution of the present paper is twofold. First, we characterize the properties of a class of escape clause models that are different from, and arguably more realistic than, those that have been considered in the literature. We show that, under certain conditions, these models can give rise to *more* equilibria than previous escape clause models, as well as cyclic or chaotic dynamics for the devaluation expectations. Second, we propose a simple empirical method by which this class of models can be brought to the data. We hope this will facilitate future empirical applications of the escape clause approach, a possibility that we illustrate by considering the experience of the French franc in 1987–1993.

The basic logic of self-fulfilling speculation in the escape clause approach is very simple. It derives from the fact that devaluation expectations increase the policymaker's desire to devalue. The most obvious way in which they do so in the real world is by raising interest rates. Faced with a dilemma between high interest rates and a devaluation, the policymaker may opt for the latter, especially if the fundamental economic situation is fragile. In fact, the policymaker may prefer a devaluation to high interest rates even though she would have maintained the fixed peg if interest rates had been low; in that case whether or not a devaluation occurs depends purely on market expectations. Escape clause models have different ways to capture this basic idea. In some models, devaluation expectations induce wage setters to predetermine high nominal wages, leading to high real wages and unemployment—unless the policymaker devalues the currency. Other models are

---

[1] Advocates of the self-fulfilling view include Eichengreen and Wyplosz (1993) and Obstfeld and Rogoff (1995) for the EMS crisis, Cole and Kehoe (1995) for the Mexican peso crisis, and Sachs and Radelet (1998) for the Asian crisis. These authors do not maintain that speculation was purely self-fulfilling and completely unrelated to the economic fundamentals, but rather that in some of the recent episodes of crisis the effect of the economic fundamentals was augmented by self-fulfilling elements. See Obstfeld (1996b) for a clear statement of this view.

[2] These models have also been called 'policy optimizing' (Isard, 1995), 'endogenous policy' (Buiter et al., 1998) and 'New Crisis' models (Krugman, 1996). See Jeanne (in press) or Flood and Marion (1998) for discussions of the escape clause approach to currency crises.

[3] An exception is Jeanne (1997).

O. Jeanne, P. Masson / Journal of International Economics 50 (2000) 327–350          329

based on the fiscal effects of devaluation expectations. High interest rates increase the burden of public debt, inducing the policymaker to inflate and devalue rather than raising taxes. Such assumptions may seem rather special, and obviously do not capture some important channels by which devaluation expectations make themselves costly for policymakers in the real world. But, one may argue, they are meant to make the models tractable and the essence of the argument should carry over in different and more complex environments.

In a recent paper, however, Krugman (1996) argues that the insights of the escape clause literature do not survive the injection of more realism in the models' assumptions. Krugman presents a model in which devaluation expectations make themselves costly by raising the ex ante interest rate, and finds that if the fundamentals deteriorate deterministically over time multiple equilibria do not arise. The date of the crisis is uniquely determined, following a backward induction logic that is similar to the same author's 1979 article on speculative attacks — allowing him to question the theoretical specificity of the second generation approach. As noted by Kehoe (1996) and Obstfeld (1996b) in their comments on Krugman's paper, this result hinges crucially on the precise timing with which devaluation expectations affect the policymaker's decision. In Krugman's model the policymaker's decision is effectively sensitive to the devaluation expectations formed by market participants at the time of the crisis, while in previous models the same decision is dependent on the expectations formed before the crisis. This apparently innocuous difference in timing seems to alter the properties of the model to a surprising extent — a puzzle on which this paper attempts to shed some light.

The analysis of this paper is based on a framework that is a reduced form for a broad class of models, including that in Krugman (1996). We completely characterize the equilibria and give a simple criterion for their multiplicity. We show that while this class of models does not give rise to multiple equilibria when the economic fundamentals are non-stationary stochastic processes or exhibit a deterministic trend (this is a generalization of Krugman's result), they may also give rise to an *arbitrarily large* number of equilibria if a condition on the fundamentals is satisfied. This property is in sharp contrast with the models of Obstfeld (1994, 1996a), Velasco (1996) or Jeanne (1997), where the number of equilibria is no larger than three. Next, we consider a hybrid model, in which the policymaker's devaluation decision is affected by the devaluation expectations formed both in the current and previous periods. We show that in this case, the devaluations expectations are not uniquely determined in general, and that their dynamics can become cyclic or chaotic.[4]

The second part of the paper addresses the question of the empirical applicability of the escape clause approach to currency crises. We show that the class of

---

[4]De Grauwe et al. (1993) study chaotic dynamics in foreign exchange markets, which result in their model from mechanistic trading rules rather than being associated with rational expectations.

330      *O. Jeanne, P. Masson / Journal of International Economics 50 (2000) 327–350*

models that we consider in this paper can be brought to the data using a standard econometric approach, the Markov-switching regimes model developed by Hamilton and others. The Markov-switching model has been applied to a number of economic phenomena, including the business cycle (Hamilton, 1989), the term structure of interest rates (Hamilton, 1988), the dynamics of floating exchange rates (Kaminsky and Peruga, 1990; Van Norden, 1996), and more recently currency crises (Martinez-Peria, 1998; Piard, 1997; Psaradakis et al., 1998). We show here that a linearization of our model gives a Markov-switching regimes model for the devaluation probability, in which the switch across regimes corresponds to jumps between different equilibria. This provides some theoretical justification for the use of the Markov-switching regimes approach in empirical work on currency crises, and can also help to assess the empirical plausibility of the multiple equilibria hypothesis. To illustrate, we estimate a Markov-switching regimes model for the French franc over the period 1987–1993, and find that a model allowing for sunspots performs better than a purely fundamental-based model, in particular by improving the relationship between the economic fundamentals and the devaluation expectations.

The paper is structured as follows. Section 2 presents the model and investigates its properties. Section 3 relates our model with the Markov-switching regimes model, which is estimated on French data. Section 4 concludes.

## 2. The model

This section presents a stylised model of a fixed exchange rate peg. Like in Krugman (1996) or Morris and Shin (1998), the model is essentially a reduced form representation of the policymaker's decision whether or not to defend the fixed peg. After a statement of the assumptions in Section 2.1, we study the equilibria in which devaluation expectations are determined uniquely by the fundamentals in Section 2.2, before examining the conditions under which self-fulfilling speculation might arise (Section 2.3). Section 2.4 scrutinizes the possibility of cyclic and chaotic dynamics in the devaluation expectations.

### 2.1. Assumptions

Consider a country that has committed to a fixed exchange rate peg, but can at each period exercise an escape clause and devalue. The domestic policymaker decides whether or not to devalue by comparing the benefits and costs of maintaining the fixed peg. She devalues if the net benefit of the fixed peg is negative. We assume that the net benefit of the fixed peg at time $t$ can be written in reduced form:

$$B(\phi_t, \pi_t) \tag{1}$$

O. Jeanne, P. Masson / Journal of International Economics 50 (2000) 327–350    331

where $\phi_t$ is a variable reflecting the exogenous economic fundamentals,[5] and $\pi_t = \int_0^1 \pi_t^i \, di$ is the average estimate at $t$ of the probability of a devaluation at $t+1$ formed by a continuum of atomistic speculators $i \in [0,1]$. We assume that the net benefit of the fixed peg is a continuously differentiable function of both variables, increasing with the level of the fundamental and decreasing with the devaluation probability ($B_1 > 0$, $B_2 < 0$). We also make the (technical) assumption that whatever the level of the devaluation probability, there is a level of the fundamental at which the policymaker is indifferent between devaluing or not, i.e. $\forall \, \pi, \, \exists \, \phi, \, B(\phi, \, \pi) = 0$.

This formulation is meant to represent in a compact way the idea that, while the net benefit of a fixed peg depends on the economic fundamentals, it is also sensitive to devaluation expectations through the level of interest rates. Other things equal, higher devaluation expectations mean that the monetary authorities must set the interest rate at a higher level, which makes the fixed peg more costly through a number of channels (lower economic activity, fragilization of the banking sector, higher interest burden on the public debt, etc.). Krugman (1996) presents a simple model in which devaluation expectations depress output by raising the ex ante interest rate, and the net benefit of the fixed peg for the policymaker can be written like Eq. (1) in reduced form.

The dynamics of the system are driven by the exogenous fundamental variable, $\phi$. We assume that this variable is stochastic, and that its movements are well described by a Markov process with a transition cumulative distribution function $F(\cdot, \, \cdot)$:

$$F(\phi, \phi') = \text{Prob}[\phi_{t+1} < \phi' | \phi_t = \phi] \tag{2}$$

We assume $F_1 \leq 0$, which may be interpreted as a requirement that the fundamental not be negatively autocorrelated (in the sense that an increase in the current value of the fundamental shifts the cumulative distribution function of the next period fundamental in the same direction).

The devaluation probability is the endogenous variable of the model. In order to understand how it is determined, let us first consider the problem at the level of an individual atomistic speculator, $i$, who makes his own assessment of the devaluation probability, $\pi^i$, taking as given the expectations of other speculators. Being rational, the speculator will estimate the devaluation probability as the mathematical probability that the net benefit of the fixed peg will be negative in the next period:

$$\pi_t^i = \text{Prob}[B(\phi_{t+1}, \pi_{t+1}) < 0 | \phi_t] \tag{3}$$

---

[5]Variable $\phi_t$ reflects all the exogenous economic factors influencing the policymaker's decision whether or not to devalue at date $t$, including the past values or the expected future values of the economic fundamentals.

where the probability is assessed conditionally on the current level of the fundamental variable. This equation shows a property which is quite important for the logic of self-fulfilling speculation in this model: the expectations of a rational speculator are forward looking, and depend not only on the speculator's beliefs about the future fundamentals but also on his beliefs about the future beliefs of other speculators. A rational speculator knows that the expectations of other speculators will influence the cost of maintaining the fixed peg at the next period and so the objective probability of a devaluation.

Assuming that all the speculators are rational and share common knowledge of the same information set,[6] we can drop index $i$ and write the devaluation probability estimated by the representative speculator at time $t$ as:

$$\pi_t = \text{Prob}[B(\phi_{t+1}, \pi_{t+1}) < 0 | \phi_t] \tag{4}$$

This equation summarizes the relationship between the fundamentals and the devaluation expectations implied by the model assumptions. Characterizing the equilibrium devaluation expectations means finding the stochastic processes $\pi$ that are solutions to Eq. (4) for a given exogenous process of the fundamental, $\phi$.

## 2.2. Fundamental-based equilibria

In a fundamental-based equilibrium the state of the economy is uniquely determined by the exogenous fundamental $\phi_t$. There is a critical level of the fundamental, $\phi^*$, under which the policymaker opts out, and above which she maintains the fixed peg. This level is determined as a fixed point in the mappings between the speculators' expectations and the policymaker's policy. Let us denote by $\phi^{*e}$ the level of the fundamental under which speculators expect the policymaker to devalue. Then each speculator estimates the devaluation probability at time $t$ as the probability that the fundamental will fall short of $\phi^{*e}$ at the following period:

$$\pi_t = \text{Prob}[\phi_{t+1} < \phi^{*e} | \phi_t] = F(\phi_t, \phi^{*e}) \tag{5}$$

Conversely, the policymaker's problem is to determine the optimal triggering level of the fundamental given the speculators' expectations. The level chosen by the policymaker, $\phi^*$, is such that the net benefit function:

---

[6]The assumption of common knowledge is not innocuous. As Morris and Shin (1998) have shown in a recent paper, the absence of common knowledge can remove the multiplicity of equilibria in escape clause models of currency crises.

O. Jeanne, P. Masson / Journal of International Economics 50 (2000) 327–350        333

$$\phi \mapsto B(\phi, F(\phi, \phi^{*e})) \tag{6}$$

takes negative values for $\phi$ lower than $\phi^*$ and positive values for $\phi$ larger than $\phi^*$. Since the net benefit function is a strictly increasing function of the fundamental, $\phi^*$ is the (unique) level of the fundamental at which the net benefit is equal to zero. We denote by $H(\phi^{*e})$ this level.[7]

In a rational expectations equilibrium the beliefs of speculators must be true, i.e. $\phi^*$ must be a fixed point of function $H(\cdot)$:

$$\phi^* = H(\phi^*) \tag{7}$$

This equation says that the level of the fundamental under which speculators expect the policymaker to devalue is the same as the level under which the policymaker effectively chooses to devalue. It always has one solution, which ensures the existence of at least one fundamental-based equilibrium.[8] But it may also have multiple solutions. To illustrate, Fig. 1 shows a case[9] where there are three possible levels of the critical benefit threshold $\phi_I^* < \phi_{II}^* < \phi_{III}^*$. This multiplicity is made possible by the fact that function $H(\cdot)$ is increasing, or in other words, that there is a *strategic complementarity* between the market expectations about the policymaker's devaluation rule and the rule that is actually chosen by the policymaker. By increasing their estimate of the critical threshold triggering the devaluation $\phi^{*e}$, speculators force the policymaker to bear the cost of higher devaluation expectations, inducing her to revise the actual threshold $\phi^*$ upwards. As a result, fundamental-based equilibria with different devaluation rules—and different average levels of devaluation expectations—may coexist.

### 2.3. Sunspot equilibria

The multiplicity of fundamental-based equilibria makes it possible to construct equilibria in which the economy jumps across states with different levels of devaluation expectations. A priori, the jumps between states may be related to the

---

[7]The *existence* of $H(\phi^{*e})$ is ensured by the following argument. The net benefit function Eq. (6) is bounded from below by $B(\phi, 1)$ and from above by $B(\phi, 0)$. Because of our technical assumption on $B(\cdot, \cdot)$ we know that there exist $\phi^0$ and $\phi^1$ such that $B(\phi^0, 0) = B(\phi^1, 1) = 0$. It is then not difficult to check that, by continuity of the net benefit function, there is at least one $\phi^*$, between $\phi^0$ and $\phi^1$, for which the net benefit is zero.

[8]This results from the fact that $H(\cdot)$ is continuous and bounded by $\phi^0$ and $\phi^1$.

[9]Fig. 1 was constructed assuming that the net benefit function is given by $B(\phi, \pi) = 1 + 0.3\phi - 2\pi$ and that $\phi_t$ is identically, independently and normally distributed, centered on $\phi = 1$ with variance 0.25. For well-behaved fundamental processes—that is, in which the innovation has a probability distribution function that is bell-shaped and symmetric—the number of solutions is limited to three, but it can be larger in general.

334       *O. Jeanne, P. Masson / Journal of International Economics 50 (2000) 327–350*

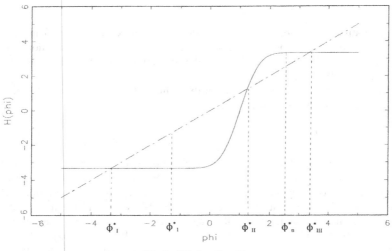

Fig. 1. Solution for $\phi^*$.

fundamentals, but this is not necessarily the case; they may also be driven by extrinsic uncertainty—a sunspot variable which coordinates the private sector expectations on one state or the other. We now proceed to construct such sunspot equilibria.

A sunspot equilibrium is formally defined as follows. We assume that the economy can be in $n$ states $s = 1, \ldots, n$, which differ from each other by the level of the fundamental triggering devaluation. We assume that if the state at time $t$ is $s$, the policymaker opts out if and only if $\phi_t < \phi_s^*$. The threshold fundamental levels are ranked by increasing order, i.e. $\phi_1^* < \phi_2^* < \cdots < \phi_n^*$, which means that if the policymaker devalues when the state is $s$, she also devalues for any state higher than $s$. Like in Jeanne (1997), the transition across states is assumed to follow a Markov process independent of the fundamentals, characterized by the transition matrix $\Theta = [\theta(i, j)]_{1 \le i,j \le n}$.

Two clarifying remarks are worth making at this juncture. First, it is important to note that the jumps in $\phi^*$ do not reflect any change in the policymaker's preferences or type. They correspond to changes in the policymaker's *decision rule* that are induced purely by shifts in the speculators' expectations. Second, the $\phi_s^*$ are a priori not the same as the critical thresholds of the fundamental-based equilibria, i.e. the $\phi^*$ solutions to Eq. (7). This equation does not take into account the speculators' expectations about future state shifts, which play an important role in shaping sunspot equilibria.

In a sunspot equilibrium the devaluation probability depends jointly on the state and the fundamental variable. It is equal to the sum of the probabilities of a

O. Jeanne, P. Masson / Journal of International Economics 50 (2000) 327–350      335

devaluation in the next period weighted by the transition probabilities from the current to the future states, i.e.:

$$\pi_t = \sum_{s=1}^{n} \theta(s_t, s) F(\phi_t, \phi_s^*) \tag{8}$$

Given these expectations, the net benefit function of the policymaker now depends jointly on the current state, the probabilities of a transition to other states and the corresponding fundamental threshold levels. In state $s$ the net benefit function is given by:

$$\phi \mapsto B\left( \phi, \sum_{s'=1}^{n} \theta(s, s') F(\phi, \phi_{s'}^*) \right)$$

Again, the policymaker chooses $\phi_s^*$ as the unique level of $\phi$ for which the net benefit is equal to zero. We denote by $H_s(\phi_1^*, \ldots, \phi_n^*)$ this level, which, in a rational expectations equilibrium, should satisfy the fixed point equations:

$$\forall s = 1, \ldots, n, \quad \phi_s^* = H_s(\phi_1^*, \ldots, \phi_n^*) \tag{9}$$

We characterize a sunspot equilibrium by a vector $(\phi_1^*, \ldots, \phi_n^*)'$ that satisfies the $n$ constraints Eq. (9). One can note that the fundamental-based equilibria may be viewed as degenerate cases of the sunspot ones, corresponding to $\Theta$ equal to the identity matrix. In that case, the economy never jumps, and always remains in its initial state. Eq. (9) reduces to Eq. (7) for all states $s$, and the $\phi_s^*$ are necessarily equal to $\phi_I^*$, $\phi_{II}^*$ or $\phi_{III}^*$. Of course, we are more interested in non-degenerate cases, in which the economy actually jumps between different states, and it is the latter type of sunspot equilibria on which we focus henceforth.

Proposition 1 gives a simple criterion for the existence of sunspot equilibria (see proof in Appendix A).

**Proposition 1.** *Sunspot equilibria exist if and only if there are multiple fundamental-based equilibria, i.e. multiple solutions to Eq. (7). Moreover, if this condition is satisfied, it is possible to construct sunspot equilibria with any number of states $n$.*

One might have expected the number of states to be the same as the number of solutions to Eq. (7). The last part of Proposition 1 shows this conjecture to be wrong. In fact, the number of states can be arbitrarily large. This implies that we can take the states arbitrarily close to each other, and in the limit define the set of states as a continuum. The intuition (and the proof of Proposition 1) relies on the fact that in a given sunspot equilibrium it is always possible to 'stack' new states between the existing ones. We show in the proof how one can construct a new state as a convex combination of two existing states.

336     *O. Jeanne, P. Masson / Journal of International Economics 50 (2000) 327–350*

This property is in sharp contrast with the second-generation models of Obstfeld (1994, 1996), Jeanne (1997) and Velasco (1996), where the number of states is no larger than three. The difference comes from the assumptions concerning the timing of devaluation expectations. In other papers, the net benefit of the fixed exchange rate system at a given period depends on the devaluation expectations formed in the preceding period. In our reduced-form notation, this corresponds to the assumption that the net benefit at time $t$ can be written $B(\phi_t, \pi_{t-1})$, so that Eq. (4) is replaced by

$$\pi_t = \text{Prob}[B(\phi_{t+1}, \pi_t) < 0 | \phi_t] \tag{10}$$

This equation can have multiple solutions since both sides are increasing with $\pi_t$. But it is a closed-loop equation that involves the value of the devaluation probability at period $t$ only, and for well-behaved fundamental processes the number of possible values for the devaluation probability is no larger than three. By contrast, our model, like Krugman's (1996) one, assumes that the net benefit of the fixed peg depends on the current period expectations about the future, which makes the determination of the devaluation probability an open-loop problem and enlarges considerably the set of equilibria.

Whether or not sunspot equilibria exist depends on the shape of function $H(\cdot)$, which in turn depends in a complex way on the policymaker's net benefit function and the stochastic process followed by the fundamental. It is possible, however, to state a condition on the fundamental process that is necessary for the multiplicity of equilibria. This condition is related to $F(\phi, \phi)$, the probability that the fundamental will be lower than $\phi$ the next period when it is equal to $\phi$ in the current period, or in other words, the probability of a decrease in the fundamental.

**Corollary 1.** *For sunspot equilibria to exist the probability of a decrease in the fundamental, $F(\phi, \phi)$, must be strictly increasing with the fundamental, $\phi$, at least over some range.*

To see why the corollary is true, let us consider two different fundamental-based equilibria, say I and II. In equilibrium II the point where the policymaker is indifferent between devaluing and maintaining the fixed peg is reached for a higher level of the fundamental than in equilibrium I. But in both equilibria, when the fundamental is exactly equal to the threshold level triggering a devaluation, the devaluation probability is exactly the same as the probability of a decrease in the fundamental between the current and next period. Hence it must be the case that:

$$F(\phi_I^*, \phi_I^*) < F(\phi_{II}^*, \phi_{II}^*)$$

which is possible only if $F(\phi, \phi)$ is strictly increasing with $\phi$, at least over some range.

*O. Jeanne, P. Masson / Journal of International Economics 50 (2000) 327–350*     337

As a negative corollary to the previous result, one can derive a number of conditions under which self-fulfilling speculation *cannot* arise in our model.

**Corollary 2.** *Assume that one of the following assumptions is satisfied: (i) the fundamental variable is always decreasing, i.e.* $\mathrm{Prob}_t[\phi_{t+1} < \phi_t] = 1$; *(ii) the fundamental variable is always increasing i.e.* $\mathrm{Prob}_t[\phi_{t+1} < \phi_t] = 0$; *(iii) the fundamental variable follows a random walk, with* $\mathrm{Prob}_t[\phi_{t+1} < \phi_t] = 1/2$; *then sunspot equilibria do not exist.*

The proof of the corollary is that $F(\cdot, \cdot) = 1, 0, 1/2$ in cases (i), (ii) and (iii), respectively, so that the condition stated in Corollary 1 is not satisfied. An implication of this corollary is Krugman's finding that his model does not give rise to multiple equilibria when the fundamental follows a downward deterministic trend. Krugman obtains this result by showing that if the policymaker is sure to devalue before a finite date, the effective devaluation date is uniquely determined by backward induction. The corollary shows that this result can be generalized to the case when the fundamental is always deteriorating but is stochastic, when it always improves over time, or follows a random walk.

## 2.4. A digression on cycles and chaos

As the previous section shows, the properties of an escape clause model of currency crisis are very sensitive to whether the net benefit of the fixed peg at time $t$ is affected by the devaluation expectations formed at time $t$ or at time $t - 1$. The first assumption would be natural if devaluation expectations were costly because of their impact on nominal wage-setting (as in Obstfeld, 1994, 1996a), or the ex post or lagged ex ante real interest rate (as in Eichengreen and Jeanne, 1998). The second assumption relies on the view that devaluation expectations matter because of their impact on the current ex ante real interest rate (Krugman, 1996). In the real world these channels are probably important simultaneously, which raises the question of the properties of a second-generation model in which the net benefit of the fixed peg at time $t$ depends on *both* $\pi_t$ and $\pi_{t-1}$. We show in this section that the dynamics of devaluation expectations become more complicated, and may exhibit cyclic or chaotic features.

We study a simple example based on a linear specification for the benefit function $B(\cdot, \cdot)$ and a fundamental variable that is independently and identically distributed over time

$$B(\phi_t, \pi_t) = b_0 + b_1\phi_t - b_2\pi_t - b_3\pi_{t-1} \tag{11}$$

$$\phi_t = \overline{\phi} + \epsilon_t \tag{12}$$

Then:

338        *O. Jeanne, P. Masson / Journal of International Economics 50 (2000) 327–350*

$$\pi_t = \text{Prob}[B_{t+1} < 0] \tag{13}$$

$$= G\left(\frac{-b_0 - b_1\overline{\phi} + b_2\pi_{t+1} + b_3\pi_t}{b_1}\right) \tag{14}$$

where $G(\cdot)$ is the cumulative distribution function of $\epsilon$. Hence, the dynamics of the devaluation probability are deterministic of the first order, and characterized by:

$$\pi_{t+1} = \frac{b_1 G^{-1}(\pi_t) + b_0 + b_1\overline{\phi} - b_3\pi_t}{b_2} \tag{15}$$

Fig. 2 depicts a possible shape for this relationship, obtained under the assumption that $\epsilon$ is normally distributed.[10] The intersection of the curve and the 45° line defines a level of the devaluation probability which is a fixed point of the expectational problem. However, this equilibrium is unstable because the slope of the curve at its intersection with the line is less than $-1$. Starting from a level of the devaluation probability to the left or the right of the fixed point gives rise to chaotic dynamics, illustrated in Fig. 3. It is also possible to find parameter values which, by making the slope of the curve at its intersection with the 45° line closer to $-1$, make the dynamics of the devaluation probability cyclic.

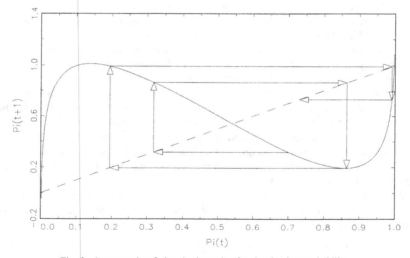

Fig. 2. An example of chaotic dynamics for devaluation probability.

[10]Figs. 2 and 3 were obtained for the specification $\pi_{t+1} = 0.76 G^{-1}(\pi_t) + 2.31 - 3.415\,\pi_t$, where $G(\cdot)$ is the c.d.f. of a standard normal with unit variance.

*O. Jeanne, P. Masson / Journal of International Economics 50 (2000) 327–350*     339

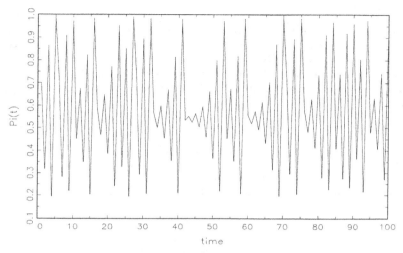

Fig. 3. Time series for $\Pi(t)$.

## 3. Multiple equilibria and Markov-switching regimes

We now proceed to the question of the empirical implementability of the escape clause approach to currency crises. The empirical literature provides ample evidence that devaluation expectations are subject to abrupt shifts that do not seem related to the economic fundamentals. This evidence has been presented by some authors in the context of the Markov-switching regimes model developed by Hamilton and others. The regime shifts are then interpreted as jumps between multiple equilibria, even though, of course, Hamilton's framework is not a structural model of multiple equilibria. We show in this section that a Markov-switching regimes model of the devaluation expectations can in fact be interpreted as a linearized reduced form of our structural model with sunspots (Section 3.1). We then illustrate the potential application of this equivalence result to empirical work by considering the experience of the French franc (Section 3.2).

### 3.1. A structural interpretation of Markov-switching regimes models

Let us consider a sunspot equilibrium of the model presented in Section 2, with $n$ states and $n$ threshold levels $\phi_1^* < \cdots < \phi_n^*$. We assume that the fundamental variable is a linear index aggregating the macroeconomic variables that are most relevant for the policymaker's choice of maintaining or not the fixed peg, plus a shock:

340     *O. Jeanne, P. Masson / Journal of International Economics 50 (2000) 327–350*

$$\phi_t = \alpha' x_t + \eta_t$$

where $\alpha = (\alpha_1, \ldots, \alpha_K)'$ is a vector of coefficients, $x_t = (x_{1t}, \ldots, x_{Kt})'$ is a vector of relevant economic fundamentals, and $\eta$ is an i.i.d. stochastic term reflecting other exogenous determinants of the policymaker's behavior.

We then linearize the model under the assumption that the fluctuations of the fundamental variable and the differences between the critical thresholds are small, i.e.:

$$\phi_t = \bar{\phi} + \delta\phi_t$$

$$\phi_s^* = \phi^* + \delta\phi_s^*$$

where $\delta\phi_t$ and $\delta\phi_s^*$ are of the first order.

Linearizing the equation for the devaluation probability, Eq. (8), gives:

$$\pi_t = \gamma_{s_t} + \beta' x_t + \nu_t, \quad s_t = 1, \ldots, n \tag{16}$$

where $\gamma_s$ is a constant that depends on the state, $\beta = (\beta_1, \ldots, \beta_K)'$ is a vector of coefficients and $\nu_t$ is an i.i.d. shock, all of which can be written as functions of the structural parameters of the model.[11]

Eq. (16) may be viewed as a Markov-switching model with $n$ regimes. Regime shifts affect the devaluation probability by changing the constant term on the right-hand side of the equation, but leave the coefficients of the fundamentals unchanged—a restriction that is not usually adopted in Markov-switching regimes models. These regime shifts can be interpreted as jumps between different states of market expectations in the underlying model with sunspots. A jump to a state of higher devaluation expectations makes the devaluation more likely and increases the constant term $\gamma$.

The likelihood of the Hamilton model is defined in the same way as the likelihood of the structural model with sunspots. In the degenerate case where there is only one state, Hamilton's model reduces to a simple linear regression of the devaluation probability on economic fundamentals, of the type estimated, e.g. by Rose and Svensson (1994). Several papers have explored how Markov-switching models with several regimes can be estimated using the maximum likelihood method, and the methods that they develop can easily be transposed to our setting.[12]

---

[11] The formula are: $\gamma_s = F(\bar{\phi}, \phi^*) + F_2(\bar{\phi}, \phi^*) \sum_{s'=1}^{n} \theta(s, s') \delta\phi_{s'}^* - F_1(\bar{\phi}, \phi^*)\bar{\phi}$, $\beta = F_1(\bar{\phi}, \phi^*) \alpha$ and $\nu_t = F_1(\bar{\phi}, \phi^*)\eta_t$.

[12] It should be noted, however, that the maximum likelihood estimation of the Hamilton model is not the same as the maximum likelihood estimation of the underlying escape clause model because the former does not take into account all the structural constraints that arise in the latter. We come back to that point at the end of Section 3.2.

O. Jeanne, P. Masson / Journal of International Economics 50 (2000) 327–350        341.

## 3.2. Empirical illustration: the French franc, 1987–1993

We illustrate the equivalence between our model and a Markov-switching regimes model by considering the example of the French franc. Some authors have argued that the speculation against the franc was self-fulfilling in 1992–1993 (see, e.g. Eichengreen and Wyplosz, 1993), and the experience of the franc has later been used as a benchmark case study of self-fulfilling speculation (Jeanne, 1997; Martinez-Peria, 1998; Piard, 1997; Psaradakis et al., 1998). Moreover the franc offers the advantage of providing a long sample period with many speculative episodes but without change of regime.

We estimated the model of Eq. (16) with two states. Our dependent variable is an estimate of the devaluation probability, in %, measured as the one-month interest differential between Euro–franc and Euro–DM instruments, after correcting for expected movement toward the center of the band using the drift adjustment method of Svensson (1993), and assuming a devaluation size of 5% (roughly the size of the average realignment of the franc in the 1979–1986 period).[13] Our sample includes monthly data between February 1987 and July 1993, which is the longest sample period without change in regime for the franc (it starts after the last franc devaluation, which took place in January 1987, and ends before the ERM band was widened to 15% in August 1993).

A key choice is the set of fundamentals. Traditional measures of exchange rate overvaluation or undervaluation focus on the balance of payments and relative prices or costs. The ERM crisis also led to consideration of a wider set of fundamentals. In second generation currency crisis models, other variables (growth, unemployment, the health of the banking sector) which may appear in the authorities' objective function are obviously relevant in forming devaluation expectations. We therefore include among the fundamentals the unemployment rate ($ur$), as well as the trade balance (as ratio to GDP, $trbal$) and the percentage deviation of the real effective exchange rate from its 1990 level ($rer$).[14] The real exchange rate is computed on the basis of unit labor costs in production; an

[13]One problem with using the drift-adjustment method is that it is derived from an implicit target zone model which is not the same as—though not necessarily inconsistent with—the escape clause model that we focus on. Introducing some features of target zones models into the escape clause approach to currency crises is an interesting research topic of its own, which goes beyond the scope of the present paper.

[14]Data are taken from the International Financial Statistics (IMF). The set of fundamentals could of course be widened further, in particular to include fiscal variables, which are critical in many speculative attack models because they explain domestic credit and hence monetary growth. However, as in most other developed economies, there is no automatic mechanism in France linking deficits to money creation, and seigniorage over this period was negligible. Moreover, the deterioration of the deficit over our sample period was largely due to cyclical factors (which are also reflected in the unemployment rate), and the public debt ratio, which remained below 50% of GDP, was not likely to have been a factor in explaining interest rates in France (unlike in Italy, where it rose to 120% of GDP).

342      O. Jeanne, P. Masson / Journal of International Economics 50 (2000) 327–350

increase in this index corresponds to a real appreciation of the franc. A time trend (*t*) is also included as a short cut to capture reputational considerations. Maintaining a fixed parity in the EMS has been justified by the desire of the policymaker to acquire an anti-inflationary reputation (e.g. Giavazzi and Giovannini, 1989), and such reputation plausibly builds gradually through time as private agents revise their beliefs about the policymaker using Bayesian learning (Masson, 1995). Variables *tbal* and *rer* are plotted in Fig. 4, while *ur* and the growth rate of output are plotted in Fig. 5.

The equation for the devaluation probability was specified as:

$$\pi_t = \gamma_{s_t} + \beta_u ur_t + \beta_t t + \beta_b trbal_t + \beta_r rer_t + \nu_t$$

where the value of the constant term depends on the state, with $s_t = 1$ or 2, and the error term $\nu$ was taken to be normally distributed, with variance $\sigma_\nu^2$. Transition between states was assumed to be governed by a Markov process, characterized by a $2 \times 2$ matrix of transition probabilities $\Theta$. The initial state also needs to be estimated, introducing a parameter $\mu = \Pr_0(s_1 = 1)$.

Estimation proceeded by first estimating the model without multiple equilibria (i.e. the purely fundamentals-based model), which can be done with ordinary least

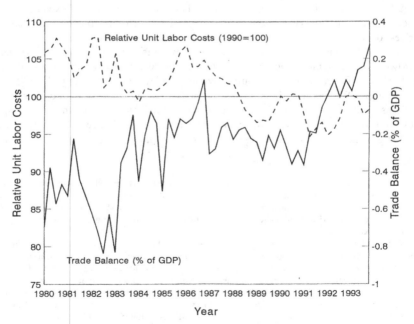

Fig. 4. Relative unit labor costs and trade balance, 1980–1993.

*O. Jeanne, P. Masson / Journal of International Economics 50 (2000) 327–350*        343

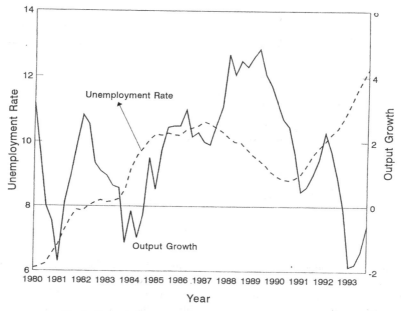

Fig. 5. Unemployment rate and output growth, 1980–1993 (%).

squares. The results are presented in column (1) of Table 1, and the forecast values for the probability of devaluing are plotted against the data in Fig. 6. The results have the expected signs for all variables except for the trade balance (a larger surplus for France should narrow the interest differential, not widen it). From Fig. 6 it can be seen that though the fitted values track the broad trend of $\pi_t$, they do not capture any of the movements associated with episodes of speculation.

Then the model was estimated with two states. Following Hamilton (1994), the EM algorithm was programmed in Gauss to get close to maximum likelihood estimates, and then Gauss's MAXLIK procedure was used to get the final estimates.[15] The estimates of the two-state model, presented in column (2) of Table 1, are more satisfactory in several respects. First, the fit of the model is considerably better, as evidenced by a lower $\sigma_\nu$ (less than half the previous one), a higher log likelihood, and substantially different values of $\gamma$ in the two states. The difference in log likelihoods (multiplied by two times the number of observations, 78), yields a test statistic of 106.58. A formal test is complicated by the fact that several parameters (in particular, the probabilities of being in the different states)

---

[15]As noted in Van Norden and Vigfusson (1996), the EM algorithm comes close to yielding maximum likelihood estimates, but does not quite reach the maximum.

Table 1
Maximum likelihood estimates of parameters (standard errors in parentheses)

|            | (1)       | (2)       |
|------------|-----------|-----------|
| $\gamma_1$ | 4.969     | 0.199     |
|            | (0.194)   | (2.114)   |
| $\gamma_2$ | –         | 3.818     |
|            |           | (2.088)   |
| $\beta_u$  | 0.183     | 0.544     |
|            | (0.371)   | (0.186)   |
| $\beta_t$  | −0.0790   | −0.0474   |
|            | (0.0135)  | (0.0086)  |
| $\beta_b$  | 1.055     | −0.425    |
|            | (0.437)   | (0.254)   |
| $\beta_r$  | 0.163     | 0.0635    |
|            | (0.171)   | (0.0920)  |
| $\sigma_v$ | 1.714     | 0.834     |
| $\mu$      | –         | 1.00      |
| $\ln L/T$  | −1.0388   | −0.3556   |

are not defined under the null of a single regime (Hamilton, 1994; Hansen, 1996). Thus it is not legitimate simply to compare the difference in log likelihoods to a $\chi^2$ with 1 degree of freedom, whose critical value at the 1% level is 6.63. An overly conservative approach would be to allow fully for the 3 extra degrees of freedom, and compare the difference in log likelihoods to a $\chi^2(4)$, whose 1% critical value is 13.28. Even this is vastly exceeded. Second, each coefficient now has its

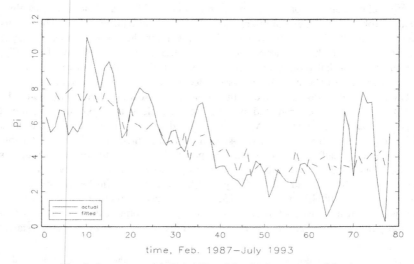

Fig. 6. One-state model: Probability of devaluation, actual and fitted.

*O. Jeanne, P. Masson / Journal of International Economics 50 (2000) 327–350*     345

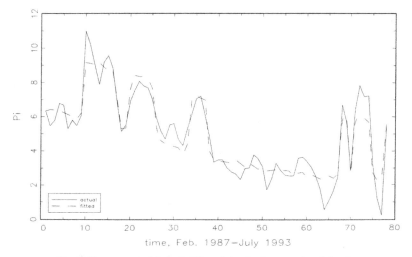

Fig. 7. Two-state model: Probability of devaluation, actual and fitted.

expected sign, including the trade balance, and all except the real exchange rate are asymptotically significant at the 10% level. Third, the plot in Fig. 7 shows that the model with multiple equilibria seems to capture well several of the episodes of sharp movements in the devaluation probability. In particular, the sharp upward moves around $t = 10$, $t = 20$ and $t = 35$, as well as the upticks after $t = 67$ (August 1992), are modelled by a jump to the second equilibrium.

The estimated $\Theta$ matrix of transition probabilities

$$\Theta = \begin{pmatrix} 0.771 & 0.229 \\ 0.145 & 0.855 \end{pmatrix}$$

shows that both states are fairly stable. This is illustrated in Fig. 8, which gives the smoothed probability estimates of being in the first state. There is clearly some persistence in the behavior of the devaluation probability, which tends to stay in one state or the other for several periods.

It should be noted that there is a sense in which the estimation of the Hamilton filter is less restricted than the estimation of the underlying escape clause model with multiple equilibria. We have *assumed*, in order to derive the former, that the underlying escape clause model had multiple equilibria. It remains to be seen whether the fundamental process that results from the estimation warrants such an assumption. Developing the techniques that would allow us to do so is a topic for future research. We now conclude the paper by outlining other interesting directions of research, after a brief summary of our results.

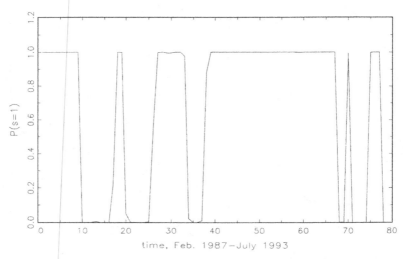

Fig. 8. Two-state model: Smoothed probability of being in state 1.

## 4. Concluding comments

This paper has investigated the properties of a class of escape clause models of currency crises in which the policymaker's objective function is influenced by the current period devaluation expectations of speculators. We found that, contrary to Krugman's (1996) claim, these models are not inconsistent with multiple equilibria, and can even give rise to a richer set of equilibria than other escape clause models of currency crises. We also showed that the model is amenable to empirical analysis using a standard econometric technique in time series analysis, the Markov-switching regimes model. We found that the model gives a substantially better account of the recent experience of the French franc when it gives a role to sunspots, in particular by tracking better the episodes of speculation—interpreting them as self-fulfilling jumps in the beliefs of foreign exchange market participants. It would be interesting to study whether the better performance of the sunspot model is an empirical regularity that holds for currencies other than the franc.

However, we would hasten to acknowledge that there remains considerable scope for further development. Even those economists who support the thesis of self-fulfilling speculation express some dissatisfaction with the state of the art of modeling multiple equilibria. In particular, the assumption that the economy jumps from one equilibrium to another following the realization of an extraneous shock raises a number of questions. To the extent that the sunspot variable instantaneously coordinates the expectations of all market participants, one would like to relate

*O. Jeanne, P. Masson / Journal of International Economics 50 (2000) 327–350*        347

this variable to an event that is publicly observable. It would be interesting, in this respect, to see whether the transitions between states that are identified by the Markov-switching technique are correlated with political events or other news, but this would require extending the analysis to a higher data frequency than monthly. A more radical criticism is that the selection of the equilibria should not be based on an hypothetical variable, but rather on an explicit modeling of the dynamics of the beliefs of heterogeneous market participants. From this point of view, it would be interesting to see what the approach of Morris and Shin (1998) can teach us about the determination of equilibria in our setting.

Finally, some extensions of our model have potentially interesting properties, like cyclical or chaotic dynamics, that we have only touched upon in this paper. It is noteworthy that in our model, these chaotic dynamics are perfectly consistent with the rationality of the foreign exchange market participants, and in particular do not require some of them to follow ad hoc trading rules. Whether these non-linear dynamics give a good account of devaluation expectations is an interesting question for future research.

## Acknowledgements

The views expressed are those of the authors and do not represent those of the IMF. This paper benefitted from comments received in a number of seminars. We are especially grateful to Giuseppe Bertola, Ricardo Caballero, Bob Flood, Berthold Herrendorf, Peter Isard, Nancy Marion, Paolo Pesenti, Ken Rogoff, Andrew Rose, Larry Schembri, Andrés Velasco, Michael Woodford and two anonymous referees for helpful comments. We also thank Freyan Panthaki for research assistance.

## Appendix A. Proof of Proposition 1

We first consider a sunspot equilibrium characterized by a vector $(\phi_1^*, \ldots, \phi_n^*)'$ with $\phi_1^* < \cdots < \phi_n^*$ and a Markov matrix $\Theta$, and show that Eq. (7) must have multiple solutions. Assume that the economy is in state 1. If speculators were sure that the state remained 1 in the next period, the policymaker's devaluation threshold would be $H(\phi_1^*)$. But in a sunspot equilibrium the probability that the economy shifts to higher states in the next period raises speculators' devaluation expectations, and increases the fundamental threshold chosen by the policymaker to a level, $H_1(\phi_1^*, \ldots, \phi_n^*)$, which is higher than $H(\phi_1^*)$. Hence:

$$\phi_1^* = H_1(\phi_1^*, \ldots, \phi_n^*) > H(\phi_1^*)$$

and similarly one can show that $\phi_n^* = H_n(\phi_1^*, \ldots, \phi_n^*) < H(\phi_n^*)$. Then Fig. 1

makes clear that $H(\phi_1^*) < \phi_1^*$ and $H(\phi_n^*) > \phi_n^*$ can be consistent with $\phi_1^* < \phi_n^*$ if and only if there are multiple solutions to Eq. (7), and $\phi_1^* \in \,]\phi_I^*, \phi_{II}^*[$ and $\phi_n^* \in \,]\phi_{II}^*, \phi^*_{III}[$.

We now show that it is always possible to add a new state to a given sunspot equilibrium. This will prove that the multiplicity of solutions to Eq. (7) is not only necessary but also sufficient, by showing how it is possible to construct a sunspot equilibrium by adding states between the fundamental-based equilibria. It will also prove, by induction, that the number of states can be arbitrarily large.

We construct an additional state as a convex combination of an arbitrarily chosen pair of states. For the sake of notational convenience, we consider states 1 and 2, and denote by $3/2$ the new intermediate state. We choose arbitrarily a fundamental threshold $\phi_{3/2}^*$ between $\phi_1^*$ and $\phi_2^*$ and construct a new state with this threshold by choosing appropriate transition probabilities.

We need to find a $(n+1) \times (n+1)$ Markov matrix $\Theta'$ that satisfies Eq. (9) for states $s = 1, 3/2, 2, \ldots, n$. Let us assume that in the new equilibrium the transition probabilities involving states other than 1, $3/2$, and 2 are unchanged, i.e. $\forall s$ and $s' \neq 3/2$, $\theta'(s, s') = \theta(s, s')$ if $s$ or $s' \notin \{1, 2\}$. We also assume that the economy can jump to state $3/2$ only from state 1 or 2, i.e. $\forall s \notin \{1, 3/2, 2\}$, $\theta'(s, 3/2) = 0$. Then Eq. (9) is satisfied for all $s$ different from 1, 2 and $3/2$, so that we can restrict the attention to the latter states. One must find transition probabilities such that the net benefit is equal to 0 when $\phi = \phi_s^*$ in each state $s = 1, 3/2, 2$. Let us first consider states 1 and 2. The sum of the transition probabilities from states 1 and 2 must remain unchanged:

$$\theta'(s, 1) + \theta'(s, 3/2) + \theta'(s, 2) = \theta(s, 1) + \theta(s, 2) \tag{A.1}$$

and the introduction of the new state should not change the devaluation probability when the fundamental is equal to the threshold level, so that:

$$\theta'(s, 1)F(\phi_s^*, \phi_1^*) + \theta'(s, 3/2)F(\phi_s^*, \phi_{3/2}^*) + \theta'(s, 2)F(\phi_s^*, \phi_2^*)$$
$$= \theta(s, 1)F(\phi_s^*, \phi_1^*) + \theta(s, 2)F(\phi_s^*, \phi_2^*)$$

for each state $s = 1, 2$. It is not difficult to find $\theta'(s, 1), \theta'(s, 3/2)$ and $\theta'(s, 1)$ between 0 and 1 satisfying the two equations above. One simply needs to substitute out $\theta'(s, 3/2)$ in the second equation using the first one, which gives a relationship between $\theta'(s, 1)$ and $\theta'(s, 2)$ that is satisfied by an infinity of pairs of probabilities.

The fixed point equation for the new state is:

$$B\left(\phi_{3/2}^*, \sum_{s=1,3/2,2,\ldots,n} \theta'(3/2, s)F(\phi_{3/2}^*, \phi_s^*)\right) = 0 \tag{A.2}$$

Let us assume that the probabilities of transition from state $3/2$ are weighted averages of the probabilities of transition from states 1 and 2, i.e. $\forall s = 1, 3/2, 2, \ldots, n$, $\theta'(3/2, s) = \lambda\theta'(1, s) + (1 - \lambda)\theta(2, s)$, where $\lambda$ is a parameter between 0

*O. Jeanne, P. Masson / Journal of International Economics 50 (2000) 327–350*     349

and 1. If the transition probabilities from state $3/2$ were the same as in state 1, i.e. if $\lambda$ was equal to 1, then the l.h.s. of Eq. (A.2) would be positive (this results from $\phi^*_{3/2} > \phi^*_1$, $F(\phi^*_{3/2}, \phi^*_s) \leq F(\phi^*_1, \phi^*_s)$ and the fixed point equation for state 1). Similarly, one can show that if the transition probabilities were the same as in state 2, the l.h.s. would be negative. This implies, by continuity, that there is one $\lambda$ between 0 and 1 for which Eq. (A.2) is satisfied. **Q.E.D.**

## References

Buiter, W., Corsetti, G., Pesenti, P., 1998. Interpreting the ERM crisis: Country specific and systemic issues, Princeton Studies in International Finance 84.

Cole, H., Kehoe, T., 1995. A self-fulfilling model of Mexico's 1994–1995 debt crisis. Journal of International Economics 41, 309–330.

De Grauwe, P., Dewachter, H., Embrechts, M., 1993. Exchange Rate Theory: Chaotic Models of Foreign Exchange Markets, Blackwell, Cambridge, MA.

Eichengreen, B., Jeanne, O., 1998. Currency crisis and unemployment: Sterling in 1931, NBER Working Paper No. 6563.

Eichengreen, B., Wyplosz, C., 1993. The unstable EMS. Brookings Papers on Economic Activity 1, 51–124.

Flood, R., Marion, N., 1998, Perspectives on the currency crises literature, NBER Working Paper No. 6380.

Giavazzi, F., Giovannini, A., 1989. Managing Exchange Rate Flexibility: The European Monetary System, MIT Press, Cambridge, MA.

Hamilton, J.D., 1994. Time Series Analysis, Princeton University Press, Princeton.

Hamilton, J.D., 1988. Rational-expectations econometric analysis of changes in regime: An investigation of the term structure of interest rates. Journal of Economic Dynamics and Control 12, 385–423.

Hamilton, J.D., 1989. A new approach to the economic analysis of nonstationary time series and the business cycle. Econometrica 57, 357–384.

Hansen, B.E., 1996. Inference when a nuisance parameter is not identified under the null hypothesis. Econometrica 64, 413–430.

Isard, P., 1995. Exchange Rate Economics, Cambridge University Press, Cambridge, UK.

Jeanne, O., 1997. Are currency crises self-fulfilling? A test. Journal of International Economics 43, 263–286.

Jeanne, O., in press. Currency crises: A perspective on recent theoretical developments, Princeton Studies in International Finance.

Kaminsky, G., Peruga, R., 1990. Can a time-varying risk premium explain excess returns in the forward market for foreign exchange? Journal of International Economics 28, 47–70.

Kehoe, T., 1996. Comment on Krugman, Are currency crises self-fulfilling? NBER Macroeconomics Annual, MIT Press, Cambridge, MA.

Krugman, P., 1996. Are currency crises self-fulfilling? NBER Macroeconomics Annual, MIT Press, Cambridge, MA.

Martinez-Peria, M.S., 1998. A regime switching approach to the study of speculative attacks: A focus on EMS crises, Mimeo, Department of Economics, UC Berkeley.

Masson, P.R., 1995. Gaining and losing ERM credibility: The case of the United Kingdom. Economic Journal 105, 571–582.

Morris, S., Shin, H.S., 1998. Unique equilibrium in a model of self-fulfilling currency attacks. American Economic Review 88, 587–597.

Obstfeld, M., 1994. The logic of currency crises. Cahiers économiques et monétaires 43, 189–214.

Obstfeld, M., 1996. Models of currency crises with self-fulfilling features. European Economic Review 40, 1037–1047.

Obstfeld, M., 1996b. Comment on Krugman, Are currency crises self-fulfilling? NBER Macroeconomics Annual, MIT Press, Cambridge, MA.

Obstfeld, M., Rogoff, K., 1995. The mirage of fixed exchange rates. Journal of Economic Perspectives 9, 73–96.

Piard, S., 1997. Currency crises on the ERM: The experience of the French franc, Mimeo, London Guildhall University.

Psaradakis, Z., Sola, M., Tronzano, M., 1998. Target zone credibility and economic fundamentals, Mimeo, Birbeck College.

Rose, A., Svensson, L., 1994. European exchange rate credibility before the fall. European Economic Review 38, 1185–1216.

Sachs, J., Radelet, S., 1998. The onset of the East Asian financial crisis, Mimeo, Harvard Institute for International Development.

Svensson, L., 1993. Assessing target zone credibility: Mean reversion and devaluation expectations in the ERM, 1979–92. European Economic Review 37, 763–802.

Van Norden, S., Vigfusson, R., 1996. Regime-switching models: A guide to the Bank of Canada Gauss procedures, Working Paper 96-3, Bank of Canada, Ottawa.

Van Norden, S., 1996. Regime switching as a test for exchange rate bubbles. Journal of Applied Econometrics 11, 219–251.

Velasco, A., 1996. Fixed exchange rates: Credibility, flexibility and multiplicity. European Economic Review 40, 1023–1035.

# 7

# The Normal, the Fat-Tailed, and the Contagious

## Modeling Changes in Emerging-Market Bond Spreads with Endogenous Liquidity

Paul R. Masson, Shubha Chakravarty, and Tim Gulden

## 1. INTRODUCTION

Despite extensive study of capital flows to developing countries, it is safe to assert that there remain a number of issues about which there is not yet a clear consensus among economists.[1] Three important issues stand out. First, though there are many models of balance of payments crises, there is little agreement in particular cases on the dominant cause. Specifically, are crises the results of poor economic fundamentals, or are they self-fulfilling, triggered by a rush for the exits by investors?[2] Are the relevant economic fundamentals excessive monetary expansion, government deficits, or financial-sector problems? Second, does a crisis in one country trigger one in another? As is the case for a financial crisis in a single country, here also it is necessary to identify the relevant set of fundamentals, since there are numerous linkages that would explain the co-movement in financial vari-

Masson, Brookings Institution and University of Toronto, Paul.Masson@Rotman .Utoronto.ca; Chakravarty, Brookings Institution and Columbia University, shubha _c@yahoo.com; Gulden, Brookings Institution and University of Maryland, tgulden@umd.edu. This chapter is a revised and abridged version of the paper presented at a conference on "International Financial Contagion: Theories and Evidence" in Cambridge, UK (30–31 May 2003). It has benefited from comments received there and at a seminar at Brookings. We are grateful to Heather Milkiewicz for research assistance, to Adrian de la Garza for providing the emerging-market spread data, and to Rob Axtell, Martin Evans, and Carol Graham for comments and encouragement; Ben Klenow provided a valuable alternative source for excess kurtosis in the model. We would also like to acknowledge our debt to Elizabeth Littlefield and Michael Mauboussin for sharing their knowledge of how the market works. Jon Parker provided help with ASCAPE programming.

ables across countries. This leads to the third issue: what are the causes of co-movement—macroeconomic fundamentals, or instead financial contagion operating through various channels, including shifts in investor attitudes, balance-sheet effects, or regional portfolio rebalancing triggered by a crisis in one country? In other words, is co-movement excessive?

In this chapter, we do not test statistically among the various channels that have been advanced in the literature, but rather simulate a simple model of balance of payments crises, focusing on both interacting expectations and varying liquidity as important features affecting emerging-market bonds. We posit a simple model of currency crises (which admits of both fundamental and self-fulfilling triggers of crises) where investors hold both emerging-market and developed-country assets. Thus, portfolio rebalancing could, in principle, lead to co-movement in asset prices. We depart from the assumption made in most models of contagion, namely, the assumption that there is a representative agent forming rational expectations. Instead, investors form expectations on the basis both of their past experience and of imitation of other (more successful) investors. These assumptions are sufficient to produce interesting dynamics, quite independent of the fundamentals, and we study their implications for triggering crises and causing contagion. This work is in the tradition of (multi-)agent-based models, which have been widely applied in a number of disciplines; some of that work is briefly surveyed below.

Our aim is also to see whether such a model can replicate in more detail the properties of the distributions of interest rates on emerging-market bonds. While there is a considerable literature on the structure of returns in various developed-country financial markets (e.g., Mandelbrot 1963; Mantegna and Stanley 1995; and Bouchaud and Potters 2000), emerging-market bonds have received less attention. In a companion paper (Masson 2003), daily data for JP Morgan's Emerging Market Bond Indices Global (EMBIG)[3] were analyzed for the twenty or so countries for which data were available. The following properties were identified on the basis of statistical analysis of the distributions of daily changes in spreads relative to U.S. Treasury securities. First, the distribution is very much not normally distributed, but rather exhibits fat tails, indicating that extreme events are much more likely than for the normal. This is a stylized fact that is significant, because it may allow one to distinguish among models of financial crises and contagion. Second, changes in spreads are serially correlated, indicating a possible departure from market efficiency. This applies to almost all emerging-market bonds, and typically the first-order serial correlation coefficient is positive, and significant. Third, there is evidence of contagion, defined as excessive co-movement: changes in spreads (and hence asset returns) are considerably more correlated across countries than are macroeconomic fundamentals defined to include trade between countries.

Agent-based computational approaches have advanced understanding of what causes heavy-tailed price movements. Lux and Marchesi (1999) demonstrated that multi-agent models can produce heavy-tailed distributions without assuming similarly distributed movements in fundamentals. Farmer and Joshi (2002) showed that market structure plays a large part in determining market behavior, and Farmer et al. (2004) showed that liquidity can drive the production of heavy-tailed price movements. MacKenzie (2003) investigated empirically the social structure of emerging-market investment decisions, providing support for the theory that imitation may be a major mechanism in producing heavy-tailed returns and excessive comovement between markets with uncorrelated fundamentals.

While this area of research is often associated with collaborations between economists and physicists, evolutionary biology has become increasingly influential in understanding market dynamics. Gandolfi, Gandolfi, and Barash (2002) provides a survey of these linkages. Farmer (2002) demonstrates that useful parallels can be drawn between multi-agent financial market models and standard models in population biology, where survival depends on "fitness." Blume and Easley (2002) examine fitness dynamics in a market setting, demonstrating that market selection favors profit-maximizing firms, but leads to systems that are much less stable than standard profit-maximizing models would predict.

In this chapter, we simulate various parameterizations of a model of investment in emerging markets in order to see what features are necessary to replicate these stylized facts. This model is an extension of the single-country model in Arifovic and Masson (2004). It combines a simple balance of payments crisis model with hypotheses concerning the formation of expectations by investors. In particular, we assume that investors form and update their expectations on the basis of the success (or otherwise) of their investment strategies. If the latter are successful (in the sense of giving a better return than some randomly chosen comparator), then the investor retains the expectation and strategy; otherwise, the investor adopts the comparator's strategy. In addition, investors at times experiment by randomly choosing a new rule. Thus, the investors in the model do not have information about economic fundamentals (the evolution of the trade balance and foreign exchange reserves), but adapt their strategies on the basis of past results. This has the potential of producing bandwagon effects— that is, serial correlation of changes of asset holdings and spreads, as expectations of excess returns for a particular asset become self-fulfilling, reinforcing that asset's attractiveness. Finally, both economic fundamentals and investor behavior contribute to triggering crises, which occur when a country's reserves go to zero, forcing it to default; this can occur as a result of a bad shock to the trade balance or because a sufficient number of investors withdraw their capital (a "sudden stop," in Calvo's words[4]). The model, when implemented for a single emerging-market bond, has some success in producing an alternation of booms and crashes in emerging markets, similar to actual data (see Arifovic and Masson).

The model also succeeds in producing serial correlation of changes in spreads, as is present in the actual data. It is clear that the "bounded rationality" of investors means that past success in investing reinforces strategies in a way that produces serially correlated changes in returns. To the extent that imitation occurs also, there will be herding (i.e., reinforcement of strategies across investors). In Arifovic and Masson (2004), that herding is the cause of booms and crashes in investment in emerging markets.

However, the model in Arifovic and Masson (2004) does not include more than one emerging-market bond, and several are needed to model contagion across markets. Moreover, that model assumes that all liabilities are short-term, so that the liquidity of a secondary market does not come into play. It turns out that a simple extension of the model to two emerging-market bonds with market-clearing prices is not able to replicate two of the stylized facts mentioned above: the basic model could not produce fat-tailed distributions, nor did co-movement in interest rate spreads for pairs of emerging-market countries emerge when the fundamentals were not themselves correlated. However, an extension of the model to include lack of liquidity is able to reproduce these two properties of the actual data, excess kurtosis and excessive co-movements across countries. We present below simulations of various parameterizations of the basic model without varying liquidity; while the first two moments of the distribution can easily be reproduced, the fourth moment is much smaller than in the real-world data, indicating that the simulated distribution has much thinner tails than the actual one. Indeed, simulated changes are in some cases even more thin-tailed than the normal. Furthermore, correlations in emerging-market spreads are small, even when the fundamentals are assumed to be highly correlated. Instead, the model would predict small negative correlations, as portfolio shifts out of one asset, would, other things equal, produce inflows into the others. It is clear that herding behavior, which is consistent with positive serial correlation in returns on individual country bonds, need not produce contagion, which requires some cross-country linkage based on economic fundamentals, correlated expectations, shifts in attitudes to risk, or portfolio rebalancing affecting the whole asset class.

The complete model includes a market in emerging-market bonds in which liquidity is provided by a market maker. Following the literature, market makers' bid-ask spreads are assumed to vary positively with the volatility of asset prices, not only in that security but also in others, while the market maker's midmarket price varies inversely with the size of the inventory held of that security. The changing degree of liquidity in the market provides a possible explanation of extreme movements of interest rates. Market practitioners point to the fact that at times of crisis, the market "dries up," as everyone attempts to get out at the same time. Moreover, market makers, who typically deal in a number of different securities, react to losses in one market by increasing their bid-ask spreads for the other bonds in which they deal. Thus, lack of liquidity may spill over to other emerging-market bonds.

This version of the model is capable of producing the excessive kurtosis and excess co-movement that is present in the actual data. While it is not the only possible explanation—and we discuss an alternative model that is capable of producing the excess kurtosis and contagion—it explores a plausible channel that has so far received little attention in the literature. We think that it deserves further exploration, both on the side of modeling as well as in detailed study of the way the trading in emerging-market bonds works. The microstructure of trading in emerging-market bonds seems to be a promising area for future research, and one that has so far received little attention, unlike the foreign exchange market (see, e.g., Evans and Lyons 2002).

The plan of the chapter is as follows. The next section describes the basic model, which draws on Arifovic and Masson 2004. Section 3 details the statistical properties of the distribution of simulated emerging-market spreads using various parameterizations of the model with a single emerging-market bond; for none of them does excess kurtosis approach that in the actual data. Section 4 simulates the same model with two emerging-market bonds, noting that despite herding behavior (resulting from investors imitating other successful investors), there is no correlation of spreads across countries. Section 5 introduces a more general model with two-period emerging-market bonds, which can be traded in the period before they mature. This model is shown, when liquidity as provided by a market maker is endogenous, to produce excess kurtosis and excessive co-movement. Section 6 concludes.

## 2. A MODEL OF EMERGING-MARKET CRISES

We proceed to describe a canonical balance of payments crisis model, and in the next section examine to what extent it can replicate the actual data. In this model, all capital flows are assumed to take the form of purchases or sales of the debt of the emerging-market government. The model links the ability of a country to service its debts to the existence of non-negative reserves: once reserves hit zero, a default is triggered, leading to losses by investors. The evolution of the balance of payments (i.e., the sum of the trade balance, minus interest payments abroad, plus net capital inflows) is the key to the ability of a country to repay its borrowings, and the interest on them.

Foreign investors choose from a very simple menu of investments: in the one-emerging-market case (to be generalized to several, below), they form expectations of the probability of a default on emerging-market debt, and choose to invest either in the safe (U.S. Treasury) security, paying a known and constant return $r^*$, or the emerging-market bond, paying $r_t$. The amount that they invest this period in the emerging-market bond, summed across all investors, is denoted $D_t$.

A default occurs at $t$ if reserves would have gone negative. The basic balance of payments equation in the model is

$$R_t = R_{t-1} + D_t - (1 + r_{t-1})D_{t-1} + T_t,$$   (1)

where $R_t$ are reserves and $T_t$ is the trade balance.[5] The trade balance is a stochastic process that in this model constitutes the economic fundamental.

Investors form expectations of the probability of default. Let investor $i$'s estimated probability be $\pi_t^i$ and expected size of the default be $\delta_t^i$. We assume that the market interest rate is set to be equal to the U.S. rate plus the average of all $n$ investors' expectations.[6] More exactly, the market rate plus unity is a geometric average over unity plus the expected probability times the size of devaluation, times unity plus the U.S. rate:

$$1 + r_t = (1 + r^*)\left( \prod_{i=1}^{n}(1 + \pi_t^i \delta_t^i) \right)^{1/n} \tag{2}$$

This formulation allows us to determine both the interest rate, which reflects average expectations, and the quantity of capital flowing to emerging markets, which reflects the skewness of the expectations of default. To illustrate this, assume that risk aversion is zero, so that an investor puts all his or her money in either the safe asset or the emerging-market bond, whichever pays the higher expected return. If an investor then has a more optimistic assessment of the probability (and size) of default than the average embodied in $r_t$, all money will be placed in emerging-market bonds (negative holdings of either asset are ruled out). If the investor is less optimistic, then all wealth will be put into the safe asset. In these circumstances, the skewness of the distribution of expectations across investors will determine the amount that is invested in emerging markets: positive skewness of the distribution of devaluation expectations will indicate that more than half of investors are to the left of the average (hence more optimistic), so that investment in emerging markets will be higher than in the case of negative skewness (see Arifovic and Masson 2004).

Investors are assumed not to observe the economic fundamental (the trade balance) or reserves. While an extreme assumption, it reflects a reality noted by observers of this market, namely, the ignorance of many investors in emerging-market bonds (who then "woke up" to the flaws of the Asian Tiger economies after the crises occurred—see Goldstein 1998). Starting from some distribution of initial priors, expectations are updated on the basis of past investment returns, with an element of imitation and experimentation. In particular, if investor $i$ puts a proportion $x_t^i$ into the emerging-market bond (and the rest into the safe asset), by analogy with evolutionary biology (Blume and Easley 2002; Gandolfi, Gandolfi, and Barash 2002; Bowles and Hammerstein 2003) one can define "fitness" as

$$\mu_t^i \equiv (1 - x_t^i)(1 + r^*) + \frac{x_t^i(1 + r_t)}{(1 + \delta_t)} - 1,$$

where $\delta_t$ is the actual default size (or zero, if no default) in period $t$. The variable $\mu_t^i$ is in fact the realized rate of return on investor $i$'s portfolio. Each investor is assumed to observe the expectations and fitness of another investor, chosen at random.[7] Investor $i$, in updating the expected probability and size of default ($\pi_t^i$, $\delta_t^i$), will compare the fitness of his or her own expectations with those of a randomly chosen comparator (where the probability of being picked depends on relative fitness—i.e., more successful rules are more likely to be imitated[8]); if the latter's fitness is greater, then the comparator's expectations will be adopted; if less than or equal, then the investor's own will be retained. In addition, with some probability $p_{ex}$ the investor would simply discard their expected probability of default $\pi_t^i$ and pick a new one randomly, drawn from a uniform distribution on the interval $[0, \pi^{max}]$, and similarly for the size of default, if it is endogenous. However, in the simulations below we assume for simplicity that the size of default is fixed and known, because, for instance, a default triggers fixed costs that are independent of the amount of the shortfall of reserves. So, in this case, both expected and actual default size (if one occurs) are known and equal to $\bar{\delta}$. We will henceforth assume this to be the case.

Investors' wealth is endogenous and evolves over time, depending on investor strategy and the rate of return:

$$W_t^i = (1 + \mu_{t-1}^i)W_{t-1}^i - \bar{r}W_{t-1}^i \tag{3}$$

where the last term is consumption out of wealth (at a constant, exogenous rate $\bar{r}$). The model is completed by a stochastic process for the trade balance. This specifies the trade balance as an AR[1] model:

$$T_t = \alpha + \beta T_{t-1} + u_t \tag{4}$$

where $u_t \sim N(0, \sigma^2)$. Estimates based on annual data for various countries are found in Masson (1999). An isomorphic model would replace the balance of payments equation by the government's budget constraint, impose an upper bound on debt (provoking default if reached), and replace the trade equation with a stochastic process on the primary (non-interest) government deficit. Such a model would give qualitatively similar results.

The simplest version of the model is as described above. However, there are two further complications that need to be explained: (a) portfolio selection when investors are risk averse, and (b) conversion of the model from an annual frequency to the monthly or daily frequency that matches our empirical data for emerging-market spreads. These complications are briefly discussed here; details are given in the appendices.

To account for risk aversion, we assume that investors maximize expected utility. Substituting into the first-order conditions a second-order Taylor's expansion of the utility function, we obtain the familiar mean-variance model of choice between a riskless asset and one or several risky assets. For the case of just one emerging-market bond, the resulting expression for the proportion of the portfolio held in the emerging-market bond will be given by

$$x_t^i = \frac{b^i \left( r_t - \dfrac{1+r}{1+\bar{\delta}}\pi_t^i\bar{\delta} - r^* \right)}{\pi_t^i(1 - \pi_t^i)\bar{\delta}^2}. \tag{5}$$

The expression in the denominator is the variance of the return on the risky asset, while the numerator (multiplied by a parameter $b^i$ that is inversely proportional to a measure of risk aversion) is the expected yield differential in favor of the risky asset, if positive.

If $0 < x_t^i < 1$, then the proportion accounted for by the emerging-market bond in $i$'s portfolio is given by equation (5); if not, then $x_t^i = 0$ or $x_t^i = 1$. In the limiting case of zero risk aversion ($b^i \to \infty$), investors merely select the asset yielding the highest expected return (given the constraints $0 \le x_t^i \le 1$). The general case is discussed in Appendix A.

For the model to be useful it needs to integrate high-frequency financial markets with lower frequency economic fundamentals. Appendix B discusses the approach taken, namely to convert equation (4) to a monthly or daily autoregression on the assumption that the true stochastic process in fact operates at the higher frequency. In addition, adjustments have to be made to make stocks and flows consistent. Interest rates have to be scaled appropriately, as does the probability of default. At a daily frequency, it makes little sense to update expectations on the basis of one-period returns; thus, we specify a memory horizon $h \ge 1$ over which past returns are averaged when comparing fitness with a comparator.[9] Finally, we take account of the possibility that not all investors are active at a daily frequency; we specify a probability $p_{inv}$ that an investor will update expectations and alter his or her portfolio in any given period.

## 3.   RESULTS OF A SIMPLE MODEL WITH ONE EMERGING-MARKET BOND AND A SAFE ASSET

The model is essentially that of Arifovic and Masson (2004), calibrated to the reserves and external debt of Argentina in 1996, and using a stochastic equation for the trade balance that is estimated with historical data.[10] As in Arifovic and Masson, the model produces a succession of booms and crashes. However, as we will see, it does not produce a distribution for the changes in spreads that has tails as fat as those in the actual data.

The model was first converted to a daily frequency, using the method described in Appendix B. This produced the following equation for the trade balance (as a percentage of GDP as are the other variables):

$$T_t = 0.23282 + 0.99867T_{t-1} + \varepsilon_t \tag{6}$$

where $\sigma_\varepsilon = 0.73198$ is the standard deviation of shocks to the trade balance, calculated as a percentage of GDP, so that the typical trade balance shock corresponds to roughly three-quarters of a percent of GDP. A crisis is triggered if the country's reserves would otherwise go below a certain threshold, here assumed to be zero. A crisis is best interpreted as a (possibly partial) default[11] on contracted debt in a proportion $0 \le \bar{\delta}/(1 + \delta) \le 1$ that prevents reserves from going negative. It is assumed that $\delta = 1$, so that a default reduces the value of debt by half.

We first summarize in table 1 the properties of the actual data on emerging-market spreads for the periods of data availability between 1994 and 2002, for the emerging-market countries for which JP Morgan

Table 1. Summary Statistics for the Distribution of Actual Changes in Emerging-Market
         Spreads, All Countries (Spread Data in Percentage Points)

| Summary Statistics | Daily | Monthly |
|---|---|---|
| Mean | 0.00214 | −0.0219 |
| Standard deviation | 0.4832 | 0.5585 |
| Skewness | −0.305 | −5.70 |
| Excess Kurtosis | 86.06 | 82.34 |
| Largest | 11.54 | 4.09 |
| Smallest | −10.70 | −8.46 |
| Jarque-Bera test for normality | 8,592,384 | 8,015,985 |
| Number of observations | 27,842 | 1,297 |

*Note:* Countries are Argentina, Bulgaria, Brazil, Colombia, Ecuador, Korea, Morocco, Mexico,
Nigeria, Panama, Peru, the Philippines, Poland, Qatar, Russia, Turkey, Ukraine, Venezuela, and
South Africa. Daily data spanned 31 December 1993 to 19 July 2002, or shorter periods when a
country's data was not available for the whole period.

collected data (the countries and time periods are detailed in Masson 2003, which also presents a more detailed analysis). Both the daily and monthly (month-end to month-end) changes exhibit a large amount of excess kurtosis in comparison to the normal (whose kurtosis is 3.0). Interestingly, the distribution is nearly symmetric, and the mean change is close to zero. As well as skewness and kurtosis, the table reports the Jarque-Bera test statistic of the null hypothesis of normality, based on those two moments,[12] and the maximum and minimum change in the spread.

The distribution of simulated daily changes in emerging-market spreads over the U.S. Treasury bill rate is given in table 2, for simulation runs of length 28,000 days (of which the first 100 were dropped to minimize the effects of initial conditions). It can be seen that unlike the actual data for changes in spreads, the simulations reported in the first four lines do not produce fat tails. In fact, the distribution has thin tails, not fat tails, since the kurtosis is less than the value of 3 that characterizes the normal. Skewness, although small, is consistently positive. As a result, normality is rejected at a very small $p$-value, using the Jarque-Bera test. It is also the case that the simulations tend to produce serial correlation in changes in spreads (not reported); since this stylized fact is easy to replicate, we do not dwell on it further.

Table 2 explores whether the absence of fat tails is robust to changing the model's parameters. The table presents statistics for simulations with alternative values for risk aversion, the probability of experimentation, the probability of investing in a given period, the maximum value for the probability of default, the standard deviation of shocks to the trade balance, and the endogeneity of wealth. Increasing the value of $\pi^{max}$ from 0.1 to 0.5 causes dramatic increases in the dispersion of changes in spreads, while introducing risk aversion also has that effect, but more moderately. In contrast, decreasing the probability of experimentation, not surprisingly, lowers volatility. Other changes reported in table 2 have relatively modest impacts. In particular, a striking result is that multiplying by 10 the standard

**Table 2. One Emerging Market Monthly Model: Simulated Effects of Daily Changes in Parameters on the Distribution of Changes in Emerging-Market Spreads, in Percentage Points (27,900 Observations)**

| Memory Length | Parameter Values | | | | | Wealth Endogenous | Distribution Statistics | | | | | |
| | $P_{ex}$ | $P_{inv}$ | $\pi^{max}$ | $b^{max}$ | $\sigma_\varepsilon$ | | Range | Mean[a] | Std. Dev. | Skewness | Kurtosis | Jarque-Bera |
| --- | --- | --- | --- | --- | --- | --- | --- | --- | --- | --- | --- | --- |
| 1. 1 | 0.333 | 0.9 | 0.1 | ∞ | 0.730 | N | (−1.26, 1.59) | 0.0004 | 0.364 | 0.049 | −0.119 | 27.6 |
| 2. 1 | 0.333 | 0.9 | 0.1 | ∞ | 0.730 | N | (−1.25, 1.52) | 0.0006 | 0.366 | 0.045 | −0.117 | 25.3 |
| 3. 5 | 0.333 | 0.9 | 0.1 | ∞ | 0.730 | N | (−1.25, 1.45) | 0.0005 | 0.348 | 0.016 | −0.053 | 4.5 |
| 4. 5 | 0.333 | 0.9 | 0.5 | ∞ | 0.730 | N | (−7.86, 6.68) | −0.0020 | 1.731 | 0.018 | −0.031 | 2.6 |
| 5. 5 | 0.333 | 0.9 | 0.5 | 5 | 0.730 | N | (−6.32, 6.62) | 0.0060 | 1.539 | 0.052 | 0.032 | 13.8 |
| 6. 5 | 0.333 | 0.9 | 0.5 | 5 | 7.320 | Y | (−6.37, 7.18) | −0.0015 | 1.537 | 0.070 | 0.033 | 24.1 |
| 7. 5 | 0.167 | 0.9 | 0.5 | 5 | 0.730 | Y | (−5.96, 5.42) | −0.0005 | 1.328 | 0.005 | 0.042 | 2.2 |
| 8. 5 | 0.167 | 0.5 | 0.1 | 5 | 0.730 | Y | (−7.10, 6.42) | 0.0081 | 1.520 | 0.067 | 0.176 | 56.9 |
| 9. 5 | 0.167 | 0.5 | 0.1 | 1 | 0.730 | Y | (−8.07, 7.67) | 0.0119 | 1.723 | 0.029 | 0.081 | 11.5 |
| 10. 5 | 0.167 | 0.5 | 0.1 | 100 | 0.730 | Y | (−6.24, 6.97) | 0.0048 | 1.426 | 0.145 | 0.179 | 135.0 |

*Note:* See text for explanation of variables.
[a] Multiplied by 10,000.

deviation of shocks to the trade balance (row 6) scarcely affects the distribution of the change in spreads. Thus, the fluctuations in the model—capital flows into and out of emerging markets that provoke occasional crashes and spikes in spreads—result here from shifting expectations rather than economic fundamentals (see also Arifovic and Masson 2004).

None of the above changes has a great effect on skewness or excess kurtosis, though the latter is positive in some cases. The Jarque-Bera test sometimes, but not always, rejects normality, as before (the critical value at the 1% level is 9.21). Thus, though these changes affect the range and variance of the distribution of changes in spreads, in all cases the distribution does not exhibit significantly fat tails. The model as it stands does not seem able to replicate this stylized fact, one that is strongly present in the actual data. Our results contrast with the view expressed by Cont and Bouchaud (2000) to the effect that herd behavior (which we have present in our model in the form of imitation) is sufficient to produce fat tails in returns.

## 4.  SIMULATING A MODEL WITH SEVERAL EMERGING-MARKET BONDS

We then proceed to simulate a model in which there is more than one emerging-market bond, in order to consider contagion phenomena. It is an important stylized fact that actual returns on emerging-market debt seem to be highly correlated—perhaps more so than would be dictated by economic fundamentals, and an extensive literature discusses why crises might occur together in several emerging-market countries. In the data (see Masson 2003), changes in emerging-market spreads are indeed highly correlated—though this may not be the same as the co-occurrence of crises.[13] This is a feature that we would hope our model with several emerging market countries could reproduce.

As detailed in Appendix A, in this case investors need to formulate estimates of the covariance of defaults among emerging-market countries when allocating their portfolios. We take the correlation between them (or correlation matrix, in the case of more than two risky assets), but not the variances, as given; that is, investors do not update their priors concerning the extent that returns move together. One would expect that the perceived correlation would be a key parameter for explaining the existence of contagion.

The simulations were performed with a model with only two emerging-market countries, each of them with parameters identical to the case of one emerging market described above, with uncorrelated shocks to the trade balance. Because the added complexity of the model slowed execution time, and in order to approximate more closely the typical time horizons of investors, we simulated at a monthly, not daily, frequency. Time aggregation will tend to reduce excess kurtosis, but in the actual data it is still present at a monthly frequency (see table 1).

An interesting issue is whether it is investors' beliefs that emerging-market bonds are similar that induces contemporaneous crises. A variant

Table 3. Two Emerging Markets: Simulated Distribution of Monthly Changes in Spreads, in Percentage Points (900 Observations)

| Perceived Correlation of Defaults | −1.0 | −0.5 | 0.0 | 0.5 | 1.0 |
|---|---|---|---|---|---|
| Country 1 | | | | | |
| Mean | −0.0004 | −0.0003 | −0.0002 | −0.0002 | −0.0004 |
| Standard deviation | 1.893 | 1.648 | 1.691 | 1.664 | 1.642 |
| Skewness | −0.0000 | −0.0038 | 0.0208 | 0.0119 | 0.0349 |
| Excess Kurtosis | 0.2133 | 0.0954 | 0.0978 | 0.0851 | 0.1571 |
| Country 2 | | | | | |
| Mean | −0.0002 | 0.0001 | −0.0000 | −0.0002 | −0.0000 |
| Standard deviation | 1.898 | 1.650 | 1.679 | 1.652 | 1.642 |
| Skewness | −0.0110 | 0.0462 | 0.0366 | 0.0048 | 0.0291 |
| Excess Kurtosis | 0.3432 | 0.1458 | 0.0856 | 0.0758 | 0.1409 |
| Correlation of simulated changes in spreads | −0.0083 | −0.0833 | −0.0929 | −0.1021 | 0.0066 |

of this argument has been used to explain the East Asian crisis, namely the "wake up call hypothesis" (Goldstein 1998): a crisis in one country (Thailand) made investors realize that there were fundamental problems in neighboring countries with similar institutions—or investors may have been misled into thinking there were, even though this was not the case. If the latter, true economic fundamentals might be uncorrelated, though investors treated them as being correlated. Investors might either overestimate the degree of correlation, or think that other investors' portfolio shifts would produce correlation where none existed. Such behavior might conceivably produce a self-fulfilling, rational expectations equilibrium, in which there was contagion across emerging-market bonds.

Table 3 gives the effect of varying the perceived correlation in the defaults by the two banks.[14] This determines the expected degree of covariance of their returns; all investors assume the same (unchanging) correlation, though investors continue to formulate different expectations of the probability of default. While it is unrealistic to suppose investors all perceive the same correlation, this polar case is considered to see whether a case can be made for self-fulfilling correlations as a source of contagion. The table reports on simulations where that correlation is fixed at a value that goes from −1.0 to +1.0. To repeat, the covariance of the two countries' macroeconomic fundamentals in these simulations is actually zero: innovations to the two emerging markets' trade accounts in their balance of payments are in fact uncorrelated.

The striking result is that for most of the values of the perceived correlation coefficient—even when it is positive—the correlation of returns is negative. Thus, there seems to be no self-fulfilling element to expectations here: even if investors believe that crises will occur simultaneously in the two emerging markets, this does not provoke co-movement of their spreads relative to U.S. Treasuries. Thus, this conjectured co-movement is not sufficient to explain any contagion phenomenon, quite to the contrary. The explanation for the negative co-movement in spreads is simple: since the two assets are substitutes in an investor's portfolio, there is a tendency to increase holdings of one when the other asset is viewed as having a greater chance to default. This portfolio substitution effect dominates any effect resulting from treating the two assets as somehow members of the same risk class. Indeed, the effect of conjecturing a negative correlation among their returns makes investors want to hold both assets, since doing so reduces overall portfolio risk. The reason for this can be seen in equation (A4) of Appendix A. A more negative correlation, other things equal, increases demands for the two securities. Paradoxically, this may thus produce positive correlation in their defaults, not the negative one that was conjectured, since by varying holdings in tandem investors will provoke contemporaneous booms and crises. The converse applies when investors conjecture positive correlations. However, these effects again are very small on the joint distribution of emerging-market spreads, producing only very slight differences in their correlations. Moreover, differences in the latter are not systematically related to the perceived correlations of default.[15]

In sum, the simple model with two emerging markets does not fit the stylized facts better than the model with one market, since in addition to producing kurtosis that is little different from that for the normal for each of the simulations in table 3, it does not provide an explanation for contagion. Thus, the model needs to be either replaced or extended in order to provide an adequate depiction of regularities in emerging-market debt. In the next section we consider an extension that models the varying liquidity of the market through the introduction of a market maker who varies the bid-ask spread as a function of the market's volatility and the market maker's own inventory position.

## 5.    ENDOGENOUS LIQUIDITY: INTRODUCING A SECONDARY MARKET AND A MARKET MAKER

Conversations with market professionals suggest that emerging-market bonds suffer from periods of pervasive illiquidity, and that this applies across a range of countries rather than being localized in just a single country facing difficulties in its balance of payments.[16] We therefore expand the model by introducing a secondary market in emerging-market debt; bonds are now assumed to have two periods to maturity (except the U.S. asset, which takes the form of cash). Investors purchase debt from emerging-market governments when they are issued (the primary market), with rates of interest determined as described above. However, if investors want to sell before maturity, or to buy a bond with only one period remaining until maturity, they need to deal in the secondary market with a market maker who quotes a buy and a sell price, which differ by the bid-ask spread, and whose average price reflects the size of the market maker's inventory of the security.

There is an extensive literature modeling the behavior of market makers.[17] Market makers are usually assumed to avoid taking speculative positions, making their income by trading, not investing. Therefore, the size of their inventory of securities has an important role in influencing the size of their bid-ask spread (O'Hara and Oldfield 1986). Shen and Starr (2002) develop a model of optimal market maker behavior in which the spread depends positively on the security price's volatility, the volatility of order flow, and the market maker's net inventory position. We follow them in making liquidity (which is inversely related to the size of bid-ask spreads) depend on the market maker's costs, which rise with increasing volatility. We extend their model by including more than one security. We also assume (as do Shen and Starr) that threat of entry leads to zero profits in the long run. Thus, the model mimics competitive behavior (though for simplicity we include only a single market maker in the model). However, the Shen-Starr model takes the evolution of prices over time as exogenous. This is not useful for our purposes, since market makers deal sequentially with many investors and could acquire unbounded inventory positions unless they adjusted the price. Instead, market makers in our model make decisions both on the price level and on the bid-ask spread; we assume that these decisions are separable.

We proceed to describe the investor's decision tree and the role of the market maker.

### 5.1  Investor

Instead of three assets—the riskless U.S. bond and two emerging-market bonds—we now have five, since investors hold emerging-market bonds with remaining terms to maturity of one and two periods. However, the two maturities of bond issued by a given country are viewed as perfect substitutes, since the probability of default is the same in both periods and the investor does not face stochastic consumption shocks, so is indifferent to the term to maturity.[18] Thus, at the beginning of each period, each investor calculates optimal holdings $(x_0, x_1, x_2)$ of U.S., emerging-market 1, and emerging-market 2 bonds, respectively, as described in Appendix A. After having redeemed maturing bonds, the investor has holdings $(\omega_1, \omega_2)$ of emerging-market bonds, which are compared with desired holdings. Let $\Delta_j = x_j - \omega_j$ (we omit here the index $i$ that characterizes the investor).

If $\Delta_j > 0$, the investor buys $\Delta$ one-period bonds from the market maker or new two-period bonds directly from the emerging-market country, depending on whether

$$\frac{(1 + r_{j,-1})^2}{p_j^b} > 1 + r_j.$$

That is, the investor chooses the bond with the highest return (since bonds pay two periods' interest at maturity, the market maker's selling price on a one-period bond $p_j^b$ has to reflect accrued interest).

If $\Delta_j < 0$, then the investor sells $-\Delta_j$ to the market maker, unless

$$\frac{(1 + r_{j,-1})^2}{p_j^s} < 1 + r^*.$$

That is, the investor liquidates excess holdings unless the market maker's price is so low that the return to holding on to them is greater than the return from investing in the safe asset. Since the investor may be risk averse and demand a premium for holding risky assets (which is already embodied in the desired allocation between the safe asset and the two risky asset classes), this rule of thumb sets a conservative lower bound to the price an investor will accept.

### 5.2  Market Maker

The market maker is assumed to be a middleman who covers costs but takes no speculative position, aiming only to minimize exposure, long or short. Assuming that there are the same quadratic costs to deviating from zero holdings in either bond (as in Shen and Starr 2002), the market maker's bid-ask spread could depend on the volatilities in the two markets. We parameterize the weight given to the own-volatility and the other bond's volatility using the $\xi$ parameter; we allow for various possibilities. In the base-case simulations reported below, we assume equal weights on the two volatilities; but, as we shall see below, allowing no volatility spillovers produces similar simulation results.

We calculate volatilities as exponentially weighted averages of the absolute value of the change in the rate in the primary market; a fixed window with equal weights would be an alternative, but one that requires storing a larger volume of past data. The constant $A$ is chosen to roughly enforce the zero long-run profit constraint, as would occur under competition among market makers, even though for convenience we model only a single market maker; any excess profits are remitted to the emerging-market governments in equal shares (and hence augment their reserves). Thus, the market maker could be thought of as an agent of the emerging-market governments. The bid-ask spread is set at the beginning of each period. Within each period, the market maker deals sequentially with investors who want to transact, quoting a buy or a sell price. The market maker (who does not initially hold an inventory of bonds) is not prevented from going short, but adjusts the price as a result of transactions in order not to accumulate too-large long or short positions. Thus,

$$\text{spread}_t = A + B\left[(1 - \xi)\,\text{vol}_{1t} + \xi\,\text{vol}_{2t}\right]$$

$$\text{vol}_{jt} = (1 - \gamma)\sum_{k=1}^{\infty}\gamma^{k-1}\,|\Delta r_{j,t-k}|$$

$$\text{price}_{jt} = (1 + r_{j,t-1})e^{-\theta X_{jt}}$$

where $A, B, \xi, \gamma,$ and $\theta$ are positive parameters, $\text{vol}_{jt}$ is the volatility of rate $j$, $\Delta r_{j,t}$ is the one-period change in the primary market interest rate set on bond $j$, and $X_{jt}$ is the market maker's net holdings of security $j$. In the limit

$\gamma \to 0$ volatility depends only on the absolute value of the change in the rate in the most recent period; $\gamma = 1$ weights all past periods the same. When $\xi = 0$, only the security's own volatility influences the spread; when $\xi = 1/2$ (the benchmark case), the two securities' volatilities have an equal effect.

We also study the cases where liquidity is not an issue (i.e., bid-ask spreads are zero), and where, on the contrary, there is no liquidity in the secondary market (i.e., investors have to hold their bonds for the full two periods until maturity). These two cases are nested in the model: in the first case, by $A = B = 0$; in the case of no liquidity, by $A$ large enough that investors choose never to transact. In the first case we also increase the value of $\theta$ and term it "market clearing," even though because of the sequential nature of transactions the market maker does not play the role of a Walrasian auctioneer who first polls all investors for their excess demand schedules and then finds a market-clearing price.

The spread is fixed at the beginning of the period, while the market maker's price varies within the period, depending at each point on the inventory position that has resulted in transactions with investors. Thus the market maker buys at $p_{jt}^b$ and sells at $p_{jt}^s$, where the prices are given by

$$p_{jt}^b = \text{price}_{jt} \, (1 - \text{spread}_t)$$

$$p_{jt}^s = \text{price}_{jt} \, (1 + \text{spread}_t)$$

The market maker's holdings evolve through transactions with each investor. After dealing with investor $i$,

$$X_{jt}^{(i)} = X_{jt}^{(i-1)} - \Delta_{jt}^{(i)} \, \text{price}_{jt}^{(i)} \, [1 + \text{sign}(\Delta_{jt}^{(i)}) \, \text{spread}_t]$$

The latter term depends on whether the transaction is a buy or a sell—that is, on the sign of the investor's excess demand. In fact, the simulations randomize the order in which investors transact with the market maker so that investors $i - 1, i, i + 1 \ldots$ vary from period to period. At the end of each period of buying and selling with all the investors who want to transact, the market maker either covers a short position by buying one-period bonds from the emerging-market country, or holds a long position until it matures in the following period.

First, we consider the two polar cases, perfect market clearing (zero bid-ask spreads) and no liquidity (infinite bid-ask spreads), as well as an intermediate parameterization with endogenous liquidity in which investors can, for a price, transact in the secondary market. Summary statistics for both primary and secondary markets—that is, the interest rate on new issues and their equivalent on one-period-old bonds that correspond to transactions with the market maker—are reported in table 4, where all the simulations were run over 1,800 periods (months). The same seed was used across cases, so that the results are comparable and are not due to the random numbers chosen.[19] The first 500 simulated periods were ignored in each case—a longer period than before because this model seemed more sensitive to initial conditions.

**Table 4. Effect of Endogenous Liquidity versus No Liquidity and Market Clearing: Summary Statistics for Monthly Changes in Emerging-Market Spreads, Primary and Secondary Markets, in Percentage Points**

| | No Liquidity | | | | Market Clearing | | | | Endogenous Liquidity | | | |
| | Secondary Market | | Primary Market | | Secondary Market | | Primary Market | | Secondary Market | | Primary Market | |
| | Country 1 | Country 2 | Country 1 | Country 2 | Country 1 | Country 2 | Country 1 | Country 2 | Country 1 | Country 2 | Country 1 | Country 2 |
|---|---|---|---|---|---|---|---|---|---|---|---|---|
| Mean | n.a. | n.a. | 0.002 | −0.002 | 0.000 | 0.000 | 0.000 | 0.000 | −0.001 | 0.000 | 0.000 | −0.001 |
| Standard deviation | n.a. | n.a. | 1.456 | 1.517 | 6.631 | 14.506 | 0.543 | 0.646 | 1.047 | 1.195 | 0.449 | 0.445 |
| Skewness | n.a. | n.a. | 0.380 | 0.630 | 0.103 | 0.100 | 0.014 | 6.204 | −0.009 | 0.264 | −0.478 | −0.442 |
| Excess Kurtosis | n.a. | n.a. | 3.983 | 4.085 | 17.078 | 12.119 | 15.058 | 133.242 | 4.758 | 13.476 | 3.233 | 4.200 |
| Jarque-Bera | n.a. | n.a. | 891 | 990 | 15,800 | 7,958 | 12,282 | 969,984 | 1,226 | 9,852 | 616 | 994 |
| Largest | n.a. | n.a. | 8.02 | 8.84 | 48.27 | 96.53 | 5.40 | 13.13 | 4.35 | 10.08 | 2.09 | 2.31 |
| Smallest | n.a. | n.a. | −6.07 | −8.40 | −47.04 | −95.21 | −4.56 | −3.58 | −4.79 | −7.91 | −2.72 | −3.03 |
| Correlation | n.a. | | −0.423 | | 0.430 | | 0.565 | | 0.121 | | 0.592 | |

There is a stark difference in the results for the three cases. The no-liquidity case (the left panel) gives tails that are greater than the normal, but modestly so: kurtosis is around 4. Changes in spreads for the two emerging-market countries are negatively correlated, as in the results described above. In contrast, both the market clearing case and the intermediate endogenous-liquidity case, in which liquidity is provided by the market maker but varies endogenously depending on historical volatility, produce considerably fatter tails than the normal.[20] Though it would be expected that the secondary market would exhibit the larger kurtosis, excess kurtosis applies to both the primary and secondary markets, though the determination of interest rates in the primary market has formally not been changed. Instead, it seems that transactions in the secondary market, by affecting the amounts held of primary securities, increase the likelihood of large changes in primary interest rates. Though not reported, it is the case that there is always positive correlation, for a given emerging-market country, between the change in spreads in primary and secondary markets. It is even true in the market-clearing case that for one of the countries, kurtosis is greater in the primary than the secondary market, but this seems to be an artifact due to the specific seed used. The market-clearing case also exhibits great instability of interest rates, as shown by the very large standard deviations and ranges of fluctuation in secondary markets. Finally, the correlation between the two countries' changes in spreads, instead of being negative (the no liquidity case), is now strongly positive.

In order to elucidate the factors contributing to the excess kurtosis and positive correlation, we simulate the model with different parameters for market-maker and investor behavior, with the results reported in table 5 (the values taken by these parameters in table 4 are given in brackets).

We first explore whether making spreads depend on the other country's volatility ($\xi > 0$) is crucial to the positive correlation discovered in table 4. The first panel reports results with $\xi = 0$. It is still the case that there is positive correlation in changes in the two emerging-market spreads. Thus, an active secondary market is a feature that contributes to the observed co-movement in emerging-market interest rates, whether there are volatility spillovers or not. In these simulations, the economic fundamentals are nonstochastic and uncorrelated, so there is no reason for co-movement in changes in their interest rates. As we saw above, investors' portfolio behavior was insufficient to produce co-movement (and in fact produced negative correlation), but the introduction of a liquid secondary market is able to do so.

In addition, we revisit the issue of how investors' expectations formation might influence the results, by varying key parameters relative to the basic market-maker case. To summarize the formation of expectations of the probability of default, each investor either compares beliefs to those of one or several randomly chosen comparators (two in table 4)—where an investor is more likely to be chosen as a comparator the higher is their

Table 5.  Effect of Key Parameters on Simulations with Market Maker: Summary Statistics for Monthly Changes in Emerging-Market Spreads, in Percentage Points

| | Zeta = 0 (0.5) | | | | Number of Comparators = 1 (2) | | | | Number of Comparators = 5 (2) | | | |
| | Secondary Market | | Primary Market | | Secondary Market | | Primary Market | | Secondary Market | | Primary Market | |
| | Country 1 | Country 2 | Country 1 | Country 2 | Country 1 | Country 2 | Country 1 | Country 2 | Country 1 | Country 2 | Country 1 | Country 2 |
|---|---|---|---|---|---|---|---|---|---|---|---|---|
| Mean | 0.001 | 0.002 | 0.000 | 0.000 | 0.000 | 0.000 | 0.000 | 0.000 | 0.008 | 0.008 | 0.008 | 0.008 |
| Standard deviation | 0.922 | 2.071 | 0.603 | 0.669 | 0.627 | 0.962 | 0.433 | 0.397 | 1.479 | 2.527 | 0.913 | 0.908 |
| Skewness | 0.377 | 0.498 | 0.641 | 0.015 | 1.267 | 0.302 | 2.150 | 1.003 | 0.753 | 0.025 | 0.549 | 0.588 |
| Excess Kurtosis | 5.3115 | 11.070 | 16.471 | 9.748 | 40.639 | 17.111 | 32.780 | 11.962 | 8.651 | 20.448 | 10.667 | 16.245 |
| Jarque-Bera | 1,559 | 6,692 | 14,784 | 5,147 | 89,805 | 15,879 | 59,205 | 7,969 | 4,177 | 22,648 | 6,229 | 14,370 |
| Largest | 5.11 | 17.67 | 5.32 | 5.42 | 8.09 | 7.64 | 6.05 | 4.10 | 10.29 | 23.04 | 6.69 | 7.19 |
| Smallest | -4.55 | -12.31 | -4.73 | -3.94 | -7.04 | -6.91 | -2.48 | -1.60 | -8.14 | -23.68 | -6.00 | -7.08 |
| Correlation | 0.149 | | 0.039 | | 0.232 | | 0.585 | | 0.132 | | 0.276 | |

| | Investor Memory = 12 Months (2) | | | | Maximum Probability of Default = 0.5 (0.2) | | | | Probability of Experimentation = 0.333 (0.05) | | | |
| | Secondary Market | | Primary Market | | Secondary Market | | Primary Market | | Secondary Market | | Primary Market | |
| | Country 1 | Country 2 | Country 1 | Country 2 | Country 1 | Country 2 | Country 1 | Country 2 | Country 1 | Country 2 | Country 1 | Country 2 |
|---|---|---|---|---|---|---|---|---|---|---|---|---|
| Mean | -0.002 | 0.002 | 0.001 | 0.003 | -0.001 | -0.011 | 0.004 | -0.007 | 0.001 | 0.001 | 0.002 | -0.001 |
| Standard deviation | 3.514 | 3.711 | 1.095 | 0.955 | 7.672 | 7.300 | 3.687 | 3.833 | 8.923 | 7.478 | 1.511 | 1.483 |
| Skewness | 0.077 | 0.047 | 1.231 | 0.608 | -0.098 | -0.010 | 1.190 | 0.699 | 0.030 | -0.032 | 0.796 | 0.732 |
| Excess Kurtosis | 52.337 | 33.515 | 10.243 | 7.839 | 19.722 | 14.664 | 9.170 | 4.794 | 5.454 | 8.889 | 2.013 | 1.107 |
| Jarque-Bera | 148,373 | 60,843 | 6,011 | 3,409 | 21,071 | 11,648 | 4,862 | 1,351 | 1,611 | 4,280 | 357 | 182 |
| Largest | 36.96 | 42.67 | 8.21 | 6.34 | 59.63 | 56.98 | 27.23 | 23.76 | 42.52 | 41.14 | 6.98 | 6.08 |
| Smallest | -38.99 | -42.16 | -6.32 | -4.83 | -69.45 | -61.29 | -18.37 | -18.37 | -44.72 | -41.45 | -4.76 | -3.85 |
| Correlation | -0.081 | | -0.255 | | -0.130 | | -0.119 | | -0.194 | | -0.582 | |

fitness—or, with probability $p_{ex}$ (0.05), experiments by randomly choosing a new chosen strategy. Fitness is calculated over a particular horizon for past returns, which we call "investor memory"; in the simulations of table 4, investor memory is set at two months. Expectations of the default probability are assumed bounded; that bound is the "maximum probability of default" (0.2), labelled $\pi^{max}$ in earlier simulations.

In table 5, we see whether changing each of these parameters in turn significantly affects the distribution of returns; the other parameters in each case are set to their values in the endogenous-liquidity case of table 4.[21] We summarize the results as follows. First, the number of comparators matters for kurtosis but not in a monotonic way. It seems that having both fewer (1) and more (5) comparators (relative to 2) increases the possibility of large and sudden shifts of opinion, producing occasional larger interest rate movements. Second, longer investor memory (12 rather than 2 months) also increases kurtosis, but reverses the positive correlation. Third, increasing the upper bound on the expected probability of default $\pi^{max}$ (to 0.5) increases the variance of the distribution (not surprisingly, since expectations now take values over a wider range) but does not significantly affect kurtosis. More surprisingly, however, the correlation properties of the changes in the two emerging-market countries' returns change from positive to negative. It appears that allowing for higher interest rates (associated with greater expected probability of default) qualitatively affects outcomes. Fourth, increasing the probability of experimentation (to 0.333) substantially reduces kurtosis in the primary market. In this case, there is not enough imitation causing the herd behavior that is an important source of financial crises (and large changes in interest rates). Also interesting is that more experimentation reverses the positive correlation that emerged in the market-maker model.

Despite its apparent simplicity, the model is complicated enough that changes in parameters produce nontrivial consequences that cannot be easily be inferred. Clearly, further investigation is needed to map out the regions in the parameter space where the phenomena of interest, excess kurtosis and positive correlation of changes in emerging-market returns, occur. It is also true that other information structures are possible and relevant (see, e.g., Watts 1999), and are worth exploring in the context of our model. For instance, there could be a group of trend setters (e.g., Goldman Sachs, Tiger Fund, or other large investment banks or hedge funds) whose strategies are widely watched and imitated. Or it could be that imitation is regional, with traders in New York, London, and Tokyo constituting separate groups. Exploring these possible networks among traders may be a subject of our future research, which we would hope to make precise by interviews with actual market participants. It may also be worth considering different access to information; market makers (and big investment banks generally, regardless of whether they make a market in a particular security) are widely believed to benefit from superior knowledge relative to other investors (in part because of their contacts with emerging-market countries and their role as underwriters). Agent-based models are particularly useful for studying such interactions (see, e.g., Epstein and Axtell 1996).

We would nevertheless conclude on the basis of our preliminary results that the introduction of a market maker and changing liquidity makes a significant step toward reproducing the stylized facts describing the actual data for emerging-market spreads. There are two crucial linkages here that help to reproduce some of the features of the actual data on emerging-market spreads, and would be present in any reasonable model of liquidity provision and portfolio selection. The first linkage results from the assumption that the market maker's bid-ask spread increases with volatility. However, having the market maker respond to volatility in one market by raising bid-ask spreads in the other market as well is not a necessary feature to produce the co-movements we see in the simulations—similar properties emerge when $\xi = 0$. Second, investors choose to retain their holdings in emerging-market debt when liquidity is too low—that is, when the prices at which they can sell are too unattractive (relative to holding on to their bonds). In any model of optimal portfolio selection, there will be prices at which investors will refuse to transact in the secondary market, and hence their initial holdings will matter. When expectations shift suddenly in the same direction, low liquidity will mean that prices need to adjust a lot in order to make it possible for investors to trade and get closer to their desired portfolio positions. Being locked into their holdings may cause them to incur large losses if there is a subsequent default, and this will then change the dynamic of their expectations formation and their desired bond holdings next period. The endogeneity of spreads is also important in causing serially correlated effects. Iori (2002) finds that if thresholds defining a no-trading range are constant over time (or zero), then volatility clustering does not occur in her model.

## 6.  CONCLUDING COMMENTS

We have identified various important features of the data for interest rates on emerging-market debt and formulated a model, which, after being extended to include endogenous liquidity, is able to replicate some of those features—in particular, fat tails in the distribution of the changes in spreads (against U.S. Treasury securities) and positive correlation between changes in emerging-market interest rates (even though the economic fundamentals are assumed uncorrelated in the simulation model). The analysis is necessarily exploratory and suggestive, rather than definitive. Nothing proves that some other model, even a reasonably parsimonious one like the one presented here, may not replicate the stylized facts as well as, or better than, this one.[22] And despite its simplicity, there needs to be more exploration of the effects of changing parameters or structure in order to understand the essential factors at work. We have identified the networks involved in imitation as a promising avenue to explore. Our model, like other models of heterogeneous agents, has interesting interactions between cross-sectional variability and time series volatility. Moreover, frictions that inhibit continuous rearranging of portfolios produce non-convexities with interesting distributional implications.[23] We hope to understand better in future work the key aspects of heterogeneity that produced the observed time series properties.

Other financial models have also produced returns with fat tails—for instance, through assuming that there are two types of traders, noise traders and fundamentalists, whose numbers vary in some fashion (see, e.g., Lux 1998 and Lux and Marchesi 1999). Most of the analysis to date has been applied to equity, foreign exchange, or developed country bond markets, all of which are deep and liquid. Studying the emerging debt markets is valuable in itself, not least because sharp movements in rates are associated with fears of (and the occurrence of) large defaults and currency devaluations. But, in addition, periods of illiquidity in these markets are much more of an issue than for advanced country financial markets, and contagion across markets has generated more concern also. Indeed, Rigobon (2002) finds that the upgrade of Mexico by rating agencies increased the universe of potential investors, and significantly decreased co-movements with other emerging markets. He therefore ascribes an important role to liquidity factors in explaining contagion. We hope to obtain market-participant data that confirms the link between volatility and illiquidity. In any case, the results of our chapter suggest that endogenous liquidity can, in and of itself, produce some of these features, and hence warrants further research in the context of emerging-market fluctuations.

## APPENDIX A: INVESTOR PORTFOLIO SELECTION WITH RISK AVERSION

We consider here the case with one riskless asset and two risky assets; it generalizes easily to the case of several risky assets. Portfolio return $R$ is given by

$$R^i = x_0^i r^* + x_1^i \left( \frac{1 + r_1}{1 + \delta_1} - 1 \right) + x_2^i \left( \frac{1 + r_2}{1 + d_2} - 1 \right), \tag{A1}$$

where $r^*$, $r_1$, and $r_2$ are the interest rates on the riskless (U.S.) asset, and on emerging-market bonds 1 and 2, respectively. Realized default proportions are denoted $\delta_1$, $\delta_2$ on assets 1 and 2, respectively. Portfolio proportions $x_j^i$ sum to 1 for each investor $i$, so we can also write the portfolio return as

$$R^i = r^* + x_1^i \left( \frac{1 + r_1}{1 + \delta_1} - 1 - r^* \right) + x_2^i \left( \frac{1 + r_2}{1 + \delta_2} - 1 - r^* \right). \tag{A2}$$

By assumption, the investor maximizes a utility function $U^i(R^i)$ with respect to $x_1^i$, $x_2^i$, given expectations of default $\delta_j^i = E^i(\delta_j)$. The first-order conditions are

$$E^i\left[U'^i(R)\left(\frac{1+r_1}{1+\delta_1} - 1 - r^*\right)\right] = 0$$

$$E^i\left[U'^i(R)\left(\frac{1+r_2}{1+\delta_2} - 1 - r^*\right)\right] = 0$$

We expand $U^i$ in a second-order Taylor's expansion around the expected return

$$\overline{R}^i \equiv E^i(R^i) = r^* + x_1^i(\mu_1 - r^*) + x_2^i(\mu_2 - r^*)$$

where $\mu_j^i \equiv E^i[(1 + r_j)/(1 + \delta_j) - 1]$:

$$U'^i(\overline{R})(\mu_1^i - r^*) + U''^i(\overline{R})(x_1^i \, var_1^i + x_2^i \, cov_{12}^i) = 0$$

$$U'^i(\overline{R})(\mu_2^i - r^*) + U''^i(\overline{R})(x_1^i \, cov_{12}^i + x_1^i \, var_2^i) = 0 \qquad (A3)$$

and

$$var_j^i \equiv E^i\left(\frac{1+r_j}{1+\delta_j} - \mu_j^i\right)^2$$

$$cov_{12}^i \equiv E^i\left[\left(\frac{1+r_1}{1+\delta_1} - \mu_1^i\right)\left(\frac{1+r_2}{1+\delta_2} - \mu_2^i\right)\right].$$

Writing

$$V^i \equiv \begin{bmatrix} var_1^i & cov_{12}^i \\ cov_{12}^i & var_2^i \end{bmatrix}, \, x^i \equiv \begin{bmatrix} x_1^i \\ x_2^i \end{bmatrix}, \, \mu^i \equiv \begin{bmatrix} \mu_1^i \\ \mu_2^i \end{bmatrix}$$

and letting

$$b^i \equiv -\frac{U'^i(\overline{R}^i)}{U''^i(\overline{R}^i)}$$

the first-order conditions can be solved to yield

$$x^i = b^i V^{i^{-1}}(\mu^i - r^*). \qquad (A4)$$

As is well known from portfolio theory, the composition of the risky asset portfolio will not depend on the degree of risk aversion (the inverse of $b^i$)—that is, the portfolio proportions captured by ratio $x_1^i/x_2^i$ will be independent of $b^i$. However, the proportion of the total portfolio held in the safe asset will depend inversely on $b^i$. In the limit as $b^i \to 0$, $x^i \to 0$ and all wealth is held in the safe asset. In the simulations, $b^i$ varies across investors, and is initialized by drawing from a uniform distribution in a prespecified range.

The expected return on each bond depends on the expected default. Default size is assumed known and exogenous (and $\overline{\delta} = 1$, which implies that default reduces the value of the bond by half), so the key variable is each investor's estimate of the probability of default on bond $j$, $\pi_j^i$, which varies from investor to investor. So $E^i(\delta_j) = \pi_j^i\overline{\delta}$, and the expected return for a given investor can be written

$$\mu_j^i = \pi_j^i\left(\frac{1 + r_j}{1 + \delta} - 1\right) + (1 - \pi_j^i)r_j = r_j - \frac{1 + r_j}{1 + \delta}\,\pi_j^i\bar{\delta},$$

its variance

$$\text{var}_j^i = E^i\left(\frac{1 + r_j}{1 + \delta_j} - 1 - \mu_j^i\right)^2 = \pi_j^i\left(\frac{1 + r_j}{1 + \delta} - 1 - \mu_j^i\right)^2 + (1 - \pi_j^i)(r_j - \mu_j^i)^2,$$

and the covariance between bonds 1 and 2

$$\text{cov}_{12}^i = E^i\left[\left(\frac{1 + r_1}{1 + \delta_1} - 1 - \mu_1^i\right)\left(\frac{1 + r_2}{1 + \delta_2} - 1 - \mu_2^i\right)\right] = \rho_{12}^i\sqrt{\text{var}_1^i\,\text{var}_2^i},$$

where $\rho_{12}^i$ is the investor $i$'s estimate of the correlation between the two assets' returns. In the simulations, this correlation is a fixed parameter that is assumed to describe the expectations of all investors.

### APPENDIX B: CURRENCY CRASH MODELS AT DIFFERENT FREQUENCIES

Instead of equation (1), the flows $T_t$ need to be divided by $n$, where $n$ is either 12 (monthly) or 365 (daily):

$$R_t = R_{t-1} + D_t - (1 + r_{t-1})D_{t-1} + \frac{T_t}{n} \tag{A5}$$

All interest rates need to be converted from annual to a monthly or daily frequency:

$$1 + r_t^{(n)} = (1 + r_t)^{1/n}$$

where $r_t$ on the RHS stands for the annual data, $r_t^{(n)}$ on the LHS stands for the monthly or daily data. As for the probability of a default, let $\pi_t^i$ be the probability over the coming year, and $\pi_t^{i(n)}$ for a fraction $1/n$ of the year. Assuming that the probability of a default in each of the months or days is independent of the others, then

$$1 + \pi_t^{i(n)} = (1 + \pi_t^i)^{1/n}.$$

Another problem is the trade-balance equation, however, because the lagged endogenous variable now refers to the previous *month's* value, not the previous *year's*. Persistence should be greater at higher frequency, and so should be the coefficient on the lagged endogenous variable. Suppose that the true adjustment takes place at the higher frequency, as in the following equation:

$$T_t = a + bT_{t-1} + \varepsilon_t \tag{A6}$$

If we go to a lower frequency (e.g., the time period is twice as long),

$$T_t = a + b(a + bT_{t-2} + \varepsilon_{t-1}) + \varepsilon_t$$
$$= a(1 + b) + b^2T_{t-2} + b\varepsilon_{t-1} + \varepsilon_t.$$

More generally, if the time period is $n$ times as long as the initial (high-frequency) data, then

$$T_t = a(1 + b + \ldots + b^{n-1}) + b^n T_{t-n} + \varepsilon_t + b\varepsilon_{t-1} + \ldots + b^{n-1}\varepsilon_{t-n+1}$$

$$= a\frac{1 - b^n}{1 - b} + b^n T_{t-n} + \varepsilon_t + b\varepsilon_{t-1} + \ldots + b^{n-1}\varepsilon_{t-n+1}$$

It is this equation that is assumed to have resulted in the coefficient estimates from annual data, say,

$$T_s = \alpha + \beta T_{s-1} + u_s$$

where $s$ is indexed by years. If we infer back from the lower frequency data we can calculate what the coefficients in (A6) should be from:

$$a\frac{1 - b^n}{1 - b} = \alpha, \quad b^n = \beta$$

Similarly, the variance of the shocks to the trade balance needs to be adjusted downward using

$$\sigma_\varepsilon^2 = \frac{1 - b}{1 - b^n}\sigma_u^2.$$

## NOTES

1. A sampling of the recent literature is contained in Claessens and Forbes (2001).

2. See for instance, the debate between Obstfeld, on the one hand, and Krugman and Garber, on the other, about the causes of the Mexican crisis of 1994–95 (see Krugman 1996). Krugman, however, changed his position following the Asian crisis, now admitting that there were self-fulfilling elements.

3. See JP Morgan Securities, Inc. (1999) for the methodology of EMBIG.

4. See Calvo (1998).

5. Reserves could also be assumed to earn interest, but since the U.S. rate is assumed constant this complication adds little to the model.

6. The basic model thus assumes risk neutrality. When investors are risk averse, a risk premium that reflects the average across investors is embodied in the market return on the emerging-market bond.

7. Other information structures are of course possible; for instance, only particularly visible investors (like hedge funds) known to have expertise could serve as comparators. We discuss this possibility in the concluding section.

8. As in Arifovic and Masson (2004), if returns are negative, the underlying expectations are not imitated.

9. Sections 4 and 5 report on simulations at a monthly frequency, however.

10. See Masson (1999).

11. However, it can also be interpreted as a devaluation that lowers the foreign currency value of debt contracted in domestic currency. See Masson (1999).

12. It is distributed as a chi-square with 2 degrees of freedom.

13. In particular, our simulations of the market-maker model described below produce high correlations of changes in spreads, but not the co-occurrence of defaults.

14. We simulated 1,000 months (corresponding roughly to the pooled sample of actual data), but dropped the first 100 observations.

15. An alternative, which we have not tried, is to make investors' expectations of the probabilities of default in the two emerging markets move in tandem. This would, by construction, force their interest rates to move together.

16. One definition of liquidity is the narrowness of the bid-ask spread; another is based on the volume of transactions (see Duffie and Singleton 2003). Unfortunately, data for neither measure are publicly available on a consistent basis for emerging-market bonds. In future work, we hope to obtain proprietary data from market participants on spreads, as well as quantitative data on the volume of transactions.

· 17. LeBaron (2001) discusses alternative market structures for agent-based financial models, including models with market makers, while Farmer and Joshi (2002) study the interaction of investors with different trading strategies in a model with market makers.

18. However, the actual occurrence of default may differ since, if reserves go to zero, the borrower defaults on bonds that mature in that period, while they may (if reserves are positive by then) not default on second-period bonds.

19. In addition, here the simulations for simplicity impose a zero U.S. interest rate and a zero rate of consumption on the part of investors; the trade balances for both emerging-market countries are also zero. As a result, the sum of the net worth of emerging-market governments and investors is a constant (market makers' net worth is also constant, since they remit profits to governments).

20. All of the market maker simulations use a value of $\theta = 0.0001$. The market-clearing case increases this parameter by an order of magnitude, to $\theta = 0.001$.

21. These simulations are done using the same random seed as in table 4, but in order to examine sensitivity to random draws we redid simulations with ten different realizations of the random variables. These simulations are available from the authors.

22. For example, Ben Klemens (personal communication, 3 November 2003) has produced excess kurtosis in the distribution of spreads by modifying this model such that each investor revises expectations of default in light of market consensus as revealed in the secondary market price. The rationale for such a model is described in Klemens (2003).

23. There is an analogy here with the literature on income inequality and growth (see Galor and Zeira 1993).

## REFERENCES

Arifovic, J., and P. R. Masson, 2004, Heterogeneity and Evolution of Expectations in a Model of Currency Crisis, *Nonlinear Dynamics, Psychology, and Life Sciences* 8, 231–258.

Blume, L. E., and D. Easley, 2002, Optimality and Natural Selection in Markets, *Journal of Economic Theory* 107, 95–135.

Bouchaud, J.-P., and M. Potters, 2000, *Theory of Financial Risks: From Statistical Physics to Risk Management* (Cambridge University Press, Cambridge).

Bowles, S., and P. Hammerstein, 2003, Does Market Theory Apply to Biology? in P. Hammerstein, ed., *Genetic and Cultural Evolution of Cooperation* (MIT Press, Cambridge).

Calvo, G. A., 1998, Capital Flows and Capital-Market Crises: The Simple Economics of Sudden Stops, *Journal of Applied Economics* 1, 35–54.

Claessens, S., and K. J. Forbes, 2001, *International Financial Contagion* (Kluwer Academic, Boston).

Cont, R., and J.-P. Bouchaud, 2000, Herd Behavior and Aggregate Fluctuations in Financial Markets, *Macroeconomic Dynamics* 4, 170–196.

Duffie, D., and K. J. Singleton, 2003. *Credit Risk: Pricing, Measurement, and Management* (Princeton University Press, Princeton, NJ).

Epstein, J. M., and R. L. Axtell, 1996. *Growing Artificial Societies, Social Science from the Bottom Up* (Brookings Institution Press, Washington, DC).

Evans, M. D. D., and R. K. Lyons, 2002, Informational Integration and Fx Trading, *Journal of International Money and Finance* 21, 807–831.

Farmer, J. D., 2002, Market Force, Ecology and Evolution, *Industrial and Corporate Change* 11, 895–953.

Farmer, J. D., L. Gillemot, F. Lillo, S. Mike, and A. Sen, 2004, What Really Causes Large Price Changes? *Quantitative Finance* 4, 383–397.

Farmer, J. D., and S. Joshi, 2002, The Price Dynamics of Common Trading Strategies, *Journal of Economic Behavior and Organization* 49, 149–171.

Galor, O., and J. Zeira, 1993, Income-Distribution and Macroeconomics, *Review of Economic Studies* 60, 35–52.

Gandolfi, A. E., A. S. Gandolfi, and D. P. Barash, 2002, *Economics as an Evolutionary Science: From Utility to Fitness* (Transaction, New Brunswick, NJ).

Goldstein, M., 1998, The Asian Financial Crisis: Causes, Cures, and Systemic Implications, in *Policy Analyses in International Economics* (Institute for International Economics, Washington, DC).

Iori, G., 2002, A Microsimulation of Traders Activity in the Stock Market: The Role of Heterogeneity, Agents' Interactions and Trade Frictions, *Journal of Economic Behavior and Organization* 49, 269–285.

J.P. Morgan Securities, Inc., 1999, *Introducing the J.P. Morgan Emerging Markets Bond Index Global (EMBI Global)* (J.P. Morgan Securities, Inc., Emerging Market Research, New York).

Klemens, B., 2003, Preferences with a Social Component, Department of Humanities and Social Sciences (California Institute of Technology, Ph.D. dissertation, Pasadena, CA).

Krugman, P., 1996, Are Currency Crises Self-Fulfilling? *National Bureau of Economic Research Macroeconomics Annual* 345–378.

LeBaron, B., 2001, A Builder's Guide to Agent-Based Financial Markets, *Quantitative Finance* 1, 254–261.

Lux, T., 1998, The Socio-Economic Dynamics of Speculative Markets: Interacting Agents, Chaos, and the Fat Tails of Return Distributions, *Journal of Economic Behavior and Organization* 33, 143–165.

Lux, T., and M. Marchesi, 1999, Scaling and Criticality in a Stochastic Multi-Agent Model of a Financial Market, *Nature* 397, 498–500.

MacKenzie, D., 2003, Long-Term Capital Management and the Sociology of Arbitrage, *Economy and Society* 32, 349–380.

Mandelbrot, B. B., 1963, The Variation of Certain Speculative Prices, *Journal of Business* 36, 394–419.

Mantegna, R. N., and H. E. Stanley, 1995, Scaling Behavior in the Dynamics of an Economic Index, *Nature* 376, 46–49.

Masson, P. R., 1999, Contagion: Macroeconomic Models with Multiple Equilibria, *Journal of International Money and Finance* 18, 587–602.

———, 2003, Empirical Regularities in Emerging Market Bond Spreads, *unpublished manuscript*.

O'Hara, M., and G. S. Oldfield, 1986, The Microeconomics of Market Making, *Journal of Financial and Quantitative Analysis* 21, 361–376.

Rigobon, R., 2002, The Curse of Non-Investment Grade Countries, *Journal of Development Economics* 69, 423–449.

Shen, P., and R. M. Starr, 2002, Market-Makers' Supply and Pricing of Financial Market Liquidity, *Economics Letters* 76, 53–58.

Watts, D. J., 1999, *Small Worlds: The Dynamics of Networks between Order and Randomness* (Princeton University Press, Princeton, NJ).

# Part III

# Fiscal Policy in Currency Unions

ELSEVIER        European Economic Review 39 (1995) 253–274

EUROPEAN
ECONOMIC
REVIEW

# Fiscal flows in the United States and Canada: Lessons for monetary union in Europe ☆

Tamim Bayoumi *, Paul R. Masson

*International Monetary Fund, Research Department Washington, DC 20431, USA*

Received June 1992, final version received April 1993

## Abstract

Regional flows of federal taxes and transfers within the United States and Canada are used to analyze long-term fiscal flows (the redistributive element) and short-term responses to regional business cycles (the stabilization element). In the United States, long-run flows amount to 22 cents in the dollar while the stabilization effect is 31 cents in the dollar. In Canada the redistributive effect is larger (39 cents) and the stabilization effect smaller (17 cents). Federal flows appears to depend on the institutional structure of the country concerned; however, in both countries the redistributive element is considerably larger than the amounts involved in the EC Structural Funds program. As for stabilization, national fiscal policies in the EC appear to have been as effective as federal governments in the United States and Canada in cushioning shocks to incomes.

*Keywords:* Fiscal policy; European Monetary Union

*JEL classification:* H11, H23, H77

☆ We are grateful to Andy Atkeson for the U.S. data, to Youkyong Kwon for research assistance, and to Barry Eichengreen, Daniel Gros, Stephen Hall, Bruce Montador, Jean Pisani-Ferry, Steven Poloz, Jürgen von Hagen, and two anonymous referees for discussion and comments. Part of this work was done while Tamim Bayoumi was visiting the Bank of England, whose support he gratefully acknowledges. The views expressed here are personal to the authors and do not represent those of the International Monetary Fund.

* Corresponding author.

254         *T. Bayoumi, P.R. Masson / European Economic Review 39 (1995) 253–274*

# 1. Introduction

The Maastricht Treaty on Economic and Monetary Union (EMU) provides for the establishment of a common currency area among EC countries, but not a common fiscal policy. Some have argued (notably, Sala-i-Martin and Sachs, 1992) that a community-wide tax and transfer system would be desirable in order to cushion asymmetric shocks, since member countries in a monetary union are not able to use the exchange rate instrument for that purpose. Indeed, according to those authors, such a federal system may be essential for the survival of EMU. [1] Sala-i-Martin and Sachs estimate that federal taxes and transfers in the United States offset 30–35 percent of deviations of per capita income from the national average. In contrast, the EC currently has no fiscal mechanisms at the Community level for offsetting short-run, or cyclical, fluctuations – such as unemployment insurance or an EC-wide income tax. However, the Sala-i-Martin and Sachs analysis has not gone unchallenged. In particular, von Hagen (1992) estimates the income offset from federal taxes and transfers to be only 10 percent, making it a much less important factor in protecting against asymmetric shocks. Others have argued that even a modest EC budget could nevertheless finance a substantial cushioning of national shocks if it were properly designed (Italianer and Pisani-Ferry, 1992).

Another aspect of fiscal policy in a federal system is the capacity to make continuing income transfers from richer to poorer countries or regions. The role of such transfers varies. Regional transfers can, in principle, finance investment needed to promote the development of poorer parts of a monetary union, which might not be forthcoming in the absence of government intervention because of various market failures. Over time, productivity levels of residents of these regions would be raised toward the national average, and there would be convergence of living standards. Alternatively, income transfers may just supplement the income of those who have chosen to live in peripheral regions which have low productivity due to climatic or geographic disadvantages; in this case, income transfers may discourage labor mobility and convergence of productivity but be justified on equity grounds and because outmigration has social costs that are not incorporated in private decisions (Boadway and Flatters, 1982). The EC has acknowledged that there is a problem with respect to long-term regional income differentials, and has fashioned several programs aimed at reducing them. In particular, in 1988 the EC agreed to double the size of the transfers from 'structural funds' by 1992, [2] and the Maastricht Treaty provides for the establishment of a 'cohesion fund' to help

---

[1] There is a large literature on fiscal federalism. See, for example, Krasnik (1986), and Rosen (1986, 1988).

[2] See Gordon (1991) for a detailed description of the operation of these structural funds.

*T. Bayoumi, P.R. Masson / European Economic Review 39 (1995) 253–274*        255

poorer regions. Nevertheless, the size of these EC transfers is still quite limited compared to some federations. In Canada, for instance, the constitution explicitly grants to the federal government a responsibility for 'equalization' – transfers from rich to poor provinces in order to enable them to provide similar government services at similar tax rates.

This paper extends the existing literature in several respects. *First*, we supplement the U.S. data with data for Canada, another federation with a different division of powers between national and regional governments. *Second*, in analyzing their experience, we use both cross-sectional and time-series evidence, in order to distinguish between redistribution and stabilization. It is important to attempt to distinguish empirically the two functions (see EC Commission, 1977, 1990; von Hagen, 1992); the results of Sala-i-Martin and Sachs (1992) however combine the two. *Third*, we decompose the effect of the federal system in a way that more accurately captures the respective roles of taxes and transfers. In contrast to Sala-i-Martin and Sachs (1992), we find a major stabilization role for transfers. *Fourth*, we go on to compare these estimates with estimates of the ability of EC countries to stabilize *national* per capita income relative to the EC average – in the absence of a federal system. Our estimates suggest that independent national fiscal policies are able to perform a similar degree of stabilization as operates within the two federations that we consider. Therefore, there we find no case on stabilization grounds for an EC-wide fiscal policy.

As for the importance of redistribution, our cross-sectional estimates differ considerably between the United States and Canada. Given that the real effects of the choice of an exchange rate regime concern mainly short-run flexibility of relative wages and prices (including the real exchange rate), but not their long-run values, we see little reason to argue that redistribution must necessarily accompany monetary union. We see the differences between the United States and Canada as primarily the result of *political* choices, not economic necessities. [3] Nevertheless, we would argue that EC countries should address the precise form that economic union is intended to take, since other aspects of European integration (including EMU) are likely to lead to calls for greater 'solidarity' among member countries.

The plan of the paper is as follows. The next section considers how to measure the importance of redistribution and stabilization. Section 3 then looks at data for the United States and Canada, using cross-sectional regressions for long-run redistribution and time series regressions to uncover fiscal responses to short-term, cyclical fluctuations in personal income. In Section 4 the extent of stabilization accomplished by national governments in the EC is examined. Section 5 contains conclusions and implications.

---

[3] See also Masson and Mélitz (1991).

256        T. Bayoumi, P.R. Masson / European Economic Review 39 (1995) 253-274

## 2. Measuring redistribution and stabilization

### 2.1. Long-term redistribution

There are many reasons why a federal fiscal system may tend to support the relative income of poor regions and reduce that of rich regions. For example, to the extent that taxes are higher in regions with higher incomes, they will tend to equalize after-tax incomes across regions. Businesses also pay taxes which are likely to be related to income. Similarly, to the extent that poor regions are in more social need, their residents are more likely to receive personal transfer payments associated with the alleviation of poverty (such as social security payments). Finally the government may deliberately redistribute income for political reasons, such as social cohesion.

The importance of the redistributive flows can be measured by cross-sectional regressions which estimate the relationship between personal income after federal taxes and transfers and pretax personal income. [4] By using data averaged over long time periods, these regressions abstract from short-term cyclical factors. The regression coefficients obtained give a direct measure of the degree to which the federal tax system reduces inequalities in incomes. In addition, by running intermediate regressions it is possible to estimate the contribution of different elements in the fiscal system (such as the federal tax system, personal transfers, etc.) to the overall total.

The importance of federal fiscal flows in redistributing income across regions is estimated using cross-section regressions of the following form:

$$(Y - TAX + TRAN)_i / (Y - TAX + TRAN) = \alpha + \beta Y_i / Y + \epsilon_i, \qquad (1)$$

where $Y$ is per capita personal income before all federal taxes and transfers; $TAX$ and $TRAN$ are per capita federal taxes and transfers, respectively; and subscript $i$ refers to the individual states or provinces while unsubscripted variables indicate the national average. The equation measures the relationship between personal income before and after the influence of federal fiscal flows. The difference between the coefficient $\beta$ and unity represents the size of the offset to personal income caused by these flows. Hence, for example, a coefficient of 0.80 indicates that 80 percent of the initial differences in relative incomes remains after federal fiscal payments have been taken into account, i.e. that the federal government in the United States or Canada redistributes 20 cents of any dollar difference between richer and poorer states or provinces.

---

[4] Throughout, the definition of personal income has been adjusted to exclude federal transfer payments.

*T. Bayoumi, P.R. Masson / European Economic Review 39 (1995) 253–274* 257

## 2.2. Fiscal stabilization

The stabilization role of federal fiscal flows measures the impact of the federal fiscal system in response to temporary deviations in income from an underlying growth path, as opposed to redistribution, which involves flows associated with long-term income differentials. In the empirical results reported below, stabilization is captured by estimating time series models on data which are detrended by first-differencing in order to remove the low frequency fluctuations that are the basis for redistribution. [5] Dickey–Fuller tests indicate that the levels data are generally nonstationary whether or not a time trend is included, but that the first-differences are stationary.

The stabilization role was estimated using the following system of equations:

$$\Delta\{ ( Y - TAX + TRAN )_i / ( Y - TAX + TRAN )\}_t = \alpha_i + \beta_i \Delta\{Y_i/Y\}_t + \epsilon_{it},$$

$$(2)$$

where $i$ ranges over regions and $t$ over time. In order to limit the number of observations and to conform to other studies, regional data were used for the United States (using the eight regions defined by the U.S. Bureau of Economic Analysis) rather than the state-by-state data; for Canada data for the provinces were used. [6]

Our specification is somewhat different from the specification used in earlier work in this area (EC Commission, 1977; Sala-i-Martin and Sachs, 1992; von Hagen, 1992; Masson and Taylor, 1992). In these papers, regressions were run relating tax and transfer payments (including grants) to movements in pretax personal income (both measured relative to the national average). The elasticities from these regressions were then used to estimate the size of the stabilization effects upon income. The reasons for using our specification are twofold. First, it provides a more direct method of evaluating the overall effect of stabilization; rather than using auxiliary results to infer the effect, it is estimated directly. Second, the elasticities approach may well overstate the role of taxes in stabilization and understate the importance of transfers because of the role of the cycle.

---

[5] It could be argued that *redistribution* occurs also in response to high frequency fluctuations; however, the paper makes the identification assumption that the two roles can be distinguished as described.

[6] To the extent that the regional time series are co-integrated (as they should be if redistribution operates), it is arguable that an error correction mechanism should be added to the estimating equation, in which case both redistribution and stabilization could be estimated from the time-series regression. Experiments with this type of functional form provided similar results to Eq. (2) on the first-differenced variables, while the long-run coefficients were not well determined. Hence the separate cross-section and time-series results are reported.

258            *T. Bayoumi, P.R. Masson / European Economic Review 39 (1995) 253–274*

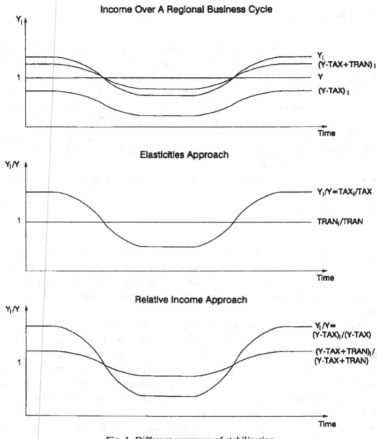

Fig. 1. Different measures of stabilization.

*Notes:* Assumptions: $TAX_i = tY_i$; $TRAN_i = TRAN$; subscripts represent regional per capita values.

This last point is best illustrated with an example. [7] Consider an economy with a large number of identical regions where the federal government levies a national income tax and provides regional transfers. We will assume that the tax is proportional to income and that the transfer payments are defined at a fixed per capita level, independent of the level of activity. The first panel in Fig. 1 shows the path of federal taxes and transfers over a regional business cycle. As activity

---

[7] The example we use involves changes over time. However, it is easy to see that the same arguments operate in cross-sectional comparisons.

T. Bayoumi, P.R. Masson / European Economic Review 39 (1995) 253–274          259

relative to the national aggregate falls, tax payments are reduced by the same percentage while transfer payments remain at their former level; in the upswing the opposite happens. Clearly, in this economy it is the federal transfer payments which are providing insurance against the regional cycle, since tax payments simply mirror the overall cycle.

The next panel shows how this stabilization would be estimated using the elasticities approach adopted by other authors. Per capita regional tax payments $(TAX_i)$ as a ratio to national per capita tax payments $(TAX)$ vary with the cycle, while the same ratio for transfers $(TRAN_i/TRAN)$ does not. As a result, the elasticities approach would attribute any stabilization that occurs to the tax system, not to transfers. The third panel illustrates the approach adopted in this paper. It shows the ratio of regional and national incomes, adjusted for taxes $((Y - TAX)_i/(Y - TAX))$, and adjusted for taxes plus transfers $((Y - TAX + TRAN)_i/(Y - TAX + TRAN))$. The post-tax income ratio varies in exactly the same way as the pre-tax ratio, while the ratio including transfers has a smaller cyclical variation. As a result, the estimation based on these ratios correctly ascribes the stabilizing effects of the fiscal system to federal transfers, not to the tax system. This illustrates the advantages of our approach as compared with the elasticities approach (both give the same overall effect from taxes and transfers together). However, while we believe our approach to be superior, there are inevitable ambiguities involved in ascribing parts of the overall stabilization effect to any particular part of the fiscal system, because spending and raising revenue cannot be divorced (on the assumption that the government must satisfy an intertemporal budget constraint).

## 3. Estimates for the United States and Canada

It is important to compare the United States to another federal system in order to gauge the generality of any conclusions. Canada is a good benchmark, because there are important differences with the United States. On the one hand, Canada has a considerably looser federation than the United States, and its federal taxes make up only about half the percentage of income that they do in the United States. [8] Compared to U.S. states, most of which have balanced budget provisions, [9] Canadian provinces have considerable fiscal freedom, which they can, and do, use to operate their own counter-cyclical policy. On the other hand, the Canadian

---

[8] In Canada, though personal income tax rates are set by the provinces, taxes are based on federal taxable income and are collected by the federal government for all provinces except Québec. Hence federal tax changes induce automatic changes in provincial government revenues, unless there are discretionary changes in provincial tax rates or tax credits.

[9] Advisory Council on Intergovernmental Relations (1991) has details of these constraints. All states except Vermont have some type of formal balanced budget requirement. For an analysis of the effects of these constraints on states' borrowing costs, see Goldstein and Woglom (1992).

260        *T. Bayoumi, P.R. Masson / European Economic Review 39 (1995) 253–274*

Table 1
Redistribution through federal fiscal flows: cross-sectional regressions for the United States and Canada [a]

| Adjustment to income | United States (1969–86) | | Canada (1965–88) | |
|---|---|---|---|---|
| | $\beta$ | $R^2$ | $\beta$ | $R^2$ |
| Taxes | 0.934 | 0.995 | 0.976 | 0.996 |
| | (0.010) | | (0.021) | |
| Taxes and social | 0.923 | 0.969 | – | – |
| insurance | (0.024) | | | |
| Taxes, social insurance | 0.824 | 0.944 | 0.824 | 0.996 |
| and transfers | (0.029) | | (0.018) | |
| Taxes, social insurance, | 0.781 | 0.945 | 0.608 | 0.987 |
| transfers and grants | (0.028) | | (0.025) | |

[a] Data are averages over the relevant time periods. Number of observations: 48 for the United States, 10 for Canada. See appendix for data definitions. Standard errors are in parentheses.

welfare system is more highly developed, and the Canadian constitution gives the federal government a responsibility for 'equalization' transfers to poorer provinces in order to enable them to provide similar levels of government services at similar tax rates. Hence, while the stabilization role of the Canadian federal government in the economy may be smaller, it may have a more important role in the redistribution of regional incomes. The Appendix gives a summary of the data, indicating the size of the various flows.

### 3.1. Redistribution

Table 1 shows the results from estimating Eq. (1) using data averaged over the longest periods for which the relevant variables were available. The first column indicates how the dependent variable is calculated, in particular, what adjustment was made to the pretax personal income data. Hence, the first row shows the results when pretax income is adjusted by federal taxes, the second the results when adjusted by both federal taxes and social insurance payments, etc. The regressions were estimated using ordinary least squares on data for the continental 48 states and the 10 Canadian provinces.

### 3.1.1. United States

The bottom row of Table 1 shows the results when all federal fiscal flows are included. For the United States, the coefficient on pretax income, $\beta$, is estimated at 0.781, with a standard error of 0.028. This indicates that, on average, U.S. federal fiscal flows reduce long-term income inequalities by some 22 cents in the dollar. Fig. 2, panel A, shows a scatter plot of the raw data, with pre-tax relative personal income on the vertical axis and personal income adjusted for all federal flows on the horizontal axis. It is clear from the chart that there is an extremely close connection between the two series, which is essentially linear. This explains

*T. Bayoumi, P.R. Masson / European Economic Review 39 (1995) 253–274* 261

## (A) Redistribution Across US States

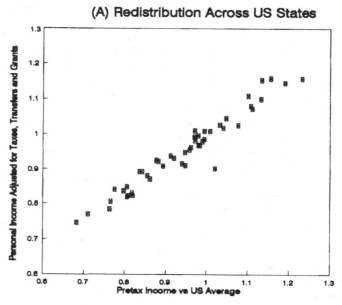

## (B) Redistribution Across Canadian Provinces

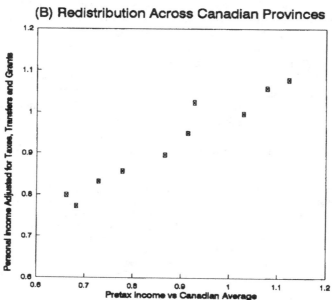

Fig. 2. Federal fiscal flows and personal income.

the relatively low standard error on the estimate of $\beta$ and good fit of the equation, as indicated by the $R^2$ statistics.

The regression results reported in the first three rows of the Table give an indication of the relative importance of the individual elements in the overall redistributive process. Since these elements (federal taxes, social insurance payments, personal transfers, and grants to state and local government) are added in successively, the difference between the coefficient estimates indicates the effect of including that fiscal flow in the regression.

All parts of the U.S. federal fiscal system have a role in redistributing income, as can be seen from the steady reduction in the estimates of $\beta$ as one moves down the Table. The largest roles in this redistribution are due to federal taxes and transfers (which reduce inequalities by some $6\frac{1}{2}$ cents and 10 cents in the dollar, respectively), with the contribution from federal grants being 4 cents, and social insurance payments contributing a relatively small 1 cent in the dollar. The results accord with intuition; for example the relatively small role for social insurance payments presumably reflects the flat rate nature of this payment, as opposed to the progressive nature of the federal income tax. [10] Given the relatively small role played by federal grants in the redistributive process, the issue of whether they should be interpreted as giving support for personal income or not does not have a large effect on the results. [11] Even if all grants were excluded from the analysis, the redistributive effect would still be 18 cents in the dollar.

The results in the left panel of Table 1 are for the full period 1969–86. As documented by other authors (U.S. Department of Commerce, 1984; Barro and Sala-i-Martin, 1992), this period has seen a significant reduction in regional income differentials in the United States. It is therefore of some interest to see whether the redistributive elements of the fiscal system have changed in tandem with this narrowing of regional inequalities. [12] However, cross-sectional regressions using data averages for three sub-periods; 1963–69, 1970–79, and 1980–86 (not reported) give results for the subperiods that are relatively similar, with no evidence of a statistically significant shift in the coefficients. There does appear to be a tendency for the role of U.S. federal transfers to have increased in importance, from 8 cents in the dollar in the 1960s to nearer 12 cents in the dollar in the

---

[10] The EC Commission (1977, Vol. 2, p. 130) estimates the level of redistribution in the United States to be slightly higher than our estimates (23–28 cents in the dollar); the main difference appears to be the larger estimated role for personal transfers, which they estimate to contribute 12–14 cents in the dollar, as opposed to 10 cents in our analysis. The significant role played by transfers and grants in the equation is noteworthy, since other empirical results (Sala-i-Martin and Sachs, 1992; von Hagen, 1992) did not find a significant role for these elements.

[11] Data on total government expenditure were also included in a variant of the regression, but the results suggested that these other government expenditures play no systematic role in redistributing income.

[12] Of course, there have also been changes in the tax and transfer system over this period, hence the results may also reflect changes in discretionary behavior.

*T. Bayoumi, P.R. Masson / European Economic Review 39 (1995) 253–274*        263

1980s. Overall, however, it appears that the redistributive effect of the federal fiscal system has stayed relatively constant over time.

### 3.1.2. Canada

Results for Canada are shown in the right panel of Table 1, using data on personal income, personal direct taxes, federal transfers to persons, and grants to other levels of government. [13] The basic data are given in panel B of Fig. 1, which shows a scatter plot of relative personal incomes before and after personal taxes, transfers, and grants. Panel B indicates that, as is the case for the U.S. data in panel A, there is a close (essentially linear) relationship between the variables.

These regression results also indicate that all of the elements of the fiscal system produce significant redistribution. Direct taxes provide an estimated 2 cents in the dollar of redistribution, somewhat smaller than in the United States. Transfers provide around 15 cents in the dollar of redistribution, and grants 22 cents, much larger than in the United States, presumably reflecting more highly developed social services and the effect of the equalization grants. At 39 cents in the dollar, the total effect in Canada is almost double that in the United States. The large role for federal grants to provincial and local governments in this regression is particularly notable since it contrasts with the United States.

We checked these results using data on gross provincial product and broader measures of taxes and transfers that include those paid and received by businesses. The estimated redistributive effect of the Canadian fiscal system was somewhat smaller (30 cents). The reduction is broad based, in that the contribution of all of the components of the fiscal system shrink. Since the main difference between personal incomes and GDP is corporate retained earnings, and there is no clear reason why the government should wish to redistribute such income, this rescaling is to be expected. Personal incomes make up some 75–80 percent of total product in Canada, hence these results are broadly consistent with the view that the parts of the fiscal system which are not associated with the personal sector have no role in redistributing income. [14]

Results across different time periods (not reported) indicate that there is little difference in the extent of redistribution between the 1970s and the 1980s; however the data do show somewhat lower levels of redistribution in the 1960s (28 cents as opposed to 41 cents in the 1970s and 44 cents in the 1980s). This rise over time is almost entirely attributable to the larger role of transfer payments in

[13] As in the case of the U.S. data, the use of data in total grants will overstate the overall effect on personal incomes, since not all grants are directed at the personal sector. Social insurance payments are not available separately, and they are included with transfers, except for public pension plan contributions and benefits which are excluded.

[14] These estimates are very similar to the redistributive effect reported in EC Commission (1977) of 28–32 cents in the dollar, although the role of transfers is larger, and that of government grants smaller than in this earlier study.

264          *T. Bayoumi, P.R. Masson / European Economic Review 39 (1995) 253–274*

Table 2
Stabilization through federal fiscal flows: Time-series regressions for the United States and Canada [a]

| Adjustment to income | United States (1965–86) | | | Canada (1967–88) | | |
|---|---|---|---|---|---|---|
| | $\beta$ | $R^2$ | DW | $\beta$ | $R^2$ | DW |
| Taxes | 0.927 | 0.90– | 1.60– | 0.966 | 0.94– | 1.17– |
| | (0.011) | 0.98 | 2.71 | (0.010) | 0.99 | 2.89 |
| Taxes and social | 0.914 | 0.85– | 1.69– | – | – | – |
| insurance | (0.014) | 0.97 | 2.66 | | | |
| Taxes, social insurance | 0.770 | 0.77– | 1.46– | 0.857 | 0.57– | 0.78– |
| and transfers | (0.015) | 0.97 | 2.99 | (0.012) | 0.98 | 1.90 |
| Taxes, social insurance, | 0.698 | 0.69– | 1.55– | 0.826 | 0.52– | 1.72– |
| transfers and grants[b] | (0.018) | 0.96 | 2.81 | (0.022) | 0.96 | 2.34 |

[a] Estimated using three-stage least squares across 8 U.S. regions and 9 Canadian provinces. See Appendix for data definitions. $R^2$ and DW are given as ranges across regions and provinces. The instruments used were a constant term, a time trend, and the first lag of the change in pretax personal income for each region or province. Standard errors in parentheses.
[b] Sample period is 1971–86 for the United States, 1967–88 for Canada.

redistribution in the 1970s and 1980s, as a result of the general expansion of federally-sponsored social programs over this period.

## 3.2. Stabilization

### 3.2.1. United States

Table 2 reports the results from estimating Eq. (2). The equations were estimated using three-stage least squares since there is the possibility that changes in fiscal variables will themselves affect pretax incomes by stimulating the regional economy; [15] the instruments used were a constant, a time trend and the first lags of the change in the regional pretax income series. The value of $\beta$ is constrained to be equal across regions, but the constant terms (the $\alpha_i$'s) are allowed to vary across regions. [16]

Turning first to the regressions involving only taxes, the first row reports a point estimate of $\beta$ of 0.927, indicating that for each one dollar that pre-tax

---

[15] This problem does not arise in the cross-sectional regressions since the data are averages over very long time periods.

[16] The estimates of the $\alpha_i$'s, which are not reported, were all insignificant in this and all other regressions run using this first-difference formulation. (Since the $\alpha_i$'s can vary across regions, there is no econometric problem associated with the fact that the average across regions equals the national figure, except for possible efficiency gains from imposing the constraint. However, standard errors of our estimates of beta are small.)

*T. Bayoumi, P.R. Masson / European Economic Review 39 (1995) 253–274*          265

incomes change, post-tax incomes vary by only 93 cents, hence taxes stabilize incomes by 7 cents in the dollar, almost identical to the estimate of the redistributive effect from the cross-sectional regression. The descriptive statistics for the individual equations are satisfactory here and for the other regressions; $R^2$ values indicate that a high proportion of the variance is explained by the regression, while the Durbin–Watson statistics do not indicate any problem of misspecification. Tests using the QLR statistic (Gallant and Jorgenson, 1979) indicate that the constraint that the coefficient $\beta$ is the same across regions cannot be rejected for any of the regressions.

When the dependent variable is adjusted for taxes, personal transfers, and grants, the constrained coefficient takes a value of 0.698. Thus, stabilization of short-term fluctuations rises to 30 cents in the dollar, larger than the 22 cent estimate of the redistributive effects provided by the cross-sectional regressions, reflecting the fact that personal transfers and grants vary more in response to short-term fluctuations than to long-term income differentials. [17] Comparing the results with those from Table 1, it can be seen that personal transfers play a larger role in stabilization of short-term economic fluctuations than they do in reducing long-term income differentials, while the role of U.S. federal taxes, social insurance payments, and grants appears similar across the two sets of regressions.

Comparing the results reported here with those reported in earlier studies using U.S. data by Sala-i-Martin and Sachs (SS) and von Hagen (vH), two features stand out. In terms of the *size* of the stabilization effects, our estimate of 30 cents in the dollar is within the range suggested by SS, who estimated a value of 30–35 cents, but very different from the estimate of under 10 cents in the dollar produced by vH. [18] We are uncertain as to why our results are so greatly at variance with vH, except that he used a different data set and estimation procedure. [19] In terms of the *composition* of the stabilization effects, the results in this paper are radically different from both of the earlier studies, which concluded that almost all of the stabilization comes from the tax system and very little from transfers. Our results indicate that transfers are, if anything, the largest component in stabilization. As discussed above, the elasticity procedure used by both SS and vH may have tended to overstate the role of tax payments.

---

[17] Estimates of $\beta$ from the individual regions indicate some heterogeneity across regions. In contrast to the results using only taxes, these coefficient estimates tend to be larger than the constrained coefficients (again the restriction of equality cannot be rejected, however).

[18] The EC Commission (1977, Vol. 1, p. 35) quotes a figure of 1/2 to 2/3 as the regional stabilization effect in the U.K. and France, but no further details are given.

[19] VH used state-by-state data over a rather shorter time period (1981–86). In addition, he excluded social security payments, used gross state product as his activity variable, and estimated a slightly different functional form than SS.

266          *T. Bayoumi, P.R. Masson / European Economic Review 39 (1995) 253–274*

### 3.2.2. Canada

The right panel of Table 2 presents estimates of the federal stabilization role in Canada. [20] In contrast to the United States, the personal income regressions for Canada indicate that when taxes, transfers, and grants are included, federal fiscal flows have a smaller role in the stabilization of personal income than they have in its long-term redistribution. At 17 cents in the dollar, the overall stabilization role of the federal government is considerably smaller than in the United States. The descriptive statistics indicate a good fit and few signs of autocorrelation, except possibly in the case of the regressions net of taxes and personal transfer payments.

## 4. Redistribution and stabilization in the EC

It is useful to compare the results for the United States and Canada with redistribution and stabilization across EC states. Redistribution across EC states is primarily carried out through the EC budget. [21] The small size of this budget (EC budgetary receipts were 1.1 percent of EC GDP in 1992), and the wide differences in income levels across EC countries, means that the potential for redistribution across EC states is small. It is sufficient to examine the data in order to get a rough estimate of the redistributive impact of the EC budget; in any case, cross-sectional regressions of the type used across U.S. and Canadian regions are unlikely to produce accurate estimates for such small flows.

One part of the EC budget which is clearly directly aimed at redistribution across states is the EC Structural Funds program, which aims to transfer resources to regions whose incomes are persistently below the EC average. Gordon (1991) using pre-1989 data estimates that a $1 fall in a member state's per capita income increases Structural Fund transfers by about $0.01. Doubling this estimate to account for the increase in the Structural Funds, implemented over 1989–93, and allowing for induced changes in EC taxes, Gordon comes up with an estimate of $0.03. The European Council recently decided a 41 percent increase in resources for structural policies, including the Cohesion Fund created in the context of the Maastricht Treaty on EMU, to take place over 1993–99 (EC Commission, 1993). However, even on the most generous of estimates of the EC transfers, the level of

---

[20] Regressions in which all the coefficients were allowed to vary across regions produced broadly similar results, although in this and other regressions the coefficients for individual provinces showed a fairly wide range of values. In Table 2 only data for the 9 largest provinces were used; Prince Edward Island, with a population of only about 100,000, disproportionately influenced the results, and was dropped from the sample. An alternative would be to use weighted least squares, with weights reflecting population.

[21] In theory, redistribution could occur through direct revenue sharing agreements across member states, of the type that operate between German Länder, but there are no proposals for such a system in the EC.

*T. Bayoumi, P.R. Masson / European Economic Review 39 (1995) 253–274*          267

Table 3
Stabilization across the EC through national fiscal flows: time-series regressions [a]

| Adjustment to income | Five EC Countries (1972–89) | | |
|---|---|---|---|
| | $\beta$ | $R^2$ | DW |
| Taxes | 0.896 (0.134) | 0.55–0.81 | 1.25–2.39 |
| Taxes and transfers | 0.692 (0.114) | 0.45–0.83 | 1.32–2.47 |

[a] Estimated using three-stage least squares across 5 EC countries; Germany, France, the United Kingdom, the Netherlands and Belgium. $R^2$ and DW are given as ranges across all countries. The instruments used were a constant term, a time trend, and the first lag of the change in pretax personal income for each country. Standard errors in parentheses.

redistribution in the EC is clearly nowhere near the levels we have estimated for either the U.S. or Canada, nor is it likely to approach them in the future. [22] Another important part of the EC budget is the Common Agricultural Policy (CAP), but this program is not designed to redistribute toward poorer areas, but rather to support a particular sector; consequently, some of the richer countries (France, Denmark) are among the larger beneficiaries.

Unlike redistribution, which requires cooperation across countries, stabilization of cyclical movements in income across EC states can be carried out at the national level. Notwithstanding the EC growth initiative announced at the December 1992 Edinburgh summit (EIB loans for infrastructure investment, and increased national spending, totalling ECU 35 billion), the EC has virtually no stabilization role. In order to measure the level of national stabilization, annual data were collected on personal income, taxes, transfers and population for Germany, France, the United Kingdom, the Netherlands and Belgium from the *OECD National Accounts* for the period 1970–89. [23] Per capita levels of personal income before and after taxes and transfers in dollars were then calculated, using PPP exchange rates against the dollar obtained from the same source, and divided by the average per capita level for all five countries to obtain a similar data set to that used for the U.S. and Canada.

Before reporting the estimated levels of stabilization it is important to note a difference between the data for EC countries and the data for U.S. and Canadian regions. Changes in federal fiscal policies have a limited impact on data for the U.S. and Canadian regions, measured relative to the national aggregate, since all

---

[22] Bureau and Champsaur (1992).

[23] These were the only countries for which the full data set could be obtained. The tax and transfer data refer to all levels of government since it was not possible to distinguish between central and local government.

of the regions in each country face the same policy change. This is not true for the EC data since each country operates an independent fiscal policy, and hence changes in the fiscal system in one country do not reflect a common EC policy change. This has two implications for the results. First, it is essential to use instrumental variable techniques in order to eliminate the endogenous impact of discretionary changes in national fiscal policies. Second, the coefficient estimates for the EC will inevitably be less precise than those for the U.S. or Canada due to the addition of noise in the data caused by differential changes in national fiscal policies.

Table 3 shows the results from estimating Eq. (2) across these five countries using three stage least squares. [24] The estimate of $\beta$ for taxes and transfers together is 0.69, implying that, on average, taxes and transfers reduce fluctuations by 31 cents in the dollar in these countries. This is very similar to the estimate obtained for the United States, and higher than that found for Canada. The coefficient on the regression when income is only adjusted for direct taxes is 0.90, implying that 10 cents of the stabilization comes from the direct tax system, with the other 20 cents coming from transfers. This ratio of two-to-one in the relative impact of taxes and transfers is very similar to the results found in Table 2 for the United States and Canada.

The cross-equation restriction of equality across the countries cannot be rejected in either regression. This partly reflects the relative imprecision of the estimates of $\beta$; the standard errors associated with the coefficients are both over 0.1, much higher than those associated with the equivalent U.S. and Canadian regressions. Despite this imprecision, the point estimate associated with income adjusted for taxes and transfers is significantly different from unity (the value at which no stabilization would occur) at the 1 percent significance level. National fiscal authorities create similar levels of stabilization across the EC to that produced by the U.S. and Canadian federal governments across regions of those countries. We have, of course, left out from the analyses of the United States and Canada the stabilization roles of states and provinces, which are needed to make them fully comparable to those for the EC. However, our purpose is more limited, namely to show that the *federal* stabilization role in the United States and Canada can be carried out by EC national governments – a fortiori, the latter can also exercise the fiscal powers of states and provinces.

## 5. Conclusions

This paper has investigated the role of federal fiscal flows in the United States and Canada in reducing long-term income differentials across regions (the redis-

---

[24] As with the earlier estimates, the instruments were a constant, a time trend and the first lags of the change in relative personal income in each country.

*T. Bayoumi, P.R. Masson / European Economic Review 39 (1995) 253–274* 269

tributive role) and in reducing short-term regional business cycle fluctuations (the stabilization role). The former effects are investigated using cross-sectional regressions, the latter using time-series estimates. The ability of EC countries to perform these roles is then discussed.

The results indicate that the size of federal fiscal transfers varies with the type of function (stabilization or redistribution) and across countries. In the United States, where there is no federal mandate to equalize per capita incomes, redistributive flows from all federal sources [25] amount to around 22 cents in the dollar, while stabilization flows are somewhat larger at around 30 cents in the dollar. In Canada, where the federal government is a smaller factor in the economy but has certain responsibilities to 'equalize' the levels of government services provided across regions, the redistribution flows are around double those in the United States (39 cents in the dollar) but the stabilization flows are smaller (17 cents in the dollar). Taxes and transfers both play important roles in these flows. In the EC, there is no 'fiscal federalism'; the EC budget is small and redistribution is limited. However, national governments carry out stabilization of personal income using domestic fiscal instruments to an extent comparable to that in the United States and Canada.

These results suggest three considerations that may be relevant in the context of EMU. First, the size of the federal flows varies significantly depending on the institutional structure of the country concerned, so that neither the United States nor Canada provides a 'blueprint' for the EC. In Canada, where the individual provinces have more fiscal independence than U.S. states, the flows related to federal stabilization are smaller. Similarly, the relative size of redistributive flows appears to reflect the differing roles of the two federal governments; the Canadian federal government does considerably more to equalize long-term income differentials than the U.S. Government.

Second, the stabilization performed by national governments in the EC is comparable to that which occurs in the U.S. or Canadian federal fiscal systems. Therefore, there does not seem to be a case for a federal system among EC countries on stabilization grounds, unless increasing integration limits their ability to carry out stabilization policies (for instance, because of increasing tax harmonization and factor mobility), an issue which is beyond the scope of the paper.

Third, both federations however have significant redistributive functions. Even in the case of the United States, where there is no specific requirement for the federal government to equalize incomes, the federal fiscal system reduces long-term income differentials by 22 cents out of every dollar, which is considerably larger than the amounts involved in the EC Structural and Cohesion Funds. Clearly it is a political choice as to how much redistribution should occur across countries, rather than an economic necessity related to monetary union. However, political pres-

---

[25] Taxes, transfers and grants to state and local governments.

sures for such redistribution may grow in the EC in response other forces leading to increased integration, in particular the Single Market and EMU itself.

## Appendix: Fiscal flows in the United States and Canada

### A.1. U.S. data

Detailed data on personal incomes by state are available on an annual basis from the Commerce Department. In addition to pre-tax personal incomes, it is also possible to get data on payments of direct federal taxes and social insurance payments. [26] These make up the vast majority of federal tax revenues. The two important sources which are missing are corporate tax payments and indirect taxes and excise duties, which make up some 20 percent of federal revenues. In addition, the personal income tables provide data on personal transfer payments. [27] Unfortunately, these flows are reported in terms of function (e.g. unemployment compensation, medical benefits, etc.) rather than source (federal, state, or local), hence the level of federal transfers has to be constructed by making assumptions as to the source of the payments. [28]

Finally, data on federal grants to state and local government were also collected. Clearly, not all government grants are directed at the personal sector, and hence the inclusion of all grants may imply some overestimation of the objectives of the federal government in redistributing personal income. [29] A more accurate method of measuring the impact of federal grants might involve deflating federal grants by state product rather than personal income. However, since personal incomes make up some 80 percent of state product, this bias is unlikely to be large, and hence no adjustment was made. The data on personal taxes, social insurance and transfers are available from 1963–86, while those on government grants are only available from 1969. Transfers and grants together make up some 65 percent of U.S. government expenditure, with the balance going to wages and salaries and government procurement. Data on federal wages and salaries and procurement by state were collected from 1981 onwards.

---

[26] Von Hagen (1992), in a similar study, excludes social security payments on the grounds that they redistribute incomes over time as well as across regions. Since they play little role in the empirical results, we do not believe that our choice to include such payments is critical to our results.

[27] Transfers to other sectors and interest payments on the national debt are not included in the figures.

[28] Two estimates of federal transfers were constructed: a 'broad' measure which was made up of all government transfers except for state and local government payments for unemployment and retirement, and a 'narrow' definition which summed federal payments for civilian retirement, unemployment and education with total payments for old age, medical benefits and veterans' affairs, all of which are dominated by the federal government. In practice, the results using the two measures were virtually identical, and hence only results using the 'broad' measure are reported.

[29] Though such grants may not be targeted at redistribution, they may have that effect in practice.

*T. Bayoumi, P.R. Masson / European Economic Review 39 (1995) 253–274* 271

The time-series regressions use data aggregated into regions. The regions are those defined by the Bureau of Economic Analysis (BEA), namely New England, the Mid East, Great Lakes, Plains, South East, South West, Rocky Mountains and Far West.

## A.2. Canadian data

Data on personal incomes, [30] federal personal direct taxes, federal transfers to persons, and federal government grants to provincial and local governments were collected for each of the 10 Canadian provinces. [31] In addition to these data from the personal income accounts, as a check, data were also collected on total provincial output (GDP), total federal taxes (the sum of federal personal and business taxes, both direct and indirect), total federal transfers (the sum of federal personal and business transfers), and grants to other levels of government. These data allow a broader estimate of the overall impact of the federal fiscal system to be calculated, including direct effects on both the personal and business sectors and indirect effects on them through grants to provinces and municipalities that allow equalization of provincial taxes and services. [32] However, since we are primarily interested in how personal income is affected, we do not report regression results using these measures in the tables, but only refer to them in passing in the text.

## A.3. Comparison of the two countries' data

Table A.1 compares the structure of the tax and transfer systems in the U.S. and Canada. It reports payments of taxes and levels of transfers as a percentage of GDP at five-year intervals starting in 1965, differentiating between federal fiscal flows and those flows to or from other levels of government. [33]

---

[30] Adjusted to exclude federal transfers, as in the case of the U.S. data.

[31] The data correspond to those collected for the U.S. states, except that social insurance payments are not reported separately. Employer and employee contributions to public service pensions plans and to unemployment insurance are included with direct taxes, while federal transfers to persons include unemployment insurance benefits, public service pensions, old age security, and miscellaneous other transfers. However, Canada and Québec pension plan (CPP/QPP) contributions and benefits are excluded from our data. Moreover, interest payments made by the federal government to persons are not available on a provincial breakdown, and are also excluded.

[32] However, we continue to leave out CPP/QPP payments and receipts and federal debt interest payments on the grounds that they do not involve deliberate federal policy either to stabilize cyclical income fluctuations or to redistribute income across provinces, though they may have the latter effect in practice, increasing our already large estimate of redistribution in Canada.

[33] The data come from national accounts sources. For Canada they are identical with the provincial data used in the estimation, while in the case of the United States there are some differences since the personal income accounts use slightly different definitions of some variables.

Table A.1
U.S. and Canada: Taxes and transfers (as a percentage of GDP)[a]

| | Direct taxes | | | | | Indirect taxes | | Net transfers (excluding interest payments) | | | | |
|---|---|---|---|---|---|---|---|---|---|---|---|---|
| | Paid by persons | | Paid by business | | Social insurance | Federal | Other | Federal to persons | Federal to business | Other to persons | Other to business | Federal to other |
| | Federal | Other | Federal | Other | | | | | | | | |
| *United States of America* | | | | | | | | | | | | |
| 1965 | 7.6 | 1.2 | 4.1 | 0.3 | 3.8 | 2.4 | 6.6 | 4.3 | 0.5 | 1.3 | −0.4 | 1.6 |
| 1970 | 9.1 | 1.7 | 3.0 | 0.4 | 5.2 | 1.9 | 7.4 | 6.1 | 0.6 | 2.0 | −0.4 | 2.4 |
| 1975 | 7.9 | 2.0 | 2.7 | 0.5 | 6.4 | 1.5 | 7.3 | 9.3 | 0.4 | 2.5 | −0.3 | 3.4 |
| 1980 | 9.5 | 2.1 | 2.6 | 0.5 | 6.9 | 1.5 | 6.4 | 9.1 | 0.4 | 2.4 | −0.2 | 3.3 |
| 1985 | 8.5 | 2.3 | 1.9 | 0.5 | 7.7 | 1.5 | 6.7 | 9.1 | 0.5 | 2.5 | −0.3 | 2.5 |
| 1990 | 8.7 | 2.5 | 2.0 | 0.4 | 8.1 | 1.2 | 6.8 | 9.0 | 0.4 | 3.0 | −0.4 | 2.4 |
| *Canada* | | | | | | | | | | | | |
| 1965 | 5.8 | 1.9 | 3.8 | 0.9 | – | 5.6 | 7.7 | 4.0 | 0.8 | 1.9 | 0.2 | 2.5 |
| 1970 | 8.3 | 3.4 | 3.4 | 0.9 | 1.5 | 4.5 | 8.9 | 4.6 | 0.8 | 3.2 | 0.3 | 3.8 |
| 1975 | 8.9 | 4.1 | 4.4 | 1.2 | 1.6 | 4.6 | 7.8 | 6.2 | 2.1 | 3.3 | 0.7 | 4.5 |
| 1980 | 7.6 | 5.1 | 3.9 | 1.2 | 1.8 | 4.0 | 7.5 | 5.3 | 2.1 | 3.7 | 0.9 | 4.1 |
| 1985 | 8.9 | 5.6 | 3.3 | 0.8 | 2.1 | 4.0 | 8.3 | 6.6 | 2.0 | 4.1 | 1.3 | 4.5 |
| 1990 | 10.9 | 7.2 | 1.6 | 0.8 | 2.3 | 3.9 | 9.0 | 6.3 | 0.9 | 4.2 | 1.1 | 4.0 |

[a] For Canada, social insurance payments are defined as the sum of payments to the federal and Quebec pension funds. For the U.S, the data comes from the national accounts, which differ slightly in terms of definition and coverage from the regional data used in the estimation.
*Source:* U.S. and Canadian National Accounts

*T. Bayoumi, P.R. Masson / European Economic Review 39 (1995) 253–274*     273

Comparing the data for the two countries, some differences in the fiscal system are clear. Focusing first on direct taxes, the most obvious differences are the importance of social insurance payments in the U.S. fiscal system and the relative importance of taxes paid to other levels of government in the Canadian system. The Canadian system also relies more heavily on indirect taxes than the U.S. system, particularly at the federal level. Turning to transfer payments, the Canadian data show a much larger role for transfers from the federal government to other levels of government than do the U.S. data, presumably reflecting the role of the federal government in equating provision of local services. In addition, as with direct taxes, non-federal levels of government play a larger role in making transfer payments to the private sector in Canada.

## References

Advisory Council on Intergovernmental Relations, 1991, Significant features of fiscal federalism: Vol. 1.: Budget processes and tax systems (ACIR, Washington, DC).

Barro, Robert and Xavier Sala-i-Martin, 1992, Convergence, Journal of Political Economy, Vol. 100, no. 2, 223–251.

Bayoumi, T. and B. Eichengreen, 1993, Shocking news about European Monetary Union, in: F. Giovannini and F. Torres, eds., The transition to economic and monetary union in Europe (Cambridge University Press, Cambridge).

Boadway, Robin and Frank Flatters, 1982, Efficiency and equalization payments in a federal system of government: A synthesis and extension of recent results, Canadian Journal of Economics 15, 613–623.

Bureau, Dominique and Paul Champsaur, 1992, Federalisme budgétaire et unification économique européenne, Observations et Diagnostics Economiques 40, April, 87–99.

Cohen, Daniel and Charles Wyplosz, 1989, The European Monetary Union: An agnostic evaluation, in: R. Bryant, D. Currie, J. Frenkel, P. Masson and R. Portes, eds., Macroeconomic policies in an interdependent world (International Monetary Fund, Washington, DC).

EC Commission, 1977, Report of the study group on the role of public finance in European integration, collection of studies, Economic and Financial Series, nos. A12/B13 (European Economic Community, Brussels).

EC Commission, 1990, One market, one money, European Economy, no. 44, Oct.

EC Commission, 1993, Annual report for 1993 (Commission of the European Communities, Brussels) Feb.

Gallant, A. Ronald and Dale Jorgenson, 1979, Statistical inference for a system of simultaneous, non-linear, implicit equations in the context of maximum likelihood estimation, Journal of Econometrics 11, 275–302.

Goldstein, Morris, and Geoffrey Woglom, 1992, Market-based fiscal discipline in monetary unions: Evidence from the U.S. municipal bond market, in: Matthew Canzoneri, Vittorio Grilli and Paul R. Masson, eds., Establishing a central bank: Issues in Europe and lessons from the U.S. (Cambridge University Press, Cambridge) 226–260.

Italianer, Alexander and Jean Pisani-Ferry, 1992, Systèmes budgétaires et amortissement des chocs régionaux: Implications pour l'Union économique et monétaire, Economic Prospective Internationale 51 (3rd Quarter), 49–69.

Kenen, Peter B., 1969, The theory of optimal currency areas: An eclectic view, in: R. Mundell and A. Swoboda, eds., Monetary problems of the international economy (University of Chicago Press, Chicago, IL).

Krasnick, Mark, 1986, Fiscal federalism (University of Toronto Press, Toronto).

Masson, Paul R. and Jacques Mélitz, 1991, Fiscal policy independence in a European Monetary Union, Open Economies Review 2, 113–136.

Masson, Paul R. and Mark P. Taylor, 1993, Common currency areas and currency unions: An analysis of the issues, Parts I and II, Journal of International and Comparative Economies 1. nos. 3–4, 231–250 and 265–294.

Rosen, Harvey S., ed., 1986, Studies in state and local public finance (University of Chicago Press, Chicago, IL).

Rosen, Harvey S., ed., 1988, Fiscal federalism: Quantitative studies (University of Chicago Press, Chicago, IL).

Sala-i-Martin, Xavier and Jeffrey Sachs, 1992, Fiscal federalism and optimum currency areas: Evidence for Europe from the United States, in: Matthew Canzoneri, Vittorio Grilli and Paul R. Masson, eds., Establishing a central bank: Issues in Europe and lessons from the U.S. (Cambridge University Press, Cambridge) 195–219.

U.S. Department of Commerce, 1984, State personal income: Estimates for 1929–1982 (USGPO, Washington, DC) Feb.

von Hagen, Jürgen, 1992, Fiscal arrangements in a monetary union: Evidence from the U.S., in: Don Fair and Christian de Boissieux, eds., Fiscal policy, taxes and the financial system in an increasingly integrated Europe (Kluwer, Deventer).

*The Economic Journal*, **108** ( *July*), 1026–1045. © Royal Economic Society 1998. Published by Blackwell Publishers, 108 Cowley Road, Oxford OX4 1JF, UK and 350 Main Street, Malden, MA 02148, USA.

# LIABILITY-CREATING VERSUS NON-LIABILITY-CREATING FISCAL STABILISATION POLICIES: RICARDIAN EQUIVALENCE, FISCAL STABILISATION, AND EMU*

*Tamim Bayoumi and Paul R. Masson*

This paper looks at theoretical and empirical issues associated with the operation of fiscal stabilisers within an economy. It argues that such stabilisers operate most effectively at a national, rather than local, level. As differing cycles across regions tend to offset each other for the country as a whole, national fiscal stabilisers are not associated with the same increase in future tax liabilities for the region as local ones. Accordingly, the negative impact from the Ricardian effects associated with these tax liabilities is smaller. Empirical work on data across Canadian provinces indicates that local stabilisers are only $\frac{1}{3}$ to $\frac{1}{2}$ as effective as national stabilisers which create no future tax liability.

Plans to create a single European currency have generated work in many areas of economics, as researchers try to assess both the implications and the advisability of this undertaking. One of these areas has been the operation of fiscal stabilisers. Without the monetary flexibility provided by separate currencies, labour mobility, wage flexibility, and fiscal stabilisers all represent potentially important ways of reducing the impact of idiosyncratic cyclical disturbances across regions of the projected currency union.[1] The function of fiscal stabilisation policies in monetary unions has already generated an extensive academic literature, going back to Mundell (1961) and Kenen (1969).[2] In the European context, it has also been the subject of an official report, European Commission (1977), and the Commission has more recently published a collection of papers devoted to the fiscal requirements for the successful operation of EMU.[3]

The recent debate in Europe on the role of fiscal stabilisers after EMU has not, however, focused on the appropriate size of fiscal stabilisers, important though that question might be. Rather, the central issue has been the level of government which should be used to operate them. Within existing national currency unions, most fiscal stabilisation is carried out at the national (federal)

* Earlier versions of this paper were presented at two conferences, the first organised by CEPREMAP, the French Ministry of the Economy and Finance, and MAD, 'Should We Rebuild Built-in Stabilisers,' Paris, January 8–10, 1996, and the second sponsored by the Bank of Israel, Hebrew University, the International Fund, and Tel-Aviv University, 'Optimum Currency Areas: The Current Agenda for International Monetary and Fiscal Integration,' Tel-Aviv, December 4–6, 1996. We are grateful to Jeff Gable for research assistance, to Assaf Razin for helpful discussions, and to participants at the conferences for comments, in particular, Elise Brezis, Daniel Cohen, Jacques Mélitz, Jean Pisani-Ferry, Jürgen von Hagen and Martin Weale. The views expressed here are personal to the authors and do not necessarily represent those of the International Monetary Fund.

[1] Cohen and Wyplosz (1989), for instance, argue that EMU could be put at risk by transitory, asymmetric shocks.

[2] For a survey, see Masson and Taylor (1993).

[3] European Commission (1993).

level, rather than at lower levels of government.[4] Empirical estimates of the
size of federal fiscal stabilisers within the United States and other countries
generally find them to be significant, with fiscal flows offsetting as much as
20–30% of the initial reduction in income.[5] As far as EMU is concerned, the
logical counterpart to this behaviour within countries would be to give a
significant role in fiscal stabilisation to a central authority of the Union. This is
not, however, the approach which the EU countries intend to adopt, with
several of them resisting any moves toward federalism. Rather, fiscal stabilisation within the new currency union will be primarily carried out at the level of
the nation state.[6]

A question which naturally arises is whether the level of government at
which fiscal stabilisation occurs has any effect on its net impact. This paper
argues that there are good reasons for believing that there is such a difference.
When local governments provide fiscal stabilisation within their own region
there is a direct impact on the level of local government debt. To the extent
that citizens take account of the future tax liabilities implicit in this increase in
debt in their current saving decisions, they will partially offset the fiscal boost
provided by the government. If a federal government provides stabilisation
across a number of regions all experiencing different disturbances, however,
the impact on federal debt will tend to cancel out, there will be no expectation
of future tax liabilities, and hence there will be less of a private sector offset to
fiscal stabilisation.

The issue is best seen in the context of the Ricardian equivalence proposition originally due to Barro (1974). In the extreme case of complete Ricardian
equivalence, local governments are unable to provide fiscal stabilisation within
their locality, as their actions will be offset by the private sector. To the extent
that deficits across differing regions cancel out, however, federal governments
*can* provide fiscal stabilisation across regions (although not for the economy as
a whole) as fiscal insurance is being provided across regions rather than across
time, unless the shocks they respond to are perfectly correlated and the
regional cycles perfectly synchronised, which is unlikely. The same logic can be
used to argue that federal stabilisers will be more effective than local ones even
in the more realistic case where Ricardian effects are only partial.

This issue has several implications for the design of federal systems, and the
allocation of powers between central and lower levels of government. There is
an extensive literature on fiscal federalism, which discusses, among other
issues, at what level public goods should be provided, the implications of factor

[4] Bayoumi and Eichengreen (1995). They also provide evidence that the level of centralisation of
government matters, with the role of lower levels of government in offsetting the cycle tending to be
larger for federal governments than for non-federal ones.
[5] Sala-I-Martin and Sachs (1992), Bayoumi and Masson (1995), and Goodhart and Smith (1993).
Significantly lower estimates of the size of fiscal stabilisers in the United States, however, are found by
von Hagen (1992).
[6] Several schemes have been proposed for providing fiscal stabilisation at the EU-wide level with little
increase in the EU budget by a highly directed set of fiscal transfers (Pisani-Ferry *et al.* 1993; Mélitz and
Vori, 1992). However, there does not appear to be any interest by national policy makers in adopting
such a scheme at present.

© Royal Economic Society 1998

mobility for taxation, and the extent services should be equalised across states through federal taxes and transfers (Tiebout, 1956; Musgrave, 1960). The role of redistribution within a federation has been extensively discussed, and it is recognised that redistribution is the *ex post* result of insurance (e.g., Rawls, 1971). As concerns macroeconomic stabilisation, Oates (1972) argues that fiscal stabilisation policy is more effective at the national, rather than local, level, for two reasons: (1) small local economies are highly open, and hence leakages are greater; and (2) since capital flows freely within a country, Keynesian deficit finance will 'tend to saddle the community with an external debt ... [which, in later years], will necessitate a transfer of real income from the residents of the community to outsiders.' (Oates, 1972, p. 5.) Recent work on fiscal federalism by Persson and Tabellini (1996*a*, *b*) studies the tradeoffs between risk sharing on the one hand and moral hazard and redistribution on the other.

To our knowledge, however, the link between the effectiveness of stabilisation policy and the fact that in a federation the taxes used to finance it do not fall solely on the region experiencing a negative shock has not been discussed in the literature. Several points need to be recognised concerning the need for, and effectiveness of, stabilisation policy. First, the need for regional stabilisation depends on the existence of asymmetric regional shocks—something that is assumed away by Oates in point (1) above. Second, the shocks to income can be even more localised—e.g., affect only an individual—and a tax and transfer system would help to cushion them. But such shocks would not show up at even the regional level, much less the national one. Third, factor mobility within a federation tends to increase the effectiveness of regional stabilisation policies, to the extent that residents of that region do not expect to have to pay the future taxes. However, it also constrains the ability of regions to incur debt because of investor concerns that they may not be able to service it. Fourth, if Ricardian equivalence holds perfectly, then the need for government stabilisation policy is diminished; consumption should vary only in response to permanent income, and cyclical income fluctuations could only be the result of myopia or lags affecting other components of demand, e.g., investment. But in the face of partial Ricardian equivalence, stabilisation policy would retain its justification, and the issue of its effectiveness would remain.

The link with insurance also raises the issue whether private financial markets and capital flows can provide a substitute for a federal stabilisation policy. In principle, private insurers could insure individuals for income shocks, or states could do so for shocks to their region by holding a diversified portfolio of claims on other income streams. In practice, it does not seem that this is empirically important; even within the United States, where there are no barriers to capital flows, the bulk of consumers do not appear to use private capital markets to insulate their consumption flow from fluctuations in regional income (Atkeson and Bayoumi, 1993). Such private insurance may not be available because of adverse selection problems: governments can solve these problems through enforcement of the tax laws, making the *ex post* redistribution compulsory (Sinn, 1995).

The implication of our results for EMU is that stabilisation by national governments is likely to produce less bang for the same buck than an equivalent EU-wide policy. However, while the sign of the effect is unambiguous, the potential size of the effect is unclear. Existing estimates of the size of the Ricardian offset to fiscal policy, and hence the potential increase in the stabilisation bang from a federal policy, vary widely.[7] We look at this issue directly using data on fiscal policy across differing levels of government for Canadian provinces. The impact of changes in federal fiscal deficits on private consumption is contrasted with the impact of changes in fiscal deficits by lower levels of government. The results indicate that idiosyncratic shocks are cushioned more effectively by federal fiscal policy that involves a degree of redistribution across provinces.

The plan for the remainder of this paper is as follows. The next section outlines in more detail the theoretical argument about why fiscal stabilisation at the federal level may be more effective than its local counterpart. Section 2 introduces the Canadian data, provides a brief discussion of the system of fiscal federalism in Canada, and reports estimates of the degree to which different levels of government stabilise output over the provincial business cycle. Section 3 explores whether there are significant differences in the effectiveness of fiscal stabilisation across these different levels of government. Section 4 concludes.

## 1. Theoretical Considerations

In order to consider the different effects of stabilisation policies at federal and regional levels, it is useful to sketch out their implications in the widely-used model of partial Ricardian equivalence due to Yaari (1965), Blanchard (1985) and Frenkel and Razin (1987). In this model, uncertain lifetimes produce a higher discount rate for the consumer than for the government.[8] A constant probability of death that is independent of age allows aggregation of all individuals into a representative consumer. It can be shown that the resulting consumption path is not independent of the choice between taxes and debt financing.[9]

In this model, if consumers maximise utility which is logarithmic, income is exogenous, and taxes are lump sum, consumption can be written:

$$C_t = \rho \left\{ B_t + \sum_{i=0}^{\infty} [(1 + r)(1 + \delta)]^{-i} E_t(Y_{t+i} - T_{t+i}) \right\} \tag{1}$$

---

[7] See Bernheim (1987) and Seater (1993) for surveys.

[8] Though it is true that governments last only a few years, they typically honour the debt incurred by previous governments. Risk of default would raise the government's borrowing cost—perhaps even above the private sector's discount rate. In practice, however, consumers cannot borrow at as low a rate as governments except in exceptional circumstances.

[9] In the special case where the birth rate and the probability of death are zero, however, Ricardian equivalence holds.

where $\rho \geqslant 0$ is the rate of time preference, $r$ is the interest rate (assumed constant), $\delta$ is a constant probability of death, $Y$ is income, and $T$ and $B$ are taxes and beginning-of-period government debt, respectively. The government satisfies an intertemporal budget constraint which implies that the bond stock equals the discounted present value of taxes minus government spending, $G$:

$$B_t = \sum_{i=0}^{\infty} (1+r)^{-i} \mathrm{E}_t(T_{t+i} - G_{t+i}). \tag{2}$$

Consider now the case of a federation of several regions (labelled provinces, and indexed by $j$), with both regional and federal fiscal policies. Now, consumption in region $j$ depends on the paths of both sets of fiscal variables, where an '$F$' superscript will denote federal taxes or spending, '$R$' regional taxes or spending, and $B_j^F$ and $B_j^R$ the region $j$ claims on federal and provincial governments (rates of time preference and mortality as well as interest rates are assumed to be identical across regions and over time):

$$C_{tj} = \rho \left\{ B_{tj}^F + B_{tj}^R + \sum_{i=0}^{\infty} [(1+r)(1+\delta)]^{-i} \mathrm{E}_t(Y_{t+ij} - T_{t+ij}^F - T_{t+ij}^R \right\} \tag{3}$$

subject to two budget constraints

$$\sum_j B_{tj}^F = \sum_{i=0}^{\infty} (1+r)^{-i} \mathrm{E}_t \left[ \sum_j (T_{t+ij}^F - G_{t+ij}^F) \right] \tag{4}$$

and

$$B_{tj}^R = \sum_{i=0}^{\infty} (1+r)^{-i} \mathrm{E}_t(T_{t+ij}^R - G_{t+ij}^R). \tag{5}$$

The important thing to note is that federal fiscal policy satisfies a budget constraint that is both inter-temporal and inter-regional; the region benefitting from an excess of spending over taxes (i.e., a deficit) need not incur budget surpluses later. Equivalently, federal deficits in a region need not involve the creation of a future regional tax liability, whose anticipated service would weaken stimulative effects in the region, because the deficits would be compensated, at least in part, by surpluses elsewhere and because debt service would be shared with other regions. The fact that there was *ex post* redistribution would therefore increase the effectiveness of federal deficits in stabilising regional consumption in the face of shocks to income. In contrast, regional deficits do create a future tax liability which needs to be serviced in the region, and this has depressing effects on consumption today.

The above discussion implies that we need to distinguish federal flows between those that create a future tax liability for the region and those that do not create such a liability (involving redistribution), as well as distinguishing federal from regional flows. This we do in the empirical section. For the moment, and to illustrate formally the points made above, we assume that *all* federal fiscal policy is non-liability-creating, and, in particular, involves a balanced national budget. Moreover, in expected values, 'federal' fiscal policy is assumed to be balanced in each region; there are no expected gainers or losers *ex ante*. Thus, for any period $t$ and region $j$

$$\sum_j T^F_{tj} = \sum_j G^F_{tj} \tag{6}$$

and

$$E_t(T^F_{t+ij} - G^F_{t+ij}) = 0, \ i \geqslant 1. \tag{7}$$

In contrast, regional deficits involve accumulation of a liability which needs to be repaid. We will assume that this repayment takes place in the following period. To simplify the presentation we will assume that there is no debt initially. Then, the regional budget constraint (5) implies that

$$G^R_{t+1j} - T^R_{t+1j} = -(1+r)(G^R_{tj} - T^R_{tj}). \tag{8}$$

Now, consumption in region $j$ can be expressed in terms of the two types of (primary) deficits (the $j$ subscript is omitted henceforth)

$$DEF^F_t = G^F_t - T^F_t$$
$$DEF^R_t = G^R_t - T^R_t \tag{9}$$

as follows

$$C_t = \rho \left\{ \sum_{i=0}^{\infty} [(1+r)(1+\delta)]^{-i} E_t(Y_{t+i} - G^R_{t+i} - G^F_{t+i}) + DEF^F_t + \frac{\delta}{1+\delta} DEF^R_t \right\}. \tag{10}$$

Because future *federal* deficits are solely redistributive, and their expected value is zero, they do not offset the stimulus to current consumption. In contrast, future *regional* deficits partially offset the stimulus to consumption from running a regional deficit in the current period, $DEF^R_t$.[10]

In conclusion, federal fiscal policy is shown to be more effective in stimulating consumption (and hence in carrying out stabilisation policy) than its regional equivalent. Moreover, it retains its effectiveness even when $\delta = 0$ and Ricardian equivalence holds. In this case, it is clear from (10) that only the path for regional government spending affects consumption, not the choice between regional taxes and bond issues (i.e., the timing of taxes).

## 2. Data and Estimation Issues

The theory outlined above implies that inter-regional automatic stabilisers provided by the federal government which create no new regional tax liability (because net receipts by one region are offset by net payments from another)

---

[10] Alternatively, suppose that the surplus is delayed until period $t + \tau$. In this case, it can easily be shown that the last term on the RHS of (10) is instead $DEF^R_t[1 - 1/(1+\delta)^\tau]$, so the effect on consumption of $DEF^R_t$ is still less than that of $DEF^F_t$, though closer to it. The possibility that period $t + \tau$ would be infinitely delayed (and hence that $1 - 1/(1+\delta)^\tau \to 1$) is ruled out by the transversality condition.

will be more effective at changing regional demand than equivalent stabilisers provided by regional governments. The reason is that the Ricardian offset, in which private individuals foresee the impact of fiscal policy on future tax liabilities and therefore reduce consumption accordingly, will not fully operate in the federal context to the extent that deficits in one region are offset by surpluses in another and that any debt servicing is shared with other regions.

The obvious method of testing such a proposition is to compare the impact of federal deficits on consumption across regions within a country with the impact of deficits of lower levels of government. Few countries provide the necessary regional detail in their fiscal accounts. Canada, however, does provide such data. Specifically, Statistics Canada publishes detailed fiscal accounts by province for all significant levels of government (federal, provincial, local, hospitals, and pension plans) in the *Provincial Economic Accounts* (various issues).[11] In addition, the same source provides data on gross provincial product (the provincial equivalent of GDP) and on the major subcategories of spending, such as private consumption, public consumption and investment. These accounts, therefore, provide all of the data necessary to look at the relative impact of automatic stabilisers at different levels of government across provinces within Canada.

The nominal *Provincial Economic Accounts* start in 1961 and the latest data available to us were for 1993. However, some of the fiscal data for the early 1960s appeared unreliable, so that the estimation period was limited to 1966–93, implying 28 years of annual data by province. Some of the data on lower levels of government were missing for one province, British Columbia, as well as for the Yukon and Northwest Territories. Accordingly, these regions were dropped, leaving a total of nine provinces in the analysis.[12] To increase the power of the empirical tests, the data were generally estimated as a panel, combining the data across different provinces into a single stacked time-series regression.

The five different levels of government identified in the Canadian provincial accounts were aggregated into those levels of government whose debt liability is incurred on a national basis and those whose debt liability is province specific. Accordingly, the fiscal accounts for the federal government were aggregated with those for the two public pension plans (the Canada Pension Plan and the Quebec Pension Plan).[13] The fiscal accounts for the other three lower levels of government—provincial governments, hospitals (which are the responsibility of the provincial governments) and local government—were aggregated together. For simplicity, the two resulting aggregates will be

[11] All parts of the deficit, including such components as debt interest payments, are allocated across provinces.

[12] Alberta, Manitoba, New Brunswick, Newfoundland, Nova Scotia, Ontario, Prince Edward Island, Quebec, and Saskatchewan.

[13] It was decided to treat the Canada and Quebec pension plans (CPP and QPP) in the same way. The QPP is run at the provincial level, while the CPP covers Canadians in all provinces except Quebec. Despite this difference, the provisions of the two Plans are essentially identical. As membership in the two Plans is also transferable depending on the province in which an individual is resident, to all intents and purposes the CPP and QPP represent a single, national, pension policy.

referred to hereafter as the federal and provincial levels of government, respectively.

It should be noted that the federal fiscal accounts include equalisation grants that explicitly aim to transfer tax revenues from richer provinces to poorer ones, in order to enable the latter to provide similar levels of government services without imposing crippling taxes on their residents. On some occasions, the sets of provinces gaining and losing, as well as the size of the transfers, have changed on account of asymmetric shocks. We would argue that this endogenous response of equalisation grants clearly should be attributed to fiscal federalism, and should properly be picked up in any test of the effectiveness of federal stabilisation policy. This is the case in the regressions reported below.

Before looking at the impact of fiscal deficits upon aggregate demand, it is useful to compare the extent that different levels of government provide automatic stabilisers in the face of provincial business cycles. Accordingly, the change in the fiscal deficit was regressed on the change in gross provincial product (GPP). To make the data comparable across different provinces and to take account of the secular growth of the economy, both sides of the equation were deflated by trend output.[14] This produced the following regression:

$$\Delta(DEF_j^k / YPOT_j)_t = \alpha_j + \beta \Delta(Y_j / YPOT_j)_t, \qquad (11)$$

where $DEF_j^k$ is the fiscal deficit of province $j$, superscript $k$ is the level of government (national or provincial), and $YPOT_j$ and $Y_j$ are potential and actual gross provincial product (in nominal terms), respectively, of province $j$. First differences are used so as to abstract from any secular trends that may be present in the data.

Two concepts of the fiscal deficit were used in the estimation, namely the negative of net lending and the negative of gross saving. Net lending measures the total amount of funds lent (or borrowed) by the government over a given period, while gross saving takes borrowing for government investment out of this total. The correct concept to use depends upon the return provided by government investment. If the investment is expected to generate a market return for the government, then borrowing for investment will generate no expected future tax liability, and gross saving should be used to measure the Ricardian offset. By contrast, if the investment produces no budgetary return, then net lending should be used.

Table 1 indicates that, using federal saving to measure the fiscal position, each \$1 reduction in gross provincial product produces an offsetting increase in the federal deficit attributed to that province of 29 cents, and that this parameter is highly statistically significant. Using federal net lending to

[14] Potential output in nominal terms was calculated as the fitted values of a regression of real gross provincial product on an exponential trend and then multiplied by the implicit price deflator. As no provincial product deflators are available from the *Provincial Economic Accounts*, implicit consumption deflators were used to calculate real provincial product. These deflators are province-specific back to 1971, before which the deflator was spliced on to the aggregate Canadian CPI series.

### Table 1

*Sensitivity of Fiscal Variables to the Cycle*

$$\Delta(DEF_j^k / YPOT_j)_t = \alpha_i + \beta\Delta(Y_t / YPOT_j)_t$$

| | Federal | | Provincial | |
|---|---|---|---|---|
| Dependent variable | Coefficient on output | F-test of parameter equality across provinces | Coefficient on output | F-test parameter equality across provinces |
| Minus gross saving | −0.29 (0.03)** | 0.62 | −0.10 (0.02)** | 0.81 |
| Minus net lending | −0.28 (0.03)** | 0.64 | −0.09 (0.02)** | 0.64 |
| Government consumption | −0.01 (0.01) | 0.30 | 0.00 (0.02) | 0.50 |
| Government investment | −0.01 (0.01) | 0.90 | −0.01 (0.01) | 0.66 |

*Notes*: Estimated constant terms are not reported. Standard errors are reported in parentheses. One and two asterisks indicate that the coefficient or test is significant at the 5 and 1% significance level, respectively.

measure the fiscal position produces an almost identical estimate (28 cents in the dollar), indicating that federal government investment plays little role over the cycle. This supposition is confirmed by regressions which measure the response of real federal government consumption and real federal government investment to the cycle; they indicate that neither federal consumption nor investment plays a significant cyclical role. This role is therefore limited to taxes and transfer payments. F-tests of the stability of the parameters across the individual regressions, also reported in the table, indicate that the restrictions that behaviour is the same across all provinces can be accepted.

The table reports similar results for provincial governments. The results indicate that a one dollar reduction in GPP increases the provincial fiscal deficit by 9–10 cents, depending upon the definition that is used. Again, these responses are highly statistically significant at conventional levels, indicating that both levels of government provide some level of stabilisation. Overall, fiscal automatic stabilisers total about 40 cents in the dollar, with the federal government providing three-quarters of this total, and lower levels of government the remaining quarter.[15]

Having established that fiscal positions at both levels of government vary significantly over the cycle, we turn to estimating the impact of deficits at different levels of government on private consumption. While recognising that this is only one channel through which the government can influence the cycle, private consumption is by far the largest component of aggregate

[15] These results can be compared to those reported in earlier studies. Bayoumi and Eichengreen (1995) use a similar econometric approach to estimate the counter-cyclical fiscal changes in Canada at different levels of government using national, rather than provincial, data. Their estimates of the cyclical offsets were 34 cents in the dollar for the federal government (including pension plans), and 17 cents in the dollar for provincial governments, broadly similar to the estimated coefficients reported above. Bayoumi and Masson (1995) measure the federal government fiscal offset at only 18 cents for every dollar fall in personal income by province. The difference may reflect the different concept of income used in the study.

demand. The relationship between consumption and government policy therefore appears to be of particular significance.

We start from the Euler equation for consumption behaviour discussed by Hall (1978). This equation says that, for an infinitely lived forward looking consumer with no liquidity constraints, a constant real rate of interest, and (implicitly) no difference between private and government discount rates, the growth in consumption should be unrelated to any predictable current or past data (as anticipated events are already incorporated into the consumer's assessment of permanent income), although it can be affected by unexpected current data. This equation can be thought of as the empirical equivalent of a full Ricardian model.

The Euler equation approach has generated a large empirical literature, much of which has dealt with the issue of whether consumption depends on predictable changes in current income. The weight of existing empirical results indicates that it does, although the reason for this dependence— whether it reflects liquidity constraints or precautionary saving—remains in dispute.[16] A simple method of taking this dependence into account is to assume the existence of a proportion of individuals whose consumption tracks current income rather than permanent income (Campbell and Mankiw, 1989, 1990). This implies that the change in current income, suitably instrumented so as to take account of the dependence of permanent income on unexpected changes in current income, should be included in the regression. Again normalising by trend real GPP, this produces the following estimating equation

$$\Delta(C_j/YPOT_j)_t = \alpha_j + \beta\Delta(Y_j/YPOT_j)_t, \tag{12}$$

where $C$ is private consumption and $Y$ is income.

To measure the impact of fiscal stabilisation on consumption we add the fiscal variables suggested by the Blanchard-Yaari framework discussed earlier. This implies that consumption should depend positively both on deficits which do not create a future regional tax liability (hereafter called non-liability-creating deficits) and, to a lesser extent, on deficits which do create such a liability (hereafter called liability-creating deficits). It should also depend negatively on pre-existing levels of debt (as the date at which this debt is anticipated to be repaid comes nearer, the negative impact of the required future fiscal surpluses on future discounted income rises), and negatively on levels of government consumption. As the specification uses first differences of consumption, this implies including the change in both liability-creating and non-liability-creating deficits (for the impact of current deficits), first lags of liability-creating deficits (for the impact of past debt, as the change in debt is equal to the deficit), and the change in government consumption.

---

[16] See Browning and Lusardi (1995) for a survey of (largely U.S.) microeconomic evidence. Other recent papers dealing with these issues include Zeldes (1989), Carroll (1992), Townsend (1994), and Hubbard *et al.* (1994, 1995).

Implementing this specification requires differentiating the non-liability-creating part of the federal fiscal deficit from the liability-creating part, which in turn requires a model of the incidence of federal taxes. Accordingly, we ran a cross-sectional regression of the average of federal revenues per capita for each province relative to the Canadian average over 1970–90 on the average level of *per capita* GPP, also measured relative to the Canadian average over the same period. This regression produced the following results

$$TAX_j^{FED}/POP_j = \underset{(0.12)}{-0.11} + \underset{(0.13)}{1.06} \ (Y_j/POP_j). \tag{13}$$

The coefficient on GPP is close to, and insignificantly different from, unity, and the constant term is insignificantly different from zero, which indicates that the Canadian federal taxes are approximately proportional to income.[17] Accordingly, the share of the overall Canadian deficit which the taxpayers in any province can be expected to shoulder in the future (the liability-creating part of the deficit) can be assumed to be equal to their share of trend income, $(YPOT_j/YPOT_{CA})DEF_{CA}^{FED}$, while the part of the federal deficit for which they can assume they will not be responsible (the non-liability-creating part of the deficit) is the province-specific federal deficit less this value,

$$[DEF_j^{FED} - (YPOT_j/YPOT_{CA})DEF_{CA}^{FED}]_t. \tag{14}$$

The liability-creating part of the federal deficit will be subject to a Ricardian offset, as consumers anticipate the future impact of the deficit on their taxes. By contrast, the non-liability-creating part of the deficit does not generate any expectation of future regional tax liabilities, so that this part of the deficit should have a larger impact on that province's consumption. Finally, changes in the provincial deficit ($DEF_j^{PRV}$), are exactly like deficits which cause a change in federal debt at the national level. Increases in the deficit being run by provincial and local levels of governments produce a future tax liability that must be serviced by residents of the province, and hence produce a Ricardian offset.

The final estimating equation was therefore

$$\Delta C_{jt} = \alpha_j + \beta \Delta Y_{jt} + \delta \Delta G_{jt} + \pi \Delta [DEF_j^{FED} - DEF_{CA}^{FED}(YPOT_j/YPOT_{CA})]_t$$

$$+ \lambda \Delta [DEF_{CA}^{FED}(YPOT_j/YPOT_{CA})]_t + \eta \Delta DEF_{jt}^{PRV} \tag{15}$$

$$+ \phi [DEF_{CA}^{FED}(YPOT_j/YPOT_{CA})]_{t-1} + \gamma DEF_{jt-1}^{PRV}.$$

As in (12), all of the variables are divided by trend provincial output ($YPOT_j$), so that the trend increase in the size of the economy over time did not create heteroscedasticity in the estimated residuals.

The theoretical framework implies that the coefficients ($\lambda$ and $\eta$) on the

---

[17] These results use total revenues from individuals and businesses. Bayoumi and Masson (1995), who report similar regression results using personal taxation, also find that personal taxes are approximately proportional to personal income.

change in the federal deficit at the national level and the provincial deficit should be equal as both variables reflect actions which create future tax liabilities for residents of the province,[18] while the coefficient on the province-specific part of the federal deficit ($\pi$) should be larger than $\lambda$ or $\eta$, as it does not create future tax liabilities for the region. The coefficients on lagged federal and provincial deficits ($\phi$ and $\gamma$), which represent the negative impact of past debt accumulation, should also be equal,[19] while the anticipated sign of the coefficient on government consumption ($\delta$) is also negative. (Note, however, that its magnitude need not equal the coefficient on income, as the income term includes the impact of liquidity constraints.) Finally, the constant terms were allowed to vary by province so as to take account of province-specific differences in consumption behaviour.

Two further data issues arise in implementing this equation. One is whether the income variable should include the impact of personal taxes and transfers or not. A measure such as personal disposable income, which includes the effect of personal taxes and transfers, will tend to lower the estimated impact of fiscal stabilisers, as some of the impact of fiscal policy will already be captured by changes in income. For this reason, we focus primarily on results using gross provincial product as our measure of income, as it is clearly not directly affected by changes in fiscal deficits.[20] As a check on the robustness of the results, however, we also report regressions using personal disposable income.

Another data issue has to do with the provincial impact of business taxes. Using the total deficit to measure the fiscal position of the government involves an implicit assumption that business taxes only affect residents of the province in which they are levied. However, there are a number of reasons why such taxes may by paid by non-residents.[21] We therefore estimate the model using alternative measures of deficits which both include and exclude direct business taxes.[22] For the sake of brevity, the reported empirical work is limited to regressions involving gross provincial product and total deficits, and personal disposable income and deficits excluding business taxes.

Instrumental variable techniques were used in the estimation, as unexpected changes in income can be associated with changes in permanent income, implying a correlation between unanticipated changes in income and the error

---

[18] This ignores the fact that individuals can avoid future provincial taxes by moving elsewhere in Canada. In the empirical work we find that we cannot reject the equality of the coefficients on the two liability-creating deficits, suggesting that mobility within Canada is not a very significant factor in determining the effects of provincial fiscal policy on the path of consumption.

[19] This assumes that the expected time at which the debt will be repaid is the same across both levels of government.

[20] Gross provincial product is calculated from the income side as the sum of domestic labour income, profits (including unincorporated enterprises and farms), net investment income, indirect taxes less subsidies, and capital consumption allowances. It is therefore a good proxy for changes in provincial personal incomes, although it does include corporate retained earnings.

[21] For example, if these taxes are incorporated in output prices and the goods are sold in another province.

[22] Data on indirect business taxes were not available.

© Royal Economic Society 1998

term. The fiscal variables were also instrumented as the fiscal position varies with income. In addition to the province-specific constant terms, the instruments used were the first and second lags of the change in income, the changes in the three fiscal deficits (the federal deficit at the national level, the province-specific federal deficit, and the provincial deficit), and the change in consumption, plus the lagged difference between consumption and income.[23] Assuming some predictability in the cycle, current changes in income and fiscal stance should be useful in predicting future changes in these variables. In addition, since the consumption model underlying our approach is the permanent income model, it follows that current consumption will summarise agents' information about the future path of income, thus the change in consumption and the relationship of the level of consumption compared to income should be useful in predicting future income (Campbell, 1987). Given the relatively large number of instruments and the fact that government consumption does not vary significantly with income (Table 1), government consumption was not instrumented.

## 3. Empirical Results

The results from regressing (15) using gross provincial product and total deficits are shown in the first column of Table 2. As the coefficient estimates for the fiscal variables were very similar whether gross saving or net lending was used to measure the fiscal stance, only results for gross saving (with sign reversed, so that it corresponds to the deficit) are reported.[24]

The coefficients on the fiscal and income variables are almost all correctly signed. The parameter estimates indicate that every dollar increase in the federal deficit which is specific to the province in question raises private consumption by (a highly significant) 44 cents. An equivalent increase in the federal deficit at the national level or in the provincial deficit raises consumption by 16 cents in the dollar (although neither of these coefficients is significant at conventional levels). The results for the lagged deficits, which measure the impact of past debt accumulation, show some variation. The coefficient on the lagged federal deficit is small, incorrectly signed, and insignificant, while that on the lagged provincial deficit, which is marginally significant at the 5% level, has the correct negative sign and indicates that each dollar in past accumulated provincial debt lowers consumption by 11 cents in the dollar. Raising government consumption by a dollar is estimated to lower private consumption by 13 cents, although the coefficient is not significant at conventional levels. Finally, the coefficient on the change in real GDP is 0.31,

---

[23] The instruments were differentiated by province by multiplying them by the province-specific dummy variables. Hence, each province had, in essence, its own forecasting equations. In all cases, variables are divided by potential output.

[24] Experiments adding changes in government investment were also carried out, but the results were unpromising and are not reported. Adding government investment to the regressions was the one case in which the coefficients varied significantly depending upon the definition of the deficit that was used.

Table 2

*Estimating the Impact of Fiscal Stabilisation on Private Consumption*

Equation (15)

|  | Basic regression | Restricted regression |
|---|---|---|
| *Coefficients of* | | |
| Change in federal deficit: | | |
| Non-liability-creating (province-specific) | 0.44 (0.08)** | 0.45 (0.08)** |
| Liability-creating (national level) | 0.16 (0.13) | |
|  | | 0.20 (0.09)* |
| Change in provincial deficit | 0.16 (0.11) | |
| Lagged national federal deficit | 0.03 (0.05) | |
|  | | −0.03 (0.04) |
| Lagged provincial deficit | −0.11 (0.06)* | |
| Change in government consumption | −0.13 (0.11) | −0.17 (0.11) |
| Change in income | 0.31 (0.04)** | 0.32 (0.04)** |
| *Statistics* | | |
| $R^2$ | 0.41 | 0.39 |
| Wald tests of: | | |
| Equality of changes in all fiscal deficits $\chi^2(2)$ | 13.1** | |
| Equality of changes in liability-creating deficits $\chi^2(1)$ | 0.0 | |
| Equality of changes in liability- and non-liability-creating deficits $\chi^2(1)$ | | 10.7** |
| Equality of lagged deficits $\chi^2(1)$ | 3.5 | |

*Notes*: Estimated constant terms are not reported. For the instrument list, see the text. One and two asterisks indicate that the coefficient or test is different from zero at the 5 or 1% significance level, respectively.

indicating that about one third of the predicted change in income comes through onto consumption.

The results conform to the prediction of the model. An increase in the fiscal deficit which does not involve a higher future tax liability for the province—measured by the province-specific part of the federal deficit—has a larger impact on consumption than an equivalent increase in deficits which do produce such a liability. Wald tests confirm that the coefficients on the three fiscal variables are significantly different from each other, but that the coefficients on the two forms of deficit spending which create future tax liabilities (the federal deficit at the national level and the provincial deficit) are not significantly different from each other. In addition, a Wald test also finds no significant difference between the coefficients on the two lagged deficit variables. The parameter restrictions predicted by the theoretical model are thus confirmed.

The second column in the table therefore reports the results from a restricted regression in which the coefficients on the change and the lagged levels of the federal deficit at the national level and the provincial deficit are made equal. The results indicate that changes in the deficit that do not create future regional tax liabilities raise consumption by 45 cents in the dollar, while those that do create such liabilities raise consumption by (a significant) 20 cents in the dollar. A Wald test indicates that the two coefficients are different from each other at the 1% level of significance. The results imply that liability-creating fiscal deficits have only about one half of the impact on consumption of non-liability-creating deficits. The coefficient on the lagged value of both federal and provincial deficits indicates that each extra dollar in existing debt lowers consumption by 3 cents, although it is not significant at conventional levels. Similarly, the coefficient on government consumption remains correctly signed but insignificant. The coefficient on changes in income, by contrast, continues to be large and highly significant.

Several variants on the basic model were estimated to test the robustness of these results. First, a more general specification was estimated in which each coefficient on the independent variables was allowed to vary by province. A Wald test of the restriction that the coefficients on the fiscal variables and real output were equal across provinces was accepted, indicating no significant variation in behaviour across provinces.[25] Next, the equation was rerun using ordinary least squares to see how important the use of instrumental variables was to the estimation results. The results, reported in column 1 of Table 3, indicate that the absolute sizes of the coefficients on the change in the fiscal variables (including government consumption) all fall. Apparently, positive shocks to consumption (and income) show up as lower deficits, which, if not allowed for using instrumental variables, lower the implied stabilisation effects. However, the Wald tests indicate that the difference between the coefficient on liability-creating and non-liability-creating fiscal policy remains large and significant.

The equation was also re-estimated with second and third lags of the instruments (column 2 of Table 3), rather than first and second lags. The concern with using first lags in the instruments is that, to the extent that consumption follows a random walk, time averaging can induce a correlation between the change in consumption and its first lag.[26] The coefficient on the province-specific federal balance is somewhat smaller than in the base case regression; however, the basic message is very similar. In particular, the impact of non-liability-creating deficits remains significantly larger than that of lia-bility-creating ones. The restricted regression (not reported) indicates an impact on private consumption from liability-creating fiscal policy that is 16 cents in the dollar, half the 32 cents estimated for non-liability-creating policy.

Next, the change in government consumption and the lagged values of the deficits were dropped from the specification, to see if the results were robust to the exclusion of these additional (and generally insignificant) variables. The results, shown in column 3 of Table 3, continue to show a large difference between the impact of liability-creating and non-liability-creating deficits.

[25] As there were so many independent variables, this regression was run using only the changes in the deficits and the change in income. The $\chi^2(32)$ statistic was 27.6, compared to a critical value at the 5% level of 44.0.
[26] Working (1960).

Table 3

*Results from Alternative Assumptions*

*Equation (15)*

|  | Ordinary least squares | Different instruments | Simpler specification |
|---|---|---|---|
| *Coefficients of* | | | |
| Change in federal deficit: | | | |
| Non-liability-creating (province-specific) | 0.31 (0.05)** | 0.32 (0.08)** | 0.48 (0.07)** |
| Liability-creating (national level) | 0.01 (0.08) | 0.08 (0.12) | 0.13 (0.11) |
| Change in provincial deficit | 0.08 (0.07) | 0.16 (0.11) | 0.18 (0.08)* |
| Lagged national federal deficit | 0.03 (0.04) | 0.02 (0.05) | |
| Lagged provincial deficit | −0.10 (0.05)* | 0.09 (0.06) | |
| Change in government consumption | 0.00 (0.09) | −0.06 (0.11) | |
| Change in income | 0.24 (0.03)** | 0.26 (0.04)** | 0.31 (0.03)** |
| *Statistics* | | | |
| $R^2$ | 0.42 | 0.41 | 0.39 |
| Wald test of: | | | |
| Equality of all fiscal parameters $\chi^2(2)$ | 20.6** | 6.2* | 16.5** |
| Equality of liability-creating deficits $\chi^2(1)$ | 0.4 | 0.4 | 0.2 |

*Notes*: See Table 2.

We also looked at different definitions of income and deficits. Table 4 shows results from estimating the same regressions as in Table 2, but using personal disposable income to measure of income and excluding direct business taxes from the definition of the deficit. The results are qualitatively similar to those in Table 2. Both non-liability-creating and liability-creating deficits affect consumption, with non-liability-creating deficits having a significantly larger impact. The main difference in the results is that the coefficients on the fiscal variables are considerably smaller using this data set than the earlier one, plausibly reflecting the fact that some of the impact of personal taxes and transfers is coming through changes in personal disposable income.[27] By contrast, the coefficient on income is very similar across the two sets of regressions.

We also experimented with adjusting the regressions to take account of the possibility that the tax system is progressive. Rather than assuming that each province's future tax burdens move in proportion to its output, so the liability-creating element of the federal deficit for any province is $(YPOT_j/YPOT_{CA})DEF_{CA}^{FED}$, in the alternative regressions this initial estimate

[27] This supposition is supported by intermediate regressions (not reported) which use gross provincial product to measure income and deficits excluding direct business taxes for fiscal policy. The resulting impacts of non-liability-creating deficits from these regressions are more similar to those using gross provincial product and total deficits than those using personal disposable income and deficits adjusted for debt. (The results for liability-creating deficits are less clear.)

Table 4

*Estimates Using Personal Disposable Income and Excluding Direct Business Taxes*

*Equation (15)*

| | Basic regression | Restricted regression |
|---|---|---|
| *Coefficients of* | | |
| Change in federal deficit: | | |
| Non-liability-creating (province-specific) | 0.25 (0.06)** | 0.24 (0.06)** |
| Liability-creating (national level) | −0.07 (0.12) | |
| Change in provincial deficit | 0.06 (0.03)* | 0.05 (0.03)* |
| Lagged national federal deficit | 0.09 (0.05) | |
| Lagged provincial deficit | −0.04 (0.02)* | −0.02 (0.02) |
| Change in government consumption | 0.00 (0.09) | −0.07 (0.09) |
| Change in income | 0.35 (0.05)** | 0.33 (0.05)** |
| *Statistics* | | |
| $R^2$ | 0.34 | 0.32 |
| Wald tests of: | | |
| Equality of changes in all fiscal deficits $\chi^2(2)$ | 11.2** | |
| Equality of changes in liability-creating deficits $\chi^2(1)$ | 1.0 | |
| Equality of changes in liability- and non-liability-creating deficits $\chi^2(1)$ | | 10.1** |
| Equality of lagged deficits $\chi^2(1)$ | 5.1* | |

*Notes*: See Table 2.

was multiplied by the average value of *per capita* income in that province relative to Canada as a whole. This procedure raises the implied elasticity of *per capita* taxes to *per capita* income from one to two. For example, in the case of Ontario, where GPP *per capita* averaged 10% more than in the country as a whole, instead of assuming that *per capita* taxes are 10% higher than the average, under the new weighting scheme they were assumed to be 21% (1 plus 10% squared) higher. The non-liability-creating part of the federal deficit was then adjusted accordingly.

The results from these regressions (not reported for the sake of brevity) are very similar to those reported in Table 2. In the restricted regression, the impact of liability-creating deficits on consumption is estimated to be 43 cents in the dollar while that on non-liability-creating deficits is estimated to be 15 cents in the dollar, with the difference between the coefficients being significant at the 1% level. Hence, the results appear robust to reasonable changes in our assumption about the incidence of future tax liabilities.

Finally, we also investigated the relative variances of our three components of fiscal stabilisation, the liability-creating federal deficit, the non-liability-creating federal deficit, and the provincial deficit (all measured as a proportion to trend GDP). The idea was to assess the relative importance of variations in non-liability-creating deficits compared to liability-creating ones. Clearly, if non-liability-creating deficits are relatively unimportant for overall fiscal policy then their superiority as a way of providing automatic stabilisers would be of limited interest. In practice, however, the non-liability-creating part of the federal deficit has a variance which is one-and-a-half times that of provincial deficits and three times that of the national federal deficit. As these variables are approximately orthogonal, this implies that about half of the variation in fiscal deficits across Canadian provinces is non-liability-creating.

## 4. Conclusions

The debate in Europe has focussed on the lack of fiscal stabilisation at the EU level, in contrast to the existence of important fiscal stabilisers at the federal or national level in other monetary unions. Little evidence has, however, been provided concerning the effectiveness of stabilisation at different levels of government in a federation, though the issue is of obvious relevance for Europe. In this paper we examine the impact of fiscal policy in federal systems, and provide empirical evidence concerning the relative effectiveness of stabilisation at different levels of government.

It is well known that if consumers are Ricardian, automatic stabilisers operating through (nondistorting) taxes and transfers will have no effect in cushioning shocks at the national level, since they will involve creation of debt whose debt service will be anticipated by consumers. The same is true of attempts to use stabilisation policy by lower levels of government. However, as is shown here, regional stabilisers which involve redistribution across a federation can in principle be more effective because they do not create a future regional tax liability. We test this hypothesis using data for Canada, a decentralised federation which engages in fiscal stabilisation policies at both the national and provincial levels. Our regressions of private consumption on various measures of fiscal position (national liability-creating, national non-liability-creating, and provincial) allow a test of Ricardian equivalence (a zero effect for liability-creating stabilisation) as well as of the greater effectiveness of non-liability-creating flows.

Our empirical results confirm that the anticipated larger impact on consumption of fiscal deficits which do not create a future regional tax liability compared to deficits which do create such a liability appears to hold empirically. In all cases, the two coefficients are significantly different from each other. Most estimates imply that liability-creating deficits are somewhat less than half as effective as non-liability-creating ones. Though we (barely) reject Ricardian equivalence for the liability-creating policies, our much stronger result is that stabilisation policy within a federal system that involves some degree of redistribution is much more effective in cushioning shocks to consumption.

We would interpret this evidence as providing another argument for Europe to consider expanding fiscal policy at the Union level, rather than relying on national fiscal policies to offset idiosyncratic shocks. As pointed out by others, effective fiscal stabilisation is all the more important in EMU, given the loss of the exchange rate instrument for that purpose—especially since other shock absorbers, like labour mobility, are unlikely to be very important. While monetary union will not reduce the effectiveness of existing national automatic stabilisers, such stabilisers can be expected to operate more efficiently if they are EU based, rather than operating solely at a national level.

However, one also needs to acknowledge that there are difficulties in designing fiscal stabilisation at the EU level that would not involve important persistent transfers of revenue from some countries to others (Von Hagen and Hammond, 1996). Therefore, EU fiscal stabilisation might be politically unacceptable. Finally, since in practice taxes are not lump sum, the distorting effects of higher tax rates also need to be taken into account when considering this option.

*International Monetary Fund*

*Date of receipt of first submission: April 1996*
*Date of receipt of final typescript: April 1997*

## References

Atkeson, Andrew, and Bayoumi, Tamim (1993), 'Do private capital markets insure regional risk? Evidence from the United States and Europe,' *Open Economies Review*, vol. 4, pp. 303–24.
Barro, Robert J. (1974), 'Are government bonds net wealth?' *Journal of Political Economy*, vol. 82, pp. 1095–117.
Bayoumi, Tamim and Eichengreen, Barry (1995), 'Restraining yourself: fiscal rules and stabilization,' *IMF Staff Papers*, vol. 42, no. 1, pp. 32–48.
Bayoumi, Tamim and Masson, Paul R. (1994), 'What can the fiscal systems in the United States and Canada tell us about EMU?' in (Paul Welfens, ed.) *European Monetary Integration*, Second Edition Berlin: Springer-Verlag.
Bayoumi, Tamim and Masson, Paul R. (1995), 'Fiscal flows in the United States and Canada: lessons for monetary union in Europe,' *European Economic Review*, vol. 39, pp. 253–74.
Bernheim, B. D. (1987), 'Ricardian equivalence: an evaluation of theory and evidence,' in *NBER Macroeconomics Annual 1987*, Cambridge, MA: MIT Press.
Blanchard, Olivier J. (1985), 'Debt, deficits and finite horizons,' *Journal of Political Economy*, vol. 93 (April), pp. 223–47.
Boadway, Robin W. and Hobson, Paul A. R. (1993), *Intergovernmental Fiscal Relations in Canada*, Canadian Tax Foundation Paper No. 96, Canadian Tax Foundation, Toronto, Canada.
Browning, Martin and Lusardi, Annamaria (1995), 'Household saving: micro theories and micro facts,' Dartmouth College Working Paper 95–19.
Campbell, John (1987), 'Does the saving anticipate declining labor income? An alternative test of the permanent income model,' *Econometrica*, vol. 55, pp. 1249–74.
Campbell, John and Mankiw, Gregory (1989), 'Consumption, income, and interest rates: reinterpreting the time series evidence,' *NBER Macroeconomics Annual 1989*, (O. Blanchard, and S. Fischer, eds.) Cambridge, MA: MIT Press.
Campbell, John and Mankiw, Gregory (1990), 'Permanent income, current income and consumption,' *Journal of Business and Economic Statistics* (July), pp. 265–79.
Carroll, Christopher (1992), 'Buffer stock saving and the permanent income hypothesis,' mimeo, Federal Reserve Board.
Cohen, Daniel and Wyplosz, Charles (1989), 'The European Monetary Union: an agnostic evaluation,' in (R. C. Bryant *et al.*, eds.) *Macroeconomic Policies in an Interdependent World*, Washington, D.C.: International Monetary Fund, pp. 311–37.
Courchene, Thomas J. (1993), 'Reflections on Canadian federalism: are there implications for European Economic and Monetary Union?' European Commission (1993), pp. 123–166.
European Commission (1977), *Report of the Study Group on the Role of Public Finance in European Integration*, collection of studies, Economic and Financial Series Nos. A12/B13, Brussels: European Economic Community.
European Commission (1993), *European Economy: The Economics of Community Public Finance*, Reports and Studies, no. 5.

Frenkel, Jacob A. and Razin, Assaf (1987), *Fiscal Policies and the World Economy*, Cambridge, MA: MIT Press.

Goodhart, Charles A. E. and Smith, Stephen (1993), 'Stabilization,' in European Commission (1993), pp. 417–55.

Hall, Robert E. (1978) 'Stochastic implications of the life-cycle hypothesis,' *Journal of Political Economy*, vol. 86, pp. 971–87.

Hubbard, R. Glenn, Skinner, Jonathan and Zeldes, Stephen P. (1994), 'The importance of precautionary motives in explaining individual and aggregate saving,' *Carnegie-Rochester Conference Series on Public Policy*, vol. 40, pp. 59–126 (June).

Hubbard, R. Glenn, Skinner, Jonathan and Zeldes, Stephen P. (1995), 'Precautionary saving and social insurance,' forthcoming *Journal of Political Economy*.

Ip, Irene K. (1993), 'Putting a new face on fiscal federalism,' in (Peter M. Leslie, Kenneth Norrie and Irene K. Ip), *A Partnership in Trouble: Renegotiating Fiscal Federalism*, Policy Study 18, C.D. Howe Institute, Ottawa: Renouf Publishing.

Kenen, Peter B. (1969), 'The theory of optimal currency areas: an eclectic view,' in (R. Mundell and A. Swoboda, eds.) *Monetary Problems of the International Economy*, Chicago: University of Chicago Press.

Masson, Paul R. and Taylor, Mark P. (1993), 'Currency unions: a survey of the issues,' in (P. R. Masson and M. P. Taylor, eds.) *Policy Issues in the Operation of Currency Unions*, Cambridge and New York: Cambridge University Press, pp. 3–51.

Mélitz, Jacques and Vori, S. (1992), 'National insurance against unevenly distributed shocks,' CEPR Discussion Paper no. 697.

Mundell, Robert A. (1961), 'A theory of optimum currency areas,' *American Economic Review*, vol. 51 (September), pp. 657–65.

Musgrave, Richard A. (1960), 'Approaches to fiscal theory of political federalism,' in *Public Finances: Needs, Sources and Utilization*, A Conference of the Universities - National Bureau Committee for Economic Research, Princeton: Princeton University Press.

Oates, Wallace E. (1972), *Fiscal Federalism*, New York: Harcourt Brace Jovanovich.

Persson, Torsten and Tabellini, Guido (1996a), 'Federal fiscal constitutions: risk sharing and moral hazard,' *Econometrica*, vol. 64 (May), pp. 623–46.

Persson, Torsten and Tabellini, Guido (1996b), 'Federal fiscal constitutions: risk sharing and redistribution,' *Journal of Political Economy*, vol. 104 (October), pp. 979–1009.

Pisani-Ferry, Jean, Italianer, Alexander and Lescure, Roland (1993), 'Stabilization properties of budgetary systems,' *European Economy: The Economics of Community Public Finance*, Reports and Studies, no. 5, pp. 511–38.

Rawls, John (1971), *A Theory of Justice*, Cambridge, MA: Harvard University Press.

Sala-I-Martin, Xavier, and Sachs, Jeffrey (1992), 'Fiscal federalism and optimum currency areas: evidence for Europe from the United States,' in (Matthew Canzoneri, Vittorio Grilli, and Paul R. Masson, eds.) *Establishing a Central Bank: Issues in Europe and Lessons from the U.S.*, Cambridge: Cambridge University Press, pp. 195–219.

Seater, John (1993), 'Ricardian equivalence,' *Journal of Economic Literature*, vol. 31, (March), pp. 142–90.

Sinn, Hans-Werner (1995), 'The subsidiarity principle and market failure in systems competition,' paper presented to a conference 'Competition or Harmonization? Fiscal Policy, Regulation, and Standards,' Munich, October 30–November 2.

Tiebout, Charles (1956), 'A pure theory of local expenditures,' *Journal of Political Economy*, vol. 64 (October), pp. 416–24.

Townsend, Robert M. (1994), 'Risk and insurance in village India,' *Econometrica*, vol. 62, no. 3, pp. 539–92.

Von Hagen, Jürgen (1992), 'Fiscal arrangements in a monetary union: evidence from the U.S.,' in (Don Fair and Christian de Boissieux, eds.) *Fiscal Policy, Taxes and the Financial System in an Increasingly Integrated Europe*, Deventer: Kluwer.

Von Hagen, Jürgen, and Hammond, George (1996), 'Insurance against asymmetric shocks in a European Monetary Union,' paper presented at a conference 'Should We Rebuild Built-in Stabilizers,' Paris, January 8–10.

Working, H. (1960), 'Note on the correlation of first differences of averages of a random chain', *Econometrica*, vol. 28, pp. 916–8.

Yaari, M. E. (1965), 'The uncertain lifetime, life insurance and the theory of the consumer,' *Review of Economic Studies*, vol. 32, pp. 137–50.

Zeldes, Stephen P. (1989), 'Consumption and liquidity constraints: an empirical investigation,' *Journal of Political Economy*, vol. 97, pp. 305–46.

# Monetary union in West Africa: who might gain, who might lose, and why?

Xavier Debrun    *IMF Research Department*
Paul Masson    *University of Toronto and Brookings Institution*
Catherine Pattillo    *IMF Research Department*

*Abstract.* We develop a model in which governments' financing needs exceed the socially optimal level because public resources are diverted to serve the narrow interests of the group in power. From a social welfare perspective, this results in undue pressure on the central bank to extract seigniorage. Monetary policy also suffers from an expansive bias, owing to the authorities' inability to precommit to price stability. Such a conjecture about the fiscal-monetary policy mix appears quite relevant in Africa, with deep implications for the incentives of fiscally heterogeneous countries to form a currency union. We calibrate the model to data for West Africa and use it to assess proposed ECOWAS monetary unions. Fiscal heterogeneity indeed appears critical in shaping regional currency blocs that would be mutually beneficial for all their members. In particular, Nigeria's membership in the configurations currently envisaged would not be in the interests of other ECOWAS countries unless it were accompanied by effective containment on Nigeria's financing needs. JEL classification: E58, E61, E62, F33

*Union monétaire en Afrique de l'Ouest : qui pourrait gagner, qui pourrait perdre, et pourquoi?* Les auteurs développent un modèle dans lequel les besoins financiers des gouvernements dépassent le niveau socialement optimal parce que des ressources publiques sont détournées de manière à servir les intérêts étroits du groupe au pouvoir. Dans une perspective de bien-être social, cela entraîne des pressions indues sur la banque centrale pour qu'elle extraie du seigneuriage. La politique monétaire souffre

Without implication, we would like to thank Ousmane Doré, Dominique Guillaume, Benoît Anne, Charalambos Tsangarides, and the participants at the conference on the 'Feasibility of Monetary Unions in African Regional Economic Communities,' organized by the UN Economic Commission for Africa (Accra, Ghana, 8–10 October 2002) for useful comments and discussions and Heather Milkiewicz for research assistance. We are also grateful to two anonymous referees for detailed comments that led to substantial improvements in the paper. The views expressed in this article do not commit any official institution. Email:cpattillo@imf.org

Canadian Journal of Economics / Revue canadienne d'Economique, Vol. 38, No. 2
May / mai 2005. Printed in Canada / Imprimé au Canada

0008-4085 / 05 / 454–481 / © Canadian Economics Association

aussi à cause d'un biais vers l'expansion monétaire du à l'incapacité des autorités à s'engager à maintenir la stabilité des prix. Une telle conjecture sur le pattern des politiques fiscale et monétaire paraît pertinente en Afrique, et cela a des profondes implications sur les incitations de pays fiscalement hétérogènes à former une union monétaire. On calibre le modèle pour l'ajuster aux données de l'Afrique de l'Ouest et on l'utilise pour évaluer les unions monétaires de l'ECOWAS. L'hétérogénéité fiscale apparaît critique dans la définition de zones monétaires mutuellement bénéfiques pour tous les membres. En particulier, la participation du Nigeria dans les configurations qui sont envisagées pour le moment ne serait pas dans l'intérêt des autres pays de l'ECO-WAS, à moins que celles-ci s'accompagnent d'une restriction effective des besoins financiers du Nigeria.

## 1. Introduction

The elimination of national currencies and their replacement by a common regional currency continues to be a topical subject. It has inspired much research, mainly in the European context, but other regions are now considering the advisability of such a project. The reasons for doing so range from wanting to promote regional solidarity and integration to a fear that independent national currencies may be subject to destabilizing speculation. One example is a project to create a common currency – the *eco* – among 13 countries of West Africa. This project has the particularity that the region already includes a monetary union, the West African Economic and Monetary Union (WAEMU),[1] and those countries that are not members of it propose to create a second monetary zone (the West African Monetary Zone, or WAMZ) by July 2005, with the intention of subsequently merging it with WAEMU.[2] Figure 1 shows the overlapping membership of the CFA franc zone, ECOWAS, and WAMZ.

In this paper, we analyse the main costs and benefits of the proposed monetary unions in West Africa using a simple theoretical framework[3] calibrated to reflect some of the region's key economic and political features. The analysis encompasses traditional 'Optimum Currency Area' (OCA) arguments as well as the role of commitment problems in macroeconomic policy, placing a special emphasis on the distortions generated by politically motivated decision makers. More specifically, we assume that governments in power tend to channel public resources towards socially useless activities and that they are ineffective at raising sufficient tax revenues. With politically dependent central banks, such distortions affect

---

1 WAEMU, which is part of the CFA franc zone, has eight members, namely, Benin, Burkina Faso, Côte d'Ivoire, Guinea-Bissau, Mali, Niger, Senegal, and Togo.
2 These countries are among the fifteen countries forming the Economic Community of West African States (ECOWAS). The five countries participating in the WAMZ project currently have their own independent currencies: Gambia, Ghana, Guinea, Nigeria, and Sierra Leone. In addition to these five and the eight WAEMU countries, ECOWAS has two other members: Liberia, which has so far declined to participate in the project, and Cape Verde, whose currency is linked to the euro.
3 It draws on a theoretical model presented in Debrun (2003).

456   X. Debrun, P. Masson, and C. Pattillo

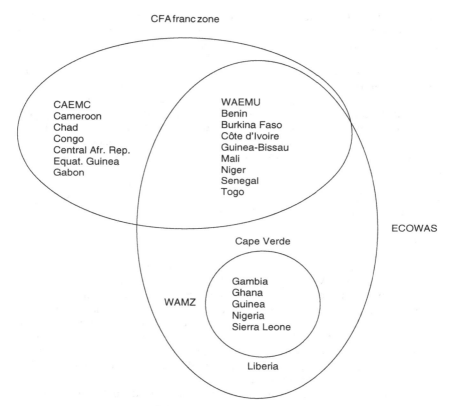

FIGURE 1   Membership of CFA franc zone and ECOWAS

monetary policy through the authorities' incentive to extract seigniorage. Differences in fiscal distortions affect incentives for countries to join a given monetary union, and the willingness of existing members to accept new entrants. This aspect is arguably of considerably greater importance in Africa than in Europe, and we present some evidence below on the extent of fiscal distortions.

We consider only the direct effect of monetary unification, not the possible use of supranational institutions to establish anti-inflationary credibility, for instance, through an external guarantee of a peg to a hard currency. In the model, net gains or losses from joining a monetary union depend on the correlation of shocks to the terms of trade (TOT) of members of the union, the political distortions affecting fiscal policy, and the degree of economic integration between them. We calibrate the model to data for West African countries, and examine the desirability of forming a monetary union, either among all the ECOWAS countries,[4] or among a subset of them. Since the parameters cannot be precisely pinned down, a sensitivity analysis is undertaken in order to see if the results about the feasibility of monetary unions are robust in the face of plausible variations of the parameters.

It needs to be recognized, of course, that there may be other incentives to join a monetary union, such as the desire to foster regional integration, for example, through trade creation. In addition, the peg of the CFA franc to the euro and the guarantee of convertibility provided by the French treasury give an extra element of stability to the existing WAEMU zone that would presumably not be extended to a greater West African currency. We do not attempt to model this in the present paper, but we discuss below how initiatives to form a wider monetary union might affect its stability.

In the second section of the paper we summarize the theoretical model, while in section 3 we describe its calibration. The simulation results are presented and discussed in section 4. Section 5 concludes.

## 2. The model

In this section we summarize the key features of the theoretical model supporting the simulations.[5] We keep the model as simple as possible and rely on the mainstream literature on European monetary integration, in particular Beetsma and Bovenberg (1998, 1999) and Martin (1995). The relevance of that strand of literature for our exercise is two-fold. First, it emphasizes the role of commitment problems in macroeconomic policy, an aspect that is particularly relevant in Africa, where credible institutional fixes (i.e., central bank independence and fiscal rules) are harder to implement than in other regions. Second, it is based on straightforward extensions of the highly flexible Barro-Gordon (1983) framework, which allows for neat analytical solutions, while at the same time addressing the interaction between monetary and fiscal policies and international policy coordination. This approach is well suited to shed light on regional efforts to build a multilateral monetary union similar to the one envisaged in West Africa. The present multilateral focus sharply contrasts with the treatment of currency unions proposed by Alesina and Barro (2002), who view monetary integration as a process of dollarization in which inflation-prone countries adopt 'hard' currencies in a *bilateral* 'client-anchor' relationship. Another key difference is that Alesina and Barro (2002)

---

4 Guinea-Bissau and Liberia are not considered because of data availability problems and because the former has been a member of WAEMU only since 1997 and the latter is not a participant in the WAMZ project. Cape Verde is not considered either, since it is not a participant in WAMZ and its interest in the wider ECOWAS currency union is unclear.

5 See Debrun (2003) for systematic comparisons with the relevant literature. A technical appendix with the key derivations is available from the authors upon request. For a survey of the recent literature on monetary and fiscal policies in a currency union, see Beetsma and Debrun (2004).

458   X. Debrun, P. Masson, and C. Pattillo

emphasize the induced increase in bilateral trade among the members of a currency union, a dimension that is admittedly less relevant in the African context (see section 3).

We consider a static, $n$-good, $n$-country economic area, which is assumed to be small vis-à-vis the rest of the world. Countries differ only by the size of their GDP, the political distortion affecting fiscal policy design, and random supply shocks. We use log-linear specifications, where each variable represents a relative deviation from an arbitrary steady state. Variables or parameters indexed by the subscript $i$ are country specific, the other variables or parameters being identical across countries. All parameters are positive.

As in the related literature, a supply function relates (the log of) output ($y$) to *unexpected* inflation ($\pi_i - \pi_i^e$). Following Alesina and Tabellini (1987) and many subsequent papers, an ad valorem tax of $\tau\%$ on firms' value added reduces output below its full-employment level (standardized to zero). Individual policies also influence neighbouring countries, creating a policy coordination problem (Hamada 1985). To focus on the key difference between autonomy and participation in a monetary union, we restrict the coordination problem to monetary policy[6] and assume that, under flexible exchange rates, a monetary expansion in a given country has a contractionary impact on the other countries in the region. Hence, non-coordinated monetary policies entail excessive inflation because of mutually fruitless attempts to offset the negative impact of the neighbours' expansion (Hamada 1985; Canzoneri and Gray 1985; or Canzoneri and Henderson 1991). Martin (1995) provides one possible rationale for negative externalities on the supply side,[7] claiming that multinationals established in different countries constantly reshuffle production in favour of plants located in countries with low real wages achieved through loose monetary policies.

Another rationale that may be particularly relevant in Western Africa is the existence of bottlenecks in the supply of conventional intermediate goods traded at the regional level. Those bottlenecks mainly reflect limited local production capacity (as is often the case for cement or refined petroleum products, for instance) and inefficient port and transportation infrastructures (a fact that concerns all intermediate goods imported from overseas such as machinery or vehicles). The technical appendix formally derives a supply function consistent with the case of an intermediate good imported from

---

6 For recent discussions of fiscal coordination problems in monetary unions, see, for instance, Beetsma, Debrun and Klassen (2001), Andersen (2002), or Uhlig (2002) and the references therein.

7 Multi-country models in the 'new open economy macroeconomics' literature tend to emphasize the terms of trade as the international transmission channel of monetary policy. A monetary expansion worsens the terms of trade, creating a positive spillover for neighbouring countries (see, e.g., Clarida, Galì, and Gertler 2002 and the references therein). In reality, such effects should materialize only for 'large' countries in the trade-theoretic sense and can be deemed negligible for our analysis of a group of small economies whose policy choices do not influence their terms of trade.

overseas at a fixed dollar price. In the short-medium run, inefficient port and transportation infrastructures make the supply of that good imperfectly elastic so that its local currency price reflects not only nominal exchange rate fluctuations vis-à-vis the dollar but also pressure from domestic demand. Hence, an unexpected monetary expansion in one country stimulates the demand by domestic firms, driving up the price of the intermediate good beyond the rate of depreciation. If intra-regional exchange rates do not overshoot, countries that did not engineer the same monetary stimulus face higher local currency price for the intermediate good that results in a contraction of their domestic output.

The magnitude of such spillovers depends on the size of the country initiating the monetary expansion and on the importance of formal and informal trade between that country and its neighbours. This explains why we later link our supply-side externality to the intensity of intra-regional trade flows. In practice though, it is very difficult to quantify cross-border spillovers in Western Africa. A recent case study of the regional economic impact of the political crisis in Côte d'Ivoire nevertheless suggests that they might be quite significant for immediate neighbors (see Doré, Anne, and Engmann 2003).

In the supply function (1), the externality is captured by parameters $\theta_{i,k}$, representing the marginal effect of a monetary policy action in country $k$ on output in country $i$. We also assume that output is subject to a country-specific terms-of-trade shock $\varepsilon_i$, which is zero-mean, non-autocorrelated, and with finite variance $\sigma^2_{\varepsilon_i}$.

$$y_i = c(\pi_i - \pi_i^e - \tau_i) - \sum_{k \neq i, k=1}^{n} \theta_{i,k} c(\pi_k - \pi_k^e) + \varepsilon_i, \qquad i = 1, \ldots, n. \quad (1)$$

Following Alesina and Tabellini (1987) and most of the subsequent literature, we impose a one-period budget constraint approximated by equation (2).

$$g_i = \mu\pi_i + \tau_i - \delta_i, \qquad i = 1, \ldots, n, \qquad (2)$$

where $g_i$ and $\tau_i$ are the ratios of socially beneficial government spending and fiscal revenues to GDP, respectively, and $\mu$ is the inflation tax base. The fixed parameter $\delta_i$ accounts for country-specific inefficiencies affecting fiscal policy design, such as tax collection costs, the appropriation of tax revenues by corrupt officials, and the allocation of scarce public resources to socially wasteful projects.[8] In sum, it symbolizes the dead-weight loss of institutional inefficiencies

---

8 Inefficiencies in developing countries' fiscal policy design are well documented (Gupta, Honjo, and Verhoeven 1997, 2000; Mauro, 1998; Robinson and Torvik, 2002). Hefeker (2003) adopts a similar specification of fiscal inefficiency. An obvious alternative to our constant total distortion would be to introduce 'iceberg costs,' thereby assuming a constant *marginal* distortion. However, the fixed-cost conjecture has overwhelming advantages in terms of tractability. As the solution of the model with iceberg costs yields similar results, we do not expect the analysis of monetary integration under this assumption to be qualitatively different.

460   X. Debrun, P. Masson, and C. Pattillo

affecting fiscal policy (as a proportion of total output) and therefore comes as a wedge between the actual tax payments made by firms (which distort production; see equation (1)) and seigniorage revenues on the one hand, and the socially useful government spending on the other hand (see equation (3)).

To preserve analytical tractability, and in common with much of the related literature, we assume that policymakers maximize utility functions generalizing Barro and Gordon (1983).[9]

$$U_i^G = \frac{1}{2}\left\{-a(\pi_i - \tilde{\pi}(\varepsilon_i))^2 - b\tau_i^2 - \gamma(g_i - \tilde{g}_i)^2\right\} + y_i, \qquad i = 1, \ldots, n. \quad (3)$$

Equation (3) implies that the marginal benefit (cost) of output gain (loss) is constant whereas deviations of inflation, taxes and expenditure from 'ideal' levels (denoted by a tilde and assumed to be zero in the case of taxes) are increasingly costly. Since the linearity in $y_i$ precludes output stabilization policies (i.e., the variance of output does not directly matter to policymakers), we follow Muscatelli (1998) and restore an implicit trade-off between the variability of inflation and the variability of output by making the socially desirable inflation rate contingent on supply shocks as follows: $\tilde{\pi}(\varepsilon_i) = -\eta\varepsilon_i$ with $\eta > 0$. A negative (positive) output shock thus incites the policymaker to tolerate positive (negative) inflation.

With autonomous monetary policies, policymakers independently choose effective tax rates $\tau_i$ and inflation rates $\pi_i$ maximizing (3). Policy choices are made simultaneously by all governments, taking the neighbours' policies as given (Nash conjecture[10]), which implicitly supposes flexible exchange rates, as illustrated in the technical appendix. The optimal, time-consistent policy mix is derived under standard assumptions, that is, complete information, rational expectations and the following sequence of events: (i) binding nominal wage contracts are signed, (ii) shocks are realized and perfectly observed by all, and (iii) monetary and fiscal policies are decided. Under monetary autonomy, the time-consistent policy mix (denoted by a star superscript) for any country $i$ can be characterized as follows (see the technical appendix for details):

$$\pi_i^* = \frac{\gamma\mu b}{\Lambda}(\tilde{g}_i + \delta_i) + \frac{(b+\gamma)+\gamma\mu}{\Lambda}c - \frac{a(b+\gamma)\eta}{\Lambda}\varepsilon_i, \qquad i = 1, \ldots, n \quad (4)$$

$$\tau_i^* = \frac{\gamma a}{\Lambda}(\tilde{g}_i + \delta_i) - \frac{\gamma\mu(1+\mu)+a}{\Lambda}c + \frac{a\gamma\mu\eta}{\Lambda}\varepsilon_i \quad (5)$$

---

9   The quasi-linear specification brings about additional algebraic simplifications (see Alesina, Angeloni, and Etro 2001; Muscatelli 1998; and Debrun 2001).

10   The determination of monetary and fiscal policies might also be envisaged as a Stackelberg leadership game in which credible commitments on fiscal policy actions (e.g., through a formal budgetary process) are made *before* monetary policy is chosen (See Beetsma and Bovenberg 1998; and Beetsma, Debrun and Klaassen, 2001). However, this presupposes a degree of pre-commitment that we deem unlikely in the specific context considered in this paper.

$$g_i^* = \frac{\gamma(a + \mu^2 b)}{\Lambda} \tilde{g}_i - \frac{ab}{\Lambda} \delta_i + \frac{b\mu - a}{\Lambda} c - \frac{ab\mu\eta}{\Lambda} \varepsilon_i \qquad (6)$$

or equivalently,

$$g_i^* + \delta_i = \left[\frac{\gamma a + \gamma \mu^2 b}{\Lambda}\right][\tilde{g}_i + \delta_i] + \left[\frac{b\mu - a}{\Lambda}\right] c + \left[\frac{-a\eta\mu b}{\Lambda}\right]\varepsilon_i,$$

with $\Lambda = a(b + \gamma) + \gamma\mu^2 b > 0$.

Key features of the equilibrium are the following. First, the average inflation rate is unambiguously positive, indicating that tax revenues are on average too low to completely finance the socially beneficial expenditure ($\tilde{g}_i$) and to make up for the institutional dead-weight loss ($\delta_i$). Second, distortionary tax rates ($\tau_i$) increase with the socially desirable amounts of public spending and the institutional dead-weight loss $\delta_i$, and decrease with the marginal effect of policy instruments ($\tau_i$ and $\pi_i$) on output ($c$). Indeed, $c$ measures the marginal output cost of taxes but also the marginal output gain from unexpected inflation; so higher $c$ leads to higher equilibrium inflation, greater seigniorage revenues, and, correspondingly, less reliance on tax revenues. Third, equilibrium government spending increases with the desired public spending level $\tilde{g}_i$ and decreases with the direct and indirect (output) costs of taxation and inflation. Also, the resources wasted in inefficient tax collection or socially useless projects ($\delta_i$) further reduce the equilibrium level of socially beneficial spending ($g_i$).

In equations (4) and (5), the terms in $\tilde{g}_i + \delta_i$ characterize the trade-off between the direct relative utility costs of collecting revenues (through either inflation or distortionary taxes), on the one hand, and the need to finance socially useful expenditure *and* to make up for wasted resources, on the other hand. To simplify discussions involving that trade-off, we will hereafter refer to $\tilde{g}_i + \delta_i$ as government $i$'s *unconstrained financing needs* (UFN). In the same equations, the terms in $c$ capture the typical Barro-Gordon inflation bias and an additional incentive to rely on inflationary financing stemming from the output cost of distortionary taxation. The inflation bias distorts the ex ante optimal outcome that would prevail if the policymakers were able to make credible commitments on inflation,[11] and in doing so, relaxes the budget constraint, allowing higher spending and lower taxes which in turn lead to greater output. In other words, the distortion resulting from the lack of commitment shifts the burden of financing expenditure from taxation to inflation (see also Alesina and Tabellini 1987).

In a monetary union (MU), monetary policy is decided by a common central bank (CCB) whose actions maximize a GDP-weighted average of individual policymakers' utility functions (see equation (7)).

---

11 The 'commitment' solution is discussed in Debrun (2003).

462   X. Debrun, P. Masson, and C. Pattillo

$$U^{CCB} = \sum_{i=1}^{n} \omega_i U_i^G, \tag{7}$$

with $\omega_i > 0$, $\forall i$ and $\Sigma_{i=1}^n \omega_i = 1$

It is crucial at this stage to note that we seek to isolate the 'pure' effect of monetary unification on policy outcomes. Therefore, we refrain from considering the delegation of national monetary power to a supranational central bank as an external fix to domestic institutional weaknesses; instead, we assume that the CCB is subject to the same type of political pressures as a national central bank would be. The only difference is that, in a monetary union, individual pressures are diluted according to the relative weight of the country in the joint decision process.

The time-consistent policy mix is described by the equations (8) to (10), where a subscript $MU$ stands for monetary union and a subscript $A$ designates cross-country, $\omega$-weighted averages, that is $x_A = \Sigma_{i=1}^n \omega_i x_i$ for $x \in \{\tilde{g},\delta,\varepsilon\}$, while

$$\theta_A = \sum_{i \in N} \sum_{j \in N} \omega_i \theta_{i,j} \Big/ \sum_{i \in N} \omega_i, .$$

where the set $N$ represents the countries in the monetary union and $\theta_{i,i}=0$. Hence, $\theta_A$ captures the extent to which monetary unification leads to internalize the monetary policy externalities prevailing under autonomous policymaking.

For simplicity of exposition, we reproduce here only the solution for a monetary union among the $n$ countries.[12] Moreover, to ease comparisons with the case of autonomy, it is useful to introduce the parameter $\Psi_i = \tilde{g}_A/\tilde{g}_i$, which captures the discrepancy between country $i$'s spending objective and the aggregate spending objective considered by the CCB. If different from 1, the common monetary policy fails to achieve the optimal trade-off between tax and monetary financing for country $i$. Finally, we will also assume that $\delta_A/\delta_i = \Psi_i$, which is tantamount to saying that the impact of institutional failures on fiscal policies is strictly proportional to the desired size of the government (as captured by $\tilde{g}_i$). That assumption – supported by the empirical evidence reported in table 1 – proves convenient in the welfare analysis because it allows expressing the equations of interest in terms of the government's unconstrained financing need (UFN) as a whole.

$$\pi^*_{MU} = \frac{\gamma\mu b}{\Lambda}(\tilde{g}_A + \delta_A) + \frac{(1-\theta_A)(b+\gamma)+\gamma\mu}{\Lambda}c - \frac{a(b+\gamma)\eta}{\Lambda}\varepsilon_A \tag{8}$$

$$\tau^*_{i,MU} = \left[\frac{a\gamma}{\Lambda} + \frac{\gamma^2\mu^2 b[1-\Psi_i]}{(b+\gamma)\Lambda}\right](\tilde{g}_i + \delta_i) - \frac{\gamma\mu(1-\theta_A+\mu)+a}{\Lambda}c + \frac{a\gamma\mu\eta}{\Lambda}\varepsilon_A \tag{9}$$

12 Debrun (2003) develops the general solution where only a subset of countries would form a monetary union.

$$g^*_{i,\,MU} = \left[\frac{\gamma\mu^2 b^2 \Psi_i}{(b+\gamma)\Lambda}\right](\tilde{g}_i + \delta_i) + (b+\gamma)^{-1}(\gamma\,\tilde{g}_i - b\delta_i) + \frac{(1-\theta_A)b\mu - a}{\Lambda}c$$

$$-\frac{ab\mu\eta}{\Lambda}\varepsilon_A, \qquad (10)$$

or equivalently,

$$\Leftrightarrow g^*_{i,\,MU} + \delta_i = \left[\frac{a\gamma(b+\gamma) + \gamma\mu^2 b(b\Psi_i + \gamma)}{(b+\gamma)\Lambda}\right][\tilde{g}_i + \delta_i] + \left[\frac{(1-\theta_A)b\mu - a}{\Lambda}\right]c$$

$$-\left[\frac{ab\mu\eta}{\Lambda}\right]\varepsilon_i.$$

From equation (8), we see that the common monetary policy (inflation rate) depends on the average UFN in the area, while it only stabilizes the average supply shock. The properties of the equilibrium policy mix reflect the fact that the gains from monetary unification essentially depend on the ability of the new regime to address the excessive inflation problem and the implications of the latter on fiscal strategies. Specifically, the CCB is able to credibly reduce average inflation with respect to autonomy because it internalizes the adverse external effects of individual monetary expansions. In that sense, monetary unification serves as a partial surrogate to the credible appointment of a conservative central banker. With the CCB now determining seigniorage revenues according to union-wide objectives, policymakers need to adjust national tax and expenditure choices.

Having obtained closed-form solutions for the time-consistent policy mix under autonomy and monetary union, we can derive the net welfare effect of participating in the monetary union against the alternative of autonomous monetary policy. Denoting by $E_{-1}$ mathematical expectations taken before the first stage of the game, the net welfare effect of monetary integration for some country $i$ is defined as follows:

$$E_{-1}G_i(n) \equiv E_{-1}U_i^G\big|_{MU} - E_{-1}U_i^G\big|_{Autonomy}$$

$$= \frac{\theta_A(2 - \theta_A)(b+\gamma)}{2\Lambda}c^2$$

$$+ \frac{\gamma\mu b(1 - \Psi_i)(\tilde{g}_i + \delta_i)}{\Lambda}\left[(1 - \theta_A)c - \frac{\gamma\mu b(1 - \Psi_i)(\tilde{g}_i + \delta_i)}{2(b+\gamma)}\right]$$

$$- \frac{a^2\eta^2(b+\gamma)(1 - \omega_i)^2}{2\Lambda}\left[\sigma^2_{\varepsilon_i} + \sigma^2_{\bar{\varepsilon}_{-i}} - 2\,\text{cov}\,(\varepsilon_i, \bar{\varepsilon}_{-i})\right], \qquad (11)$$

where $\sigma^2_x$ symbolizes the variance of a random variable $x$ and $\bar{\varepsilon}_{-i} = \Sigma_{k \neq i}(\omega_k/1 - \omega_i)\varepsilon_k$ (the GDP-weighted average of supply shocks across

464    X. Debrun, P. Masson, and C. Pattillo

the $n-1$ other member states of the monetary union) so that $\varepsilon_A = \omega_i \varepsilon_i + (1 - \omega_i) \bar{\varepsilon}_{-i}$.

The first line of the right-hand side of (11) is strictly positive, showing the unambiguous benefits from a lower Barro-Gordon inflationary bias. The second line summarizes the effect of cross-country differences in governments' financing needs. The latter is country specific and ambiguous. It ultimately depends on the sign and magnitude of the discrepancy between an individual government's UFN and the union's average. On the one hand, cross country differences in UFN contribute to decrease individual welfare because the union-wide inflation rate will only by chance coincide with a country's desired trade-off between seigniorage and tax revenues. On the other hand, profligate governments (i.e., with a relatively high UFN, or $\Psi_i < 1$) benefit from the participation of more fiscally conservative partners (i.e., countries with lower UFN, or $\Psi_i > 1$) because the latter impose some restraint on the CCB, thereby amplifying the reduction in the average inflation rate profligate countries expect from monetary unification. Correspondingly, countries with small UFN suffer from the pressure exerted by others on the CCB to produce greater monetary financing, thereby mitigating the gains from CCB's pseudo-conservatism. Also notice that the relative importance of these effects on governments' utility increases when the impact of unification on monetary discipline is smaller – that is, when $(1 - \theta_A)$ is larger. Net losses due to fiscal heterogeneity may thus more than offset the gains derived from the pseudo-conservatism of the CCB. As the model assumes that the pressure exerted by a country on the CCB is proportional to its size, the joint cross-country distribution of sizes and financing needs should be critical to determine the equilibrium configuration of monetary unions in the region.

The third line of (11) accounts for the suboptimal stabilization of country-specific shocks by the CCB. That term is equal to zero if and only if $\sigma_{\varepsilon_i}^2 = \sigma_{\bar{\varepsilon}_{-i}}^2$ and corr $(\varepsilon_i, \bar{\varepsilon}_{-i}) = 1$.

Overall, equation (11) indicates that the decision to form a monetary union rests on a trade-off between the benefits of having a supranational currency intrinsically more stable than the national currency and the costs associated with idiosyncrasies.[13] In addition to shock asymmetry, our model emphasizes the differences in the financing needs by governments of potential member states.

## 3. Calibration

The model summarized above implies that for any country, the net gains from joining a monetary union depend on: (1) differences in governments' financing needs; (2) the correlation of their shocks with those of other members; and (3) the strength of negative monetary policy externalities (which depends on the

---

[13] In their study of international unions, Alesina, Angeloni, and Etro (2001) also note: 'central to the political economy of all unions is the existence of a tension between the heterogeneity of individual countries' preferences and the advantage of taking certain decisions in common.'

intensity of trade linkages). Size differences among countries also influence the prospects of particular monetary union configurations. Broadly, the stylized facts on these points in West Africa are as follows. (1) Concerning fiscal policy, WAEMU countries had higher revenue, lower spending, lower deficits (as ratios to GDP), and substantially lower inflation relative to WAMZ countries on average during 1996–2000 (appendix table A1).[14] Our calculation of the fiscal policy distortion discussed below also uses an institutional quality index, which varies substantially across the countries (see table 1). (2) Terms of trade (TOT) shocks (measured by standard deviations of changes in the TOT) are large and are typically not well correlated across the ECOWAS countries (table A2), owing in large part to differences in commodity exports. In particular, as Nigeria is the only net oil exporter, its TOT changes are negatively correlated on average with those of the rest of the countries. Note also that the correlations tend to be higher for the WAEMU countries among themselves than either the correlation of WAEMU with non-WAEMU countries or the correlations among non-WAEMU countries. (3) Internal trade within the ECOWAS region is relatively small, at a little over 10% of the average of exports and imports (Masson and Pattillo 2001), indicating that the level of the monetary policy externality in the model is relatively low. The WAEMU countries, however, trade considerably more among themselves than do the WAMZ countries, in part because of the pre-existing monetary union among WAEMU countries and of the inevitably more intense trade flows between coastal and landlocked countries in the WAEMU.[15]

Besides the negative supply-side externality conjectured in the model, negative spillover effects of unexpected inflationary shocks or depreciations on output in neighbouring countries may in practice also operate through demand-side channels. The latter may be relevant in the case of Nigeria and its neighbours, for example, since Nigeria has substantial parallel trade with the WAEMU countries bordering it. In particular, Nigeria and Niger share a long, porous border over which substantial amounts of livestock, food products, textiles, and small manufactures are traded. Depreciations in Nigeria or other changes in Nigeria's trade and exchange rate policies have significant effects on cross-border trade, real exchange rates on the naira/CFA parallel market, and real incomes in Niger (Dissou and Dorosh 1998).

There is broad consistency between the model's predictions about the monetary-fiscal policy mix and the experience in West Africa. The model predicts that after

14 Of course, period averages can conceal large variability. For example, while fiscal performance in WAEMU generally improved in the post-devaluation period 1994–7, there has been marked deterioration since then, partly owing to unfavourable terms of trade developments, but also caused by weak policies in several countries (Doré and Masson 2002). While Nigeria's fiscal position varies substantially with the volatile oil price cycles, the 1996–2000 period is not particularly atypical. Oil prices were in the moderate range, except in 2000, when they were high.

15 All WAMZ countries have access to sea. As documented in Doré, Anne, and Engmann (2003, table 13), the share of imports from Côte d'Ivoire is much larger for its landlocked neighbours than for those having access to sea.

466   X. Debrun, P. Masson, and C. Pattillo

joining a monetary union, countries would have lower inflation, further implying that expenditure would be financed with higher taxes. Some supporting evidence, noted above, comes from the comparison of the WAEMU countries with their WAMZ neighbours that have retained substantial monetary autonomy. Inflation is substantially lower and revenues are higher in the WAEMU countries (table A1). Although each is a special case, it is also interesting to look at the inflation experiences of countries that were not continuously part of the CFA franc. These include Mali, which left the franc zone at independence but rejoined it in 1984; Equatorial Guinea, a former Spanish colony, which joined the Central African currency zone in 1985; and Guinea-Bissau, a former Portuguese colony which joined WAEMU in 1997. For all three countries, table A3 shows that inflation has been dramatically lower in the period after joining the CFA zone relative to a pre-monetary union period beginning in 1970. The comparison is even more stark when 1994–5, the two years influenced by the CFA franc devaluation, are excluded.

To calibrate the model, we need to determine values for parameters related to the supply function (equation (1)), the government budget constraint (equation (2)), and the government utility function (equation (3)). Some of these parameters are country specific, and others are assumed to be the same for all countries. In this section as well as the next, we discuss the sensitivity of our results to alternative parameterizations.

Looking first at the log-linear supply function (1), we calibrate the term $\sigma_{\varepsilon_i}$ so that it properly reflects the impact of term-of-trade variability on domestic output.[16] It is appropriate to scale the variance of the terms of trade by the degree of openness of the economy, because changes in the trade balance affect output in proportion to the importance of trade for the economy.[17,18]

One of the potentially important considerations in discussing the costs of monetary unions is the asymmetry of shocks facing participating countries. This asymmetry is measured by the extent to which the correlation matrix of terms of trade shocks (table A2) departs from the unit matrix. In fact, as we

16 Kose and Riezman (2001) provide evidence of the importance of terms of trade shocks for African economies.
17 Writing the level of output as the sum of domestic demand ($DD$) and net exports ($p_X X - p_M M$), $Y = DD + p_X X - p_M M$, we see that, if trade is initially balanced and we normalize the initial price indices to equal unity, it is the case in differential form that

$$\frac{dY}{Y} = \frac{dDD}{Y} + \frac{d(X-M)}{Y} + \frac{X}{Y}\left(\frac{dp_X}{p_X} - \frac{dp_M}{p_M}\right).$$

The last term in parentheses is the change in the terms of trade. If trade is not balanced, then the expression can be written in terms of the average of exports and imports, and a further term in the sum of changes in the price of imports and exports appears, multiplied by the trade balance. We ignore the latter term as being of second order; the standard deviation of the TOT shocks is thus scaled by openness to get the relevant $\sigma_\varepsilon$ (see columns 1–3 of appendix table A2).
18 Openness is calculated from exports and imports of goods and services taken either from the *Balance of Payments Yearbook 2001*, the *Direction of Trade Statistics Yearbook 2001* (DOT), or *International Financial Statistics*. Generally, the sources agreed, but in some cases data were missing or a very low ratio suggested data problems, so an alternative source was used.

shall see below, asymmetry of external shocks does not play a great role in the analysis, even when we calculate openness as the sum (not the average) of exports and imports, divided by GDP.

Turning to the externality parameters, we calibrate the $\theta_{i,k}$s to the data for country $i$'s exports to country $k$, scaled by the GDP of country $i$, since we are considering the supply function for country $i$. This matrix is given in table A4, and is based on IMF Direction of Trade Statistics data, taken for 1999 or the most recent year for which data were available. There are many zeros, which may be because of missing data rather than the absence of trade. Moreover, informal trade is, by definition, omitted, so we make an ad hoc adjustment for it by increasing all the $\theta_{i,k}$ by 25%.[19]

Another parameter deriving from the supply function is $\theta_A$, which depends on the composition of the monetary union: it is a GDP-weighted average of the trade linkages among the various countries that are included, scaled by the total GDP of the zone. We obtain $\theta_A = 0.0399$ for the WAEMU and $\theta_A = 0.0591$ for the full ECOWAS monetary union. The scale of the externality parameter is critical for the existence of feasible monetary unions. Indeed, absent that feature (i.e., for $\theta_A = 0$), fiscal heterogeneity would always entail net welfare losses for all countries with relatively low financing needs, as can be seen from setting $\theta_A = 0$ in equation (11) – the first terms on the right-hand side would be zero, while the other two terms would be unambiguously negative for all countries with $\Psi_i > 1$. Thus, increasing this parameter by 25% has a positive effect on expected utility levels under a monetary union, although this ad hoc adjustment in externality parameters turns out to have no qualitative impact on the simulation results.

Second, turning to the government instantaneous budget constraint (equation (2)), data for inflation and government spending and taxes as ratios to GDP are readily available (table A1) and allow calculation of $\mu$, the hypothetical tax base on which to apply the inflation tax in order to balance the government's budget. Since the model requires this parameter to be the same for all countries, we calculate it from the average for the five non-WAEMU countries in our sample:[20] the deficit (with sign reversed), divided by inflation, provides the estimate: $\mu = 7.64/15.23 = 0.50$. An alternative would be to use the money/income ratio, but doing so would hardly be consistent with the no-borrowing constraint of equation (2) and might not capture all the sources of seigniorage.

Third, we have emphasized the effects of political distortions on the design of fiscal policy, assuming that resources were diverted from socially productive ends to benefit private interests. For any amount of socially desirable spending $\tilde{g}_i$, that fiscal wedge increases the government's financing needs by $\delta_i\%$ of

19  This adjustment is fairly conservative, in the light of existing estimates of the size of informal trade. As monetary policy externalities are proportional to trade openness, the adjustment increases the benefits from monetary unification, but leaves unchanged the costs of heterogeneity (asymmetric shocks and country-specific fiscal regime).

20  These countries are the closest to the regime of monetary discretion assumed in the theoretical model.

468    X. Debrun, P. Masson, and C. Pattillo

GDP, resulting in higher inflation and tax rates. As the analysis in the previous section shows, the UFN is the relevant concept to study the equilibrium policy mix in the context of our model.

Estimating UFN is challenging because its components ($\tilde{g}_i$ and $\delta_i$) are unobservable. Taking expenditures on health and education as the best possible proxies for the socially beneficial expenditure entering in $g_i$, we turn to the data to identify and eventually estimate the systematic *underspending* on those specific items predicted by our theoretical model as being a result of $\delta_i$ (see equation (6)). In line with a growing literature on the economic impact of institutions (e.g., Mauro, 1998; Gupta, Davoodi, and Tiongson 2000), our own regressions explaining government expenditure on health and education in a cross-section of African countries (as of 1999) confirm that countries with poor institutions (and therefore more diversion) spend relatively *less* on health and education, than countries with good institutions.

To estimate the extent of resource diversion in the countries of our sample, we compare actual outlays on health and education with the expenditure levels predicted by the empirical equations under the highest possible ranking of our index of institutional quality, implicitly assuming that 'perfect' institutions lead to zero diversion[21] (see 'no diversion' columns in table 1). For each sector, resource diversion is thus the difference between the actual and the hypothetical figures.

Since social (and governments') *objectives* in terms of public spending (that is $\tilde{g}_i$) are unobservable as well, we take *actual* public expenditure as a proxy of the desired level of socially beneficial spending. We thereby assume that the population would ideally like its government to allocate 100% of actual outlays on items it deems desirable, which seems both legitimate and plausible. To obtain the UFN, we thus increase actual public spending (our proxy for $\tilde{g}_i$) by a factor $\left(1 + \left[\delta_i^{HE}/2\left(g_i^{HE} + \delta_i^{HE}\right)\right]\right)$, which is (one plus half of)[22] the estimated resource diversion in percentage of the no-diversion spending levels (third and fifth columns in table 1).

Fourth, the utility function parameters are directly borrowed from Debrun, Masson, and Pattillo (2002), whose slightly different specification allowed us to calibrate $a$, $b$, and $\gamma$ directly on the basis of observed fiscal data for countries in the region.[23] Appendix I in Debrun, Masson, and Pattillo (2002) describes in detail the calibration of utility function parameters $a$, $b$, and $\gamma$ as functions of $c$. Normalizing $c = 1$, we derived the following baseline values for the other parameters: $a = 0.9657$, $b = 9.0759$, $\gamma = 1.7723$.

Testing sensitivity of the simulations to halving and doubling each of the three parameters in turn, keeping the others constant (see Debrun, Masson, and Pattillo 2002) showed that although the magnitude of the gains differed

---

21  Admittedly, perfect institutions are not of this world. The same is probably true for the absence of political distortions in the policymaking process.
22  We apply only half of the estimated diversion to be conservative in our estimates.
23  It should be noted, however, that the welfare effects of monetary unification are identical to those calculated in Debrun, Masson, and Pattillo (2002).

TABLE 1
Expenditure on priority sectors: estimates of the diversion effect (in percentage of GDP)

| | ICRG Institutional quality index (1) | Health (1999) | | Education (1999) | | Diversion in percent of no diversion (6) | Government spending | |
|---|---|---|---|---|---|---|---|---|
| | | Actual (2) | No diversion (3) | Actual (4) | No diversion (5) | | Actual[a] (7) | UFN (8) |
| Country | | | | in percentage of GDP | | | | |
| Benin[b] | n.a. | n.a. | n.a. | n.a. | n.a. | n.a. | 18.5 | 21.6 |
| Burkina Faso | 4.3 | 1.2 | 2.6 | 2.0 | 2.9 | 42.2 | 24.9 | 30.2 |
| Côte d'Ivoire | 5.5 | 1.2 | 2.3 | 5.5 | 6.2 | 21.5 | 20.8 | 23.0 |
| Gambia, The | 5.6 | 1.6 | 2.6 | 2.6 | 3.2 | 29.3 | 24.5 | 28.1 |
| Ghana | 5.6 | 1.4 | 2.7 | n.a. | n.a. | 47.7 | 28.2 | 35.0 |
| Guinea | 4.6 | 2.1 | 3.3 | 1.6 | 2.4 | 35.7 | 16.4 | 19.3 |
| Mali | 3.4 | 1.9 | 3.4 | 2.2 | 3.2 | 38.2 | 22.8 | 27.2 |
| Niger | 4.0 | 1.4 | 2.8 | n.a. | n.a. | 49.9 | 16.1 | 20.1 |
| Nigeria | 4.2 | 0.7 | 2.4 | n.a. | n.a. | 70.6 | 31.4 | 42.5 |
| Senegal | 5.3 | 2.6 | 3.6 | 3.6 | 4.3 | 21.6 | 20.2 | 22.4 |
| Sierra Leone | 3.0 | 1.0 | 2.7 | 1.1 | 2.2 | 57.6 | 20.1 | 25.9 |
| Togo | 3.4 | 1.1 | 2.8 | 4.2 | 5.2 | 34.0 | 19.7 | 23.0 |
| ECOWAS average | 4.4 | 1.5 | 2.8 | 2.8 | 3.7 | 40.8 | 22.0 | 26.5 |
| WAEMU average | 4.7 | 1.6 | 2.9 | 3.5 | 4.4 | 34.6 | 20.4 | 23.9 |
| WAMZ average | 4.6 | 1.4 | 2.7 | 1.7 | 2.6 | 48.5 | 22.8 | 30.2 |

NOTES: The health expenditure regression includes a constant, the log of GDP per capita at PPP (average 1990–7), an index of institutional quality (simple average of ICRG indices for political stability, democratic accountability and corruption, ranging from 0–10, higher numbers indicating better institutions), a dummy identifying countries with HIV/AIDS prevalence rate above 10%, life expectancy and infant mortality. The sample consists of 34 African countries and estimates were obtained by OLS. No institutional data were available for Benin. The education expenditure regression includes a constant, the log of GDP per capita at PPP (average 1984–98), illiteracy and an interaction variable between illiteracy and institutional quality (simple average of ICRG indices for political stability, democratic accountability, corruption, rule of law, and bureaucratic quality). Here, the sample only consists of 24 African countries, owing to missing data. Averages across countries are unweighted.
a Average over 1996–2000
b For Benin, the spending target is based on WAEMU average diversion.

considerably from the baseline case presented below, signs were preserved in 80% of the cases, indicating that incentives to join a monetary union were relatively robust to substantial deviations from the set of baseline parameters.

## 4. Simulations

Table 2 gives the net gains from a monetary union among existing WAEMU member states for the countries individually, using baseline parameter values. Since the theoretical model assumes that the common central bank follows discretionary strategies, those results ignore the utility value of the particular

470   X. Debrun, P. Masson, and C. Pattillo

TABLE 2
WAEMU: net benefits[a]

| Country | ω | Gain rel. to indep. | Correlation | Ψ |
|---|---|---|---|---|
| Benin | 0.0824 | 0.0217 | 0.6911 | 1.0939 |
| Burkina Faso | 0.0985 | 0.0793 | 0.6009 | 0.7847 |
| Côte d'Ivoire | 0.4137 | 0.0349 | 0.7737 | 1.0300 |
| Mali | 0.0987 | 0.0609 | 0.4905 | 0.8719 |
| Niger | 0.0729 | 0.0148 | −0.3161 | 1.1780 |
| Senegal | 0.1816 | 0.0310 | 0.8331 | 1.0581 |
| Togo | 0.0521 | 0.0346 | 0.5628 | 1.0276 |

[a] Parameters are $a = 0.9657$, $b = 9.0759$, $\gamma = 1.7723$, $c = 1$, $\eta = 1$, $\mu = 0.50$, $\theta_A = 0.0399$.

commitment technology available to the BCEAO – WAEMU's central bank – namely, a peg between the CFA franc and the euro guaranteed by the French Treasury. Such an arrangement has specific origins that are quite distinct from the constitution of a monetary union.[24]

Table 2 indicates that participation in a monetary union is better than independent policies (and separate currencies) for all of the WAEMU member states. The magnitude of the gains, which are to be interpreted as permanent log changes in GDP equivalents (see equation (3)), are sizeable. It can be seen that the countries with the most profligate fiscal policies (values of Ψ smaller than unity), in particular Burkina Faso and Mali, are the greatest gainers relative to independent monetary policies, while the most fiscally conservative member states – Benin and Niger – post relatively small gains. As illustrated by table 4, below, this reflects the fact that the traditional pillar of OCA analysis – the requirement of some symmetry in the shocks – is nowhere near as important here as differences in spending propensities in determining net gains from monetary unification. Again, one should keep in mind that this assessment is made under the assumption that the common central bank follows discretionary strategies, and that, unlike the actual situation of the WAEMU countries, the exchange rate of the common currency can adjust to exogenous shocks. Admittedly, the utility impact of shocks would be larger than suggested by table 4 if the decision to form the monetary union was paired with the decision to adopt an external peg for the region's currency. While fiscally profligate countries benefit from a central bank they perceive as less accommodative, the fiscally conservative member states suffer from the excessive monetary financing those less conservative countries manage to extract. This partly explains why Niger finds its participation only marginally beneficial (also because of the effect of the negative correlation of its shocks

24 A similar agreement, but not in the context of monetary union, has been extended to Cape Verde by Portugal, to maintain an exchange rate link with the euro.

TABLE 3
ECOWAS monetary union: net benefits for participants[a]

| Country | $\omega$ | Gain. rel. to indep. | Correlation | $\Psi$ | Gain rel. to WAEMU |
|---|---|---|---|---|---|
| Benin | 0.0340 | −0.0175 | 0.2677 | 1.4922 | −0.0392 |
| Burkina Faso | 0.0406 | 0.0425 | 0.1979 | 1.0704 | −0.0367 |
| Côte d'Ivoire | 0.1706 | −0.0042 | 0.0508 | 1.4051 | −0.0390 |
| Mali | 0.0407 | 0.0236 | 0.1523 | 1.1893 | −0.0373 |
| Niger | 0.0301 | −0.0242 | −0.2465 | 1.6069 | −0.0390 |
| Senegal | 0.0749 | −0.0075 | 0.3455 | 1.4434 | −0.0386 |
| Togo | 0.0215 | −0.0032 | 0.4255 | 1.4017 | −0.0378 |
| Gambia | 0.0061 | 0.0238 | 0.2277 | 1.1499 | n.a. |
| Ghana | 0.1078 | 0.0692 | −0.2748 | 0.9232 | n.a. |
| Guinea | 0.0597 | −0.0275 | 0.5914 | 1.6706 | n.a. |
| Nigeria | 0.4037 | 0.1155 | 0.9429 | 0.7594 | n.a. |
| Sierra Leone | 0.0104 | 0.0147 | −0.1986 | 1.2447 | n.a. |

[a] Parameters as in table 2, except $\theta_A = 0.0591$

with the rest of the union), while Burkina Faso and Mali record above average gains with respect to monetary autonomy.

Table 3 does a welfare calculation for a monetary union among the full set of ECOWAS countries. The same factors as those cited above explain why Burkina Faso and Mali are the only WAEMU member states that would prefer participation in a full ECOWAS monetary union over independent monetary policies (we will consider below whether this is the relevant comparison), while all but one (Guinea) of the non-WAEMU countries would prefer monetary union. Not surprisingly, Guinea has the lowest financing needs (UFN) among non-WAEMU countries and the largest gainer among them, Nigeria, has the largest UFN.

Looking more carefully into the various ways participation in the monetary union may affect governments' utility, we calculate the net loss/gain due to the cross-country differences in the spending objectives ($A$) and the net loss due to asymmetric shocks ($B$) (see table 4). A residual term ($C$) mainly captures the net gain stemming from the reduced incentives of the CCB to boost output through unexpected inflation.

It can be seen that the disciplinary effect ($C$) is relatively large for all the countries considered. In contrast, the costs stemming from suboptimal stabilization in the presence of asymmetric shocks ($B$) are small, representing often less than 10% of $C$. As a consequence, the determining factor in the net gain or loss expected from participation in a greater ECOWAS monetary union is the country's position in the cross-country distribution of financing needs, represented by the value of $\Psi_i$. In particular, table 4 shows that the two countries characterized by $\Psi_i < 1$ (Ghana and Nigeria) exhibit a positive $A$, meaning that they take advantage of sharing a common central bank with more conservative member states. At the other end of the distribution, countries characterized by

472   X. Debrun, P. Masson, and C. Pattillo

TABLE 4
Decomposition of the net gain from a monetary union among ECOWAS countries relative to monetary autonomy

| Country | $\Psi_i$ | $A$ | $B$ | $C$ | Net gain/loss |
|---|---|---|---|---|---|
| Benin | 1.4922 | −0.0730 | −0.0068 | 0.0623 | −0.0175 |
| Burkina Faso | 1.0704 | −0.0142 | −0.0022 | 0.0589 | 0.0425 |
| Côte d'Ivoire | 1.4051 | −0.0635 | −0.0024 | 0.0617 | −0.0042 |
| Mali | 1.1893 | −0.0346 | −0.0019 | 0.0601 | 0.0236 |
| Niger | 1.6069 | −0.0840 | −0.0032 | 0.0630 | −0.0242 |
| Senegal | 1.4434 | −0.0678 | −0.0017 | 0.0620 | −0.0075 |
| Togo | 1.4017 | −0.0631 | −0.0018 | 0.0617 | −0.0032 |
| Gambia | 1.1499 | −0.0283 | −0.0077 | 0.0598 | 0.0238 |
| Ghana | 0.9232 | 0.0176 | −0.0055 | 0.0571 | 0.0692 |
| Guinea | 1.6706 | −0.0895 | −0.0012 | 0.0632 | −0.0275 |
| Nigeria | 0.7594 | 0.0655 | −0.0041 | 0.0541 | 0.1155 |
| Sierra Leone | 1.2447 | −0.0429 | −0.0030 | 0.0606 | 0.0147 |

$\Psi_i \gtrsim 1.4$ (small UFN relative to the union's average) appear to lose more from the pressures of their profligate partners on the CCB than they gain from the disciplinary effect of centralized policymaking: $|A| > C$. If trade were not scaled up by 25% to account for informal trade, then $C$ (and hence also the net gains) would be reduced by about 0.01 for all countries. As can be seen from table 4, this would not change the signs of the net gains: most countries, except Nigeria and Ghana, would lose from monetary union, while those countries would be substantial net gainers.

More relevant for WAEMU countries, however, is a comparison of the full ECOWAS monetary union with the utility derived from being members of a smaller monetary union. The last column of table 3 suggests that all WAEMU countries would record comparable losses from the full ECOWAS monetary union.[25] Of course, that comparison ignores the induced changes in the institutional architecture of the monetary union. In particular, we do not consider the value of the BCEAO's commitment to peg the CFA franc to the euro, and in practice it is unclear whether the CCB of the full ECOWAS could rely on a comparable commitment technology. Those politically sensitive and economically crucial matters could give additional incentives to WAEMU member states to resist a wider monetary union or to strictly limit its membership. In any case, even a mere extension of the WAEMU that preserved present institutional arrangements would have to be reviewed by France and its European Union partners, and it is likely that any risk of a substantial revision of the guarantee currently extended to the BCEAO would undermine the willingness of WAEMU member states to engage in a significant enlargement of the union. However, such a risk is also an opportunity for WAEMU

25 These losses would be increased if no account were taken of informal trade.

TABLE 5
WAMZ monetary union[a]

| Country | ω | Gain rel. to indep. | Correlation | Ψ |
|---------|------|---------|-------------|--------|
| Gambia | 0.0103 | −0.0592 | 0.1298 | 1.3652 |
| Ghana | 0.1833 | −0.0121 | −0.4325 | 1.0961 |
| Guinea | 0.1016 | −0.1138 | 0.6109 | 1.9835 |
| Nigeria | 0.6870 | 0.0456 | 0.9912 | 0.9016 |
| Sierra Leone | 0.0178 | −0.0702 | −0.3191 | 1.4778 |

[a] Parameters as in table 2, except $\theta_A = 0.0201$

member states in the sense that it gives them a considerable bargaining power in negotiations with potential entrants. Since our simulations clearly identify disciplinary gains as the key motivation for non-WAEMU countries (except Guinea) to join a greater ECOWAS monetary union, WAEMU countries – like Germany during the negotiation of the Maastricht Treaty[26] – might be in a position to obtain serious institutional guarantees concerning, for instance, safeguards on the statutory independence of the CCB, a monetary policy framework conducive to price stability, and the strict application of entry criteria, including the requirement for fiscal discipline.

We now turn to whether WAMZ would likely be a feasible and durable monetary union on its own. The results in table 5 indicate that it would not be so, for the same reasons that the full ECOWAS monetary union was not. All countries except Nigeria would be worse off than if they retained their own monetary policies. Nigeria has both very different terms of trade shocks and less disciplined fiscal policies than some of the other countries that are prospective members of the WAMZ. Given its size, it would dominate the monetary policy of the union, provided the union operated a discretionary monetary policy (rather than being tied to an external anchor through a currency board, for instance). In this regard, an ECOWAS monetary union would be more desirable, since Nigeria would have a somewhat smaller weight. As proposed, the WAMZ is viewed as only a way-station towards the full ECOWAS union and as a way of speeding the transition.

Finally, in table 6 we consider whether adding a single country to a monetary union made of WAEMU countries would be incentive compatible for both the entrant and the existing members. In each case, entry is in the interest of the newcomer. However, existing members would welcome only Gambia or Guinea, although for Sierra Leone, the negative effects on other countries are so small as to be negligible; hence, WAEMU members might not object to admitting Sierra Leone as well. In contrast, Nigeria and, to a much lesser

26 Debrun (2001) shows that Germany might have enjoyed a large bargaining power because other countries saw their participation in the European Monetary Union as a surrogate to building credible monetary institutions at home.

474   X. Debrun, P. Masson, and C. Pattillo

TABLE 6
Adding countries individually to WAEMU

| Country | ω | Gain rel. to indep. | Correlation | Ψ | Gain rel. to WAEMU |
|---|---|---|---|---|---|
| **Adding Gambia**[a] | | | | | |
| Benin | 0.0812 | 0.0221 | 0.6808 | 1.0969 | 0.0005 |
| Burkina Faso | 0.0971 | 0.0797 | 0.6058 | 0.7868 | 0.0005 |
| Côte d'Ivoire | 0.4077 | 0.0353 | 0.7735 | 1.0328 | 0.0005 |
| Mali | 0.0973 | 0.0614 | 0.4921 | 0.8742 | 0.0005 |
| Niger | 0.0719 | 0.0152 | −0.3251 | 1.1812 | 0.0005 |
| Senegal | 0.1790 | 0.0315 | 0.8459 | 1.0610 | 0.0005 |
| Togo | 0.0513 | 0.0350 | 0.5497 | 1.0304 | 0.0004 |
| Gambia | 0.0145 | 0.0615 | 0.4915 | 0.8452 | n.a. |
| **Adding Ghana**[b] | | | | | |
| Benin | 0.0653 | 0.0150 | 0.6104 | 1.2022 | −0.0066 |
| Burkina Faso | 0.0781 | 0.0729 | 0.4780 | 0.8623 | −0.0064 |
| Côte d'Ivoire | 0.3280 | 0.0285 | 0.8416 | 1.1319 | −0.0064 |
| Mali | 0.0783 | 0.0544 | 0.3691 | 0.9581 | −0.0065 |
| Niger | 0.0578 | 0.0081 | −0.1956 | 1.2945 | −0.0067 |
| Senegal | 0.1440 | 0.0243 | 0.6869 | 1.1628 | −0.0067 |
| Togo | 0.0413 | 0.0278 | 0.4436 | 1.1292 | −0.0067 |
| Ghana | 0.2072 | 0.1017 | 0.8466 | 0.7438 | n.a. |
| **Adding Guinea**[c] | | | | | |
| Benin | 0.0720 | 0.0227 | 0.6335 | 1.0685 | 0.0010 |
| Burkina Faso | 0.0860 | 0.0806 | 0.6426 | 0.7665 | 0.0013 |
| Côte d'Ivoire | 0.3614 | 0.0361 | 0.7206 | 1.0061 | 0.0013 |
| Mali | 0.0862 | 0.0623 | 0.5478 | 0.8516 | 0.0014 |
| Niger | 0.0637 | 0.0162 | −0.3366 | 1.1506 | 0.0015 |
| Senegal | 0.1587 | 0.0324 | 0.8844 | 1.0336 | 0.0014 |
| Togo | 0.0455 | 0.0359 | 0.5644 | 1.0337 | 0.0013 |
| Guinea | 0.1265 | 0.0117 | 0.2176 | 1.1963 | n.a. |
| **Adding Nigeria**[d] | | | | | |
| Benin | 0.0416 | −0.0382 | 0.2246 | 1.5249 | −0.0599 |
| Burkina Faso | 0.0498 | 0.0228 | 0.1548 | 1.0938 | −0.0564 |
| Côte d'Ivoire | 0.2090 | −0.0251 | −0.0539 | 1.4358 | −0.0599 |
| Mali | 0.0499 | 0.0035 | 0.1201 | 1.2153 | −0.0574 |
| Niger | 0.0369 | −0.0453 | −0.2394 | 1.6420 | −0.0601 |
| Senegal | 0.0918 | −0.0282 | 0.2764 | 1.4749 | −0.0592 |
| Togo | 0.0263 | −0.0236 | 0.3939 | 1.4324 | −0.0582 |
| Nigeria | 0.4947 | 0.0996 | 0.9746 | 0.7760 | n.a. |
| **Adding Sierra Leone**[e] | | | | | |
| Benin | 0.0804 | 0.0208 | 0.6861 | 1.0965 | −0.0009 |
| Burkina Faso | 0.0961 | 0.0784 | 0.5931 | 0.7865 | −0.0008 |
| Côte d'Ivoire | 0.4035 | 0.0340 | 0.7825 | 1.0325 | −0.0008 |
| Mali | 0.0963 | 0.0601 | 0.4809 | 0.8739 | −0.0008 |
| Niger | 0.0711 | 0.0139 | −0.3090 | 1.1808 | −0.0009 |
| Senegal | 0.1771 | 0.0301 | 0.8245 | 1.0606 | −0.0009 |
| Togo | 0.0508 | 0.0337 | 0.5622 | 1.0300 | −0.0009 |
| Sierra Leone | 0.0247 | 0.0524 | 0.5075 | 0.9147 | n.a. |

a  $\theta_A = 0.0408$.
b  $\theta_A = 0.0486$.
c  $\theta_A = 0.0377$.
d  $\theta_A = 0.0445$.
e  $\theta_A = 0.0394$.

TABLE 7
ECOWAS monetary union: net benefits for participants when Nigeria's spending distortion is equal to average

| Country | ω | Gain rel. to indep. | Correlation | Ψ | Gain rel. to WAEMU |
|---|---|---|---|---|---|
| Benin | 0.0340 | 0.0278 | 0.2677 | 1.1721 | 0.0061 |
| Burkina Faso | 0.0406 | 0.0853 | 0.1979 | 0.8408 | 0.0060 |
| Côte d'Ivoire | 0.1706 | 0.0407 | 0.0508 | 1.1037 | 0.0059 |
| Mali | 0.0407 | 0.0672 | 0.1523 | 0.9342 | 0.0063 |
| Niger | 0.0301 | 0.0215 | −0.2465 | 1.2622 | 0.0068 |
| Senegal | 0.0749 | 0.0375 | 0.3455 | 1.1338 | 0.0065 |
| Togo | 0.0215 | 0.0417 | 0.4255 | 1.1011 | 0.0071 |
| Gambia | 0.0061 | 0.0672 | 0.2277 | 0.9032 | n.a. |
| Ghana | 0.1078 | 0.1105 | −0.2748 | 0.7252 | n.a. |
| Guinea | 0.0597 | 0.0185 | 0.5914 | 1.3123 | n.a. |
| Nigeria | 0.4037 | 0.0540 | 0.9429 | 1.0000 | n.a. |
| Sierra Leone | 0.0104 | 0.0587 | −0.1986 | 0.9778 | n.a. |

extent, Ghana would have negative effects on existing members if they joined. When Nigeria is added, each of the other countries' correlations with the union's average shock goes down, while Nigeria's correlation exceeds 0.9. Nigeria's dominance in terms of size would, according to our model, grant it the greatest influence on the union's monetary policy. Through this channel, the large financing needs of Nigeria's government and Nigeria-specific shocks to its terms of trade would have significant negative externalities on other countries. Also, Ghana has the second largest UFN among WAMZ countries and would have a significant weight in the union's monetary policy. Still, the negative effect on WAEMU members from adding Nigeria would be considerably larger (about 10 times, according to our calculations) than the negative effects from adding Ghana.

As suggested earlier, changes in spending propensities at the regional level might substantially affect incentives to form monetary unions, and our analysis makes clear that specific efforts aiming at a greater degree of fiscal convergence would contribute to making larger monetary unions more desirable for all member states. One way to foster convergence of fiscal performance on mutually agreed objectives would be through the implementation of regional surveillance. As in the process that led to the creation of the European Monetary Union, membership could be made conditional upon the satisfaction of these fiscal convergence criteria. To illustrate the potential importance of such a mechanism, table 7 reports the net gains from a full ECOWAS monetary union, assuming that Nigeria's UFN is set equal to the average for the remaining 11 countries.

Interestingly enough, for all the WAEMU countries a monetary union under these conditions would be preferred to a narrower union with the same membership as the existing WAEMU, and all the non-WAEMU countries would also benefit relative to monetary autonomy. Of course, the credibility of fiscal arrangements remains an open question, especially after the

476   X. Debrun, P. Masson, and C. Pattillo

monetary union has been established and is difficult to reverse. The recent experience in the euro area suggests that substantial pressures from politically influential member states to loosen the rules would be hard to resist. But we leave these important institutional issues for future research.

## 5. Conclusions

We calibrated a model in which negative spillovers from autonomous monetary policy provide incentives for forming a monetary union; these incentives depend on the extent of trade linkages among member countries. The model also includes a fiscal distortion that causes governments to aim for financing that is higher than the socially optimal level in order to channel funds that serve the narrow interests of the group in power or to compensate for revenue losses due to inefficient tax collection. We have argued that this feature, ignored in the literature on monetary union in Europe, is potentially quite important in Africa and influences both the incentives to join a monetary union and, for existing members, the willingness to accept a new member.

Our simulations bear this out. Using actual data to calibrate the model, we find that differences in government spending propensities are more important than asymmetric shocks in determining net gains and losses from potential monetary unions. The proposed monetary union among all the countries of ECOWAS, though desirable for most of the non-WAEMU countries, is shown not to be incentive compatible for most of the existing WAEMU members in the absence of other institutional changes or gains not captured in the model. The chief reason is that Nigeria, which would have a preponderant weight in such a union, is estimated to have a high fiscal distortion. This distortion would put pressure on an ECOWAS monetary union's central bank to produce monetary financing and hence would lower the utility of these countries. An additional but less important factor is that Nigeria's terms of trade differ from those of its neighbours, and hence the average shock would have a low or negative correlation with other countries' shocks. Even though a monetary union would be in Nigeria's interest, it is difficult to see that all potential members would be willing to proceed with one, despite agreement in principle to do so.

In contrast, the membership of the other non-WAEMU countries individually would not pose the same problems, and the model suggests that in most cases they would increase the welfare of existing WAEMU countries as well as that of the prospective new members.

The problem of disparities in financing needs for the formation of a monetary union and for its ongoing monetary policy suggests that regional surveillance mechanisms could contribute to a greater degree of convergence in fiscal policies. If Nigeria's financing needs were equal to the average for the other countries, a full-ECOWAS monetary union would be incentive compatible for all countries. While the design of such regional surveillance is outside the scope of this paper, we conclude that lack of fiscal convergence, not the low level of regional trade or the asymmetry of shocks, is the primary obstacle to the creation of a well-functioning and acceptable monetary union in West Africa.

## References

Alesina, Alberto, and Robert Barro (2002) 'Currency unions,' *Quarterly Journal of Economics* 117, 409–36
Alesina, Alberto, and Guido Tabellini (1987) 'Rules and discretion with noncoordinated monetary and fiscal policies,' *Economic Inquiry* 25, 619–30
Alesina, Alberto, Ignazio Angeloni, and Federico Etro (2001) 'The political economy of international unions,' NBER Working Paper No. 8645
Andersen, Torben (2002) 'Fiscal stabilization in a monetary union with inflation targeting,' CEPR Discussion Paper No 3232, London
Barro, Robert, and David Gordon (1983) 'A positive theory of monetary policy in a natural rate model,' *Journal of Political Economy* 91, 589–610
Beetsma, Roel M.W.J., and A. Lans Bovenberg (1998) 'Monetary union without fiscal coordination may discipline policymakers,' *Journal of International Economics* 45, 239–58
— (1999) 'Does monetary unification lead to excessive debt accumulation?,' *Journal of Public Economics* No. 74, pp. 299–325
Beetsma, Roel M.W.J., and Xavier Debrun (2004) 'The interaction between monetary and fiscal policies in a monetary union: a review of recent literature,' in *Monetary Policy, Fiscal Policies and Labour Markets: Macroeconomic Policymaking in the EMU*, ed. Roel M.W.J. Beetsma, Carlo Favero, Alessandro Missale, Anton Muscatelli, Piergiovanna Natale, and Patrizio Tirelli (Cambridge: Cambridge University Press)
Beetsma, Roel M.W.J., Xavier Debrun and Franc Klaassen (2001) 'Is fiscal policy coordination in EMU desirable?' *Swedish Economic Policy Review* 8, 57–98
Canzoneri, Matthew B., and Jo Anna Gray (1985) 'Monetary policy games and the consequences of noncooperative behaviors,' *International Economic Review* 26, 547–64
Canzoneri, Matthew B., and Dale Henderson (1991) *Monetary Policy in Interdependent Economies: A Game-Theoretic Approach* (Cambridge, MA: MIT Press)
Cashin, Paul, and Catherine Pattillo (2000) 'Terms of trade shocks in Africa: are they short-lived or long-lived?' IMF Working Paper 00/72, Washington, DC
Clarida, Richard, Jordi Galí and Mark Gertler (2002) 'A simple framework for international monetary policy analysis,' *Journal of Monetary Economics* 45, 879–912
Debrun, Xavier (2001) 'Bargaining over EMU vs. EMS: why might the ECB be the twin sister of the Bundesbank,' *Economic Journal* 111, 566–90
— (2003) 'Common currencies,' unpublished paper, International Monetary Fund
Debrun, Xavier, Paul Masson, and Catherine Pattillo, (2002), 'Monetary union in West Africa: who might gain, who might lose, and why?' IMF Working Paper 02/226, Washington, DC
Dissou, Yazid, and Paul Dorosh (1998) 'Taux de change réels et échanges régionaux en Afrique de l'Ouest: une analyse en équilibre général des relations Nigeria-Niger,' *Revue d'Economie du Développement* 6, 47–77
Doré, Ousmane, and Paul Masson (2002) 'Experience with budgetary convergence in the WAEMU,' IMF Working Paper 02/108, Washington, DC
Doré, Ousmane, Benoît Anne, and Dorothy Engmann (2003) 'Regional impact of Côte d'Ivoire's 1999–2000 sociopolitical crisis: an assessment,' IMF Working Paper 03/85, Washington, DC
Gupta, Sanjeev, Keiko Honjo, and Marijn Verhoeven (1997) 'The efficiency of government expenditure: experiences from Africa,' IMF Working Paper 97/153, Washington, DC

478   X. Debrun, P. Masson, and C. Pattillo

Gupta, Sanjeev, Hamid Davoodi, and Erwin Tiongson (2000) 'Corruption and the provision of health care and education,' IMF Working Paper 00/116, Washington, DC

Hamada, Koichi (1985) *The Political Economy of International Monetary Interdependence* (Cambridge, MA: MIT Press)

Hefeker, Carsten (2003) 'Fiscal reform and monetary union in West Africa,' HWWA Discussion Paper 224, Hamburg

Kose, M. Ayhan, and Raymond Riezman (2001) 'Trade shocks and macroeconomic fluctuations in Africa,' *Journal of Development Economics* 65, 55–80

Martin, Philippe (1995) 'Free-riding, convergence and two-speed monetary unification in Europe,' *European Economic Review* 39, 1345–64

Masson, Paul, and Catherine Pattillo (2001) 'Monetary union in West Africa (ECO-WAS) – is it desirable and how could it be achieved?' IMF Occasional Paper No. 204, Washington, DC

Mauro, Paolo (1998) 'Corruption and the composition of government expenditure,' *Journal of Public Economics* 69, 263–79

Muscatelli, Anton (1998) 'Optimal inflation contracts and inflation targets with uncertain central bank preferences: accountability through independence?' *Economic Journal* 108, 529–42

Robinson, James, and Ragnar Torvik (2002) 'White elephants,' CEPR Discussion Paper 3459, London

Uhlig, Harald (2002) 'One money but many fiscal policies in Europe: what are the consequences?' CEPR Discussion Paper No 3296, London

**Appendix: West Africa: selected data**

TABLE A1

Government spending, revenue, deficits and inflation, 1996–2000, and GDP shares

|  | Revenue/GDP | Spending/GDP | Deficit/GDP[a] | Inflation[b] | Shares of GDP, $\omega^c$ |
|---|---|---|---|---|---|
| **WAEMU:** |  |  |  |  | 41.23% |
| Benin | 18.87 | 18.45 | 0.43 | 3.73 | 3.40% |
| Burkina Faso | 21.15 | 24.91 | −3.76 | 2.43 | 4.06% |
| Côte d'Ivoire | 18.69 | 20.75 | −2.06 | 2.89 | 17.06% |
| Mali | 20.21 | 22.8 | −2.59 | 1.72 | 4.07% |
| Niger | 13.09 | 16.08 | −2.98 | 2.67 | 3.01% |
| Senegal | 19.88 | 20.19 | −0.3 | 1.41 | 7.49% |
| Togo | 15.66 | 19.69 | −4.03 | 3.15 | 2.15% |
| Average | 18.22 | 20.41 | −2.19 | 2.57 |  |
| **WAMZ:** |  |  |  |  | 58.77% |
| Gambia | 19.88 | 24.49 | −4.61 | 1.93 | 0.61% |
| Ghana | 19.45 | 28.24 | −8.78 | 25.33 | 10.78% |
| Guinea | 13.79 | 16.40 | −2.61 | – | 5.97% |
| Nigeria | 17.47 | 31.43 | −13.96 | 12.27 | 40.37% |
| Sierra Leone | 11.88 | 20.14 | −8.26 | 21.37 | 1.04% |
| Average | 16.49 | 24.14 | −7.64 | 15.23 |  |
| ECOWAS average | 17.50 | 21.96 | −4.46 | 7.17 |  |
| WAEMU–WAMZ | 1.73 | −3.73 | 5.45 | −12.66 |  |

*a* if negative

*b* in percent

*c* Based on 1998 figures for GDP in U.S.$

SOURCE: *International Financial Statistics*

TABLE A2
Openness, standard deviation and correlation of terms of trade shocks

| | Openness[a] | Standard deviation of TOT shocks | | Correlation of terms of trade shocks | | | | | | | | | | | |
| | | Unscaled | Scaled | Benin | Burkina Faso | Côte d'Ivoire | Mali | Niger | Senegal | Togo | Gambia | Ghana | Guinea | Nigeria | Sierra Leone |
|---|---|---|---|---|---|---|---|---|---|---|---|---|---|---|---|
| Benin | 61% | 0.178 | 0.109 | | 0.56* | 0.22 | 0.43** | -0.03 | 0.46** | 0.28 | 0.14 | 0.33 | -0.19 | 0.07 | 0.19 |
| Burkina Faso | 43% | 0.072 | 0.031 | 0.56* | | 0.06 | 0.94** | -0.02 | 0.57* | 0.11 | 0.37 | 0.16 | 0.26 | 0.02 | 0.06 |
| Côte d'Ivoire | 82% | 0.063 | 0.052 | 0.22 | 0.06 | | -0.01 | -0.40** | 0.59* | 0.52* | 0.36 | 0.75* | -0.16 | -0.23 | 0.65* |
| Mali | 63% | 0.051 | 0.032 | 0.43** | 0.94** | -0.01 | | -0.06 | 0.48* | 0.07 | 0.26 | 0.08 | 0.32 | 0.01 | -0.05 |
| Niger | 47% | 0.064 | 0.030 | -0.03 | -0.02 | -0.40** | -0.06 | | -0.57* | -0.41** | -0.31 | 0.05 | -0.13 | -0.17 | 0.06 |
| Senegal | 67% | 0.065 | 0.043 | 0.46** | 0.57* | 0.59* | 0.48* | -0.57* | | 0.49* | 0.62* | 0.28 | 0.33 | 0.09 | 0.15 |
| Togo | 76% | 0.081 | 0.062 | 0.28 | 0.11 | 0.52* | 0.07 | -0.41** | 0.49* | | 0.03 | 0.14 | 0.07 | 0.27 | 0.26 |
| Gambia, | 154% | 0.186 | 0.286 | 0.14 | 0.37 | 0.36 | 0.26 | -0.31 | 0.62* | 0.03 | | 0.17 | 0.54* | 0.06 | 0.17 |
| Ghana | 62% | 0.111 | 0.069 | 0.33 | 0.16 | 0.75* | 0.08 | 0.05 | 0.28 | 0.14 | 0.17 | | -0.41 | -0.54* | 0.62* |
| Guinea | 39% | 0.073 | 0.029 | -0.19 | 0.26 | -0.16 | 0.32 | -0.13 | 0.33 | 0.07 | 0.54* | -0.41 | | 0.59* | -0.44 |
| Nigeria | 71% | 0.215 | 0.152 | 0.07 | 0.02 | -0.23 | 0.01 | -0.17 | 0.09 | 0.27 | 0.06 | -0.54* | 0.59* | | -0.38 |
| Sierra Leone | 45% | 0.063 | 0.028 | 0.19 | 0.06 | 0.65* | -0.05 | 0.06 | 0.15 | 0.26 | 0.17 | 0.62* | -0.44 | -0.38 | |
| Average All | | | | 0.19 | 0.24 | 0.18 | 0.19 | -0.15 | 0.27 | 0.14 | 0.19 | 0.13 | 0.06 | -0.02 | 0.10 |
| Average WAEMU | | | | 0.32 | 0.37 | 0.16 | 0.31 | -0.25 | 0.34 | 0.17 | 0.21 | 0.26 | 0.07 | 0.01 | 0.19 |
| Average Non-WAEMU | | 0.063 | | 0.08 | 0.13 | 0.20 | 0.09 | -0.07 | 0.21 | 0.11 | 0.16 | -0.03 | 0.05 | -0.05 | 0.00 |

* Significant at 5% level
** Significant at 10% level
a Calculated as the sum of exports and imports as a percent of GDP
SOURCE: Calculated from the Terms of Trade Index (1987 = 100, US$-based), World Tables (World Bank). Openness calculated from *Balance of Payments Yearbook, 2001, Direction of Trade Statistics, 2001,* and *International Financial Statistics*

480   X. Debrun, P. Masson, and C. Pattillo

TABLE A3
Inflation in three late joiners of the CFA franc zone

| | Year country joined monetary union (MU) | Average inflation in pre-MU period[a] | Average inflation in post-MU period[b] | Average inflation in post-MU period (w/o 1994–5) |
|---|---|---|---|---|
| Mali | 1984 | 11.8 | 2.9 | 0.9 |
| Equatorial Guinea | 1985 | 21.4 | 4.1 | 1.1 |
| Guinea-Bissau | 1997 | 38.3 | 4.4 | |

a From 1970 until year country joined the CFA franc zone
b From year after country joined CFA franc zone until 2001
SOURCE: IMF World Economic Outlook (WEO) database

TABLE A4

$\theta_{i,k}$: importance of inflation surprises in country at top for country at left[a]

| | Benin | Burkina | Côte d'Ivoire | Mali | Niger | Senegal | Togo | UEMOA | Gambia | Ghana | Guinea | Nigeria | Sierra Leone | WAMZ |
|---|---|---|---|---|---|---|---|---|---|---|---|---|---|---|
| Benin | 0.0000 | 0.0004 | 0.0000 | 0.0004 | 0.0021 | 0.0004 | 0.0004 | 0.0039 | 0.0000 | 0.0000 | 0.0000 | 0.0004 | 0.0000 | 0.0004 |
| Burkina Faso | 0.0004 | 0.0000 | 0.0072 | 0.0011 | 0.0011 | 0.0000 | 0.0011 | 0.0108 | 0.0000 | 0.0022 | 0.0000 | 0.0000 | 0.0000 | 0.0022 |
| Côte d'Ivoire | 0.0037 | 0.0110 | 0.0000 | 0.0195 | 0.0034 | 0.0124 | 0.0075 | 0.0576 | 0.0010 | 0.0115 | 0.0045 | 0.0034 | 0.0008 | 0.0212 |
| Mali | 0.0000 | 0.0007 | 0.0011 | 0.0000 | 0.0004 | 0.0000 | 0.0000 | 0.0022 | 0.0000 | 0.0000 | 0.0000 | 0.0011 | 0.0000 | 0.0011 |
| Niger | 0.0019 | 0.0005 | 0.0015 | 0.0000 | 0.0000 | 0.0000 | 0.0000 | 0.0039 | 0.0000 | 0.0000 | 0.0000 | 0.0369 | 0.0000 | 0.0369 |
| Senegal | 0.0047 | 0.0010 | 0.0029 | 0.0105 | 0.0002 | 0.0000 | 0.0012 | 0.0205 | 0.0043 | 0.0008 | 0.0021 | 0.0004 | 0.0004 | 0.0080 |
| Togo | 0.0333 | 0.0068 | 0.0014 | 0.0020 | 0.0048 | 0.0000 | 0.0000 | 0.0483 | 0.0000 | 0.0116 | 0.0000 | 0.0272 | 0.0000 | 0.0387 |
| Total UEMOA | 0.0043 | 0.0052 | 0.0015 | 0.0102 | 0.0020 | 0.0052 | 0.0035 | 0.0319 | 0.0012 | 0.0057 | 0.0023 | 0.0057 | 0.0004 | 0.0153 |
| Gambia | 0.0000 | 0.0000 | 0.0000 | 0.0000 | 0.0000 | 0.0000 | 0.0000 | 0.0000 | 0.0000 | 0.0000 | 0.0000 | 0.0000 | 0.0000 | 0.0000 |
| Ghana | 0.0033 | 0.0008 | 0.0003 | 0.0000 | 0.0008 | 0.0004 | 0.0382 | 0.0438 | 0.0001 | 0.0000 | 0.0000 | 0.0106 | 0.0000 | 0.0107 |
| Guinea | 0.0000 | 0.0000 | 0.0022 | 0.0000 | 0.0000 | 0.0000 | 0.0000 | 0.0022 | 0.0000 | 0.0000 | 0.0000 | 0.0017 | 0.0000 | 0.0017 |
| Nigeria | 0.0004 | 0.0006 | 0.0217 | 0.0000 | 0.0009 | 0.0097 | 0.0002 | 0.0335 | 0.0000 | 0.0197 | 0.0001 | 0.0000 | 0.0005 | 0.0203 |
| Sierra Leone | 0.0000 | 0.0000 | 0.0000 | 0.0000 | 0.0000 | 0.0000 | 0.0000 | 0.0000 | 0.0000 | 0.0000 | 0.0000 | 0.0000 | 0.0000 | 0.0000 |
| Total WAMZ | 0.0008 | 0.0006 | 0.0152 | 0.0000 | 0.0008 | 0.0067 | 0.0071 | 0.0313 | 0.0000 | 0.0135 | 0.0001 | 0.0021 | 0.0003 | 0.0161 |

a Calculated as exports of $i$ to $k$, divided by GDP of $i$.

# Part IV

# International Economic Policy Coordination and Uncertainty

# International Policy Coordination in a World with Model Uncertainty

ATISH R. GHOSH and PAUL R. MASSON*

*The design and desirability of rules for the international coordination of macroeconomic policies in a world characterized by model uncertainty are considered. The presence of model uncertainty provides additional incentive to coordinate policies, provided that policymakers recognize that they cannot know the true model. To quantify the benefits from coordination, confidence regions are specified for parameters in MINIMOD; policymakers in the United States and the rest of the world are assumed to use these ranges as subjective probability priors. It is shown that the expected value of gains from coordination of policies may be large, despite substantial parameter uncertainty.*

---

THERE IS NOW A substantial literature that establishes the conditions under which international coordination of economic policies can be expected to lead to better outcomes, and a few empirical studies that attempt to quantify those gains.[1] The consensus of these empirical studies is that there exist clear gains to policy coordination, but that their magnitude is not enormous (Oudiz and Sachs (1984), McKibbin and Sachs (1988)). Most empirical studies to date have not, however, attempted to take into account the fact that the true econometric model

* Mr. Ghosh is a graduate student at Harvard University; this paper was written while he was visiting the Research Department.

Mr. Masson is an Advisor in the Research Department. He holds a doctorate from the London School of Economics and Political Science.

The authors thank Guillermo Calvo and Swati Ghosh, as well as colleagues in the Fund, for helpful comments. Any opinions expressed are those of the authors and not those of the International Monetary Fund.

[1] For surveys of the theoretical and empirical literature, see Cooper (1986), Horne and Masson (1987), and Fischer (1987).

GHOSH, ATISH R., *International Policy Coordination in a World with Model Uncertainty* ,
International Monetary Fund Staff Papers, 35:2 (1988:June) p.230

POLICY COORDINATION WITH MODEL UNCERTAINTY          231

describing the economy is not known.[2] An exception is Frankel (1987), who shows that in this case coordination may reduce welfare.

Indeed, policymakers have long doubted the value of international macroeconomic coordination in an environment characterized by uncertainty with respect to the econometric models being used by the various national policymaking groups. Typifying this view, Martin Feldstein (1983, p. 44), then Chairman of the Council of Economic Advisers, wrote:

> Economists armed with econometric models of the major countries of the world can, under certain circumstances, identify co-ordinated policies that, quite apart from the balance-of-payments constraints, are better than the outcome of unco-ordinated country choices. But, in practice, the overwhelming uncertainty about the quantitative behaviour of individual economies and their interaction, the great difficulty of articulating policy rules in a changing environment. . . . all make any such international fine tuning unworkable.

Consistent with this view, Frankel (1987) shows that if policymakers choose their policies on the basis of one set of empirical macromodels, each one having an equal chance of being correct, and policymakers simply ignore the reality of model uncertainty, then coordinated policies may be inferior to the uncoordinated, or Nash, equilibrium.[3]

There are at least two grounds for criticism of such an approach. First, it attributes irrationality to the policymakers, since they must certainly recognize the reality of model uncertainty. Second, although such an argument appears to be an indictment of international policy coordination, it is rather an argument against the pursuit of *any* activist policy—coordinated or uncoordinated—when the effects of such policy are not known. A lesson of the literature on policy choice in the presence of parameter uncertainty[4] is that, in general, policy instruments should be used more conservatively (Brainard (1967)). Evaluation of gains to policy coordination should be done in a context in which policymakers take this lesson into account. In such a context, the ex ante gains to

---

[2] Canzoneri and Minford (1988) consider uncertainty about other countries' actions but do not treat *model* uncertainty.

[3] See also Frankel and Rockett (1986) and Holtham and Hughes Hallett (1988).

[4] In this paper, *parameter* and *model* uncertainty are treated as being the same; this is valid provided the models can be nested in a more general form, with, for instance, some parameters being zero or unity depending on which model is correct. As an example, suppose that there are two reduced-form models $Y = aX$ and $Y = bZ$; they can be nested in $Y = \alpha aX + (1 - \alpha) bZ$, where $\alpha$ equals unity if the first model is correct, and zero if the second one is correct.

GHOSH, ATISH R., *International Policy Coordination in a World with Model Uncertainty*,
International Monetary Fund Staff Papers, 35:2 (1988:June) p.230

232                ATISH R. GHOSH and PAUL R. MASSON

policy coordination must be positive; indeed, model uncertainty may
provide an additional incentive to coordinate macroeconomic policies.[5]
    In this paper the focus is on the case in which governments are as-
sumed to take explicit account of any model uncertainty when forming
optimal policies. A theoretical section shows that whether model uncertainty increases or decreases the attractiveness of coordination depends
on the source of the uncertainty in the reduced form of the model.
Uncertainty about the effects of the foreign instruments on the home
country (that is, the transmission effects) invariably raises the gains from
coordination relative to the Nash equilibrium. In contrast, uncertainty
regarding the effects of the country's own instruments on itself has
ambiguous implications for the benefits from coordination.
    The effects of model uncertainty on the ex ante expected gains from
policy coordination are then assessed in a two region econometric model
of the world economy. Uncertainty is introduced at the level of the
structural model rather than the reduced form. Uncertainty is considered with regard to parameters such as the interest elasticity of money
demand, price elasticities in import and export equations, the slope of
the Phillips curve, the degree of substitution between government and
private consumption, and the strength of accelerator effects on investment. This approach allows tracing the effect of uncertainty about
econometric estimates of key structural parameters on the reduced-form
multipliers and, ultimately, on the welfare implications of coordinated
versus uncoordinated macroeconomic policies.
    Assessment of gains to coordination involves a comparison of dynamic
programming solutions that maximize expected utility (either independently or jointly) under uncertainty about the effects of the instruments.
The welfare criterion used is the expected (ex ante) value of an objective
function in which the expectation is calculated over the prior probability
weights assigned to each model. The analysis, therefore, may be viewed
as an extension of the seminal work of Brainard (1967) to a two-player,
strategic setting. It should also be stressed that since we focus on the
expected gains from coordination, we do not have to specify, arbitrarily,
the "true" model of the world economy.
    The plan of the paper is as follows. Section I reviews some of the
theoretical arguments about the effects of model uncertainty on the
gains from policy coordination. Section II describes the econometric
model, MINIMOD, used for the simulation work and specifies confidence regions for the key structural parameters. Section III explains the
procedure used to calculate the gains from coordination under model
uncertainty. Section IV presents estimates of those gains, and Section V
offers some brief concluding remarks. An Appendix gives the derivation
of both Nash and cooperative strategies under model uncertainty.

---

[5] See Ghosh (1986a, 1986b) and Ghosh (1987).

GHOSH, ATISH R., *International Policy Coordination in a World with Model Uncertainty* ,
International Monetary Fund Staff Papers, 35:2 (1988:June) p.230

POLICY COORDINATION WITH MODEL UNCERTAINTY          233

## I. Theory of Model Uncertainty and Policy Coordination

To begin the discussion, it is useful to consider the effects of model
uncertainty on the gains from policy coordination in the simplest possible theoretical structure—one that has been widely used in the literature
on policy coordination.[6] The discussion here follows Ghosh (1987). Let
policymakers have the quadratic objective function defined over the
price level:

$$V = -\max \left(\frac{1}{2}\right)(p^2),$$

subject to the linear reduced-form equation

$$p = \theta_1 M + \theta_2 M^* + \epsilon, \quad \epsilon > 0,$$

where $p$ is the price level, $\epsilon$ is an inflation shock, $M$ is the home country's
monetary policy, and $M^*$ is the foreign country's monetary policy. It is
assumed that $\theta_1 > 0$ and $\theta_1 + \theta_2 > 0$. The coefficient $\theta_1$ represents the
effects of the home country's monetary policy on its own price level,
whereas $\theta_2$ gives the effects of the foreign instrument on the home
country's price level; these coefficients are termed *domestic* and *transmission* multipliers, respectively. A similar objective function and model
apply to the symmetric foreign country:

$$p^* = \theta_1 M^* + \theta_2 M + \epsilon, \quad \epsilon > 0.$$

Note that $\theta_1$ and $\theta_2$ again represent domestic and transmission multipliers, respectively. Under a cooperative regime a single planner maximizes a weighted average of the two countries' welfare functions:

$$W = \omega V + (1 - \omega)V^*.$$

In a world with symmetric countries, it is natural to choose the relative
welfare weight of $\omega = 0.5$ so that any gains from coordination are shared
equally. In the absence of coordination, each country maximizes its
respective objective function, $V$ or $V^*$, choosing its policies under the
assumption that the other country's policy settings are given. Because
countries are mirror images, we may concentrate on the home country
with the understanding that the effects on the foreign country are
identical.

In the absence of model uncertainty, the unique symmetric Nash
equilibrium is characterized by the following policy settings:

$$M = M^* = -\epsilon/(\theta_1 + \theta_2).$$

Similarly, under cooperation,

$$M = M^* = -\epsilon/(\theta_1 + \theta_2).$$

[6] See Oudiz and Sachs (1984) and Cooper (1986).

GHOSH, ATISH R., *International Policy Coordination in a World with Model Uncertainty* ,
International Monetary Fund Staff Papers, 35:2 (1988:June) p.230

234          ATISH R. GHOSH and PAUL R. MASSON

The Nash and cooperative equilibria coincide so that there are no 'ains from coordination in this case. Here each country has one instrument and one target so that the two countries can achieve their first-best outcomes without coordination (see Oudiz and Sachs (1984)).

Now suppose that the multipliers $\theta_1$ and $\theta_2$ are uncertain, with means $\mu_{\theta_1}$, $\mu_{\theta_2}$ and variances $\sigma_{\theta_1}^2$, $\sigma_{\theta_2}^2$, respectively. For expositional purposes it is convenient to separate the effects of uncertainty about domestic multipliers from the effects of uncertainty about transmission multipliers.[7] The objective function is now

$$V = -\max \left(\frac{1}{2}\right) E\,(p^2),$$

where the expectation is taken over the uncertain parameters. The symmetric Nash strategies are now given by

$$M = M^* = -\epsilon / (\mu_{\theta_1} + \mu_{\theta_2} + \sigma_{\theta_1}^2 / \mu_{\theta_1}), \tag{1a}$$

whereas the cooperative equilibrium is given by

$$M = M^* = -\epsilon / [\mu_{\theta_1} + \mu_{\theta_2} + (\sigma_{\theta_2}^2 + \sigma_{\theta_1}^2)/(\mu_{\theta_1} + \mu_{\theta_2})]. \tag{1b}$$

Therefore, unless

$$\mu_{\theta_1} \sigma_{\theta_2}^2 = \mu_{\theta_2} \sigma_{\theta_1}^2, \tag{1c}$$

the cooperative and Nash equilibria differ, and there would be gains from coordination.[8] When there is no uncertainty (that is, $\sigma_{\theta_1} = \sigma_{\theta_2} = 0$), then equation (1c) necessarily holds, but in general this will not be the case.

The reason that model uncertainty introduces gains from coordination has been discussed in some detail by Ghosh (1987). As Brainard (1967) has shown, under instrument uncertainty the "efficiency" of policy instruments decreases, and the optimal program calls for the modified use of policy.[9] The use of policy instruments brings the mean values of the target variables closer to their "bliss" points; however, it also increases their variances around their means. The planner therefore faces a mean-

---

[7] If parameter uncertainty is introduced at the level of the structural (as opposed to the reduced-form) model, however, the presence of domestic multiplier uncertainty will in general be associated with uncertainty about the transmission effects, so that this separation is not possible.

[8] If $\theta_1$ and $\theta_2$ are correlated, the expressions for the optimal strategies become more complicated, but the condition for efficiency of the Nash equilibrium remains the same. Note that the Nash strategy can be over- or under-interventionist relative to the cooperative policy.

[9] Brainard (1967) defined the efficiency of a policy instrument as the ratio of its mean effect to its variance.

GHOSH, ATISH R., *International Policy Coordination in a World with Model Uncertainty*,
International Monetary Fund Staff Papers, 35:2 (1988:June) p.230

POLICY COORDINATION WITH MODEL UNCERTAINTY          235

variance trade-off in the use of his instruments.[10] In the Nash equilibrium each government treats the variance from the foreign instrument as exogenous additive uncertainty; that is, as independent of its own instrument. In equilibrium, however, the foreign instrument *is* a function of the home instrument (at the symmetric equilibrium $dM^*/dM = 1$), so that the Nash player incorrectly estimates the efficiency of his instrument and chooses an inappropriate degree of intervention.[11]

From an initial equilibrium in which there are no gains from coordination, therefore, the introduction of uncertainty about either the domestic or the transmission multipliers unambiguously raises the incentive to coordinate. More generally, the effects of introducing model uncertainty into a model in which there already exist gains from coordination depend on whether there is uncertainty about the domestic or the transmission multipliers.

Consider a model in which each country has two targets, the price level and the level of output, but only one instrument, the money supply. It can be shown that increasing the degree of domestic multiplier uncertainty has ambiguous effects on the gains from policy coordination (Ghosh (1987)). For example, in the limiting case of an infinite increase in the home multiplier uncertainty (that is, where $\sigma_{\theta_1}^2 \to \infty$), the optimal policy, both under Nash and under cooperative behavior, is to refrain from any intervention whatsoever:

$$M = M^* = 0.$$

The Nash and cooperative strategies therefore converge at this point, eliminating all gains from coordination. For intermediate values, the expected gains from coordination may either be enhanced or diminished when domestic multiplier uncertainty is increased. An increase in parameter uncertainty will lead to a less active use of the policy instrument; if the Nash equilibrium is too interventionist, then an increase in domestic multiplier uncertainty by reducing the use of policy will bring the Nash equilibrium closer to the cooperative solution, thereby reducing gains from coordination. Conversely, if the Nash equilibrium is biased toward too much intervention, then an increase in domestic multiplier uncertainty may tend to increase gains from coordination.

In contrast, the effect of transmission multiplier uncertainty is un-

---

[10] Ghosh (1987) used a modified mean-variance portfolio analysis diagram to illustrate the inefficiency of the Nash strategy.

[11] There are forms of noncooperative behavior—for instance, the consistent conjectural variation equilibrium—that do account for foreign government reactions. It can be shown, however, that all noncooperative strategies will be inefficient in the face of uncertainty.

GHOSH, ATISH R., *International Policy Coordination in a World with Model Uncertainty*,
International Monetary Fund Staff Papers, 35:2 (1988:June) p.230

236                    ATISH R. GHOSH and PAUL R. MASSON

ambiguous. The divergence between the Nash and cooperative cases is
always an increasing function of the degree of transmission uncertainty—and so, correspondingly, is the gain from coordination. The
difference in impact of domestic and transmission multiplier uncertainty
will figure prominently in the discussion of quantitative estimates of
gains to coordination presented below.

## II. Structure of the Econometric Model

The model we have used to estimate the gains of policy coordination
is a small, two-region macroeconomic model called MINIMOD (see
Haas and Masson (1986)). This model contains blocks for the United
States and an aggregate of the rest-of-the-world (ROW) countries, with
about 30 equations per region. The regions are linked through uncovered interest parity and bilateral trade flows.

Since MINIMOD is nonlinear, it was first linearized around a point on
a steady-state growth path. A linear model is necessary to make the
policy optimization tractable; the essential conclusions about the effects
of model uncertainty on the gains from coordination are not, however,
specific to such a model.[12] The linearized model exhibits saddle-point
stability and has as many unstable eigenvalues as jumping variables (five
of them, corresponding to the exchange rate, two long-term bond rates,
and two inflation rates).[13] For these nonpredetermined variables, termi-
nal rather than initial conditions are imposed such that they do not grow
without bound. As a result, a unique, stable rational expectations path
exists. The linearized version of the model is a function of the structural
parameters of the original, nonlinear model, so we can give an intuitive,
economic interpretation to the effects of uncertainty about parameters.

An argument often given for policy coordination is that, because
under cooperation governments could choose the same policies they
were pursuing at the Nash equilibrium, by revealed preference, coordination must improve welfare. In MINIMOD, however, expectations are
formed rationally, and governments are assumed to be unable to commit
their actions in advance, so that private sector reaction functions faced
by the cooperative planner will, in general, differ from those faced by the
governments acting independently. As Rogoff (1985) has demonstrated,
the standard argument that coordination must be beneficial thus breaks
down in the presence of a forward-looking private sector. In particular,
monetary expansion may be more tempting when pursued jointly, since

[12] See Ghosh (1987) for a discussion of the effects of model uncertainty on the
gains from coordination in a model with general functional forms.
[13] See Masson (1987) for details.

GHOSH, ATISH R., *International Policy Coordination in a World with Model Uncertainty* ,
International Monetary Fund Staff Papers, 35:2 (1988:June) p.230

POLICY COORDINATION WITH MODEL UNCERTAINTY     **237**

exchange rate depreciation would not result. Therefore, if governments
are unable to commit themselves in advance not to pursue expansionary
policies, the private sector will include a (rational) forecast of looser
monetary policy in its wage demands, and the inflation-output trade-off
will be less favorable in the coordinated regime than in the Nash.
Whether this effect is sufficiently strong to render the gains from coordination negative depends on the specific parameters of the model. In the
simulations reported below, the gains from coordination always do turn
out to be positive, so that the possibility raised by Rogoff does not apply
to MINIMOD, at least for the policies and shocks considered.

The key structural parameters that govern both the domestic effects of
policy changes and their transmission to the foreign economy are listed
in Table 1, together with their values in MINIMOD and in two al-

Table 1.   *Parameter Values of U.S. Model for Different Simulations*

| Parameters Changed, by Simulation | Model 1 | Model 2 | Memorandum Item: Parameter Values in MINIMOD |
|---|---|---|---|
| 1.  None: Baseline | | | |
| 2.  Semi-elasticity of money demand with respect to current and lagged interest rate | | | |
|     Current | −0.4842 | −0.1948 | −0.3390 |
|     Lag 1 | −0.1859 | −0.0748 | −0.1303 |
| 3.  Degree of direct crowding out of private consumption by government expenditure | 0.3 | −0.3 | 0.0 |
| 4.  Slope of the Phillips curve: effects of current and lagged capacity utilization rate on gross national product (GNP) deflator | | | |
|     Current | 0.0405 | 0.0045 | 0.0225 |
|     Lag 1 | 0.0866 | 0.0096 | 0.0481 |
|     Lag 2 | −0.0580 | −0.0064 | −0.0322 |
| 5.  Elasticity of import demand with respect to activity | 2.9273 | 1.6273 | 2.2773 |
| 6.  Elasticity of import demand with respect to real exchange rate | −0.8226 | −0.3226 | −0.5726 |
| 7.  Elasticity of export demand with respect to foreign activity | 1.3148 | 0.2148 | 0.7648 |
| 8.  Elasticity of export demand with respect to real exchange rate | 1.3339 | 0.8739 | 1.1039 |
| 9.  Effect of gross domestic product (GDP) on investment activity | 0.0427 | 0.0134 | 0.0294 |

GHOSH, ATISH R., *International Policy Coordination in a World with Model Uncertainty* ,
International Monetary Fund Staff Papers, 35:2 (1988:June) p.230

238          ATISH R. GHOSH and PAUL R. MASSON

ternative models, intended to capture the upper (model 1) and lower
(model 2) bounds of 95 percent confidence regions. The parameters of
MINIMOD were not in most cases directly estimated; rather, they were
derived from other empirical work, primarily from the U.S. Federal
Reserve's Multicountry Model (MCM; see Stevens and others (1984)).
Uncertainty in the parameters cannot therefore be directly associated
with estimated standard errors. In any case, parameter uncertainty in
empirical models is likely to be considerably greater than estimated
standard errors because specification searches have usually been used to
achieve a good fit and to accord with prior assumptions about the size of
coefficients. A better measure of model uncertainty is the range of
estimates resulting from different estimation strategies and different
maintained hypotheses. Parameter changes will also result from different sample periods, and if parameters do change over time then this
variation, which may be important, also may not be correctly captured
by estimated standard errors in a model with constant coefficients.

     Another issue is whether parameters vary endogenously as a result of
a change in the policy regime, a possibility raised by Lucas (1976). The
Lucas critique is obviously relevant here, since policy coordination
would constitute a clear change in regime relative to the historical
period. Parameter ranges should be wide enough to allow for this
possibility.

     The first key parameter that is considered in Table 1 is the interest
elasticity of money demand in the United States. The demand for narrow
money—the M1 aggregate—has been affected in recent years by two
major structural changes: financial deregulation and technological
innovations that have changed the costs of carrying out financial transactions. Simpson (1984, pp. 261–62), described some of these changes
and concluded that

> . . . rapid financial change continues to affect the behavior of M1 and thus
> the setting of M1 growth objectives. Considerable uncertainty surrounds
> the contours of the relationship that now exists among M1, income, interest
> rates, and other economic developments and that will exist once the transi-
> tion phase has drawn to a close. . . . The preceding discussion strongly sug-
> gests that the interest elasticity of M1 demand will be much lower once the
> deregulation process has ended and that the demand to hold M1 balances
> will continue to be "noisy," especially over short periods. . . .

     The equation favored by Simpson includes an own rate of interest (in
particular, the rate on NOW accounts, which are included in M1) as well
as the market rate. He predicted that the elasticity with respect to the
overall level of the interest rates will fall over time—relative to the
"standard" elasticity of 0.10—as the proportion of M1 that is subject to

GHOSH, ATISH R., *International Policy Coordination in a World with Model Uncertainty* ,
International Monetary Fund Staff Papers, 35:2 (1988:June) p.230

POLICY COORDINATION WITH MODEL UNCERTAINTY        239

an unregulated own rate grows. He cited in opposition, however, a model developed at the Federal Reserve Bank of San Francisco, which explains strong M1 growth in the 1982–83 period not by deregulation but rather by a high interest elasticity—equal to 0.15—that is asserted not to have changed in recent years. Thus we quantify uncertainty about money demand elasticities by postulating a range of 0.05 to 0.15 for the interest elasticity: this range includes both a substantial decline from the standard elasticity and the opposing view of the San Francisco Federal Reserve Bank. This range, plus or minus half the point estimate, was applied to the MINIMOD coefficients, which are semi-elasticities and hence cannot be directly compared with Simpson's estimate. It should be noted that, since Simpson's 1984 article, the Federal Reserve Board abandoned M1 targets, citing instability in the money demand, income, and interest rate relationship.

Another parameter that is of direct relevance to the effects of policy is the degree to which government spending is a direct substitute for private consumption expenditure. If government programs can just as easily be provided directly by the private sector, then there need be no real effects from increases in government spending (provided also that the financing of that spending has no real effects—that is, Ricardian equivalence holds). In contrast, if government spending is of quite a different nature, then it should not affect the utility of private consumption. There is a parameter in MINIMOD that measures this degree of substitutability; it is provisionally set to zero so that there is no direct offset through private consumption of government spending.

Empirical estimates of the degree of offset are quite mixed. It should be emphasized the government and private spending can be either substitutes or complements. If complements, then increases in government spending tend to increase private consumption; for instance, improved roads or parks may stimulate expenditures on automobiles and induce people to travel. Several authors have discovered complementarity (Buiter and Tobin (1979), Feldstein (1982), and Kormendi (1983)); in contrast, Ahmed (1986) found substitutability (that is, a direct offset on private spending). Although the data with which the models were estimated and also the precise specification differ considerably, the studies cited above suggest a range of −0.3 to 0.3, with a midpoint at the MINIMOD estimate of zero.

Clearly a crucial feature of any model is the degree of wage-price stickiness or, alternatively, the slope of the Phillips curve. In the limiting case of perfect flexibility, monetary policy has no real effects. In MINIMOD, the degree of flexibility is captured by coefficients on the rate of capacity utilization in the equation for the rate of change of the gross

GHOSH, ATISH R., *International Policy Coordination in a World with Model Uncertainty* ,
International Monetary Fund Staff Papers, 35:2 (1988:June) p.230

240         ATISH R. GHOSH and PAUL R. MASSON

domestic product (GDP) deflator. Uncertainty about these parameters is directly related to uncertainty concerning the "sacrifice ratio" between the cumulative output loss relative to the potential needed to achieve a given reduction in the rate of inflation. The higher are the coefficients on capacity utilization, the lower is the sacrifice ratio. There is a considerable range of estimates of the sacrifice ratio; according to Sachs (1985), traditional estimates ranged from 6 to 18, with Arthur Okun's best guess (cited in Sachs) being 10. Sachs himself calculated the sacrifice ratio to be 3 in the 1982–84 disinflationary period. A reasonable range, therefore, might be 2 to 18, or plus or minus 0.8 times the point estimate. Such a range was applied to the MINIMOD coefficients in Table 1.

Trade equations have been the object of numerous empirical studies, and most have used the standard specification, or a variant of it, embodied in MINIMOD—imports by each region in volume terms depend on real domestic expenditure and on relative prices; that is, on the real exchange rate. Despite the consensus about this specification, there is still controversy about the relevant elasticities, especially about their implications for future U.S. current account deficits.[14] A comparison of seven detailed models of the U.S. current account revealed that, for both imports and exports, activity and price elasticities varied widely. For non-oil imports, income elasticities of demand ranged from 1.2 to 2.5, whereas price elasticities ranged from 0.7 to 1.2 (see Bryant and others (1987, pp. 133–34)). Similarly, for nonagricultural goods exports, foreign income elasticities range from 1.0 to 2.1, and relative price elasticities from 0.5 to 1.0. These elasticities apply to data other than those in MINIMOD: trade flows include only a subset of merchandise trade, whereas MINIMOD's trade flows include all merchandise trade as well as nonfactor services. Nevertheless, the elasticities give a good measure of the uncertainty relating to the parameters in trade equations. On the basis of the above results, the range of absorption elasticities was taken to be MINIMOD's estimate plus or minus 65 percent of the mean for imports, 55 percent for exports. Relative price elasticities were taken to include values 25 percent on either side of MINIMOD's coefficient for imports, 23 percent for exports.

A final important linkage for both monetary and fiscal policies is the accelerator effect of income variations on investment. MINIMOD's equation for the change in the capital stock is based on a conventional

---

[14] A recent conference at The Brookings Institution compared the recent tracking and future projections of several models of the U.S. current account; the implications of these results are discussed in Bryant and Holtham (1987) (see also Krugman and Baldwin (1987)). For a general survey of empirical work on trade equations, see Goldstein and Khan (1985).

GHOSH, ATISH R., *International Policy Coordination in a World with Model Uncertainty* ,
International Monetary Fund Staff Papers, 35:2 (1988:June) p.230

POLICY COORDINATION WITH MODEL UNCERTAINTY       241

lagged adjustment to the optimal level, with that level depending on
GDP and the user cost of capital. The accelerator effect thus depends on
the speed of adjustment to the optimal capital stock. Several alternative
specifications give a similar positive effect of changes in GDP on investment. Clark (1979) estimated equations with different theoretical under-
pinnings; implied estimates for the contemporaneous effects of output
ranged from 0.03 to 0.08 when his coefficients for producers' durable
equipment and for nonresidential structures were weighted together
using 1986 relative shares. Applying a similar range to the point estimate
in MINIMOD gave the range presented in Table 1 for that parameter.
   The ranges of parameter estimates are very large—larger in general
than those implied by estimated standard errors from any single model.
Although the ranges do not allow for a change in sign of the *structural*
parameter (with the exception of the direct effect of government expenditure on consumption), *reduced-form* multipliers do in fact change
signs. The range of resultant policy effects is indeed wider than that
implied by the different models considered by Frankel (1987). Therefore, the parameter uncertainty treated here is quite fundamental to the
macroeconomic outcomes from the model.

## III. Optimal Strategies Under Model Uncertainty

   Calculation of the gains from policy coordination involves comparison
of the expected utility achievable under the dynamic time-consistent
Nash equilibrium (Basar and Olsder (1982)) with that enjoyed by each
country when a single planner maximizes a weighted sum of the two
countries' welfares. In the simulations reported below, equal weights
were assigned to each country,[15] and the gains from coordination were
assessed by reference to this global welfare function.
   In the baseline simulations—where there is no model uncertainty—we
use the standard dynamic programming solution for the optimal control
of an economy with forward-looking variables (see Oudiz and Sachs
(1985)). Once model uncertainty is introduced, however, the optimal
control solution must be modified to take into account the risks associated with the use of policy. We therefore extended the algorithms of
Chow (1975) and Kendrick (1981) to deal with forward-looking variables
and strategic behavior.
   The logic of the model is as follows. In period $t$, policymakers observe
the inherited state vector $x_t$ which is predetermined; the timing con-

---

[15] For convenience, in MINIMOD the ROW region is referred to as a country.

GHOSH, ATISH R., *International Policy Coordination in a World with Model Uncertainty* ,
International Monetary Fund Staff Papers, 35:2 (1988:June) p.230

242                    ATISH R. GHOSH and PAUL R. MASSON

vention of the linearized MINIMOD is such that all nonjumping endogenous variables are determined at the beginning of the period and are
thus included in $x_t$. Policymakers then set their instruments with a view
to influencing $x_{t+1}$ and any jumping variables in period $t$, $e_t$. At the time
that policies must be decided, the true model describing the world economy is unknown, and policymakers must use their prior beliefs about the
possible models. In period $t + 1$, $x_{t+1}$ is observed, so that the model that
applied to period $t$ may be inferred. Because the realization of the true
model is assumed to be independent in each period, however, policymakers will use the same priors in the next period; updating of priors
is not required.

The home government's welfare function is assumed to be given by

$$V = \max -\left(\frac{1}{2}\right) \sum_{t=0}^{\infty} \beta^t E\left(y_t' \, \Omega \, y_t\right), \tag{2}$$

where $y_t$ is an $n$ vector of endogenous variables, measured as deviation
from the bliss point; $\Omega$ is an $(n \times n)$ matrix of utility weights; and $E(\cdot)$
is the expectation's operator. All of the model's endogenous variables are
contained within $y_t$, and the nonzero terms of $\Omega$ assign weights to those
variables targeted by the home-country planner. The foreign government maximizes a similar objective function.

The world economy's dynamics are given by

$$\begin{bmatrix} x_{t+1} \\ e_{t+1} \end{bmatrix} = \begin{bmatrix} A^i & B^i \\ D^i & F^i \end{bmatrix} \begin{bmatrix} x_t \\ e_t \end{bmatrix} + \begin{bmatrix} C^i \\ G^i \end{bmatrix} U_t, \qquad i = 1, \ldots, k, \tag{3}$$

where $i$ indexes the $k$ possible models describing the world economy;
$(A^i, B^i, C^i, D^i, F^i, G^i)$ are constant coefficient matrices for model $i$;[16] $x_t$
is a $p$ vector of predetermined variables; $e_t$ is an $m$ vector of forward-
looking variables; $e_{t+1}$ is the expectation, as of period $t$, of the jumping
variables in period $t + 1$; and $U_t$ is an $r$ vector of home and foreign policy
instruments.

In each time period there are four vectors of potentially different
probability priors assigned to each of the $k$ possible models. The home
and foreign governments use the subjective priors $\Pi_t$ and $\Pi_t^*$ to derive
their optimal policies. The private sector assigns the priors $\hat{\Pi}_t$ to the
models. Finally, there is an objective probability, $\bar{\Pi}_t$, that any given
model is the correct description of the world economy. The priors are
exogenously given and are not updated either through active or passive
learning.

[16] These matrices have dimension $[(p \times p), (p \times q), (p \times r), (q \times p), (q \times q),
(q \times r)]$ respectively.

GHOSH, ATISH R., *International Policy Coordination in a World with Model Uncertainty*,
International Monetary Fund Staff Papers, 35:2 (1988:June) p.230

POLICY COORDINATION WITH MODEL UNCERTAINTY          243

The specification of the objective probability vector, $\bar{\Pi}_t$, depends on
the treatment of model uncertainty. If it is assumed that there is a unique
correct model—say, model $j$—that describes the world economy over
the relevant horizon, but that policymakers have yet to discover it, then
$\Pi_t$ is degenerate; that is, $\Pi_t$ is a vector of zeros except for the $j$th element,
which is unity. An alternative treatment of model uncertainty, and one
that is implemented in what follows, assumes that the world economy is
too complex to be captured by a single model. Rather, the correct model
changes from period to period and may be viewed as a truly stochastic
realization from the set of $k$ possible models, where each outcome has
the associated objective probability $\bar{\pi}_t^i$.

The objective priors are used to calculate the expected welfare for
each country:

$$V = \max -\left(\frac{1}{2}\right) \sum_{t=0}^{\infty} \beta^t E\,(y_t'\,\Omega\,y_t) = \max -\left(\frac{1}{2}\right) \sum_{t=0}^{\infty} \beta^t \sum_{i=1}^{k} \bar{\pi}_t^i(y_t^{i\prime}\,\Omega\,y_t^i), \quad (4)$$

where the notation $y_t^i$ reads "the value of $y_t$ implied by model $i$," so that
$V$ represents the true mathematical expectation of the country's welfare.
Rational expectations by the private and public sectors in each country
obtain when their subjective priors coincide with the objective probabilities:

$$\hat{\pi}_t^i = \pi_t^i = \pi_t^{i*} = \bar{\pi}_t^i.$$

In the simulation analysis below, it is assumed that these conditions
of rational expectations obtain. In contrast, Frankel (1987) explicitly
assumed that policymakers do not exhibit such rational expectations.

Although equation (4) postulates an infinite horizon, it is convenient
to start with a finite-horizon problem and then let the number of periods
go to infinity.[17] Let the horizon be $T$ periods, and consider the final
period. It is assumed that by period $T$ the world economy has attained
a steady state and that all forward-looking variables have stabilized. The
world economy has inherited a state vector $x_T$, and the objective function
for the home country is

$$v_T(x_T) = \max -\left(\frac{1}{2}\right) E(y_T'\,\Omega\,y_T) = \max -\left(\frac{1}{2}\right) \sum_{i=1}^{k} \pi_T^i(y_T^{i\prime}\,\Omega\,y_T^i). \quad (5)$$

A corresponding expression gives the foreign country's objective function, $v_T^*$. Because the forward-looking variables have stabilized by
period $T$,

$$e_{T+1}^i = e_T^i, \qquad i = 1,\ldots,k, \tag{6}$$

[17] This algorithm is an extension to that used by Oudiz and Sachs (1985) in
their deterministic model; wherever possible, a similar notation has been
adopted. The Appendix provides a fuller derivation.

GHOSH, ATISH R., *International Policy Coordination in a World with Model Uncertainty* ,
International Monetary Fund Staff Papers, 35:2 (1988:June) p.230

244 ATISH R. GHOSH and PAUL R. MASSON

where, again, $e^i$ reads "the value of the forward-looking variables implied by model $i$." Substitution into the respective models yields

$$e_T^i = J_T^i x_T + K_T^i U_T, \qquad i = 1, \ldots, k, \tag{7}$$

where $J_T^i$ and $K_T^i$ are matrices specific to model $i$. In period $T$, $x_T$ does *not* have an $i$ superscript because it represents the (observed) inherited state vector. The vector of endogenous variables, $y_T^i$ is given by

$$y_T^i = \begin{bmatrix} x_T \\ e_T^i \end{bmatrix} \equiv M_T^i x_T + N_T^i U_T, \qquad i = 1, \ldots, k, \tag{8}$$

where, again, $M_T^i$ and $N_T^i$ are matrices specific to model $i$. Substituting equation (8) into equation (5) yields the objective functions.

When the countries are in a cooperative agreement, a single global planner chooses the entire vector of instruments, $U$, to maximize a weighted sum of the utility functions:

$$w_T(x_T) = \omega v_T(x_T) + (1 - \omega) v_T^*(x_T).$$

Note that the global planner uses each country's probability priors to evaluate the respective expected utilities. If $\Pi \neq \Pi^*$, then at least one of the governments does not have rational expectations. As long as the global planner uses each country's own priors in evaluating $v$ and $v^*$, however, disagreements over the true model do not preclude the possibility of coordination. Indeed, such disagreements over the prior vector can, by themselves, give rise to gains from coordination in models in which there are no other conflicts between the countries.[18] Given the linear-quadratic structure of the model, the solution to the planner's optimization problem may be written as

$$U_T^C = \Gamma_T^C x_T,$$

where the $C$ superscript denotes the cooperative solution.

When countries are acting noncooperatively, each chooses the subset of $U$ under its control—$u$ and $u^*$—to maximize $v_T(\cdot)$ and $v_T^*(\cdot)$, respectively, taking the actions of the other government as given. The resultant equilibrium may be written as

$$U_T^N = \Gamma_T^N x_T.$$

Hence, from equation (7),

$$e_T^i = (J_T^i + K_T^i \Gamma_T) x_T \equiv \theta_T^i x_T, \tag{9}$$

where $\Gamma$ denotes $\Gamma^C$ or $\Gamma^N$ as appropriate. Rational expectations of the forward-looking variables are

$$\bar{E}_T(e_T) = \sum_{i=1}^{k} \bar{\pi}_T^i \theta_T^i x_T = \bar{\theta}_T x_T. \tag{10}$$

[18] See Frankel (1987) and Ghosh (1987) for discussion.

GHOSH, ATISH R., *International Policy Coordination in a World with Model Uncertainty*,
International Monetary Fund Staff Papers, 35:2 (1988:June) p.230

POLICY COORDINATION WITH MODEL UNCERTAINTY          245

Finally, the period-$T$ value functions for the home country are

$$v_T^C(x_T) = -\left(\frac{1}{2}\right)\sum_{i=1}^{k} \bar{\pi}_T^i x_T^i (M_T^i + N_T^i \Gamma^C)' \Omega (M_T^i + N_T^i \Gamma^C) x_T$$

$$= x_T' S_T^C x_T. \tag{11}$$

Similarly, substituting for $\Gamma^N$ yields the value under noncooperative behavior:

$$v^N(x_T) = x_T' S_T^N x_T.$$

Correspondingly, for the foreign country,

$$v_T^{C^*}(x_T) = x_T' S_T^{C^*} x_T \quad\text{and}\quad v_T^{N^*}(x_T) = x_T' S_T^{N^*} x_T.$$

The functions $\Gamma_T^C$, $\Gamma_T^N$, $\bar{\theta}_T$, $S_T^C$, $S_T^{C^*}$, $S_T^N$, $S_T^{N^*}$ give the optimal policies, the evolution of the forward-looking variables, and the value functions, given that the state vector is $x_T$.

Now consider period $T-1$, to which the state vector $x_{T-1}$ has been bequeathed. At $T-1$ the home government faces the following optimization problem:

$$v_{T-1}(x_{T-1}) = \max -\left(\frac{1}{2}\right)\sum_{i=1}^{k} \pi_{T-1}^i (y_{T-1}^i{}' \Omega y_{T-1}^i) + \beta \sum_{i=1}^{k} \pi_{T-1}^i v_T(x_T^i), \tag{12}$$

where $v(\cdot)$ represents the value function under cooperative or noncooperative behavior, as appropriate. Note that $x_T^i$ now has an $i$ superscript: in period $T-1$ it is not known which $x_T$ will be bequeathed, since the model pertinent to period $T-1$ is not known. Hence, in period $T-1$, $E_{T-1}\{v_T(\cdot)\}$ is found by taking the expectation over all possible $x_T^i$. Expanding equation (12) makes this clearer:

$$v_{T-1}(x_{T-1}) = \max -\left(\frac{1}{2}\right)\sum_{i=1}^{k} \pi_{T-1}^i (y_{T-1}^i{}' \Omega y_{T-1}^i)$$

$$+ \beta \sum_{i=1}^{k} \pi_{T-1}^i \sum_{i=1}^{k} \pi_T^i x_T^i (M_T^i + N_T^i \Gamma^C)' \Omega (M_T^i + N_T^i \Gamma^C) x_T. \tag{13}$$

The inner summation—over $\pi_T$—yields the expected utility in period $T$, *given that* the inherited state vector is $x_T$. The outer summation—over $\pi_{T-1}$—yields the expectation of $v_T(x_T^i)$ over the possible $x_T^i$ bequeathed from period $T-1$.

The optimization now yields $S_{T-1}(\cdot)$, and so forth. As described in the Appendix, this procedure is repeated until stationary functions $[\theta(x), S(x), S^*(x)]$ are obtained. When these functions become stationary, the truncation error from solving a (large) but finite period problem rather than the true infinite horizon becomes negligible. From an initial state vector $x_0$, the present value of the gains from coordination accruing to the world are then given by

GHOSH, ATISH R., *International Policy Coordination in a World with Model Uncertainty* ,
International Monetary Fund Staff Papers, 35:2 (1988:June) p.230

246                     ATISH R. GHOSH and PAUL R. MASSON

$$\Psi(x_0) = \omega[v^C(x_0) - v^N(x_0)] + (1 - \omega)[v^{C^*}(x_0) - v^{N^*}(x_0)]$$
$$= \omega[x_0'(S^C - S^N)x_0] + (1 - \omega)[x_0'(S^{C^*} - S^{N^*})x_0].$$

## IV. Simulation Results

Model uncertainty about the structural parameters for the U.S. block in MINIMOD was introduced to examine its effects on the gains from coordination. Table 1 indicates which parameters were assumed uncertain in each simulation. The simulations also required specification of the utility weights and probability priors. The choice of the utility function parameters is likely not to be critical here because the primary focus is on the effects of model uncertainty relative to the baseline (no model uncertainty) results. It was assumed that policymakers in each country target GDP, the rate of change of prices, and the current account balance. The square of each of these variables, expressed as a percentage of its value at the point of linearization, enters the objective function; there are no cross-product terms.[19] The relative weights on the targets were taken to be 1, 10, 1.5, respectively. In addition, we included penalties for the use of monetary and fiscal policies, measured as a percentage deviation from the levels of the policy variables in the baseline, and assigned a relative welfare weight of 0.5 to each quadratic term. The discount factor, $\beta$, for each government was chosen to be $\beta = 0.95$, and the weight assigned to each country in the global planner's objective function was $\omega = 0.5$. Throughout the simulation exercises, we assumed that all policymakers, together with the private sector, exhibit rational expectations, and that the priors are not updated:

$$\pi_t^i = \pi_t^{*i} = \hat{\pi}_t^i = \bar{\pi}_t^i = \bar{\pi}^i, \qquad \text{for all } i, t.$$

In each of the simulations, there were two competing models (models 1 and 2 in Table 1) with probability weights $\bar{\pi}^i = 0.5$, $i = 1, 2$.

As discussed in Section I, the implications of model uncertainty for the gains from coordination depend, among other things, on whether it is the domestic multipliers that are uncertain or the transmission effects from abroad that are unknown. It is useful, therefore, to gain some understanding of how the structural parameter uncertainty translates into multiplier uncertainty in the reduced form of the model. Because the forward-looking variables are functions of the entire future sequence of policy settings, however, it is not possible—in a rational expectations setting—to define a measure of a multiplier uncertainty that is indepen-

---

[19] See Oudiz and Sachs (1984) for a similar objective function.

GHOSH, ATISH R., *International Policy Coordination in a World with Model Uncertainty* ,
International Monetary Fund Staff Papers, 35:2 (1988:June) p.230

POLICY COORDINATION WITH MODEL UNCERTAINTY          247

dent of whether governments are acting cooperatively or noncooperatively. As a partial solution to this problem, we solved for a rational
expectations path along which future monetary and fiscal policies are at
their baseline values, and concentrated on uncertainty about the impact
effects of policy. Using a recursive form of the Blanchard-Kahn (1980)
solution method, we obtained the dynamic systems:

$$z_t = \begin{bmatrix} x_{t+1} \\ e_t \end{bmatrix} = \begin{bmatrix} \Lambda_x^i \\ \Lambda_e^i \end{bmatrix} x_t + \begin{bmatrix} \Phi_x^i \\ \Phi_e^i \end{bmatrix} U_t, \qquad i = 1, \ldots, k, \qquad (14)$$

where $\Lambda^i$ and $\Phi^i$ are semireduced-form coefficients, derived under the
assumption that $U_{t+j} = 0$, for all $j > 0$. The mean value of the effect of an
instrument $u_t^M$ on a target variable $z_{t+1}^j$ is:

$$\mu_M^j = \sum_{i=1}^{k} \pi^i \Phi_{jM}^i,$$

where $\Phi_{jM}^i$ is the $(j, M)$ element of $\Phi^i$, and the average has been taken
over the $k$ possible models (here $k = 2$). Similarly, the variance of each
model's multipliers is given by

$$(\sigma_M^j)^2 = \sum_{i=1}^{k} \pi^i (\Phi_{jM}^i - \mu_M^j)^2.$$

For each target $z_t^j$, we then defined a measure of the parameter
uncertainty[20] regarding the use of instrument $u^M$ as

$$\zeta_M^j \equiv \mu_M^2 / (\mu_M^2 + \sigma_M^2),$$

so that $\zeta_M^j \in (0, 1)$ is a decreasing function of the severity of model
uncertainty. Note that $\zeta$ is a dimensionless statistic, satisfying $\zeta = 1$ when
there is no uncertainty and $\zeta \to 0$ as the effectiveness of the instrument
worsens.

Table 2 gives the $\zeta$ values for each combination of the instruments and
targets in each set of simulations. In the baseline simulation, of course,
$\zeta$ is always unity because, by construction, there is no model uncertainty.
More generally, the prevalence of model uncertainty implies that $\zeta$ will
be less than unity, at least for the effects of some of the instruments on
some of the targets. A number of points emerge from this table. First,
there is usually greatest disagreement among the models with respect to
the effects of policies—domestic or foreign—on the current account.
The greater is the welfare weight placed on the current account, the
more important will be the implications of this form of model uncertainty for the gains from coordination. Second, any uncertainty about

---

[20] This measure is a simple transformation of the coefficient of variation, which
Brainard (1967) used as a measure of policy effectiveness.

GHOSH, ATISH R., *International Policy Coordination in a World with Model Uncertainty* ,
International Monetary Fund Staff Papers, 35:2 (1988:June) p.230

248                ATISH R. GHOSH and PAUL R. MASSON

Table 2.  *Degree of Reduced-Form Model Uncertainty, ζ,
of Policy Instruments on Selected Variables*

| Simulation | Endogenous Variables[a] | Policy Variables | | | |
|---|---|---|---|---|---|
|  |  | *UG*[a] | *UM*[a] | *RG*[a] | *RM*[a] |
| 1. Baseline | *RGDP* | 1.000* | 1.000* | 1.000 | 1.000 |
|  | *UGDP* | 1.000 | 1.000 | 1.000* | 1.000* |
|  | *UCURRBAL* | 1.000 | 1.000 | 1.000 | 1.000 |
|  | *RPI* | 1.000* | 1.000* | 1.000 | 1.000 |
|  | *UPI* | 1.000 | 1.000 | 1.000* | 1.000* |
| 2. Interest semi-elasticity of U.S. money demand uncertain | *RGDP* | 0.999* | 0.859* | 0.999 | 0.999 |
|  | *UGDP* | 0.999 | 0.855 | 0.997* | 0.995* |
|  | *UCURRBAL* | 0.983 | 0.854 | 0.998 | 0.999 |
|  | *RPI* | 0.975* | 0.850* | 0.986 | 0.999 |
|  | *UPI* | 0.984 | 0.850 | 0.997* | 0.999* |
| 3. Direct crowding out effect of U.S. government spending uncertain | *RGDP* | 0.913* | 1.000* | 1.000 | 1.000 |
|  | *UGDP* | 0.920 | 1.000 | 1.000* | 1.000* |
|  | *UCURRBAL* | 0.938 | 1.000 | 1.000 | 1.000 |
|  | *RPI* | 0.869* | 1.000* | 1.000 | 1.000 |
|  | *UPI* | 0.879 | 1.000 | 1.000* | 1.000* |
| 4. Slope of U.S. Phillips curve uncertain | *RGDP* | 0.179* | 0.431* | 0.998 | 0.162 |
|  | *UGDP* | 0.966 | 0.898 | 0.912* | 0.555* |
|  | *UCURRBAL* | 0.613 | 0.265 | 0.740 | 0.366 |
|  | *RPI* | 0.471* | 0.419* | 0.467 | 0.414 |
|  | *UPI* | 0.493 | 0.410 | 0.379* | 0.412* |
| 5. Activity elasticity of U.S. imports uncertain | *RGDP* | 0.915* | 0.999* | 0.999 | 0.996 |
|  | *UGDP* | 0.996 | 0.998 | 0.999* | 0.999* |
|  | *UCURRBAL* | 0.964 | 0.968 | 0.994 | 0.978 |
|  | *RPI* | 0.827* | 0.949* | 0.917 | 0.967 |
|  | *UPI* | 0.730 | 0.967 | 0.983* | 0.970* |
| 6. Real exchange rate elasticity of U.S. imports uncertain | *RGDP* | 0.997* | 0.995* | 0.999 | 0.981 |
|  | *UGDP* | 0.999 | 0.999 | 0.999* | 0.992* |
|  | *UCURRBAL* | 0.964 | 0.994 | 0.996 | 0.942 |
|  | *RPI* | 0.940* | 0.994* | 0.773 | 0.929 |
|  | *UPI* | 0.908 | 0.990 | 0.927* | 0.939* |
| 7. Activity elasticity of rest-of-world (ROW) imports uncertain | *RGDP* | 0.999* | 0.994* | 0.999 | 0.999 |
|  | *UGDP* | 0.999 | 0.999 | 0.682* | 0.951* |
|  | *UCURRBAL* | 0.998 | 0.995 | 0.490 | 0.991 |
|  | *RPI* | 0.995* | 0.984* | 0.417 | 0.994 |
|  | *UPI* | 0.997 | 0.987 | 0.999* | 0.995* |

GHOSH, ATISH R., *International Policy Coordination in a World with Model Uncertainty* ,
International Monetary Fund Staff Papers, 35:2 (1988:June) p.230

POLICY COORDINATION WITH MODEL UNCERTAINTY          249

Table 2   (*concluded*).

| Simulation | Endogenous Variables[a] | Policy Variables | | | |
|---|---|---|---|---|---|
| | | $UG^a$ | $UM^a$ | $RG^a$ | $RM^a$ |
| 8.  Real exchange rate | RGDP | 0.998* | 0.996* | 0.999 | 0.996 |
| elasticity of ROW | UGDP | 0.999 | 0.999 | 0.999* | 0.981* |
| imports uncertain | UCURRBAL | 0.991 | 0.998 | 0.992 | 0.983 |
| | RPI | 0.958* | 0.993* | 0.880 | 0.971 |
| | UPI | 0.972 | 0.994 | 0.968* | 0.973* |
| 9.  Effect of GDP on | RGDP | 0.996* | 0.999* | 0.999 | 0.996 |
| U.S. investment | UGDP | 0.915 | 0.998 | 0.999* | 0.999* |
| uncertain | UCURRBAL | 0.964 | 0.968 | 0.994 | 0.978 |
| | RPI | 0.827* | 0.967* | 0.917 | 0.967 |
| | UPI | 0.730 | 0.949 | 0.983* | 0.970* |

Note: A value of unity ($\zeta = 1$) signifies absence of model uncertainty for that
policy instrument.
   [a] Variables are defined as follows: *UG*, U.S. fiscal policy; *UM*, U.S. monetary
policy; *RG*, ROW fiscal policy; *RM*, ROW monetary policy; *UGDP*, U.S. GDP;
*RGDP*, ROW GDP; *UCURRBAL*, U.S. current account balance; *UPI*, U.S.
consumer inflation; *RPI*, ROW consumer inflation. A single asterisk (*) denotes
transmission effect.

parameters of the home country, such as the degree of fiscal crowding
out, or the slope of the Phillips curve, is often magnified in the transmission process. For example, in simulation 3, where the degree of fiscal
crowding out in the United States is the only uncertain parameter, uncertainty about the effects of U.S. fiscal policy on ROW GDP and on ROW
inflation is greater than uncertainty surrounding the effects on U.S.
GDP or inflation.

   In the symmetrical two-country model without expectations that was
discussed in Section I, uncertainty about transmission effects—the
effects of home policy on the foreign country and vice versa—always
increased the gains from coordination, whereas uncertainty about the
domestic effects had ambiguous implications for the incentive to coordinate. (Although in the limiting cases where $\zeta = 0$ for domestic instruments, the gains from coordination are necessarily eliminated.) In
Table 2, uncertainty about the transmission multipliers has been indicated by an asterisk(*). In simulations 3 and 4, the degree of transmission uncertainty is almost always greater than the corresponding
uncertainty for the domestic targets. For these simulations, therefore,
the analysis of Section I suggests that the presence of model uncertainty
should serve to raise the gains from coordination. For the remaining

GHOSH, ATISH R., *International Policy Coordination in a World with Model Uncertainty* ,
International Monetary Fund Staff Papers, 35:2 (1988:June) p.230

250          ATISH R. GHOSH and PAUL R. MASSON

simulations, however, because domestic multiplier uncertainty is large, there is no clear presumption about the effects of model uncertainty.

The gains from coordination were calculated for a standard shock of a 1 percent decline in GDP, relative to baseline, together with a 1 percent rise in the consumer price level, again relative to baseline, in both the U.S. and ROW sectors.[21] The shock is purely transitory, occurring in the initial period and returning to zero immediately. Because of the dynamics of the model, however, effects on endogenous variables may persist for a considerable number of periods. To focus on the effects of model uncertainty per se, the gains from coordination under each set of parameter values must be normalized by the corresponding "certainty equivalent" model. Otherwise, the effects of model uncertainty cannot be distinguished from the fact that different models, when known to be realized with unit probability, imply different gains from coordination. For example, suppose that the two possible models obtain with probability $\pi^1$ and $\pi^2$, respectively,[22] and let the gains from coordination be denoted by $\Psi(\pi^1, \pi^2)$. The certainty equivalent gains from coordination, $\overline{\Psi}(\pi^1, \pi^2)$, are given by

$$\overline{\Psi}(\pi^1, \pi^2) = \pi^1 \Psi(1, 0) + \pi^2 \Psi(0, 1).$$

It should be emphasized that $\overline{\Psi}$ will not in general equal the gains under the baseline parameters in Table 1. The effects of model uncertainty are beneficial to the case for coordination if and only if

$$\Psi(\pi^1, \pi^2) > \overline{\Psi}(\pi^1, \pi^2).$$

Table 3 reports the gains from coordination under model uncertainty, $\Psi(\pi^1, \pi^2)$, and for the certainty equivalent model, $\overline{\Psi}(\pi^1, \pi^2)$, under each of the pairs of parameter values listed in Table 1. The gains reported are the total benefit accruing to the world economy over the infinite horizon and are expressed in terms of the one-quarter U.S. GDP equivalent. Thus the estimated gains in the baseline simulation, with the original MINIMOD parameters and no model uncertainty, are equivalent to the utility associated with a 19.5 percent increase in U.S. GDP sustained over one quarter. This estimate of the gains from coordination is roughly commensurate with previous empirical estimates (for example, Oudiz and Sachs (1984), who found gains of about 1 percent, but sustained over three years), although of course they depend on the specific utility function and shocks under consideration.

---

[21] In general, the joint distribution describing the error terms in the model's equations will be related to the distribution describing the parameters. With an estimated model, one could choose a drawing from these distributions that was consistent with the historical data. This was not done here, however.

[22] In particular, it is assumed that $\pi^1 = \pi^2 = 0.5$.

GHOSH, ATISH R., *International Policy Coordination in a World with Model Uncertainty* ,
International Monetary Fund Staff Papers, 35:2 (1988:June) p.230

POLICY COORDINATION WITH MODEL UNCERTAINTY          251

Table 3.   *Gains from Coordination Under Model Uncertainty*

| Simulation | Gain Under Uncertainty, $\Psi(\pi^1, \pi^2)$ | Gain Under Certainty Equivalent, $\bar{\Psi}(\pi^1, \pi^2)$ | Ratio, $\Psi(\pi^1, \pi^2)/\bar{\Psi}(\pi^1, \pi^2)$ |
|---|---|---|---|
| 1. Baseline | 19.5 | 19.5 | 1.00 |
| 2. Interest elasticity of U.S. money demand uncertain | 17.0 | 9.9 | 1.42 |
| 3. Direct crowding out effect of U.S. government spending uncertain | 29.2 | 12.2 | 2.38 |
| 4. Slope of U.S. Phillips curve uncertain | 25.1 | 10.9 | 2.29 |
| 5. Activity elasticity of U.S. imports uncertain | 23.9 | 19.2 | 1.24 |
| 6. Real exchange rate elasticity of U.S. imports uncertain | 3.4 | 12.5 | 0.27 |
| 7. Activity elasticity of ROW imports uncertain | 23.9 | 16.8 | 1.41 |
| 8. Real exchange rate elasticity of ROW imports uncertain | 19.4 | 17.1 | 1.13 |
| 9. Effect of GDP on U.S. investment uncertain | 9.6 | 17.8 | 0.53 |

From Table 3 it is apparent that the presence of model uncertainty in general raises the gains from policy coordination—in this model, and for this particular shock and objective function. Only for simulations 6 and 9, in which there is uncertainty about the real exchange rate elasticity of import demand by the United States and about the effect of U.S. GDP on U.S. investment demand, respectively, does model uncertainty serve to reduce the gains from coordination. Inspection of Table 2 reveals that in these simulations domestic multiplier uncertainty in general exceeds the corresponding transmission uncertainty. Specifically, the effects of ROW government expenditure on ROW inflation exhibit considerable parameter uncertainty in simulation 6, whereas in simulation 9 all the transmission effects are less uncertain than are the corresponding domestic multipliers. In the other simulations, however, the effect of model uncertainty is to *raise* the gains from coordination. Indeed, in simulations 3 and 4, where there is in general much greater transmission uncer-

GHOSH, ATISH R., *International Policy Coordination in a World with Model Uncertainty* ,
International Monetary Fund Staff Papers, 35:2 (1988:June) p.230

252                     ATISH R. GHOSH and PAUL R. MASSON

tainty relative to domestic uncertainty, the gains from coordination are
more than doubled; whereas for the other simulations the effects of
model uncertainty are far from negligible, at least in terms of propor-
tionate increases in the certainty equivalent gains. It is still true that, in
absolute terms, gains from policy coordination are estimated to be relatively modest.

## V. Conclusions

This paper has examined the desirability of international policy coordination in an environment characterized by model uncertainty. Rather
than use the reduced forms of different models, we chose a single two-
region macroeconometric model and introduced parameter uncertainty
at the structural level of the model. The primary advantage of such an
approach is that it allows tracing the effect of uncertainty about structural parameters on reduced-form multipliers and, in turn, on the gains
from coordination.

The major finding in this paper has been that model uncertainty, far
from precluding policy coordination, may in fact provide a strong incentive for countries to coordinate their macroeconomic policies. By contrast, in a series of articles Frankel reached exactly the opposite conclusion (Frankel (1987) and Frankel and Rockett (1986)).

The essential difference between Frankel's approach and ours is that
Frankel explicitly assumed that policymakers do not exhibit rational
expectations. Policymakers were assumed to ignore the presence of
model uncertainty in choosing their optimal plans, even though they
disagree on which is the correct model of the world economy. Within our
framework, therefore, the probability priors used by Frankel's policymakers, $\Pi$ and $\Pi^*$, do not coincide with the objective probabilities $\hat{\Pi}$.
Because the mathematical expectation of each country's welfare is evaluated at the true probability weights $\hat{\Pi}$, policymakers are effectively maximizing the wrong objective function. If in the Nash equilibrium policymakers are undertaking incorrect policies, and if under cooperation they
become more efficient at making mistakes, it is scarcely surprising that
coordination may reduce welfare.

But the general argument that ignorance of the correct model is likely
to negate gains from coordination is problematic. First, it attributes an
extraordinary degree of irrationality to policymakers to suggest that they
simply ignore model uncertainty. Second, this argument has very little to
do with policy coordination: it is simply an indictment of activist policy

GHOSH, ATISH R., *International Policy Coordination in a World with Model Uncertainty* ,
International Monetary Fund Staff Papers, 35:2 (1988:June) p.230

POLICY COORDINATION WITH MODEL UNCERTAINTY        253

when the precise effects of policy are unknown. If there is some doubt
about the effects of policies, it is clearly desirable for the authorities to
be cautious in setting those policies.

Although the gains from coordination in the baseline simulation without model uncertainty were rather modest, in simulations where policymakers explicitly recognize model uncertainty when framing their policies the gains from coordination relative to the Nash equilibrium increased considerably. Policy setting in the latter does not properly take
into account the feedback effect on overall uncertainty that results from
induced changes in foreign policies. In terms of GDP-utility equivalents,
model uncertainty can increase the gains from coordination by as much
as a factor of 2. Furthermore, in line with theoretical arguments, the
implications of uncertainty about MINIMOD parameters for the incentive to coordinate depend crucially on the source of that uncertainty.
When transmission effects are unknown, the greater is the uncertainty,
the greater are the gains from coordination. When the effects of policies
on the domestic economy are uncertain, however, model uncertainty can
either increase or decrease the gains from coordination, depending on
several other factors.

This paper has been in part methodological—exploring the design of
coordination regimes in dynamic rational expectations models in the
presence of model uncertainty—and there remain several possible extensions of our work. First, we intend to undertake more extensive simulation analyses to see how structural parameter uncertainty is embodied in
the reduced-form multipliers of such models. This extension is of considerable interest because the disagreements between multicountry
models may be reducible to econometric estimates of certain key structural parameters. Second, although we have employed a dynamic model,
we have not included any learning mechanism, whether active or passive.
It seems reasonable, however, that policymakers may start with some
vector of priors that are slowly updated until they converge to the rational (objective) probabilities over the models. If policymakers learn
about the domestic effects of their policies faster than they do about
transmission effects, an increase in the gains from coordination may
occur over time. Conversely, if policymakers attempt active learning—
that is, perturbing the economy in order to learn about it—then the Nash
equilibrium may become even more inefficient, since each government
will introduce excessive noise into the world economy.[23]

[23] Ghosh (1986b) explores this possibility in a theoretical model.

GHOSH, ATISH R., *International Policy Coordination in a World with Model Uncertainty* ,
International Monetary Fund Staff Papers, 35:2 (1988:June) p.230

254         ATISH R. GHOSH and PAUL R. MASSON

## APPENDIX

## Nash and Cooperative Strategies Under Model Uncertainty

In this Appendix the Nash and cooperative strategies under model uncertainty are derived, by using a dynamic programming solution technique.

Assume, in period $t$, that

$$v_{t+1}(x_{t+1}) = x'_{t+1} S_{t+1} x_{t+1} \tag{15}$$

$$v^*_{t+1}(x_{t+1}) = x'_{t+1} S^*_{t+1} x_{t+1} \tag{16}$$

$$E(e_{t+1}) = \theta_{t+1} x_{t+1}, \tag{17}$$

where $v(\cdot)$ is the home country's value function, and $v^*(\cdot)$ is the foreign country's value function; $x_t$ is the $p$-dimensional state vector in period $t$; $e_t$ is the $q$-dimensional vector of jumping variables; and $S$ and $S^*$ are matrices. The $k$ models are given by

$$x^i_{t+1} = A^i x_t + B^i e_t + C^i U_t \tag{18}$$

$$e^i_{t+1} = D^i x_t + F^i e^i_t + G^i U_t, \tag{19}$$

where $U_t$ is an $r$-dimensional vector of controls. Substituting equation (17) into equations (18) and (19) yields

$$e^i_t = (\theta_{t+1} B^i - F^i)^{-1} [(D^i - \theta_{t+1} A^i) x_t + (G^i - \theta_{t+1} C^i) U_t]$$

$$\equiv J^i_{t+1} x_t + K^i_{t+1} U_t$$

and

$$x_{t+1} = (A^i + B^i J^i_{t+1}) x_t + (B^i K^i_{t+1} + C^i) U_t$$

$$\equiv H^i_{t+1} x_t + L^i_{t+1} U_t$$

$$y^i_t = \begin{bmatrix} x_t \\ e^i_t \end{bmatrix} = \begin{bmatrix} I_p \\ J^i_t \end{bmatrix} x_t + \begin{bmatrix} 0 \\ K^i_{t+1} \end{bmatrix} U_t$$

$$\equiv M^i_{t+1} x_t + N^i_{t+1} U_t.$$

The home country's value function is given by

$$v_t(x_t) = \sum_{i=1}^k \pi^i [(M^i_{t+1} x_t + N^i_{t+1} U_t)' \Omega (M^i_{t+1} x_t + N^i_{t+1} U_t)$$

$$+ \beta (H^i_{t+1} x_t + L^i_{t+1} U_t)' S_{t+1} (H^i_{t+1} x_t + L^i_{t+1} U_t)],$$

where $\Omega$ is a matrix of objective function weights, and $S_{t+1}$ summarizes the future discounted utility stream. The foreign country's expected value function is given by a similar expression. Under the Nash equilibrium, each country chooses a subset of $U_t$, either $u_t$ or $u^*_t$. Let lowercase letters denote conformable partitions of $M$, $N$, $H$, and $L$. Solving for the Nash equilibrium yields

GHOSH, ATISH R., *International Policy Coordination in a World with Model Uncertainty* , International Monetary Fund Staff Papers, 35:2 (1988:June) p.230

POLICY COORDINATION WITH MODEL UNCERTAINTY      255

$$U_t^N =$$

$$- \left[ \begin{array}{c} \sum_{i=1}^{k} \pi^i (n_{t+1}^i{}' \, \Omega \, n_{t+1}^i + \beta l_{t+1}^i{}' \, S_{t+1} \, l_{t+1}^i) \; \sum_{i=1}^{k} \pi^i (n_{t+1}^i{}' \, \Omega \, n_{t+1}^{i*} + \beta l_{t+1}^i{}' \, S_{t+1} \, l_{t+1}^{i*}) \\ \sum_{i=1}^{k} \pi^i (n_{t+1}^{i*}{}' \, \Omega^* \, n_{t+1}^{i*} + \beta l_{t+1}^{i*}{}' \, S_{t+1}^* \, l_{t+1}^{i*}) \sum_{i=1}^{k} \pi^i (n_{t+1}^{i*}{}' \, \Omega^* \, n_{t+1}^i + \beta l_{t+1}^{i*}{}' \, S_{t+1}^* \, l_{t+1}^i) \end{array} \right]^{-1}$$

$$\left[ \begin{array}{c} \sum_{i=1}^{k} \pi^i (n_{t+1}^i{}' \, \Omega \, M_{t+1}^i + \beta l_{t+1}^i{}' \, S_{t+1} \, H_{t+1}^i) \\ \sum_{i=1}^{k} \pi^i (n_{t+1}^{i*}{}' \, \Omega^* \, M_{t+1}^i + \beta l_{t+1}^{i*}{}' \, S_{t+1}^* \, H_{t+1}^i) \end{array} \right] x_t = \Gamma^N x_t. \tag{20}$$

Under coordination, the corresponding first-order condition is

$$U_t^C = \left[ \sum_{i=1}^{k} \pi^i (N_{t+1}^i{}' \, \Omega^G \, N_{t+1}^i + \beta L_{t+1}^i{}' \, S_{t+1}^G \, L_{t+1}^i) \right]^{-1}$$

$$\times \left[ \sum_{i=1}^{k} \pi^i (N_{t+1}^i{}' \, \Omega^G \, M_{t+1}^i + \beta L_{t+1}^i{}' \, S_{t+1}^G \, H_{t+1}^i) \right] x_t$$

$$= \Gamma^C x_t, \tag{21}$$

where $\Omega^G$ and $S^G$ are matrices of the global planner's value function:

$$\Omega^G = \omega \Omega + (1 - \omega) \Omega^*$$
$$S^G = \omega S + (1 - \omega) S^*.$$

The home country's value function therefore becomes

$$v_t(x_t) = \sum_{i=1}^{k} \pi^i [x_t{}' (M_{t+1}^i + N_{t+1}^i \, \Gamma)' \, \Omega \, (M_{t+1}^i + N_{t+1}^i \Gamma) \, x_t$$

$$+ \beta x_t{}' (H_{t+1}^i + L_{t+1}^i \, \Gamma)' \, S_{t+1} \, (H_{t+1}^i + L_{t+1}^i \Gamma) \, x_t]$$

$$= x_t{}' \, S_t x_t, \tag{22}$$

where $\Gamma$ denotes $\Gamma^C$ or $\Gamma^N$ as appropriate. Similarly, the foreign country's value function may be written as

$$v_t^* (x_t) = x_t{}' \, S_t^* \, x_t.$$

The expected value of the forward-looking variables is

$$E_{t-1} (e_t) = \sum_{i=1}^{k} \pi^i (J_{t+1}^i x_t + K_{t+1}^i \, \Gamma x_t) \equiv \theta_t x_t. \tag{23}$$

Replacing $S_{t+1}$ by $S_t$, $S_{t+1}^*$ by $S_t^*$, and $\theta_{t+1}$ by $\theta_t$ in equation (23), we obtain recursive rules to compute the equilibria. The recursion is started by choosing $S_T = S_T = 0$ and by requiring that $e_{T+1} = e_T$.

GHOSH, ATISH R., *International Policy Coordination in a World with Model Uncertainty* ,
International Monetary Fund Staff Papers, 35:2 (1988:June) p.230

256 ATISH R. GHOSH and PAUL R. MASSON

## REFERENCES

Ahmed, Shaghil, "Temporary and Permanent Government Spending in an Open Economy," *Journal of Monetary Economics* (Amsterdam), Vol. 17 (March 1986), pp. 197–224.

Basar, Tamar, and Gert J. Olsder, *Dynamic Noncooperative Game Theory,* (London; New York: Academic, 1982).

Blanchard, Olivier, and Charles Khan, "The Solution of Linear Difference Models under Rational Expectations," *Econometrica* (Evanston, Ill.), Vol. 48 (July 1980), pp. 1305–11.

Brainard, William C., "Uncertainty and the Effectiveness of Policy," *American Economic Review* (Nashville, Tennessee), Vol. 57 (May 1967), pp. 411–25.

Bryant, Ralph, and Gerald Holtham, "The U.S. External Deficit: Diagnosis, Prognosis, and Cure," in Ralph Bryant and others, eds., *External Deficits and the Dollar: The Pit and the Pendulum* (Washington: The Brookings Institution, 1987).

Bryant, Ralph, and others, eds., *External Deficits and the Dollar: The Pit and the Pendulum* (Washington: The Brookings Institution, 1987).

Buiter, Willem H., and James Tobin, "Debt Neutrality: A Brief Review of Doctrine and Evidence," in *Social Security Versus Private Saving,* ed. by George von Furstenberg (Cambridge, Massachusetts: Ballinger, 1979), pp. 39-63.

Canzoneri, Matthew, and Patrick Minford, "Policy Interdependence: Does Strategic Behaviour Pay? An Empirical Investigation using the Liverpool World Model," in D. R. Hodgman and Geoffrey Wood, eds., *Macroeconomic Policy and Economic Interdependence* (New York: Macmillan, forthcoming, 1988); originally appeared as Discussion Paper 201 (London: Centre for Economic Policy Research, October 1987).

Chow, Gregory, *Analysis and Control of Dynamic Economic Systems* (New York: Wiley, 1975).

Clark, Peter K., "Investment in the 1970s: Theory, Performance, and Prediction," *Brookings Papers on Economic Activity: 1* (1979), The Brookings Institution (Washington), pp. 73–113.

Cooper, Richard N., "Economic Interdependencies and Coordination of Economic Policies," in Richard N. Cooper, *Economic Policy in an Interdependent World* (Cambridge, Massachusetts: MIT Press, 1986), pp. 289–331; originally published in *Handbook of International Economics*, Vol. 2, ed. by Ronald W. Jones and Peter B. Kenen (Amsterdam: North-Holland; New York: Elsevier, 1985).

Feldstein, Martin, "Government Deficits and Aggregate Demand," *Journal of Monetary Economics* (Amsterdam), Vol. 9 (January 1982), pp. 1–20.

———, "Signs of Recovery," *The Economist* (London), June 11, 1983, pp. 43–48.

Fischer, Stanley, "International Macroeconomic Policy Coordination," NBER Working Paper 2224 (Cambridge: National Bureau of Economic Research, May 1987).

GHOSH, ATISH R., *International Policy Coordination in a World with Model Uncertainty* ,
International Monetary Fund Staff Papers, 35:2 (1988:June) p.230

POLICY COORDINATION WITH MODEL UNCERTAINTY     257

Frankel, Jeffrey, "Obstacles to International Macroeconomic Policy Coordination," IMF Working Paper WP/87/29 (unpublished; Washington: International Monetary Fund, 1987).

———, and Katharine Rockett, "International Macroeconomic Policy Coordination when Policy-Makers Disagree on the Model," NBER Working Paper 2059 (Cambridge: National Bureau of Economic Research, October 1986).

Ghosh, Atish R. (1986a), "International Policy Coordination in an Uncertain World," *Economics Letters* (Amsterdam), Vol. 21, pp. 271–76.

——— (1986b), "Policy Coordination with Model Uncertainty and Active Learning," (unpublished; Cambridge, Massachusetts: Harvard University).

Ghosh, Swati, "International Policy Coordination When the Model Is Unknown" (M. Phil. Thesis; London: Oxford University, 1987).

Goldstein, Morris, and Mohsin S. Khan, "Income and Price Effects in Foreign Trade," Chapter 20 in *Handbook of International Economics*, Vol. 2, ed. by Ronald W. Jones and Peter B. Kenen (Amsterdam: North-Holland; New York: Elsevier, 1985).

Haas, Richard, and Paul R. Masson, "MINIMOD: Specification and Simulation Results," *Staff Papers*, International Monetary Fund (Washington), Vol. 33 (December 1986), pp. 722–67.

Holtham, Gerald, and Andrew Hughes Hallett, "International Policy Cooperation and Model Uncertainty," in *Global Macroeconomics: Policy Conflict and Cooperation*, ed. by Ralph Bryant and Richard Portes (New York: St. Martin's, 1988), pp. 128–84.

Horne, Jocelyn, and Paul R. Masson, "Scope and Limits of International Economic Cooperation and Policy Coordination," IMF Working Paper WP/87/24 (unpublished; Washington: International Monetary Fund, 1987); see revised version, *Staff Papers*, International Monetary Fund (Washington), Vol. 35 (June 1988), pp. 259–96.

Kendrick, David, *Stochastic Control for Economic Models* (New York: McGraw-Hill, 1981).

Kormendi, Roger C., "Government Debt, Government Spending, and Private Sector Behavior," *American Economic Review* (Nashville, Tennessee), Vol. 73 (December 1983), pp. 994–1010.

Krugman, Paul, and Richard Baldwin, "The Persistence of the U.S. Trade Deficit," *Brookings Papers on Economic Activity: 1* (1987), The Brookings Institution (Washington), pp. 1–55.

Lucas, Robert, "Econometric Policy Evaluation: A Critique," in *The Phillips Curve and Labor Markets*, Carnegie-Rochester Conference Series on Public Policy, Vol. 1, ed. by Karl Brunner and Allan H. Meltzer (Amsterdam: North-Holland, 1976), pp. 19–46.

Masson, Paul R., "The Dynamics of a Two-Country Minimodel Under Rational Expectations," *Annales d'Economie et de Statistique* (Paris), No. 6/7 (1987), pp. 37–69.

McKibbin, Warwick, and Jeffrey Sachs, "Coordination of Monetary and Fiscal Policies in the OECD," in *International Aspects of Fiscal Policy*, ed. by Jacob A. Frenkel (Chicago: University of Chicago Press, 1988).

258                    ATISH R. GHOSH and PAUL R. MASSON

Oudiz, Gilles, and Jeffrey Sachs, "Macroeconomic Policy Coordination Among
   the Industrial Economies," *Brookings Papers on Economic Activity: 1*
   (1984), The Brookings Institution (Washington), pp. 1–75.

————, "International Policy Coordination in Dynamic Macroeconomic Mod-
   els," in *International Economic Policy Coordination,* ed. by Willem H.
   Buiter and Richard C. Marston (Cambridge and New York: Cambridge
   University Press, 1985).

Rogoff, Kenneth, "Can International Monetary Policy Cooperation Be
   Counterproductive?" *Journal of International Economics* (Amsterdam),
   Vol. 18 (May 1985), pp. 199–217.

Sachs, Jeffrey, "The Dollar and the Policy Mix: 1985," *Brookings Papers on
   Economic Activity: 1* (1985), The Brookings Institution (Washington),
   pp. 117–97.

Simpson, Thomas D., "Changes in the Financial System: Implications for Monetary Policy," *Brookings Papers on Economic Activity: 1* (1984), The
   Brookings Institution (Washington), pp. 249–65.

Stevens, Guy, and others, *The U.S. Economy in an Interdependent World: A
   Multicountry Model* (Washington: Board of Governors of the Federal Reserve System, 1984).

# Model Uncertainty, Learning, and the Gains from Coordination

## By Atish R. Ghosh and Paul R. Masson*

*This paper considers gains from international economic policy coordination when there is uncertainty concerning the functioning of the world economy but also learning about the "true" model on the part of policymakers. The paper reports estimates of plausible alternative versions of a standard two-country model. Activist policy (either coordinated or uncoordinated) may produce large welfare losses in the absence of learning, if policymakers believe in the wrong model; hence, exogenous money targets and freely flexible exchange rates may be best. However, model learning (from observations on macroeconomic variables) causes coordinated policies to dominate activist uncoordinated policies or exogenous money targets. (JEL F33, F42)*

In recent years, there has been a marked increase in interest in international economic policy coordination, as evidenced by the proliferation of academic publications and of meetings of officials. Though the presumption is that policy coordination among the major industrial countries is a good thing, there exist valid doubts concerning the possibility of designing appropriate intervention and coordination rules when the effects of policies are uncertain. Speaking at the American Economic Association meetings in December 1987, Martin Feldstein noted, "Uncertainties about the actual state of the international economy and uncertainties about the effects of one country's policies on the economies of other countries make it impossible to be confident that coordinated policy shifts would actually be beneficial" (Feldstein, 1988 p. 10). Though coordinated policies may, *ex post*, turn out to have been ill-advised, the relevant question is whether they are likely to result in higher welfare on average than uncoordinated policies, despite the presence of such uncertainties.

The issue has been discussed in several recent papers, though a consensus on the implications of model uncertainty for the desirability of coordination has yet to be achieved. Jeffrey Frankel and Katharine Rockett (1988) argue that model uncertainty makes coordination too risky and that, on average, countries are as well off pursuing noncooperative policies as they are under coordination.[1] In contrast, we have argued in another paper that the existence of model uncertainty does not necessarily preclude a beneficial role for the coordination of macroeconomic policies; indeed, it may in fact provide an additional incentive to coordinate policies internationally (Ghosh and Masson, 1988; see also Ghosh and Swati Ghosh [1991]). The reason for this is that, in the choice of optimal policies, coordination will properly take into account the effects of those policies on global economic uncertainty.

The differences in conclusions stem from two essential differences in approach. First

*Department of Economics, Princeton University, Princeton, NJ 08544 and International Monetary Fund, Washington, DC 20431. We are grateful to Mike Dooley, Dale Henderson, and an anonymous referee for helpful comments. The views expressed in the paper are those of the authors alone, and in particular do not represent those of the International Monetary Fund.

[1]Gerald Holtham and Andrew Hughes Hallett (1987) show that criteria can be applied that diminish the likelihood that coordination will be bad.

is the question of whether to evaluate gains *ex ante* or *ex post*. Our earlier paper focuses on the *ex ante* expected gains from coordination, while Frankel and Rockett (1988) consider the *ex post* actual gains after arbitrarily specifying which is the true model. The second issue concerns the nature of expectations formation. In our earlier paper, policymakers are assumed to have rational expectations across the set of possible models and to take due account of the presence of model uncertainty in formulating policies, whereas in Frankel and Rockett's approach policymakers are assumed to have different subjective priors with respect to the different models, but each believes (wrongly) that he/she knows the correct model.[2]

In this paper, we reexamine the issue of model uncertainty and policy coordination, highlighting the effects of the differences in approach described above. We use variants of a simple consensus open-economy model presented in Gilles Oudiz and Jeffrey Sachs (1985), which is based on the Rudiger Dornbusch (1976) extension to the Mundell-Fleming model.[3] If the subjective priors of policymakers (and of private agents) equal the objective probabilities, the average of welfare values achieved *ex post* —presumably the relevant criterion—will equal the *ex ante* expected welfare value. This was the case in our earlier paper; here, we relax that assumption and allow subjective priors and objective probabilities to differ, as do Frankel and Rockett (but we do not allow for disagreement concerning these probabilities, as they do). We estimate alternative versions of the Oudiz-Sachs model and perform stochastic simulations on the assumptions that one or the other version is the true one and that agents assign nonzero

probabilities to each of the models; we use the *ex post* welfare criterion in evaluating the gains from coordination. However, policymakers are assumed to take account of the model uncertainty and to maximize expected utility over the range of models.

This paper also makes a significant departure from all of the earlier coordination literature in that it abandons the purely static view of model uncertainty which has hitherto been adopted. Instead, it is assumed that agents update their priors over the set of possible models in a Bayesian fashion.[4] There is an extensive literature on "learning rational expectations" (William Brock, 1972; R. M. Cyert and M. E. De Groot, 1974; Stephen De Canio, 1979; Lawrence Blume and David Easley, 1982; Blume et al., 1982; Margaret Bray, 1982; Bray and Neil Savin, 1986; Albert Marcet and Thomas Sargent, 1988). The conclusion of this literature is that least-squares learning seems to converge to rational expectations in a wide variety of circumstances but that it may also converge to an incorrect model. In particular, the paper by Blume and Easley is closest to the setup of our paper, as the authors consider Bayesian updating of prior probabilities applied to a finite set of models. They construct examples of cases in which both the true model and the wrong model are locally stable (i.e., cases in which it is possible that agents do not converge to rational expectations). It is thus of interest to analyze in an empirical macroeconomic model whether convergence to rational expectations occurs both in a cooperative and in a Nash equilibrium. Furthermore, since the process of learning affects both policy-setting and the private sector's expectation formation, it will change

---

[2] In a section entitled, "Extensions with Uncertainty," Frankel and Rockett (1988) also consider cases in which models are not believed to be correct with certainty; however, priors are not rational in that the true objective probability does not equal the subjective prior.

[3] The multicountry models surveyed by Frankel (1988) are generally elaborations of this simple model structure.

[4] Frankel and Rockett (1988 p. 318) refer to this possibility in justifying their assumption of disagreement among policymakers but do not treat it formally: "If one wishes to think of actors as perpetually processing new information in a Bayesian manner, so that their models over time would converge on any given reality in the limit, then one must admit that the speed of convergence is sufficiently slow, or else that reality is changing sufficiently rapidly, that policymakers have not been able to reach agreement on the true model."

the economy's equilibrium and hence the estimated gains from coordination.

We evaluate three regimes: a cooperative equilibrium in which monetary policies (in particular, the monetary base) are jointly chosen to maximize a weighted average of the two countries' utilities; a noncooperative, or Nash, equilibrium in which each country maximizes its own utility, taking as given the actions of the foreign government; and finally a noninterventionist "pure float" exchange-rate policy, in which each country keeps the money supply at its exogenous target level. The models we use are based on an empirically estimated, two-country (United States and an aggregate rest-of-OECD [Organization for Economic Coordination and Development]) model with a number of structural variants. Although these structural differences are seemingly minor and innocuous, the differences in the reduced-form multipliers of the models are substantial, with the degree of model uncertainty similar to that in Frankel (1988).[5] Policy conflicts between the countries arise from structural shocks to the world economy, including shocks to each country's money demand, aggregate demand, and inflation and to their joint exchange rate. In our simulation analysis, we use drawings from a joint distribution describing these shocks that is based on the empirically estimated covariance matrix.

Our main conclusions may be briefly summarized. First, if optimal policies—whether cooperative or noncooperative—assign sufficiently little weight to the true model and there is no learning, then the economy can become dynamically unstable with potentially large gains or losses from coordination. In contrast, uncoordinated policies involving freely floating exchange rates and exogenous money targets never result in dynamic instabilities in our estimated version of the Oudiz-Sachs model. Therefore, in the absence of model learning, such a

policy regime may be optimal, because it is more robust to model misspecification. We have argued previously (Ghosh and Masson, 1988) that the lesson from model uncertainty is not that coordination is bad, but that policy-setting—whether it is coordinated or not—should in some sense be more cautious. Our results here support that conclusion. Second, once Bayesian learning is allowed, optimal policies never result in dynamic instability, and even when very little initial probability is assigned to the true model, the *ex post* gains from coordination (when discounted back to the present) are *always* positive in our simulation exercises.

The reason for the latter result is simple. If policies are set to maximize *ex ante* expected utility, coordination only results in welfare deterioration *ex post* if the models are very different; in that case, however, it becomes very easy to distinguish between the models and to learn which is the true model. The subjective priors therefore quickly converge to the true model, and coordination is welfare-improving. We would not want to exaggerate the relevance of this result to real-world policy choice; instead, it highlights the inadequacy of the assumption that one model is the "true" one.[6] Nevertheless, experience of the past quarter century does provide evidence that policymakers abandon views of the world that can be seen to be wrong (such as the view that there exists a long-run trade-off between unemployment and inflation that can be exploited by aggregate demand policy) and thereby avoid the more disastrous consequences of their actions.

### I. The Empirical Model

The empirical model we adopt is a general, two-country Mundell-Fleming model with forward-looking exchange-rate expectations (see Dornbusch, 1976; Oudiz and

---

[5] The degree of model uncertainty for a particular reduced-form multiplier is measured in terms of the ratio of its squared average across models to the sum of its squared average and its variance.

[6] In the context of the quote in footnote 4, we would argue that the speed of learning is unlikely to be the source of the problem, but rather, that reality is much more complex than the models and is changing too rapidly.

468                    THE AMERICAN ECONOMIC REVIEW                    JUNE 1991

Sachs, 1985). The model was estimated using the data that are the basis for the IMF's MULTIMOD model (Masson et al., 1988). Results are presented in Table 1, using the same notation as in Oudiz and Sachs (1985). Our two "countries" are the United States and the rest of the world (ROW); data for the latter region resulted from aggregation of the remaining industrial countries in MULTIMOD.[7] The estimation period, using annual data, was 1966–1986. Aggregate demand equations were estimated using instrumental variables: the instruments included money stocks, government spending, time, and lagged prices and output.

The coefficient estimates are all of the right signs and are generally fairly well determined—in particular, the effects of the real exchange rate on U.S. aggregate demand and of U.S. GDP on rest-of-world demand, the money-demand parameters, and the change in GDP effects on the two regions' output price changes. Despite its simplicity, the model seems to fit the data fairly well. Nevertheless, residual serial correlation is evident in the money-demand equations, and the specification embodies arbitrary constraints that are open to discussion. We proceed to relax some of these restrictions below and to estimate the resulting alternative models.

The computational burden of calculating optimal policies with model learning severely restricted the number of alternative models we could introduce; in this paper, we consider three possible models. The two alternative models, models II and III, differ from the baseline model (model I) in two respects: in model II money balances are deflated by the consumer price index rather than the GDP deflator, and there is a lagged dependent variable in the money-demand

---

[7] In general, variables were aggregated by converting to a common currency and summing. GDP (gross domestic product) weights were used to aggregate interest rates. The exchange rate was taken to be the reciprocal of the MERM-weighted effective rate (Jacques Artus and Anne McGuirk, 1981) of the U.S. dollar (in index form, 1980 = 1). The rest-of-world price level and money supply are expressed in this "currency."

equation, while in model III there is also a nonvertical Phillips curve. Estimates for these models are also presented in Table 1.

A first arbitrary feature of model I relates to the proper deflator for real money balances. As William Branson and Willem Buiter (1983) point out in their discussion of the Mundell-Fleming model, the effects of monetary and fiscal policies can be importantly different depending on whether the domestic output price or a broader index that includes foreign goods is used. The Oudiz-Sachs specification, excluding as it does the effects of terms of trade, conforms in this respect to the original Mundell-Fleming model. Model II deflates money balances not by $p$ but by $p^c$. A second major area of arbitrariness in the Oudiz-Sachs model is the dynamic specification. The money-demand equation, whether specified with the output or consumption deflator, shows evidence of residual serial correlation. Most studies have allowed for the possibility that money balances adjust with a lag and have included a lagged dependent variable (see e.g., Stephen Goldfeld, 1973); this is also done in model II. The resulting money-demand equations fit considerably better than the ones in model I.

Model III includes the changes of model II and also relaxes the unitary coefficient on the lagged rate of inflation in the domestic-price-change equation. Relaxing this restriction lowers the standard errors of estimate in both the U.S. and rest-of-world equations, and the standard errors for the inflation coefficients imply rejection of the unitary coefficient for both the United States and the rest of the world. Furthermore, the change in output becomes insignificant, so we dropped this variable. Though the fit of the equations is only marginally superior to that for model I, the two specifications for the inflation equation have quite different long-run properties. The Oudiz-Sachs model exhibits no long-run trade-off between output and inflation, as in the steady state both output prices and consumer prices grow at the same, steady rate. In contrast, with a nonunitary coefficient, different rates of inflation are associated with different rates of

TABLE 1—PARAMETER ESTIMATES FOR OUDIZ-SACHS MODEL AND VARIANTS,
1966–1986 (STANDARD ERRORS IN PARENTHESES)

**Model I**

*Aggregate demand:*

$q_t = -0.114\,(p_t - e_t - p_t^*) + 0.054 q_t^* - 0.152\,(i_t - p_{t+1} + p_t) + 0.020 t + 0.300 g_t + 5.196$
    (0.050)                    (0.209)      (0.340)                        (0.009)    (0.166)    (2.298)

$[\bar{R}^2 = 0.988, \quad \sigma = 0.021, \quad DW = 1.78]$

$q_t^* = 0.167\,(p_t - e_t - p_t^*) + 0.550 q_t - 0.378\,(i_t^* - p_{t+1}^* + p_t^*) - 0.031 t + 1.614 g_t^* - 6.077$
    (0.099)                    (0.499)     (0.212)                          (0.026)    (0.477)     (6.129)

$[\bar{R}^2 = 0.992, \quad \sigma = 0.021, \quad DW = 1.16]$

*Money demand:*

$m_t - p_t = 0.225 q_t - 1.419 i_t + 3.453$
    (0.066)      (0.413)    (0.503)

$[\bar{R}^2 = 0.382, \quad \sigma = 0.038, \quad DW = 1.02]$

$m_t^* - p_t^* = 0.700 q_t^* - 1.077 i_t^* + 0.100$
    (0.078)        (0.609)    (0.616)

$[\bar{R}^2 = 0.853, \quad \sigma = 0.051, \quad DW = 0.67]$

*Consumer price index:*

$p_t^c = 0.899 p_t + (1 - 0.899)(p_t^* + e_t)$

$p_t^{c*} = 0.758 p_t^* + (1 - 0.758)(p_t - e_t)$

*Output price change:*

$p_t - p_{t-1} = (p_{t-1}^c - p_{t-2}^c) + 0.095\,[q_{t-1} - 0.027(t-1) - 7.373] + 0.309\,(q_{t-1} - q_{t-2}) - 0.009$
                                    (0.119)                                    (0.108)                      (0.004)

$[\bar{R}^2 = 0.351, \quad \sigma = 0.011, \quad DW = 2.33]$

$p_t^* - p_{t-1}^* = (p_{t-1}^{c*} - p_{t-2}^{c*}) + 0.040\,[q_{t-1}^* - 0.033(t-1) - 7.803] + 0.880\,(q_{t-1}^* - q_{t-2}^*) - 0.031$
                                        (0.088)                                    (0.204)                        (0.008)

$[\bar{R}^2 = 0.458, \quad \sigma = 0.017, \quad DW = 1.74]$

*Exchange rate:*

$e_{t+1} = e_t + i_t - i_t^* + \varepsilon$

$\{\sigma_\varepsilon = 0.026\}$

**Model II**
(All equations as for model I except the following)

*Money demand:*

$m_t - p_t^c = 0.184 q_t - 1.387 i_t + 0.680\,(m_{t-1} - p_{t-1}^c) + 0.302$
    (0.051)      (0.318)    (0.160)                          (0.857)

$[\bar{R}^2 = 0.691, \quad \sigma = 0.029, \quad DW = 1.63]$

$m_t^* - p_t^{c*} = 0.277 q_t^* - 1.579 i_t^* + 0.702\,(m_{t-1}^* - p_{t-1}^{c*}) - 0.421$
    (0.094)          (0.456)    (0.141)                            (0.494)

$[\bar{R}^2 = 0.909, \quad \sigma = 0.038, \quad DW = 1.65]$

**Model III**
(All equations as for model II except the following)

*Output price change:*

$p_t - p_{t-1} = 0.611\,(p_{t-1}^c - p_{t-2}^c) + 0.364\,[q_{t-1} - 0.027(t-1) - 7.373] + 0.022$
    (0.098)                              (0.101)                                    (0.006)

$[\bar{R}^2 = 0.783, \quad \sigma = 0.010, \quad DW = 1.95]$

$p_t^* - p_{t-1}^* = 0.238\,(p_{t-1}^{c*} - p_{t-2}^{c*}) + 0.491\,[q_{t-1}^* - 0.033(t-1) - 7.803] + 0.051$
    (0.146)                                  (0.116)                                    (0.010)

$[\bar{R}^2 = 0.761, \quad \sigma = 0.015, \quad DW = 1.44]$

**Variable Definitions**
(U.S. variables are unstarred; non-U.S. variables are starred;
all variables except $i$ and $t$ are in logs)

$e$ = nominal exchange rate (dollars per foreign currency)
$g$ = real government spending on goods and services
$i$ = nominal short-term interest rate
$m$ = monetary base
$p$ = GDP deflator
$p^c$ = deflator of domestic absorption
$q$ = real GDP
$t$ = time trend

TABLE 2—EIGENVALUES OF MODELS I–III

| Model I | Model II | Model III |
|---|---|---|
| 1.421 | 1.237 | 1.195 |
| 0.975 | 0.982 ± 0.069i | 0.942 |
| 0.936 ± 0.119i | 0.974 | 0.782 |
| −0.085 | 0.611 | 0.656 |
|  | −0.363 | 0.237 |
|  | −0.044 |  |

output growth; this possibility would be disputed by many economists, however (see e.g., Milton Friedman, 1968). On the basis of the estimation results, it may be reasonable to attribute some nonzero probability to the existence of such a trade-off.

Although the structural differences among the three models seem minor, the reduced-form multipliers differ considerably across the models, as do the dynamic properties (see Table 2 for the eigenvalues of the three models). There is one unstable eigenvalue in each case, corresponding to the one nonpredetermined variable, the exchange rate. Model II has a more complicated dynamic structure and two extra real eigenvalues, compared to model I: this is due to lags in money demand. Model III retains the money-demand equation but has a simpler adjustment process for prices.

A simple summary statistic for the degree of model uncertainty is given by the ratio

(1)        $\zeta = \mu^2 / (\mu^2 + \sigma^2)$

where $\mu$ is the mean multiplier of an instrument on a particular target and $\sigma^2$ is its variance (across the three models). This gives a dimensionless statistic which equals unity if there is no model uncertainty and approaches zero as the effectiveness of the policy instrument deteriorates, in the sense of William Brainard (1967). In a model with forward-looking variables, the multipliers depend upon the anticipation of future policies as well as current policies and therefore are not independent of the regime under consideration (it is assumed for this purpose that a policy of exogenously setting the money supply prevails).

Table 3 includes the second-year multipliers for the three models, as well as $\zeta$ values, for an exogenous permanent increase in the money supply of 4 percent. As expected from theoretical models, the transmission effects of a monetary expansion can have either sign, depending on parameter values: models I and II imply positive transmission onto foreign output, while the reverse is true of model III. Somewhat surprisingly, the second-year *domestic* output effects of a ROW money increase also are ambiguous: the negative effect on ROW output in models I and II results from the large coefficient on the lagged change in output in the ROW inflation equation, which pushes up domestic output prices by enough that the real exchange rate appreciates in the second year relative to baseline.[8] In model III, ROW output effects of a ROW monetary expansion are persistently positive. Though models I and II give the same signs for all the multipliers, their numerical values differ substantially.

It is interesting to compare the $\zeta$ values for our three models with those implied by the models in Frankel's (1988) study, also calculated for such a money-supply shock. As can be seen from Table 3, his study of 12 different models incorporates a somewhat greater degree of uncertainty about the reduced-form multipliers of a U.S. monetary expansion than our three alternative models, but the output effects of a ROW monetary expansion are more certain in Frankel's set of models than in ours.

### II. Optimal Policies Under Model Uncertainty and Model Learning

In order to calculate the average *ex post* gains from coordination with model learning, we adapt the algorithm we developed in Ghosh and Masson (1988). The logic of the model is as follows. In period $t$, the state vector $\mathbf{x}_t$ and a vector of subjective priors

---

[8]In the *first* year, the money supply increase leads to a large *increase* in ROW output, however: by 2.8 percent in model I and by 2.2 percent in model II.

TABLE 3—REDUCED-FORM MODEL MULTIPLIERS AND MEASURES OF MODEL UNCERTAINTY

| Model | Effects of U.S. money supply on: | | | | Effects of ROW money supply on: | | | |
|---|---|---|---|---|---|---|---|---|
| | U.S. $Y$ | ROW $Y$ | U.S. $P$ | ROW $P$ | U.S. $Y$ | ROW $Y$ | U.S. $P$ | ROW $P$ |
| *Second-year effects of a 4-percent monetary expansion (percentage):* | | | | | | | | |
| I | 0.5 | 1.0 | 1.2 | −2.6 | 0.2 | −0.1 | −0.8 | 3.8 |
| II | 0.2 | 0.2 | 0.9 | −1.8 | 0.1 | −0.4 | −0.6 | 3.1 |
| III | 0.5 | −0.2 | 0.8 | −0.4 | −0.2 | 0.5 | −0.5 | 1.0 |
| *Measures of model uncertainty ($\zeta$ values; percentage):*[a] | | | | | | | | |
| I–III | 88 | 31 | 97 | 75 | 4 | —[b] | 96 | 83 |
| Frankel (1988) | 68 | —[b] | 45 | 52 | 19 | 72 | 24 | 25 |

[a] Based on second-year effects; a smaller number indicates greater uncertainty.
[b] The effects were clustered around zero, giving a zero value for $\zeta$.

$\Pi_t$ (with elements $\pi_t^i$) are inherited. Policymakers choose a vector of controls (i.e., policy instruments) $u_t$ in order to influence their target vector $\tau_t$. They do not attempt active learning (i.e., performing policy experiments in order to discover which of the models is correct). At the end of period $t$, a vector of endogenous variables $\omega_{t+1}$ is observed which allows agents to update their priors, yielding $\Pi_{t+1}$.

The dynamics of the world model are assumed to be given by:

$$(2) \quad \begin{bmatrix} x_{t+1}^i \\ e_{t+1}^i \end{bmatrix} = \begin{bmatrix} A^i & B^i \\ D^i & F^i \end{bmatrix} \begin{bmatrix} x_t^i \\ e_t^i \end{bmatrix} + \begin{bmatrix} C^i \\ G^i \end{bmatrix} u_t + \begin{bmatrix} \Theta_x^i \\ \Theta_e^i \end{bmatrix} \varepsilon_t$$

for $i$ ranging over the possible models $i,\ldots,k$, and where $x$ is a vector of state variables, $e$ is a vector of jumping variables, $u$ is the vector of controls, and $\varepsilon$ is an unobserved vector white-noise shock, distributed $N(0,\Sigma)$ ($\Sigma$ is the variance-covariance matrix). $A^i$, $B^i$, $C^i$, $D^i$, $F^i$, $G^i$, $\Theta_x^i$, and $\Theta_e^i$ are constant matrices associated with model $i$.

In addition, structural equations of the models map the state variables and the forward-looking variables into a vector of targets $\tau$:

$$(3) \quad \tau_t^i = L^i x_t + M^i e_t + N^i u_t + \Theta_\tau^i \varepsilon_t.$$

Policymakers in each country are assumed to have preferences over the target vector which are represented by

$$(4) \quad v = \max\left[ -(1/2) \sum_{t=0}^{\infty} \beta^t E\{\tau_t' \Omega \tau_t\} \right]$$

and

$$(5) \quad v^* = \max\left[ -(1/2) \sum_{t=0}^{\infty} \beta^t E\{\tau_t' \Omega^* \tau_t\} \right]$$

respectively, where $\beta$ is a discount factor, $\Omega$ and $\Omega^*$ are matrices that weight the target variables, and the expectation is taken with respect to uncertainty about both the correct model and the current realization of the shock $\varepsilon_t$. We assume that, although agents do not know the true model of the world economy, they do know the variance-covariance matrix of the additive shocks.[9] Moreover, we do not allow heterogeneity of agents; both the private sectors and the governments start with the same priors across models and update them in the same fashion.

Following Oudiz and Sachs (1985), we derive the optimal linear decision rules by first calculating the dynamic programming

[9] This is a somewhat heroic assumption, but it simplifies the analysis considerably. Furthermore, our main conclusions do not appear to be excessively sensitive to the assumed variance-covariance matrix.

solution[10] for a (finite) $T$-period horizon and then increasing $T$ until stationary matrices $\Gamma$ and $\Gamma^*$ (functions of $\Pi_t$) are obtained:

$$(6) \quad \mathbf{u}_t = \Gamma(\Pi_t)\mathbf{x}_t \quad \text{and} \quad \mathbf{u}_t^* = \Gamma^*(\Pi_t)\mathbf{x}_t.$$

Moreover, this allows us to write the vector of forward-looking variables as a linear function of a matrix $\lambda$ and the state vector $\mathbf{x}_t$:

$$(7) \quad \mathbf{e}_t = \lambda(\Pi_t)\mathbf{x}_t.$$

From equations (2)–(7), we can then express the value functions as quadratic forms in $\mathbf{x}_t$ and matrices $S$ and $S^*$ (dependence on $\mathbf{x}_t$ and $\Pi_t$ is made explicit by the functional notation):

$$(8) \quad v(\mathbf{x}_t, \Pi_t) = \mathbf{x}_t'S(\Pi_t)\mathbf{x}_t$$

$$v^*(\mathbf{x}_t, \Pi_t) = \mathbf{x}_t'S^*(\Pi_t)\mathbf{x}_t.$$

Once the optimal stationary policy rules have been obtained, the model is simulated forward, and priors are updated using Bayesian inference. The forward simulation is conditional on a particular model, say model $j$, being true. Suppose that in period $t$, the world economy has inherited the state $\mathbf{x}_t$ and priors over the models are given by $\Pi_t$. The optimal policy in period $t$ for the home country is given by

$$(9) \quad \mathbf{u}_t = \Gamma(\Pi_t)\mathbf{x}_t.$$

A drawing from the shocks $\boldsymbol{\varepsilon}_t$ is made, and the state vector in $t+1$ is therefore given by

$$(10) \quad \mathbf{x}_{t+1} = \mathbf{A}^j\mathbf{x}_t + \mathbf{B}^j\lambda^j(\Pi_t)\mathbf{x}_t$$
$$+ \mathbf{C}^j\mathbf{u}_t + \Theta_x^j\boldsymbol{\varepsilon}_t.$$

At the beginning of period $t+1$, agents

observe a vector of variables $\boldsymbol{\omega}_{t+1}^i$. Each of the $k$ possible models implies a structural relationship for the observation vector $\boldsymbol{\omega}_{t+1}^i$

$$(11) \quad \boldsymbol{\omega}_{t+1}^i = \mathbf{W}_x^i\mathbf{x}_t + \mathbf{W}_e^i\mathbf{e}_t + \mathbf{W}_u^i\mathbf{u}_t + \mathbf{W}_\varepsilon^i\boldsymbol{\varepsilon}_t$$

where matrices $\mathbf{W}_x^i$, $\mathbf{W}_e^i$, $\mathbf{W}_u^i$, and $\mathbf{W}_\varepsilon^i$ are obtained from the relevant rows of (2) and it is assumed that $\mathbf{W}_\varepsilon^i$ is invertible.[11] Let $E(\boldsymbol{\omega}_{t+1}^i)$ be the expected value of $\boldsymbol{\omega}_{t+1}^i$ [evaluated at $E(\boldsymbol{\varepsilon}_t) = 0$]. The value of the shock implied by each model is therefore

$$(12) \quad \boldsymbol{\varepsilon}_t^i = \left(\mathbf{W}_\varepsilon^i\right)^{-1}\left[\boldsymbol{\omega}_{t+1}^i - E(\boldsymbol{\omega}_{t+1}^i)\right].$$

The new Bayesian priors are then given by

$$(13) \quad \pi_{t+1}^i = \frac{\Pr(\boldsymbol{\varepsilon}^i|\Sigma^i)\pi_t^i}{\left[\sum_{i=1}^k \Pr(\boldsymbol{\varepsilon}^i|\Sigma^i)\pi_t^i\right]}$$

where $\Pr(\cdot)$ is the probability that a vector shock, distributed $N(0, \Sigma^i)$, takes the value $\boldsymbol{\varepsilon}^i$. The state variables in period $t+2$ are then generated with a drawing for $\boldsymbol{\varepsilon}_{t+1}$, and the whole process is repeated.[12]

### III. Simulation Results

In addition to the model parameters, the simulation analysis requires specification of the policymakers' discount factors (chosen to be 0.95; i.e., a discount rate of 5 percent per annum), the utility weights on each target, and the relative weight each country receives in the social planner's objective function. The utility weights were taken from the revealed preference estimates of Oudiz and Sachs (1984) with policymakers assumed to target inflation and output.[13]

---

[10]The dynamic programming solution excludes trigger mechanisms and reputational strategies. It may therefore exaggerate the gains from coordination relative to Nash solutions (see Matthew Canzoneri and Dale Henderson, 1988).

[11]If agents observe fewer variables than the number of shocks in $\boldsymbol{\varepsilon}$, then they face a signal-extraction problem concerning the shocks as well as the models.
[12]Until the priors converge to the model generating the data, expectations will not be unbiased.
[13]The current-account objective in Oudiz and Sachs (1984) was ignored. The utility-function weights used were those reported in table 11 of their paper; for the rest of the world, weights for Japan and West Germany were averaged.

VOL. 81 NO. 3                    GHOSH AND MASSON: MODEL UNCERTAINTY                    473

The objective functions are as follows for the United States (unstarred) and the rest of the world (starred):[14]

(14)

$$V = E\left\{ \sum_{t-0}^{\infty} 0.95^t \left[ 0.07 q_t^2 + 0.49 (\Delta p_t^c)^2 \right] \right\}$$

(15)

$$V^* = E\left\{ \sum_{t-0}^{\infty} 0.95^t \left[ 0.045 q_t^{*2} + 0.50 (\Delta p_t^{c*})^2 \right] \right\}.$$

The world objective function is

(16)          $V_w = \alpha V + (1 - \alpha) V^*.$

In simulations reported below, $\alpha = 0.5$; each country is given equal weight in the world objective function, which is used to evaluate the outcomes of the three policy regimes.[15]

In the Nash equilibrium, the United States maximizes (14) with respect to $m_t$, and the rest of the world maximizes (15) with respect to $m_t^*$. In the cooperative regime, (16) is maximized with respect to $\{m_t, m_t^*\}$. In the floating regime, policy is

described by an exogenous money-supply target, whatever the value of the objective functions. The observation vector includes output, interest rates, and producer prices in each country and the nominal exchange rate. The optimal policies and value functions depend nonlinearly on the probabilities assigned to each of the three models. The recursive optimization had to be done on a two-dimensional grid; that is, for each possible combination $[\pi^1, \pi^2, (1 - \pi^1 - \pi^2)]$, the recursive algorithm outlined above must be solved.[16]

In the first set of simulations, all agents assign an initial probability to each model and do not update their priors (to repeat, we assume throughout that all agents in the model—both private and public—share a common set of subjective priors). The results are reported conditional on each of the three models being the true model; we also cite results for the certainty case, in which agents assign a probability of 1 to the true model. The values reported in Table 4 represent the total present value of disutility for the world economy (with equal weights on the United States and the rest of the world) and are expressed in terms of GDP equivalents. As is evident below, some of the simulations exhibit explosive behavior, and the present value of disutility may be undefined; in these cases, we have simply marked the entry "explosive." Since there is an additive random shock, $\varepsilon_t$, disutility depends upon the specific realizations (which are drawn from a normal distribution with zero mean and the estimated variance-covariance matrix of the "true" model),[17] and hence we have taken the average of ten stochastic simulations (the drawings are the same for each of the models). The optimal

---

[14] Variables $q$ and $\Delta p^c$ are output and the rate of change of consumer prices, both as deviations from the baseline.

[15] The welfare values in Table 4 are all for world welfare, using the same equally weighted objective function. There is no guarantee that both countries' welfares increase as a result of cooperation (although in most cases both do). We have verified that, in all cases where coordination improves world welfare, a set of weights could be found such that each country's welfare (averaged over the ten drawings of the shocks) was higher. In practice, when unequal weights were necessary, a greater weight had to be given to the United States than to the rest of the world in world welfare, no doubt a result of asymmetries in the multipliers reported in Table 3. Such welfare weights, however, lowered the overall gains from cooperation, when evaluated using a consistently defined objective function. Alternatively, if a mechanism for side payments existed, then both countries would always gain, even when cooperation involved maximizing the equally weighted welfare function.

[16] We used a grid of 11 equally spaced intervals. Table 4 reports a subset of those simulations, plus simulations in which a very small weight (0.045) is placed on the true model, and others in which a weight of 0.5 is placed on the true model and weights of 0.25 are placed on the alternative models.

[17] None of the estimated correlations between shocks was significant at the 5-percent level, so a diagonal variance-covariance matrix was used to generate the shocks.

TABLE 4—DISUTILITY LEVELS WITH AND WITHOUT MODEL-LEARNING

| Probabilities assigned to each model[a] | | | Regime | | |
|---|---|---|---|---|---|
| I | II | III | Cooperative | Nash | Float |
| No model-learning: | | | | | |
| 1.0* | 0.0 | 0.0 | 31 | 42 | 44 |
| 0.5* | 0.25 | 0.25 | 32 | 41 | 43 |
| 0.1* | 0.9 | 0.0 | 39 | 45 | 43 |
| 0.1* | 0.0 | 0.9 | 40 | 87 | 43 |
| 0.045* | 0.0 | 0.955 | explosive | explosive | 47 |
| 0.0 | 1.0* | 0.0 | 42 | 51 | 55 |
| 0.25 | 0.5* | 0.25 | 58 | 71 | 55 |
| 0.9 | 0.1* | 0.0 | 67 | 82 | 55 |
| 0.0 | 0.1* | 0.9 | 55 | explosive | 55 |
| 0.0 | 0.045* | 0.955 | explosive | explosive | 55 |
| 0.0 | 0.0 | 1.0* | 21 | 28 | 24 |
| 0.25 | 0.25 | 0.5* | 22 | 28 | 24 |
| 0.9 | 0.0 | 0.1* | 23 | 31 | 25 |
| 0.0 | 0.9 | 0.1* | 24 | 28 | 24 |
| Model-learning:[b] | | | | | |
| 0.5* | 0.25 | 0.25 | 31 | 41 | 44 |
| 0.1* | 0.9 | 0.0 | 31 | 41 | 44 |
| 0.1* | 0.0 | 0.9 | 31 | 41 | 44 |
| 0.045* | 0.0 | 0.955 | 31 | 41 | 44 |
| 0.25 | 0.5* | 0.25 | 42 | 51 | 56 |
| 0.9 | 0.1* | 0.0 | 42 | 52 | 56 |
| 0.0 | 0.1* | 0.9 | 41 | 53 | 55 |
| 0.0 | 0.045* | 0.955 | 42 | 51 | 55 |
| 0.25 | 0.25 | 0.5* | 21 | 28 | 24 |
| 0.9 | 0.0 | 0.1* | 21 | 29 | 24 |
| 0.0 | 0.9 | 0.1* | 22 | 28 | 24 |

[a]The correct model is indicated by an asterisk.
[b]Table entries are initial probabilities; probabilities are updated in a Bayesian fashion.

policies are designed to stabilize output and inflation against the specific random structural shocks applied to the model; as such, the optimal policies under both cooperative and noncooperative behavior are not easily interpretable and are therefore not reported.

There are two noteworthy points about the top part of Table 4 (no model learning). First, when equal weights are assigned to the competing models and a weight of 0.5 is assigned to the "true" one, the gains from coordination relative to the Nash equilibrium are not spectacular but are certainly measurably positive: they are comparable in size to those under certainty (the top line of each panel). These gains, which range from 6 percent to 13 percent of GDP, amount to a permanent increase of about half of 1

percent of GDP per year (using the 5-percent discount rate), an estimate which is in line with those of previous studies (e.g., Oudiz and Sachs [1984], who calculate welfare gains in that form to be less than 1 percent).[18] Both the Nash and the cooperative equilibria are significantly better than a pure float regime for model I; this is not true of model III, however, where floating is intermediate between the other two regimes. For model II, under certainty, the Nash equilibrium is better than floating; but with a probability of 0.5 on model II and 0.25 on models I and II, the Nash equilibrium is

[18]In Oudiz and Sachs (1984), the gains are given in terms of GDP equivalents sustained for three years.

considerably worse and the cooperative regime is somewhat worse than the pure float regime.

Second, when we assign a low probability to the true model and a high probability to one of the competing models, the cooperative regime actually yields substantially lower *ex post* welfare than the pure float regime. The situation is most critical when a large weight is attached to model III (and either model I or model II is correct); here, the cooperative solution results in (eventually) explosive behavior[19] of the economy or in large disutility. The Nash equilibrium also implies large (and in some cases, unbounded) disutility when the weights are over 90 percent on model III but one of the other models is correct. In fact, the most robust policy to follow is one of complete nonintervention. The large losses and possible instability no doubt result from the fact that model III implies a long-run trade-off between output and inflation, which activist policies (either Nash or cooperative) try to exploit—unsuccessfully, it turns out, because the true model, either model I or model II, is in fact a natural-rate model. In either case, coordination severely reduces welfare to the extent of making the sustainability of a coordinated regime infeasible. However, it is important to note that it is not only the cooperative regime that may result in low welfare when policymakers use the wrong model. For example, if model II is the true model but a high prior (0.9) is put on model III, the Nash equilibrium is highly inefficient, so that there are very large *gains* from coordination. In the cases when both cooperative and Nash equilibria exhibited instability, the disutility levels were larger and diverged more quickly for the latter.

The conclusion that emerges from the above results is therefore that a policy rule that does not require active intervention, corresponding to exogenous money supplies and floating exchange rates, is the safest policy when policymakers are uncertain about the model. Our results therefore provide some support to the advocacy of fixed rules in preference to activist policies, which Friedman has long argued may be destabilizing (see e.g., Friedman, 1948).[20]

The results suggest that, when policymakers have the wrong priors over the models and do not undertake updating, any policy intervention—coordinated or uncoordinated—can be dangerous. However, it is implausible that policymakers would not update their subjective priors when they find that their expectations about the effects of their policies are consistently invalidated. In a second set of simulations, therefore, we assume that agents update their priors over the models in the Bayesian fashion described above. The lower part of Table 4 reports the discounted present value of disutility under cooperative and noncooperative behavior, as well as the floating-exchange-rate regime with exogenous money targets, for simulations with various initial probability priors.

The important conclusion that emerges is that policies no longer become unstable, even when the initial priors attributed to the true model are very low. Furthermore, we find that coordination is always welfare-improving relative to both the Nash equilibrium and nonactivist policies. Consider, for example, the case in which agents assign a prior probability of 4.5 percent to model I and 95.5 percent to model III, when model I is the correct model. In the absence of Bayesian updating, coordination reduces welfare substantially relative to a pure float, since the coordinated regime is dynamically unstable. Bayesian learning, combined with the same initial priors, results in a welfare gain relative to both Nash equilibrium and floating.[21] With endogenous model-learn-

[19] The instability manifested itself in a failure of policy settings to converge, and in the fact that disutility levels were not bounded as the horizon was extended.

[20] There are other considerations that are relevant to the choice between fixed rules and more activist policies (see e.g., Stanley Fischer, 1988).

[21] Nevertheless, a superior policy *ex post* would have been to follow a noninterventionist policy until policymakers reduced their probability weight on the incor-

476                    THE AMERICAN ECONOMIC REVIEW                    JUNE 1991

ing, the discounted-present-value gains from coordination are all in the range of 7–15 percent of GDP.[22] The noninterventionist-policy regime now performs consistently worse than the cooperative regime but is sometimes better than the Nash equilibrium —in particular, when model III (the non-vertical Phillips curve model) is true. In this case, it would seem that the scope for beggar-thy-neighbor policies is greater; they are ruled out by both the cooperative and "floating" (i.e., nonactivist) regimes.

The examples in which policymakers (and the private sector) assign a high initial weight to model III, when in reality one of the other two models is correct, have some relevance to the history of demand management in the postwar period. Early models of the "Phillips curve" (see e.g., A. W. Phillips, 1958; Richard Lipsey, 1960) implied that there was a trade-off between the rate of change of wages or prices and the unemployment rate or output. These models no doubt helped induce central banks and treasuries to engage in demand expansion, in an attempt to buy more output growth at what was judged to be an acceptable inflation cost. The experience of accelerating inflation beginning in the late 1960's forced economists and policymakers to reconsider those models, and there has been a profound shift in policy away from short-term fine-tuning and to a concern for the medium-term inflation consequences of policy. Moreover, the rationale for the policy changes has been acceptance of natural-rate models, which do not allow for monetary stimulus to have permanent positive effects on the level of activity. Friedman (1977 p. 470) commented on the change in policy in the following terms in his Nobel lecture:

Government policy about inflation and unemployment has been at the center

of political controversy. Ideological war has raged over these matters. Yet the drastic change that has occurred in economic theory has not been a result of ideological warfare. It has not resulted from divergent political beliefs or aims. It has responded almost entirely to the force of events: brute experience proved far more potent than the strongest of political or ideological preferences.

### IV. Caveats and Discussion

Having found that, in the presence of model-learning, the cooperative regime dominates noncooperation and nonintervention in the context of our model, we tried to gauge the sensitivity of the results to our assumptions. The *ex post* performance of the coordinated regime depends on two factors: the robustness of the optimal policy to model errors; and the rate of learning of the model. Clearly, the more diverse the models are, the more likely the optimal policy based on the "wrong" priors is to result in lower welfare. We also thought that we might have assumed too little uncertainty in choosing the structurally similar models of Section III. However, in further simulations with more diverse models, we found that as the degree of model uncertainty increased (in the sense of lower $\zeta$ ratios) the rate of model-learning also increased. The intuition is straightforward: if the models are very different, then the implied observation vector of each model is also very different, and the updated priors assigned to the false models will be correspondingly low. Thus, although greater diversity between the models makes more likely the possibility of welfare-deteriorating policies, it also serves to reduce the model uncertainty (at least when there is a finite number of alternative models, as is the case here).

It is possible to decrease the rate of learning by increasing the variance of the additive shocks $\varepsilon_t$. The greater the variance of $\varepsilon_t$, the greater the noise in the updating observations and, therefore, the slower the rate of learning. We checked the sensitivity of our results by using a variance matrix with ten times the estimated standard er-

---

rect model (model III) sufficiently and then cooperated.

[22] When the world objective function uses weights that ensure that welfare averaged over the ten stochastic simulations improves in both countries as a result of cooperation, the range of gains is 1.5–15 percent.

*VOL. 81 NO. 3*        *GHOSH AND MASSON: MODEL UNCERTAINTY*        *477*

rors. Despite this large increase in error variances, however, we were unable to reverse our conclusions about the ranking of the coordinated and uncoordinated regimes in the presence of learning.

It must be emphasized, however, that our experiments assume knowledge of the variance-covariance matrix describing the shocks. Forcing agents to estimate it would introduce considerably more uncertainty and make it more difficult to infer which model was correct, as would a combination of temporary and permanent shocks.

Another caveat is that we have simplified the problem to one in which policymakers must just discover the unique unchanging model describing the economy. An alternative assumption is that agents can never perfectly anticipate the true model when setting policies, because the true model is stochastic. If the vector of subjective priors converges to the true probability that the model is realized, then the average *ex post* welfare gain will equal the *ex ante* expected welfare gain from coordination, at least in large samples. In that case, we return to the *ex ante* expected welfare criterion in which coordination is necessarily welfare-improving.[23] More realistic is the case in which the true model is changing in a nonrandom way as a result of structural shifts and in which these shifts occur frequently enough so that the distribution describing the models is never completely learned. We have yet to explore this case.

### V. Conclusions

In this paper, we have discussed whether coordination is likely to reduce the actual *ex post* level of welfare when policymakers are uncertain about the effects of policies. We have found no evidence in our simulations that policy coordination is likely to reduce welfare vis-à-vis noncooperative policies; however, a simple nonintervention

[23] This was verified in simulations in which the true model was drawn stochastically from the three possible models, each of which had equal probability, and agents undertook Bayesian learning as above.

regime, such as a pure floating exchange rate accompanied by exogenous money targets, may be the most robust policy in the presence of model uncertainty. These conclusions are of course specific to a particular model and are based here on an estimated version of the Mundell-Fleming model with sticky prices and rational exchange-rate expectations. More experimentation with other models is no doubt necessary in order to gauge whether the conclusions can be generalized.

Once we introduced endogenous model-learning, we found that coordination always results in higher welfare: though the gains from coordination are not spectacular, they appear to be significantly positive. We were unable to generate losses from coordination, even by increasing the variance of the additive noise. No doubt, the representation of the economy is much too simple. What the results suggest, however, is that the conclusion that coordination is as likely to decrease welfare as to increase it (see Frankel and Rockett, 1988) is not consistent with the joint assumptions that there is a single "true" model and that agents learn about that model in a Bayesian fashion.

### REFERENCES

**Artus, Jacques and McGuirk, Anne,** "A Revised Version of the Multilateral Exchange Rate Model," *Staff Papers* (International Monetary Fund), June 1981, *28*, 275–309.

**Blume, Lawrence E. and Easley, David,** "Learning to Be Rational," *Journal of Economic Theory*, April 1982, *26*, 340–51.

——, **Bray, Margaret and Easley, David,** "Introduction to the Stability of Rational Expectations Equilibrium," *Journal of Economic Theory*, April 1982, *26*, 313–7.

**Brainard, William C.,** "Uncertainty and the Effectiveness of Policy," *American Economic Review*, May 1967, *57*, 411–25.

**Branson, William H. and Buiter, Willem H.,** "Monetary and Fiscal Policy with Flexible Exchange Rates," in J. Bhandari and B. Putnam, eds., *Economic Interdependence and Flexible Exchange Rates*, Cambridge,

478                                    THE AMERICAN ECONOMIC REVIEW                                    JUNE 1991

MA: MIT Press, 1983, pp. 251–85.

Bray, Margaret, "Learning, Estimation, and the Stability of Rational Expectations," *Journal of Economic Theory*, April 1982, 26, 318–39.

_____ and Savin, Neil E., "Rational Expectations Equilibria, Learning, and Model Specification," *Econometrica*, September 1986, 54, 1129–60.

Brock, William A., "On Models of Expectations That Arise from Maximizing Behavior of Economic Agents Over Time," *Journal of Economic Theory*, December 1972, 5, 348–76.

Canzoneri, Matthew B. and Henderson, Dale W., "Is Sovereign Policymaking Bad?" in K. Brunner and A. H. Meltzer, eds., *Stabilization Policies and Labor Markets*, Carnegie-Rochester Conference Series on Public Policy, New York: North Holland, 1988, pp. 93–140.

Cyert, R. M. and De Groot, M. E., "Rational Expectations and Bayesian Analysis," *Journal of Political Economy*, May/June 1974, 82, 521–36.

De Canio, Stephen J., "Rational Expectations and Learning from Experience," *Quarterly Journal of Economics*, February 1979, 93, 47–57.

Dornbusch, Rudiger, "Expectations and Exchange Rate Dynamics," *Journal of Political Economy*, December 1976, 84, 1161–76.

Feldstein, Martin, "Distinguished Lecture on Economics in Government: Thinking about International Economic Coordination," *Journal of Economic Perspectives*, Spring 1988, 2, 3–13.

Fischer, Stanley, "Rules versus Discretion in Monetary Policy," NBER (Cambridge, MA) Working Paper No. 2518, February 1988.

Frankel, Jeffrey, "Ambiguous Policy Multipliers in Theory and in Empirical Models," in Ralph Bryant, Dale Henderson, Gerald Holtham, Peter Hooper, and Steven Symansky, eds., *Empirical Macroeconomics for Interdependent Economies*, Washington, DC: The Brookings Institution, 1988, pp. 17–26.

_____, and Rockett, Katharine, "International Macroeconomic Policy Coordina-

tion when Policymakers Do Not Agree on the True Model," *American Economic Review*, June 1988, 78, 318–40.

Friedman, Milton, "A Monetary and Fiscal Framework for Economic Stability," *American Economic Review*, June 1948, 38, 245–64; reprinted in Milton Friedman, *Essays in Positive Economics*, Chicago: University of Chicago Press, 1953, pp. 133–56.

_____, "The Role of Monetary Policy," *American Economic Review*, March 1968, 58, 1–17.

_____, "Inflation and Unemployment," *Journal of Political Economy*, June 1977, 85, 451–72.

Ghosh, Atish and Masson, Paul R., "International Policy Coordination in a World with Model Uncertainty," *Staff Papers* (International Monetary Fund), June 1988, 35, 230–58.

_____ and Ghosh, Swati, "Does Model Uncertainty Really Preclude International Policy Coordination?" *Journal of International Economics*, 1991, forthcoming.

Goldfeld, Stephen, "The Demand for Money Revisited," *Brookings Papers on Economic Activity*, 1973, (3), 577–637.

Holtham, Gerald and Hughes Hallett, Andrew, "International Policy Coordination and Model Uncertainty," in Ralph Bryant and Richard Portes, eds., *Global Macroeconomics: Policy Conflict and Cooperation*, London: Macmillan, 1987, pp. 128–77.

Lipsey, Richard G., "The Relation Between Unemployment and the Rate of Change of Money Wage Rates in the United Kingdom, 1862–1957: A Further Analysis," *Economica*, February 1960, 27, 1–31.

Marcet, Albert and Sargent, Thomas J., "The Fate of Systems with 'Adaptive' Expectations," *American Economic Review*, May 1988, 78, 168–72.

Masson, Paul R., Symansky, Steven, Haas, Richard and Dooley, Michael, "MULTIMOD: A Multi-Region Econometric Model," *Staff Studies for the World Economic Outlook* (Washington, DC: International Monetary Fund), July 1988, 50–104.

Oudiz, Gilles and Sachs, Jeffrey, "Macroeconomic Policy Coordination Among Industrial Economies," *Brookings Papers on Economic Activity*, 1984, (1), 1–75.

_____ **and** _____, "International Policy Coordination in Dynamic Macroeconomic Models," in Willem H. Buiter and Richard C. Marston, eds., *International Economic Policy Coordination*, Cambridge: Cambridge University Press, 1985, pp. 274–319.

Phillips, A. W., "The Relation Between Unemployment and the Rate of Change of Money Wage Rates in the United Kingdom, 1861–1957," *Economica*, November 1958, *25*, 283–99.

MASSON, PAUL R., *Portfolio Preference Uncertainty and Gains from Policy Coordination* ,
International Monetary Fund, Staff Papers, 39:1 (1992:Mar.) p.101

IMF *Staff Papers*
Vol. 39, No. 1 (March 1992)
© 1992 International Monetary Fund

# Portfolio Preference Uncertainty
# and Gains from Policy Coordination

PAUL R. MASSON*

*International policy coordination is generally considered to be made less likely—and less profitable—by uncertainty about how the economy works. This paper offers a counter example, in which investors' increased uncertainty about portfolio preference makes coordination more beneficial. Without such coordination, monetary authorities may respond to financial market uncertainty by not fully accommodating demands for increased liquidity, for fear of inducing exchange rate depreciation. Coordinated monetary expansion would minimize this danger. This result is formalized in a model incorporating an equity market; then, the stock market crash of October 1987 and its implications for monetary policy coordination are discussed.* [JEL C73, E44, E52, F31]

A LARGE LITERATURE already exists that considers the conditions under which the international coordination of economic policies could be expected to be beneficial. Several factors have been shown to influence the gains, including the "reputation" of governments—that is, their ability to precommit to fully optimal, but possibly time-inconsistent, policies (Currie, Levine, and Vidalis (1988)), the size and nature of international spillovers (Cooper (1985), Oudiz and Sachs (1984)), the nature of governments' objective functions (Martinez Oliva and Sinn (1988)), and so forth. The likelihood of policy coordination being achieved has also been debated, and many observers have expressed

* Paul R. Masson is Chief of the Economic Modeling and External Adjustment Division of the Research Department. He received his Ph.D. from the London School of Economics and Political Science. The author is grateful to Atish Ghosh and Peter Isard for discussion of the issues, to Claire Adams for expert research assistance, and to Kellett Hannah for supplying Salomon Brothers' measure of implied stock market volatility.

MASSON, PAUL R., *Portfolio Preference Uncertainty and Gains from Policy Coordination* ,
International Monetary Fund, Staff Papers, 39:1 (1992:Mar.) p.101

102                              PAUL R. MASSON

skepticism about the possibility of agreement being reached on coordinated policies when there is disagreement on how the economy functions,
and, in particular, on the effects of policies (Feldstein (1988), Frankel and
Rockett (1988)).

It is important to distinguish between two types of uncertainty: *additive*
uncertainty, which does not affect optimal policies in a linear model with
a quadratic objective function;[1] and *multiplicative* uncertainty, which
does affect them, because the incremental effects of policy changes are
uncertain (Brainard (1967)). It is therefore natural to treat disagreement
among policymakers about the appropriate model of the world economy
in a framework of multiplicative, or model, uncertainty. This was done
in Ghosh and Masson (1988), where disagreement about models was
linked to uncertainty about key parameters of a general model that nests
the various alternative views.[2] The empirical results in that paper confirmed the theoretical analysis of Ghosh and Ghosh (1991), who showed
that uncertainty about parameter values can *increase* expected gains from
coordination, especially when such uncertainty concerns the transmission
effects of policies from one country to another, rather than their domestic
effects.

This paper attempts to extend the intuition about the effects of uncertainty on expected gains from coordination[3] by considering a particular
case of multiplicative uncertainty, one in which policymakers must take
account of uncertainty concerning the preferences of investors across
portfolio shares. These portfolio shares play the same role as model
parameters, and they are assumed to be stochastic in the model used
here.

This view of investment decisions—that they contain a random component—is consistent with observed behavior in financial markets. Fluctuations in asset prices are not explainable solely by news concerning
fundamentals, but are plausibly also the result of shifts in asset preferences. This is one interpretation that can be given to the evidence of
variance-bounds tests, which suggests that the volatility of asset prices
exceeds that of fundamentals.[4] A recent example of sudden portfolio

---

[1] "Certainty equivalence" is said to apply in this case; see Simon (1956).
[2] However, disagreement over the correct model can exist even when each
policymaker is certain that he or she is right. Conversely, uncertainty about
parameter values does not imply that policymakers have different assessments of
the distributions describing those parameters.
[3] Ex post, welfare may, of course, be lower when policies are coordinated than
when they are not; however, policies are assumed to be chosen in order to
maximize expected welfare, and, on average, ex post welfare is assumed to equal
expected welfare.
[4] For such evidence, see Shiller (1981). Whether variance-bounds tests actually
demonstrate the existence of excess volatility has been questioned, however; see,
for instance, Flavin (1983) and Flood and Hodrick (1986).

MASSON, PAUL R., *Portfolio Preference Uncertainty and Gains from Policy Coordination* ,
International Monetary Fund, Staff Papers, 39:1 (1992:Mar.) p.101

shifts is associated with the generalized crash of all major stock markets
in October 1987, during which many investors dumped their shares on
the market in an attempt to shift out of stocks into other assets at virtually
any price.

Moreover, shifts in portfolio preferences that lead to sudden declines
in stock prices are often associated with increased uncertainty, as evidenced by increased volatility of stock prices. This was the experience in
the days following October 19, 1987, and also in the August 1990 sell-off.
From a macroeconomic policy perspective, the central concern in such
an environment is that the real economy will be affected, owing to
declines in real wealth and increases in the cost of capital to firms.
However, the effects of monetary and fiscal policies on ultimate target
variables are also increasingly uncertain, since these policies operate
through financial markets. The effects of uncertainty in domestic financial markets are compounded by uncertainty in foreign exchange markets: a sharp depreciation will have unfavorable effects on inflation, for
instance, and may exacerbate loss of confidence.

Greater uncertainty in financial markets may increase the need for
policy coordination because of a dilemma facing a central bank when
responding to shocks. For instance, if the central bank responded to a
stock market crash by loosening monetary policy, it might bring about a
collapse in the value of the currency. Fear of such a possibility might well
lead to an inappropriately timid monetary policy, in which monetary
expansion was kept too low. In contrast, a coordinated reduction in
interest rates by central banks would diminish the risk of sharp exchange
rate movements, while neutralizing the unfavorable effects of a generalized shift out of equities. Consistent with this, the October 1987 crash led
to coordination among central banks, or at least some consultation
among them about the need to increase liquidity, and interest rates were
lowered simultaneously in all major industrial countries.

More generally, variation over time in the amount of financial market
uncertainty may explain why coordination tends to be episodic, rather
than institutionalized.[5] In times of crisis, the outlook is uncertain, as are
the effects of policies; coordination of policies may decrease the danger
of very bad outcomes. The incentives to pull together may be strength-
ened in such circumstances. It may be that in normal times gains from
macroeconomic policy coordination are relatively small, consistent with
estimates calculated using macroeconomic models (see, for instance,
Oudiz and Sachs (1984)). However, great uncertainty about the effects
of policies may make the gains from coordination larger, for instance
when financial markets are turbulent and there is a danger that portfolio

[5] The terminology was used by Artis and Ostry (1986).

MASSON, PAUL R., *Portfolio Preference Uncertainty and Gains from Policy Coordination* , International Monetary Fund, Staff Papers, 39:1 (1992:Mar.) p.101

104                              PAUL R. MASSON

shifts may lead to large movements in asset prices and spillovers onto the real economy. Macroeconomic policy coordination may thus take on the character of "regime-preserving coordination" (Kenen (1988)), rather than a continuous attempt to maximize joint welfare, however defined.

This paper illustrates the effect of portfolio uncertainty on coordination with a simple model. Section I presents a two-country, two-good model in which the portfolio preferences of investors between domestic money and an international equity are random variables,[6] goods prices are sticky, and the value of financial wealth affects real output. It is shown in Section II that expected gains from policy coordination depend crucially on the perceived variances and covariances of the portfolio shifts. Policy at the time of the October 1987 crash is analyzed in the light of these results in Section III. Section IV presents conclusions.

## I. The Model

In order to highlight the interaction between portfolio preferences, asset prices, and real activity, a simple, short-run model of two countries is specified. Portfolio preferences are stochastic, and can differ in the two countries. Longer-run questions such as wage adjustment and capital accumulation are ignored. Moreover, in this stylized model, there are only three assets: domestic money, foreign money, and a single equity, which is a claim to a composite consumption good (that is, the equity pays a real return, which is assumed exogenous).[7] A feature of this model is thus that there is a single world equity price; this assumption reflects in extreme form the reality that comovements of equity prices across countries have been very high in recent years—and especially so at the time of the October 1987 crash.

Each of the two countries is specialized in the production of a single good but consumes both. Utility is assumed to be Cobb-Douglas, so that consumption shares are constant; in the home country, expenditure falls in proportion, $\alpha$, on home goods and $(1 - \alpha)$ on foreign goods. Consumption is assumed to be proportional to the real value of financial wealth ($W$, to be defined later), so that

---

[6] A number of articles have included equity markets in macroeconomic models; for instance, Diamond (1967) and Helpman and Razin (1978). This paper makes no attempt to model capital accumulation or to relate the riskiness of equities to technological uncertainty. What is at issue here is the risk related to shifts in portfolio preferences.

[7] Thus, the "fundamentals" are not the cause of asset price volatility. A more complicated model could make both production technology and portfolio preferences stochastic.

MASSON, PAUL R., *Portfolio Preference Uncertainty and Gains from Policy Coordination* ,
International Monetary Fund, Staff Papers, 39:1 (1992:Mar.) p.101

PORTFOLIO PREFERENCE UNCERTAINTY          105

$$C = \rho W / P. \tag{1}$$

The consumption deflator, $P$, is a geometric average of the two goods prices, where $p$ is the price of the home good, $p^*$ is the price of the foreign good, and $s$ is the price of foreign currency:

$$P = p^\alpha (sp^*)^{1-\alpha}. \tag{2}$$

Consistent with Cobb-Douglas utility, consumption is divided between the home good, $C_1$, and the foreign good, $C_2$, on the basis of fixed spending shares:

$$C_1 = \alpha (P/p) C \tag{3}$$

$$C_2 = (1 - \alpha)(P/sp^*)C. \tag{4}$$

In what follows it is assumed that for both the home and foreign countries, spending falls equally on the two goods, so that $\alpha = \frac{1}{2}$. Therefore, equations (2) and (3) can be written as follows:

$$P = (psp^*)^{1/2} \tag{5}$$

$$C_1 = 0.5(P/p)C \tag{6}$$

$$C_2 = 0.5(P/sp^*)C. \tag{7}$$

Wealth is held in the form of money, $M$, which is nontraded, and in international equities, $E$, which are a promise to pay a given amount of the composite consumption good (which is the same in the two countries since $\alpha = \alpha^* = \frac{1}{2}$), and for which there is a single world market. Money and equities are held in proportions, $m$ and $1 - m$; these proportions are random variables. The price of a real equity claim is $q$:

$$M = mW \tag{8}$$

$$qPE = (1 - m)W. \tag{9}$$

Uncertainty in portfolio preferences is reflected in the variance of $m$. Shifts in domestic portfolio preferences may or may not be correlated with shifts in the preferences of foreign investors; the degree of correlation is shown below to be crucial to gains from coordination.

A symmetric foreign country has a similar structure, indicated by starred variables. Parameters are assumed identical, except the random portfolio share parameter, $m^*$, which may not be equal to $m$ (in the next section the *distributions* describing $m$ and $m^*$ are, however, assumed to be the same). There is a single world equity price (that is, $q^* = q$), since both home and foreign equities pay returns in the same consumption basket. The counterparts of equations (1) and (5)–(9) are

MASSON, PAUL R., *Portfolio Preference Uncertainty and Gains from Policy Coordination* ,
International Monetary Fund, Staff Papers, 39:1 (1992:Mar.) p.101

106                                  PAUL R. MASSON

$$C^* = \rho W^* / P^* \tag{1'}$$

$$P^* = [(p/s)p^*]^{1/2} \tag{5'}$$

$$C_1^* = 0.5(sP^*/p)C^* \tag{6'}$$

$$C_2^* = 0.5(P^*/p^*)C^* \tag{7'}$$

$$M^* = m^*W^* \tag{8'}$$

$$qP^*E^* = (1 - m^*)W^*. \tag{9'}$$

It is assumed that output prices are sticky, and that $p$ and $p^*$ are fixed in the short run; output is determined by demand:

$$y = C_1 + C_1^* \tag{10}$$

and

$$y^* = C_2 + C_2^*. \tag{10'}$$

However, consumer prices can vary since the exchange rate, $s$, is flexible. Similarly, the price of equities, $q$, moves to equate the demand for equities and the outstanding stock of equity shares, $K + K^*$, where $K$ and $K^*$ are the initial endowments of equities at home and abroad:

$$K + K^* = E + E^*. \tag{11}$$

The exchange rate is determined by an equilibrium condition that the current account surplus equal the capital account outflow, which is equivalent to the condition that the distribution of equities between the two countries satisfy portfolio preferences. The net capital outflow, $CAP$, from the home country (that is, net purchases of equities) is equal to

$$CAP = qP(E - K), \tag{12}$$

(which is, of course, equal, from equation (11), to $-qP(E^* - K^*)$, the inflow to the foreign country, which corresponds to net sales of equities). The current account surplus, $CUR$, is the excess of domestic output over domestic absorption (that is, saving), or exports minus imports:

$$CUR = (y - C_1)p - s(y^* - C_2^*)p^*, \tag{13}$$

and the balance of payments condition is

$$CAP = CUR. \tag{14}$$

## II. Optimal Government Policy

In the context of this model, monetary policy has a role in cushioning portfolio preference shifts, which have real effects because prices are sticky and consumption depends on wealth. Under consideration will be

MASSON, PAUL R., *Portfolio Preference Uncertainty and Gains from Policy Coordination* ,
International Monetary Fund, Staff Papers, 39:1 (1992:Mar.) p.101

PORTFOLIO PREFERENCE UNCERTAINTY     107

the optimal monetary policy of a government, or central bank, that desires to minimize deviations from target output $\bar{y}$—presumably its full employment level—and from price stability, which implies that the price level equals its initial equilibrium value, $\bar{P}$. A quadratic objective function of deviations from bliss levels is postulated for tractability. Such a formulation implies a symmetric treatment of positive and negative deviations, which is probably not realistic; however, this analysis will only consider a portfolio shift out of equities into money that tends to depress output. In particular, the optimal response of the money supply to a shock to the mean value of investors' portfolio preferences is considered in the face of uncertainty about these preferences. Thus, the situation is one in which an initial portfolio shift is observed (such as the shift leading to the fall in equity prices on October 19, 1987), but there is uncertainty about *subsequent* shifts.

Suppose that the home government's objective function is

$$L = E\{(y/\bar{y} - 1)^2 + \phi(P/\bar{P} - 1)^2\} \tag{15}$$

and similarly, for the foreign government

$$L^* = E\{(y^*/\bar{y}^* - 1)^2 + \phi(P^*/\bar{P}^* - 1)^2\}. \tag{15'}$$

It is assumed that in initial equilibrium, money supplies and asset proportions are equal, so that $M = M^* = \bar{M}$ and $1/m = 1/m^* = \bar{n}$, and so $\bar{s} = 1$, and $p = p^* = 1$. Consider a shift out of equities at home and abroad, so that now

$$E(1/m) \equiv E(n) = E(n^*) = \theta\bar{n}, \tag{16}$$

with $\theta < 1$. How does the optimal setting for monetary policy in the two countries, if each takes the other's policy as given, compare to the case of joint maximization of an equally weighted global objective function, $G$, where $G = 0.5(L + L^*)$?

In the absence of uncertainty, it can be shown that the optimal response to such a shock will be—not surprisingly—to accommodate fully the increase in liquidity preference. In this case, the Appendix shows that cooperative and noncooperative policy settings are the same; they both involve an increase in money supply by the increase in money demand, so $M = M^* = \bar{M}/\theta$. If there is no uncertainty, then in this model monetary policy can completely neutralize the negative output effects of the portfolio preference shock, and the noncooperative and cooperative policies are the same. This is true because each government has as many targets as instruments; in this case, despite possible spillovers through the exchange rate, gains from policy coordination are zero.

However, if there exists uncertainty about portfolio preferences, then only in the case where the portfolio shifts in the two countries are

MASSON, PAUL R., *Portfolio Preference Uncertainty and Gains from Policy Coordination* ,
International Monetary Fund, Staff Papers, 39:1 (1992:Mar.) p.101

expected to be perfectly correlated will the two policies be the same. It can be shown (see Appendix) that, in general—unless the weight on inflation in the objective function is zero—the optimal noncooperative policy will be too contractionary, relative to the optimal, cooperative solution. The reason for this bias is the externality associated with the exchange rate (Sachs (1985)): appreciation helps in moderating domestic prices but exports inflation to the foreign country, and the latter effects are ignored in the absence of cooperation. The difference between the noncooperative and cooperative policies and, hence. the gains from policy coordination depend both on the common variance, $\sigma^2$, of portfolio preferences and on the correlation, $\kappa$, between the two countries' portfolio preference shifts—directly in the first case, and inversely in the second.

The difference between the two policies increases monotonically as the correlation declines, and is maximized when their correlation is minus unity; that is, they are perfectly negatively correlated. In this case, governments set policy with the risk that a monetary expansion may lead to a large exchange rate depreciation because portfolio preferences of domestic and foreign residents for money and equities are expected to shift in ways that reinforce their effects on the exchange rate. The depreciation is undesirable because of its price level effects.

This example provides an additional reason why policy coordination may be beneficial, compared to the traditional literature in which the effects of policies are assumed to be known. In Sachs (1985), for instance, noncooperative monetary policies are too contractionary in response to an inflation shock because exchange rate appreciation improves the output/inflation trade-off, and there are two targets and only one instrument. In the present example, the effects of policies are uncertain because of possible shifts in portfolio preference, so that even if each government has as many instruments as targets it still has an incentive to coordinate. The fact that portfolio preferences are uncertain and that they contribute to the variance of the exchange rate makes uncoordinated policies overcontractionary in the face of an increase in liquidity preference.

## III. The Stock Market Crash of October 1987

On October 19–20, 1987, the world's stock markets declined in a sudden sell-off of shares by investors. In local currency terms, stock market indices declined during the period from September 30 to October 31 by 21.5 percent in the United States, 26.1 percent in the United

MASSON, PAUL R., *Portfolio Preference Uncertainty and Gains from Policy Coordination* ,
International Monetary Fund, Staff Papers, 39:1 (1992:Mar.) p.101

PORTFOLIO PREFERENCE UNCERTAINTY           109

Kingdom, 22.9 percent in Germany, and 12.6 percent in Japan (see
Figure 1 for a visual impression of the comovements of major market
indices). Other declines were even more dramatic: 58.3 percent in Australia, and 56.3 percent in Hong Kong (Federal Reserve Bank of New
York (1988, p. 18)). To a large extent, therefore, at least during this
period world equity markets seemed globally integrated—as is assumed
in the model described above, in which there is only one equity market—
although the reasons for the common movement of prices are subject to
dispute. To some extent, this comovement may have been the result of
the gradual increase in interlisting of shares on different exchanges;
however, correlations between the main trading zones increased by a
factor of three from their levels in the previous nine months (Bertero and
Mayer (1989)). Common movements in October 1987 did not seem to
result from significant international investment flows, since cross-border
selling was relatively small (Federal Reserve Bank of New York (1988,
p. 34)). More fundamentally, then, increased economic integration and
the globalization of information led to a common reassessment of equity
prices in all major stock markets at the time of the stock market crash.

As is argued above, the question of whether equity prices move together (because they are good substitutes—for instance, because they are
claims to similar income streams) is logically separate from whether
portfolio preferences for equities shift in the same way in different countries. Confirming a generalized shift out of equities, as opposed to a shift
in investor sentiment in some countries but not in others, the sharp
decline in equity values was associated with relatively small exchange rate
movements (Figure 2). In the October 1987 crash, exchange rate movements do not seem to have been a consideration in the setting of monetary
policies.[8]

What does seem to have been a major concern influencing policy was
that the 1987 stock crash might be a replay of the 1929 one, which was
followed by the Great Depression (Schwartz (1988)). In this regard, a
high degree of uncertainty was attached to the linkage between the stock
market and the real economy—that is, the spending propensities of
consumers, whose wealth had declined, and businesses, whose investment plans might be scaled back reflecting increased caution. Also subject to increased uncertainty was the stability of the financial system:
whether the inability of individuals to cover margin calls, or of financial
institutions to transact in financial markets, would lead to bankruptcies,

---

[8] They are not mentioned, for instance, in Alan Greenspan's testimony at
hearings on "Black Monday," held by the U.S. Senate Committee on Banking,
Housing, and Urban Affairs, February 2–5, 1988. See U.S. Congress (1988).

110                              PAUL R. MASSON

Figure 1. *Stock Market Prices, January 1985 to September 1990*
(Indices: 1985 = 100)

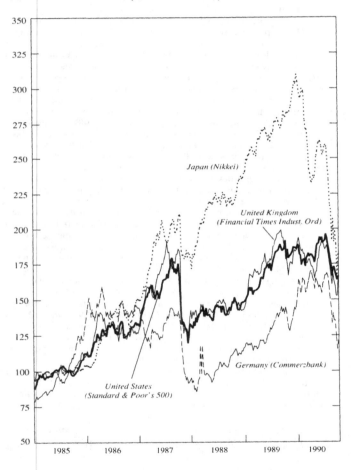

MASSON, PAUL R., *Portfolio Preference Uncertainty and Gains from Policy Coordination* ,
International Monetary Fund, Staff Papers, 39:1 (1992:Mar.) p.101

PORTFOLIO PREFERENCE UNCERTAINTY     111

Figure 2.  *U.S. Dollar Exchange Rates , January 1985 to December 1990*
(Indices: 1985 = 100)

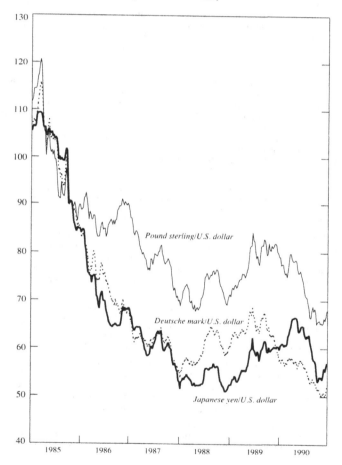

MASSON, PAUL R., *Portfolio Preference Uncertainty and Gains from Policy Coordination* ,
International Monetary Fund, Staff Papers, 39:1 (1992:Mar.) p.101

112                          PAUL R. MASSON

and whether anticipation of such problems would cause the clearing and
settlements system to collapse (Bernanke (1990)). It is hard to quantify
the increase in uncertainty; however, one measure, the expected volatility implied by a comparison of equity and options prices, showed a
dramatic increase in the United States in October 1987 (Figure 3).

Fear of financial collapse led governments and central banks to intervene by providing liquidity; moreover, they did so through closely coordinated actions. Of course, given the importance of the United States in
world financial markets, the actions of the U.S. authorities were of
paramount importance. The Federal Reserve reversed its tight monetary
stance, flooding the system with liquidity; persuaded the banks to lend
freely to securities firms; and closely monitored the situation, taking
direct action where necessary (Bernanke (1990)). However, it did not act
in isolation, according to Fed Chairman Alan Greenspan: " . . . we closely
monitored the international ramifications of the stock market crash. . . .
We communicated with officials of foreign central banks. . . . " (U.S.
Congress (1988, p. 92)). In describing the role of policy coordination
among the major industrial countries in this period, Dobson (1991) says:

> The risk in 1987 was that, in the absence of close G-7 cooperation, the
> financial crisis could have turned into an economic crisis. Had the authorities
> turned their backs and refused to cooperate among themselves, it is very
> likely that the crisis would have deepened (p. 128).

What occurred was a generalized decline in short-term interest rates
as all central banks expanded liquidity (Figure 4). To some extent, a
decline in interest rates on government paper (though not on private
claims) might be expected from a "flight to quality," but central banks
clearly favored a fall in rates, as indicated by Fed Chairman Alan
Greenspan (U.S. Congress (1988)):

> By helping to reduce irrational liquidity demands, and accommodating the
> remainder, the Federal Reserve avoided a tightening in overall pressures on
> reserve positions and an increase in short-term interest rates. In fact, we went
> even further and eased policy moderately following the stock market collapse
> in light of the greater risk to continued economic expansion (p. 90).

In sum, therefore, the October 1987 stock market crash is an example
of what appears to be a direct link between increased uncertainty and
increased policy coordination. In describing the risks to the clearing and
settlement system posed by the October 1987 crash and other events, the
Governor of the Bank of Canada stated (Crow (1990)):

> These disturbances, and others since, were effectively contained through
> co-operation among major market participants . . . [T]he temporary injec-
> tion of liquidity by central banks . . . helped to prevent the October 1987

MASSON, PAUL R., *Portfolio Preference Uncertainty and Gains from Policy Coordination* ,
International Monetary Fund, Staff Papers, 39:1 (1992:Mar.) p.101

PORTFOLIO PREFERENCE UNCERTAINTY　　　113

Figure 3. *Implied Volatility of Standard and Poor's 500,*
*January 1, 1987 to October 12, 1990*

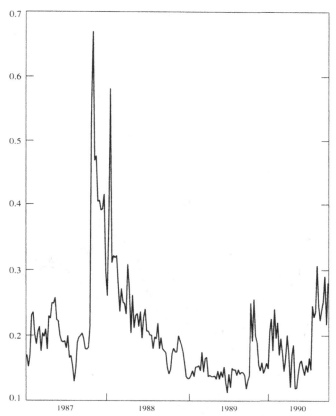

Source: Salomon Brothers.
Note: Calculated using the Black-Scholes option price formula, adjusted for
dividend payments and using the price of a put option on the Standard and Poor's
500 Stock Index and the interest rate on U.S. Treasury Bills.

MASSON, PAUL R., ***Portfolio Preference Uncertainty and Gains from Policy Coordination*** ,
International Monetary Fund, Staff Papers, 39:1 (1992:Mar.) p.101

114                          PAUL R. MASSON

Figure 4.  *Short-Term Interest Rates , January 1985 to December 1990*
(In percent per year)

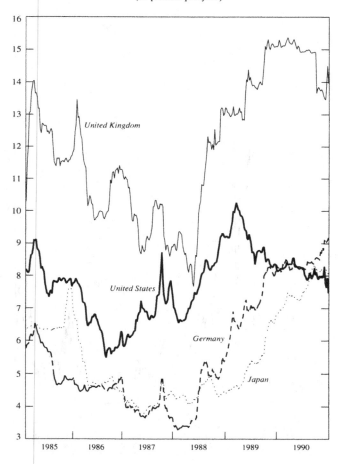

MASSON, PAUL R., *Portfolio Preference Uncertainty and Gains from Policy Coordination* ,
International Monetary Fund, Staff Papers, 39:1 (1992:Mar.) p.101

PORTFOLIO PREFERENCE UNCERTAINTY    115

financial problems from degenerating into solvency problems. In retrospect,
it is clear that the global community has come altogether too close to
situations where market difficulties could have been severe enough to inflict
lasting damage on financial markets and even on national economies (p. 2).

The model developed above has suggested that the need for policy
coordination might have been even greater if the portfolio shifts had been
less symmetric, for instance, if the fall in equity prices had been associated with severe weakness of the U.S. dollar. In this case, the Federal
Reserve might have been much less willing to expand liquidity, for fear
of adding to a run on the dollar. In cases such as these, a coordinated
decline in interest rates in all countries would diminish the risk of disrup-
tive exchange rate movements while minimizing the dangers of financial
collapse.

## IV. Conclusions

The paper has illustrated in a simple model the link between uncertain
portfolio preferences of private investors and the difference between
coordinated and uncoordinated policies. Greater uncertainty makes coordination more desirable in this example where portfolio shifts generate
variations in output and exchange rates. The analysis suggests that if the
perceived degree of uncertainty varies over time—perhaps as described
in recent articles, for instance, by Flood, Bhandari, and Horne (1989)—
then the incentives to coordinate policies will also vary. In particular, in
situations of great uncertainty, where the prevailing international monetary system is threatened, policies are more likely to be influenced by
shared goals.

In the particular source of uncertainty that is considered in the paper—
uncertainty on the part of policymakers about the portfolio preferences
of private investors—the degree of correlation across countries of portfolio shifts between equities and money is crucial in determining the gains
from policy coordination. That conclusion is likely to remain in more
general models with a wider menu of traded assets, in which portfolio
shifts may also occur between different countries' equities and bonds.
Paradoxically, if portfolio shifts are expected to be correlated across
countries—as was the case with the shift out of equities at the time of
the October 1987 crash—they may not require policy coordination to
the extent that less symmetric portfolio preference shifts would. Of
course, what is important is policymakers' anticipations of the degree
of correlation of portfolio shifts; these anticipations are unlikely to involve perfect correlation. Thus, uncertainty about investors' preferences
is at times likely to provide a powerful incentive to coordinate policies
internationally.

MASSON, PAUL R., *Portfolio Preference Uncertainty and Gains from Policy Coordination* ,
International Monetary Fund, Staff Papers, 39:1 (1992:Mar.) p.101

116                              PAUL R. MASSON

# APPENDIX

## Solution of the Model

The solution for the variables that are of interest—it is assumed that policymakers have targets for domestic output and consumer prices—can be obtained as
follows. Domestic output prices (but not consumer prices) are fixed in the current
period. From equations (5) and (5') in the text

$$P^* = P/s. \tag{17}$$

As a result, from equations (1), (8), and (17)

$$C = \rho(M/m)/P \tag{18}$$

$$C^* = s\rho(M^*/m^*)/P. \tag{18'}$$

From the conditions for goods market equilibrium, equations (10) and (10')

$$y = 0.5[\rho M/m + s\rho M^*/m^*]/p \tag{19}$$

$$y^* = 0.5[\rho(M/m)/s + \rho M^*/m^*]/p^*. \tag{19'}$$

Turning to equilibrium in financial markets, substituting equations (9) and (9')
into (11) yields

$$qP = [(1 - m)M/m + (1 - m^*)sM^*/m^*]/(K + K^*). \tag{20}$$

Now the balance of payments equilibrium can also be expressed in terms of $s$ and
$q$; from equations (12)–(14)

$$qP(E - K) = 0.5\rho(sm^*/m^* - M/m). \tag{21}$$

Substitution of equations (9) and (20) into (21) yields an expression for $s$ in terms
of money supplies, portfolio preferences, and initial endowments of equities:

$$s = \{(1 - m)[K^*/(K + K^*)]M/m + 0.5\rho M/m\}/\{(1 - m^*)$$
$$\cdot [K/(K + K^*)]M^*/m^* + 0.5\rho M^*/m^*\}. \tag{22}$$

In keeping with our assumption of symmetry, we further posit that initial endowments of the international equity are equal, so that $K/(K + K^*) = 0.5$. Therefore, the exchange rate can be written as

$$s = [(M/m)(1 - m + \rho)]/[(M^*/m^*)(1 - m^* + \rho)]. \tag{23}$$

Thus, for given portfolio preferences, the exchange rate is determined by relative
money supplies; a shift out of equities into money (an increase in $m$) will tend
to appreciate the currency (lower $s$).

Using the expression for $s$, reduced-form expressions can be derived for domestic and foreign outputs. From equation (19)

$$y = \rho(M/m)\{[1 - 0.5(m + m^*) + \rho]/(1 - m^* + \rho)\}/p \tag{24}$$

and from equation (19')

$$y^* = \rho(M^*/m^*)\{[1 - 0.5(m + m^*) + \rho]/(1 - m + \rho)\}/p^*. \tag{24'}$$

It will be assumed that it is not possible to go short in equities, so that $1 - m > 0$
and $1 - m^* > 0$. Therefore, the terms in braces in (24) and (24') are positive,

MASSON, PAUL R., **Portfolio Preference Uncertainty and Gains from Policy Coordination**,
International Monetary Fund, Staff Papers, 39:1 (1992:Mar.) p.101

PORTFOLIO PREFERENCE UNCERTAINTY          117

implying that an increase in the money supply in the home country increases output:

$$\partial y / \partial M > 0 \quad \text{and} \quad \partial y^* / \partial M^* > 0.$$

while an increase in the desire to hold domestic money decreases it:

$$\partial y / \partial m < 0 \quad \text{and} \quad \partial y^* / \partial m^* < 0.$$

In contrast, portfolio shifts abroad have the opposite effect (that is, they are negatively transmitted); it can be shown that

$$\partial y / \partial m^* > 0 \quad \text{and} \quad \partial y^* / \partial m > 0.$$

The first-order condition for optimal policy setting in the home country can be derived in the following way. Let $n = 1/m$, $n^* = 1/m^*$, and $F(n, n^*) = [(\rho + 1)n - 1]/[(\rho + 1)n^* - 1]$, and note that both the numerator and denominator of $F$ are positive, from the assumption made above that portfolio shares must be positive. From equations (23) and (24) above

$$\partial L / \partial M = E\{0.5M [n + n^*F(n, n^*)]^2 / \overline{M}^2 \bar{n}^2$$
$$- [n + n^*F(n, n^*)]/\overline{M}\bar{n} + \phi[F(n, n^*)/M^*]$$
$$- \phi[F(n, n^*)/M^*M]^{1/2}\} = 0. \tag{25}$$

Given the assumptions of symmetry, implying that $F(n^*, n) = 1/F(n, n^*)$, the foreign country's first-order condition is similar, and is not presented here.

Consider an equal change in the two countries in portfolio preferences, such that the desired wealth proportion held in the form of money rises equally—that is, $n$ and $n^*$ fall by the same amount. It is clear that, starting from the same position, the optimal policy response to the same portfolio shock will be the same in the two countries, so that $M = M^*$. Replacing $M^*$ and $M$ by $M^n$, the common noncooperative policy setting, the following is obtained from (25):

$$M^n = 2[\overline{M}\bar{n}]E[n + n^*F(n, n^*)]/E[n + n^*F(n, n^*)]^2$$
$$- [2\phi/M^n]\{EF(n, n^*) - E[F(n, n^*)]^{1/2}\}$$
$$\cdot \overline{M}^2\bar{n}^2/E[n + n^*F(n, n^*)]^2. \tag{26}$$

If, instead, the two governments coordinate and minimize a joint objective function, $G$, that gives equal weights to $L$ and $L^*$, then the first-order condition for the use of the home country's money supply instrument is

$$\partial G / \partial M = E\{0.5M[n + n^*F(n, n^*)]^2 / \overline{M}^2 \bar{n}^2$$
$$- [n + n^*F(n, n^*)]/\overline{M}\bar{n} + \phi[F(n, n^*)/M^*]$$
$$- \phi[F(n, n^*)/M^*M]^{1/2} - \phi F(n^*, n)(M^*/M^2)$$
$$+ \phi(MM^*)^{1/2}[F(n^*, n)]^{1/2}/M\} = 0. \tag{27}$$

Not surprisingly, the first-order condition for $M^*$ is symmetrical, and therefore it will not be presented. Solving (27) for the common coordinated money supply setting $M^c$

$$M^c = [2\overline{M}\bar{n}]E[n + n^*F(n, n^*)]/E[n + n^*F(n, n^*)]^2$$
$$- [\overline{M}^2\bar{n}^2\phi/M^c]\{E[F(n, n^*)] - E[F(n, n^*)]^{1/2}$$
$$- E[F(n^*, n)] + E[F(n^*, n)]^{1/2}\}. \tag{28}$$

MASSON, PAUL R., *Portfolio Preference Uncertainty and Gains from Policy Coordination* ,
International Monetary Fund, Staff Papers, 39:1 (1992:Mar.) p.101

118                                   PAUL R. MASSON

Equation (28) simplifies further in the case (assumed here) where the distributions describing portfolio preference parameters are the same in the two countries, although not necessarily their realizations. In this case, $EF(n, n^*) = EF(n^*, n)$ and $EF(n, n^*)^2 = EF(n^*, n)^2$. Therefore, the term in equation (28) between braces is zero, and the cooperative monetary policy is given by

$$M^c = [2\overline{M}\overline{n}]E[n + n^*F(n, n^*)]/E[n + n^*F(n, n^*)]^2. \qquad (29)$$

In this case, although each country's objective includes inflation and, hence indirectly, the exchange rate (and both countries' inflation targets are included symmetrically in $G$), the exchange rate plays no role in the cooperative monetary policy: the latter, given by equation (29), is independent of the value of $\phi$.

What is the effect of increased liquidity preference in the two countries under each policy regime? First, assume *absence of uncertainty*. In this case, since $n = n^* = \theta\overline{n} < \overline{n}$

$$EF(n, n^*) = EF(n^*, n) = E[F(n, n^*)]^{1/2} = E[F(n^*, n)]^{1/2} = 1$$

and

$$E[n + n^*F(n, n^*)] = 2\theta n.$$

It can be verified from equations (26) and (29) that

$$M^n = M^c = \overline{M}/\theta, \qquad (30)$$

so that both policy regimes fully accommodate the shift in liquidity preference. In the absence of uncertainty, no negative exchange rate repercussions are to be feared from a symmetric portfolio shift.

Next, consider the effect of an increase in uncertainty in the two policy regimes, starting from the initial position with a common monetary policy stance, $M = M^* = \overline{M}$, and letting $E(n) = E(n^*) = \overline{n}$. The only element of uncertainty will relate to the common variance of $n$; that is

$$E(n - \overline{n})^2 = E(n^* - \overline{n})^2 = \sigma^2.$$

In order to evaluate expressions on the right-hand sides of equations (26) and (29), first, take a second-order Taylor series expansion of $F(n, n^*)$ and $F(n, n^*)^{1/2}$ around $E(n) = \overline{n}$, and $E(n^*) = \overline{n}$, and take expectations (letting $\mathrm{var}(n) = \mathrm{var}(n^*) = \sigma^2$, $\mathrm{cov}(n, n^*) = \kappa\sigma^2$, and $\beta = [(\rho + 1)\overline{n} - 1]^{-2}$):

$$EF(n, n^*) \doteq 1 + (\rho + 1)^2\beta(1 - \kappa)\sigma^2 \qquad (31)$$

$$EF(n, n^*)^{1/2} \doteq 1 + (\rho + 1)^2\beta(1 - \kappa)\sigma^2/4. \qquad (32)$$

From approximations (31) and (32) it can be shown that

$$EF(n, n^*) - EF(n, n^*)^{1/2} \doteq 3(\rho + 1)^2\beta\sigma^2(1 - \kappa)/4 \geq 0 \qquad (33)$$

$$E[n + n^*F(n, n^*)] \doteq 2\overline{n} + (\rho + 1)\beta\sigma^2(1 - \mu) \qquad (34)$$

$$E[n + n^*F(n, n^*)]^2 \doteq 4\overline{n}^2 + 4\sigma^2 + 2[4(\rho + 1)\overline{n} - 1]\beta\sigma^2(1 - \kappa). \qquad (35)$$

From equations (26), (29), and (31)–(35), it can be shown that increased uncertainty (a larger $\sigma^2$) makes both noncooperative and cooperative policies more contractionary, but it increases the gap between them (unless $\kappa = 1$); evaluated at $\sigma^2 = 0$

$$\frac{dM^c}{d\sigma^2} - \frac{dM^n}{d\sigma^2} \doteq \frac{(\phi/2)\overline{M}}{1 + \phi/2}[(3/4)(\rho + 1) + 1/2\overline{n}](\rho + 1)\beta(1 - \kappa) > 0.$$

MASSON, PAUL R., ***Portfolio Preference Uncertainty and Gains from Policy Coordination*** ,
International Monetary Fund, Staff Papers, 39:1 (1992:Mar.) p.101

PORTFOLIO PREFERENCE UNCERTAINTY     119

Thus, a moderate amount of uncertainty will imply gains from coordination. The general case is ambiguous, however; starting from a position where $\sigma^2 > 0$, the effect of additional uncertainty cannot be signed.

## REFERENCES

Artis, Michael, and Sylvia Ostry, *International Economic Policy Coordination*, Chatham House Papers No. 30 (London: Royal Institute of International Affairs, 1986).

Bernanke, Ben S., "Clearing and Settlement During the Crash," *Review of Financial Studies*, Vol. 3, No. 1 (1990), pp. 133–51.

Bertero, Elisabetta, and Colin Mayer, "Structure and Performance: Global Interdependence of Stock Markets Around the Crash of October 1987," CEPR Discussion Paper No. 307 (London: Centre for Economic Policy Research, March 1989).

Brainard, William C., "Uncertainty and the Effectiveness of Policy," *American Economic Review*, Vol. 57 (May 1967), pp. 411–25.

Cooper, Richard N., "Economic Interdependence and Coordination of Economic Policies," in *Handbook of International Economics*, ed. by Ronald W. Jones and Peter B. Kenen, Vol. 2 (Amsterdam; New York: North-Holland, 1985).

Crow, John W., "Notes for Remarks by the Governor of the Bank of Canada at the Treasury Management Association of Canada's Eighth Annual Cash and Treasury Management Conference in Toronto on 7/11/90," *BIS Review*, No. 231 (November 26, 1990), pp. 1–6.

Currie, David, Paul Levine, and Nic Vidalis, "International Cooperation and Reputation in an Empirical Two-Bloc Model," in *Global Macroeconomics: Policy Conflict and Cooperation*, ed. by Ralph C. Bryant and Richard Portes (New York: St. Martin's Press, 1988).

Diamond, Peter A., "The Role of a Stock Market in a General Equilibrium Model with Technological Uncertainty," *American Economic Review*, Vol. 57 (September 1967), pp. 759–76.

Dobson, Wendy, *Economic Policy Coordination: Requiem or Prologue?*, Policy Analyses in International Economics No. 30 (Washington: Institute for International Economics, 1991).

Federal Reserve Bank of New York, *Quarterly Review*, Vol. 13 (Summer 1988).

Feldstein, Martin, "Distinguished Lecture on Economics in Government: Thinking about International Economic Coordination," *Journal of Economic Perspectives*, Vol. 2 (Spring 1988), pp. 3–13.

Flavin, Marjorie, "Excess Volatility in the Financial Markets: A Reassessment of the Empirical Evidence," *Journal of Political Economy*, Vol. 91 (December 1983), pp. 929–56.

Flood, Robert P., Jagdeep S. Bhandari, and Jocelyn P. Horne, "Evolution of Exchange Rate Regimes," *Staff Papers*, International Monetary Fund, Vol. 36 (December 1989), pp. 810–35.

MASSON, PAUL R., *Portfolio Preference Uncertainty and Gains from Policy Coordination* ,
International Monetary Fund, Staff Papers, 39:1 (1992:Mar.) p.101

120                                         PAUL R. MASSON

Flood, Robert P., and Robert J. Hodrick, "Asset Price Volatility, Bubbles,
    and Process Switching," *Journal of Finance*, Vol. 41 (September 1986),
    pp. 831–42.

Frankel, Jeffrey, and Katharine Rockett, "International Macroeconomic Policy
    Coordination when Policymakers Do Not Agree on the True Model," *Amer-
    ican Economic Review*, Vol. 78 (June 1988), pp. 318–40.

Ghosh, Atish R., and Swati R. Ghosh, "Does Model Uncertainty Really Pre-
    clude International Policy Coordination?" *Journal of International Econom-
    ics*, Vol. 31 (November 1991), pp. 325–40.

Ghosh, Atish R., and Paul R. Masson, "International Policy Coordination in a
    World with Model Uncertainty," *Staff Papers*, International Monetary
    Fund, Vol. 35 (June 1988), pp. 230–58.

Helpman, Elhanan, and Assaf Razin, "Uncertainty and International Trade in
    the Presence of Stock Markets," *Review of Economic Studies*, Vol. 45 (June
    1978), pp. 239–50.

Kenen, Peter B., "Exchange Rates and Policy Coordination in an Asymmetric
    Model," CEPR Discussion Paper No. 240 (London: Centre for Economic
    Policy Research, May 1988).

Martinez Oliva, Juan Carlos, and Stefan Sinn, "The Game-Theoretic Approach
    to International Policy Coordination: Assessing the Role of Targets,"
    *Weltwirtschaftliches Archiv*, Band 124, Heft 2 (1988), pp. 252–68.

Oudiz, Giles, and Jeffrey Sachs, "Macroeconomic Policy Coordination Among
    the Industrial Economies," *Brookings Papers on Economic Activity: 1*
    (Washington: The Brookings Institution, 1984).

Sachs, Jeffrey, "The Dollar and the Policy Mix: 1985," *Brookings Papers on
    Economic Activity: 1* (Washington: The Brookings Institution, 1985).

Schwartz, Anna J., "The 1987 U.S. Stock Market Crash," *Economic Affairs*,
    Vol. 8 (February/March 1988), pp. 7–10.

Shiller, Robert J., "Do Stock Prices Move Too Much To Be Justified by Subse-
    quent Changes in Dividends?" *American Economic Review*, Vol. 71 (June
    1981), pp. 421–36.

Simon, Herbert A., "Dynamic Programming Under Uncertainty with a
    Quadratic Criterion Function," *Econometrica*, Vol. 24 (January 1956),
    pp. 74–81.

U.S. Congress, Committee on Banking, Housing, and Urban Affairs, " 'Black
    Monday,' the Stock Market Crash of October 19, 1987: Hearings Before the
    Committee on Banking, Housing, and Urban Affairs, February 2, 3, 4, and
    5, 1988" (Washington: Government Printing Office, 1988).

# Conclusion: A Personal View on the Use of Economic Models in Policymaking

I was encouraged by the publishers to supply a concluding chapter with some more personal reflections on the material republished in this book, in the light of my career in official institutions (and more recently, at a university). While I will resist the temptation to write my autobiography, a few anecdotes may illuminate the ways economic analysis feeds into policy discussions, as well as how policy drives the research agenda. I will then go on to discuss the differences between academic research and policy research and speculate on the research areas that may be the most pertinent as the international monetary system evolves in the future.

## My Career at Official Institutions

My first real job as an economist was at the Bank of Canada, in Ottawa, starting in 1973 following my PhD at the London School of Economics. I was attached to the Bank for the next 11 years, though I spent four years on leave at the Organization for Economic Co-operation and Development (OECD) in Paris. The work at the Bank showed me some of the dilemmas facing monetary policy and its relative ineffectiveness. During this period, the Bank was targeting monetary aggregates, in particular, variants of M1, but inflation was trending upward despite targets being reached. In the early 1980s, one of my duties was estimating demand for money equations (used as the basis for M1 targeting), which at this time were unstable partly as a result of financial innovations. This led to requests from management to do a better job at "explaining" money demand (using dummy variables, if nothing else worked), and to identify the sources of the shocks so that a policy decision could be made on whether or not to respond to those shocks. This was largely a fruitless exercise, and it led to over-fitting a relationship which in any case was mis-specified in a number of respects. Monetary aggregates were probably not the best intermediate target anyway, in a context in which the stagflationary effects of the second oil price shock and of a very tight US monetary policy were being felt in Canada. Finally, the Governor, without consulting us staff economists, just threw in the towel and abandoned monetary targeting — or, as he put it, "we didn't abandon monetary aggregates, they abandoned us"!

My work at the OECD from 1976–79 occurred at an interesting time, since the global economy was dealing with the after effects of the first oil price shock and policymakers were trying to make sense of the system of flexible exchange rates. Chapters 1 and 2 on exchange rate determination were written at that time or shortly thereafter. During this period, the G5 was in its infancy, and the OECD was vying with other international organizations to get involved in the process. The OECD already had considerable experience in providing a forum for exchange of information and peer review of macroeconomic and exchange rate policies. The OECD had begun its work in 1960 (when the OECD took the place of the OEEC, the agency that had been set up to allow European countries to rebuild and liberalize their economies in the context of Marshall Plan aid). The OECD's Economic Policy Committee and in particular, its Working Party 3, were the prime venues for ministers and central bank governors of member countries to meet for what could be free-wheeling discussions of important policy questions. I was thus exposed to the many issues related to international transmission of policies and discussions of ways to coordinate them. Since I worked in the balance of payments division, I was involved with international monetary system issues, and I was fortunate to collaborate with others on a special project to model exchange rate determination, which was a new and stimulating exercise.

I observed at the OECD that research at an official institution could take on a very political character. Policymakers and senior officials were clearly interested in the bottom line, the actual policy recommendation, rather than how you got there. They were concerned to avoid receiving policy advice that they did not want to follow, since this might make things more difficult at home. With empirical research, there are many alternative specifications that can be tried, and the incentive is always there to choose among them the ones that higher-ups want to see. This makes it especially important that research at official institutions be subject to academic peer review. At the OECD at that time, outside publication of research was frowned upon as an unnecessary waste of an economist's time. However, outside vetting is valuable for the organization (as well for the individual who wants greater recognition for his work) as it improves the quality and credibility of the research done. I think this lesson has now been learned in most official institutions (including the OECD), and I am heartened by the extent that outside publication of research is now encouraged. This is especially true of central banks, which can afford to have a good number of economists doing background research, and it has always been true to my knowledge of the International Monetary Fund (IMF).

I moved to the IMF in 1984. During my career there, I worked mainly in the Research Department, but also on European and African issues for a period of time. In particular, I was head of the division that dealt with France, Belgium, the Netherlands, and Luxembourg in 1992–94, right at the time of the crises in the European Monetary System. As I also subsequently participated in IMF missions to the European Monetary Institute and then the European Central Bank, I met with a number of the important European policymakers in the lead-up to the creation of the euro in 1999. I was caught up in the debate on the costs and benefits of monetary union, in understanding currency crises, and in modeling the interaction of monetary and fiscal policies in a currency union. Some of this work is reprinted as Chapters 5, 6, 10, and 11.

The IMF has pursued academic-quality research from the beginning, partly because many of the issues it faced were not well understood by the economics profession, so it had to blaze new trails. Two influential models of the international economy developed at the IMF were the Mundell-Fleming model and the monetary theory of the balance of payments. A special issue celebrating the IMF *Staff Papers*' 50th anniversary recalls some of the important articles published there.

Despite its emphasis on the quality of research, in my experience, even the IMF was not immune to political pressure or indeed censorship in the publication of that research. One unfortunate author saw his article on capital flight removed from the issue of *Staff Papers* where it had already been printed, but not yet released, at the insistence of a country mentioned in the study. A new issue was printed with the offending article removed. In another incident, the Reagan Administration objected to the staff's analysis of the effects of US fiscal policy on crowding out of private sector activity and on the current account deficit, and that study never saw the light of day. The French authorities objected strenuously to any dissemination of a research study that I co-authored on the market's assessment of France's commitment to the EMS parity. My boss and I were threatened with all sorts of dire consequences. Needless to say, that article never made it into print, or even to the working paper stage. A survey article I had written with a colleague on policy coordination, which was accepted for publication in *Staff Papers*, was delayed at the insistence of the Managing Director because issues related to the G5/G7 and the IMF's involvement with them were viewed as being very sensitive at that time (the mid-1980s).

Nevertheless, I continued to analyze policy coordination and produced some articles that are reprinted as Chapters 13–15. The Fund's role as a sort of secretariat for the G7 from the mid-1980s onward made studying the interactions between the major industrial countries especially important. This period, during which I developed a multi-country model for policy analysis, MULTIMOD, was quite an interesting one from my point of view. The model helped to guide the policy advice, especially for G7 countries, and allowed the construction of scenarios of coordinated policy measures. The Research Department was also fortunate in being able to attract a large number of consultants from academe who helped supplement our more applied research with state-of-the-art theoretical analysis, making the working environment very congenial and productive.

My work in Africa, which began in the late 1990s, focussed on regional integration issues, particularly in West and Central Africa, some of whose countries participate in the CFA franc zone. My co-authors and I also assessed the desirability of a proposed monetary union that would include all the West African (ECOWAS) countries; one article based on this work is reprinted as Chapter 12. In many respects, I found analysis of African policy issues satisfying because it could have a real impact on actual policies followed. Our message was very much a cautionary one because the impetus for monetary union came mainly from the politicians wanting to make a gesture in favour of regional integration. The economic costs and benefits were not really on their radar screens. Our work helped to put them there and to stimulate a real debate on whether a common currency was really desirable. We wanted to dispel the notion that just because it was good for Europe, a common currency was necessarily good for Africa. It could be in some cases, but the safeguards against undisciplined fiscal policy, which could lead to a bad monetary policy, had to be made especially strong in Africa, and the choice of possible monetary union partners was also crucial to making a common currency work.

## Academic versus Policy Research

Research at official institutions has, I believe, become more similar to academic research in the years I have been involved with it. Should the two be the same? I do not actually think that the former (which for lack of a better term could be called policy research) should converge to the latter. I will lay out the reasons below, as well as my views about the different pitfalls that plague the two types of research.

The fundamental difference between the two is that policy research is concerned with getting the right answer, not a new or original way to analyze a particular question. In contrast, academic research often pursues issues that are thrown up by other path-breaking research. The issues involve understanding the implications of a new theory, or variants of a new technique, rather than finding and applying the best tools (new or old) to address a policy issue. As a result, many academic papers, if they draw policy conclusions, do so on the basis of some limited empirical work that applies the latest model, rather than a survey of a broad range of empirical work of various types and an attempt to assess the relevance of each of them. The emphasis is on innovation, so that academic research is especially subject to fads; during the late 1980s, there were many economists modeling target zones and many modeling inflation targeting a decade later — some of them being the same people.

The academic profession has also moved too far, in my opinion, in the direction of taking their models seriously and emphasizing the derivation of analytical results rather than empirical testing — at least in the macroeconomics field that I am most familiar with. In the interests of having a tightly specified, internally consistent general equilibrium model, the profession has tended to work with tractable setups and specific functional forms for which analytical solutions are possible, though there is really little justification for them except tractability. This is typically done in the context of a representative agent model in which the whole economy acts as if it resulted from the optimizing decisions of a single consumer and a single producer. As it is well known, the aggregation restrictions that would make micro and macro behavior consistent in a world of many agents are so stringent as to make this completely unrealistic, but this fact is simply ignored. Moreover, the assumption of rational expectations makes it very difficult to work with multiple agent models because of infinite regress concerning conjectures of how others expect you to act.

As a result, the current state-of-the-art dynamic, stochastic general equilibrium (DSGE) models are elegant and consistent, and may be useful in some contexts, but their limitations need to be kept firmly in mind. I agree with Willem Buiter (2008) that the world of these models can be overly reassuring, in particular for central banks, many of which have embraced these models from academe and used them to set policy rates. These models imply that small changes in the short-term policy rate have large effects on future output and inflation, since if they are expected to be persistent, they cause substantial changes all along the yield curve of interest rates. Credibility of monetary policy is assumed by these models not to be an issue, meaning that central banks can guide the economy along a full employment target path with low inflation by tweaking its policy rate. Because of the complexity resulting from their emphasis on internal consistency, DSGE models are especially prone to the "drunk under the lamp-post" syndrome: "if I can't see how to solve it, I won't include it in my model." The 2008–09 financial crisis has forced a re-examination of the assumptions behind DSGE models and their application to monetary policy issues.

In general, research at official institutions tends to be much closer to the data than most academic research. This is natural, since the data are often compiled at official institutions, and hence they are more easily accessible, and quirks in the data are better understood. In my view, the standards for publishing empirical academic research are too low, allowing conclusions to be drawn from casual empiricism or from sloppy and partial use of available data. There are, of course, pitfalls from being too close to the data, however. One is that one may be modeling an imperfect measure of an underlying concept, and it would be better to take a step back and consider other proxies or theories that do not have an exact representation in the data. A second pitfall is the temptation to do data mining and explain historical data to a high degree of accuracy with a model that is neither closely related to theory, nor likely to perform well in the future. More generally, as mentioned above, policy research is prone to the selective use of results to give the answer desired. This makes it especially important to subject policy research to outside scrutiny.

A danger that affects economic modelers in both academic and official institutions is that we typically think in static, ahistorical terms, and that this leads us to underestimate the magnitude of the major changes that may be in store for us. To be more specific, when I was working on MUL-TIMOD, we anchored the long run using the steady-state solution of the model. It was assumed that the model's structure, which we had estimated on the basis of recent data, would remain in place forevermore, and so eventually real variables would all grow at a steady rate (the "end of history"). Uncertainty was quantified using the estimated error variances around the unchanged structure over the recent historical period. But if we are looking out 10 or 20 years, chances are that there will be major structural changes.

Assuming an unchanged model and convergence to a steady state are common practices among modelers. Though it may be very difficult to model formally, we should at least ask ourselves the following questions: How does the fact that we may never get to a steady state change our view of the world? How should uncertainty about future structural changes lead us to modify our view of optimal policy?

I have tried to address some of this uncertainty in my past research. My work with Rex Ghosh on model uncertainty and policy coordination is one example (Chapters 13 and 14). Another set of research is based on my view that exchange rate regimes should best be thought of as in a continual state of flux, rather than converging to a single, invariant regime or pair of polar cases (regime choice is modeled in Chapters 3 and 4 as a Markov process). But clearly, much more can (and should) be done.

## Future Research Topics

My interest in studying the further evolution of economic systems has led me to consider in my current and future research the possible reform of the international monetary system. It seems to me at the time this is being written (in 2010) that there is a real chance that a concerted effort will be made to rethink and refashion the international monetary system — for the first time since the 1970s (Dailami and Masson, 2010). The current regime or "non-system" as some have called it,[1] emerged from the breakdown of the Bretton Woods system and the move to generalized floating of the major currencies. While there was an attempt by the IMF to specify the rules of the game for such a regime, in particular, to rule out currency manipulation, in practice those rules have not been enforced. As a result, all exchange rate systems, including currency boards, managed floating, and freely flexible exchange rates, have been permitted. While this non-system has been relatively robust in the face of shocks (there were no rules to be broken!), it has been accompanied by major problems: high exchange rate volatility and misalignments at times, destabilizing capital flows, and crises in emerging market countries. Contrary to the critics of floating exchange rates, higher volatility did not produce the drying up of international trade or direct investment that some had feared, but misalignments of exchange rates sometimes put severe pressures on export sectors and caused an increase in protectionism to counter those pressures.

---

[1] The first one to use this term seems to have been Williamson (1976).

When exchange rates and payments moved seriously out of line, the G5/G7/G8 attempted to coordinate policies and correct the disequilibria. This policy coordination had some occasional successes, but the current crisis has highlighted the limitations of G7/G8 coordination and led to the current pre-eminence of the G20. The G8 failed either to identify the imminent crisis or to take any measures to address its causes. This was partly due to the rise of other countries, in particular China, that were not members of the G8. That has now been corrected by the prominent role given to the G20, but it remains to be seen how effective this larger grouping will be.

In my view, it is important not just to strengthen ad hoc coordination, but also to consider enhanced and enforceable rules of the game of the monetary system as a whole. This is of course a very challenging problem — both analytical and political. Many eminent academic economists, officials, and policymakers studied reform in the years leading up to the abandonment of Bretton Woods. As early as Triffin's work in the 1950s and early 1960s (Triffin, 1960), it was understood that to depend on the United States' balance of payments deficits for increases in global liquidity built a contradiction into the system as long as the dollar in turn was convertible into gold. Those deficits were needed to supply reserves for a growing global economy, but their continuation harmed the credibility of the United States' commitment to convertibility at a fixed price for gold. In the end, it was convertibility that was abandoned, but with a US monetary policy that was producing higher inflation than other major countries could tolerate, the pegged exchange rate system had to be abandoned too.

At present, there is also disagreement among major countries about the proper stance of macroeconomic policies and the desirable levels of real exchange rates and current account positions. The United States, hard hit by the recession, has continued its zero interest rate policy and quantitative easing longer than some other countries think wise. Other developed and emerging market countries see this as being a beggar-thy-neighbour policy leading to an undervalued dollar. At the same time, the United States criticizes China for its policies limiting the flexibility of the renminbi against the dollar, and for its large current account surpluses that reflect inadequate domestic demand.

While policy coordination could in principle address these problems, there are limits on the extent that bargains can be struck on an ad hoc basis. Most difficult to achieve is agreement on targets for the "zero-sum" or "conflict" variables like the exchange rate or the current account balance:

if all countries want to boost output in response to a common global downturn, then each wants to export some of its problems to others through a weaker currency and an improved current balance. Agreements on underlying macroeconomic policies may avoid some of the direct conflict, but those policies are much more difficult to assess and monitor than are exchange rates and balances of payments. Fiscal policy especially involves many aspects and is often driven by domestic politics. Hence, success with G20 policy coordination is far from assured.

A major role of the rules of the game for the global system is to rule out by prior agreement certain types of behavior that are viewed as beggar-thy-neighbor. A return to a system like Bretton Woods with pegged exchange rates, however, seems extremely unlikely and also unwise. To make it work, countries would also have to agree to put capital flows back into Pandora's box — which would be well-nigh impossible, or abandon monetary sovereignty — which seems very unlikely. Hence, I think that alternative systems that allow some of the flexibility of the current "non-system" but also target shared international public goods need to be explored.

A promising avenue to explore could be to modify domestic inflation targeting to introduce a shared target for international prices. This could be commodity prices, wholesale prices (which would also include semi-finished manufactures), or a basket of commonly traded goods and services. By targeting a common basket — with each country targeting an index expressed in its own currency — countries could achieve both low inflation and exchange rate stability. Success in hitting the same inflation target would also be accompanied by exchange rate stability.

Certainly, there are other regimes that can be imagined that introduce an automatic element of coordination through shared targets. In my view, improvement in the system needs to go down the road of trying to reach agreement on reinforced rules, rather than relying on ad hoc coordination when things get out of line — because it may be precisely then that the conflicts between countries are greatest and their willingness to compromise is weakest. Unless well-designed rules have been decided beforehand, there will be little chance of eliminating beggar-thy-neighbor behavior.

### References

Buiter, Willem, "Central Banks and Financial Crises," paper presented at Federal Reserve Bank of Kansas City Conference, Maintaining Stability in a Changing Financial System, Jackson Hole, Wyoming, August 2008.

Dailami, Mansoor, and Paul R. Masson, "Toward a More Managed International Monetary System?" *International Journal*, Vol. 65(2) (2010), pp. 393–409.

Triffin, Robert, *Gold and the Dollar Crisis: The Future of Convertibility*, New Haven, CT: Yale University Press, 1960.

Williamson, John, "The Benefits and Costs of an International Monetary Nonsystem," in *Reflections on Jamaica, Essays in International Finance*, Edward M. Bernstein *et al.*, Vol. 115 (Princeton, NJ: Princeton University Press, 1976), pp. 54–59.